P9-DHK-360

DON'T MESS WITH MY MONEY

OTHER BOOKS BY KEN AND DARIA DOLAN

Sam's Teach Yourself e-Personal Finance Today

Smart Money

Straight Talk on Money

The Smart Money Family Financial Planner

DISCARD

Don't Mess with My Money

THE DOLANS' NO-NONSENSE LIFETIME MONEY PLAN

Ken and Daria Dolan

TIMPANOGOS HIGH SCHOOL
MEDIA CENTER

CALL # 332 DOL BOOK # 0405

CURRENCY

New York   London   Toronto   Sydney   Auckland

A CURRENCY BOOK
PUBLISHED BY DOUBLEDAY
a division of Random House, Inc.

CURRENCY is a trademark of Random House, Inc., and DOUBLEDAY is a registered
trademark of Random House, Inc.

Don't Mess with My Money was originally published in hardcover by Currency in January 2003.
Copyright © 2003 by Ken and Daria Dolan
All rights reserved

The Library of Congress has cataloged the hardcover edition of this book as follows:
Dolan, Ken.
Don't mess with my money : the Dolans' no-nonsense lifetime money plan /
Ken and Daria Dolan.—1st ed.
p.   cm.
1. Finance, Personal. I. Dolan, Daria. II. Title.
HG179.D586 2002
332.024—dc21   2002031438

ISBN 0-385-50791-7

Book design by Erin L. Matherne and Tina Thompson

PRINTED IN THE UNITED STATES OF AMERICA

First Edition: January 2003
First Currency Paperback Edition: October 2004

All trademarks are the property of their respective companies

SPECIAL SALES
Currency Books are available at special discounts for bulk purchases for sales promotions or premiums.
Special editions, including personalized covers, excerpts of existing books, and corporate imprints can be
created in large quantities for special needs. For more information, write to Special Markets, Currency
Books, specialmarkets@randomhouse.com

1 3 5 7 9 10 8 6 4 2

We dedicate this book to the victims and families of the September 11, 2001, terrorist attack on America. Their courage to persevere, to go on with their lives amid their unspeakable loss and grief, has been an enormous inspiration to us, a couple who said that we would never make the effort to write another book.

We had to do *something* to contribute to the rebirth of the indomitable American spirit that began on September 11 and continues to this day.

We hope that our message of empowerment in this book, dedicated to our fallen brethren and their families, will help our fellow Americans take greater control of their lives by making sound money decisions and, just as important, be prepared for any unexpected event or circumstance . . . and, in the process, live better lives!

CONTENTS

ACKNOWLEDGMENTS

WE WOULD LIKE TO THANK our research associate/writer, Ms. Jan Alexander. This book simply could not have happened without her. Her patience, attention to detail, and even temperament were something to behold as we put this important book together during one of the busiest periods of our lives.

A special thanks is also given to our long-suffering literary agent, George Greenfield, who would not take "no" for an answer. He kept at us in his understated and gentlemanly manner for at least three years to convince us to write this book. He is living proof that persistence pays!

Also, thanks to our listeners, whose encouragement and input helped separate this book from any other written on personal finance. We treasure your support and your loyalty.

SECTION I

The Way You Live Now

CHAPTER 1

Don't Mess with *Your* Money

MARTHA STEWART CONVICTED. . . . SEC investigates a number of mutual fund companies. . . . The accuracy of some Wall Street stock research questioned. . . . Corporate malfeasance trials are all the rage!

. . . on and on— When will it stop?!

One thing is *very* clear.

Never has it been more important to take responsibility for your own money life.

If you think Wall Street, Uncle Sam, or your cousin Ralph's "hot stock tips" is your solution for a secure financial future . . . forget it. . . . GET REAL!

You CAN do it. . . . You CAN take control. . . . You MUST take control *now*!

Our latest book is *not* the entire answer. Read it and you'll be a money expert overnight? NO. But it is a good start!!

We know what you may be thinking, as you quickly look at this: "Oh, no, not *another* money book!"

We thought most money books were the same, too—until we got *mad* at the way the economy and the corporate world have messed with *your* money.

Most money books hedge their comments to avoid insulting anyone, afraid of making waves that might come back to bite them in the butt. *Hey* . . . come on! Most money books are best used as sales pieces for the financial services business, or, better yet, as doorstops in the poorhouse to which slick salespeople so adroitly send us.

Many money books claim that they contain "all you'll ever want to know about" investing, insurance, retirement, and so on. GIVE US A BREAK! How the heck do *you* know "all" that *I* want to know?

This is a different kind of money book. We promise you that. This is a book that will show you how to fight back. We *do* claim that we pass along all you *need* (there's a big difference between want and need) to know to at least get you started in taking control of your money life and, thereby, taking control of your life.

During the last 12 months you've been hit with a lot of jive talk from certain CEOs (does that acronym stand for "Chief Embezzlement Officer"?), accountants, brokerage executive fat cats, research analysts, financial planners, bankers, credit card companies, insurance salespeople . . . and others trying to separate you from your hard-earned bucks. We know it's becoming increasingly difficult to obtain respected, trustworthy information you can use to make those important money decisions during your life.

As we've all discovered, we're on our own, folks!

But that's OK (even better) *if* you can finally find some straight information.

Do you know, for example, the right place to invest your bucks for a secure retirement when the stock market is taking punches from every direction? Do you know the best strategies for funding a 529 plan for your child's college education? Buying insurance for yourself and your family? Buying your first or second home? Finding the best credit card? Dealing with a broker/financial planner?

We have heard it all on our radio show during the past 15 years, having fielded tens of thousands of phone calls to our personal finance talk show, *The Dolans*.

We answer questions on more than 200 different topics based on both our own life experience (we've been married more than 30 years and are the parents of a recently married daughter) and more than 45 years of experience in the field of personal finance.

Our radio listeners across America immeasurably helped us write this book, with the questions that they called in to our show and with e-mail messages to us.

When we announced that we were writing a "no-holds-barred" book, we asked our listeners to tell us what specific issues they were having trouble coping with.

We were bombarded with all sorts of stories and questions.

Among our listeners' major concerns:

"How may I pick stocks that go UP!?" (What a concept!)

"My broker has taken advantage of me. . . . Can I sue—and win?"

"I'd like to level the playing field when I walk into a car dealership. . . . How can I make the best deal for ME?"

"Is it more advantageous to lease a car or buy?"

"My next-door neighbor pays less property tax than I do. . . . How can I fight my property tax assessment—and win?"

"How do I avoid buying the next Enron, Global Crossing, WorldCom, or _____ (fill in the blank)?"

"Which 'so-called' investments aren't investments at all?"

"My search is not going well . . . are there little-known sources of college financial aid?"

"Every financial pro I meet claims to know when to buy stocks/mutual funds . . . but nobody knows when to sell. Help!"

"I know there are hidden terms that my credit card company isn't telling me. . . . What are some of their tricks?"

"How do I stay covered with health insurance if I'm laid off?"

"I'm afraid my parents will be wiped out by nursing home expenses. . . . Is there anything they can do to avoid that happening?"

"A lot of my retired friends wish that they had planned better for their golden years—what can I do now to assure my secure retirement?"

"Are there some little-known strategies for getting the best price when I sell my home? How do I pay the least when I buy?"

"When I interview a broker/financial planner before I do business, I feel that I'm the one being interviewed! I want to take more control of the process. . . . What are the tough questions that I should ask and the answers I should hear?"

"I really need to get my student loan situation under control. Where do I start?"

"I am one-half of a gay couple. Can you help us with our financial planning?"

"I'm in the early stages of considering a divorce. I'm scared and don't know where to start."

"I have seen some of my friends lose their 401(k) money because of shady dealings by their companies. . . . What are some of the warning signs that MY plan may be in trouble?"

"I think that my company is short-changing my pension check every month. How do I find out if this is true ?"

. . . and more!

We'll show you how to take control, so that no one can mess with your money. Don't be discouraged by all the bad news around you—if you take charge and know where to go for advice, you *can* get back on track. We work with people across the country every day, helping them distinguish between a good money strategy and a bad one, between good money advice and bad advice.

Buckle up . . . here we go!

CHAPTER 2

The Dolans' Financial Checkup

WE'RE MAD AS HELL, and you will be, too, by the time you finish this chapter. It took foreign terrorists to shatter America's innocence, but the American dream was shattered from within at the start of the twenty-first century.

Greedy corporate leaders lied—yes, out and out LIED—about company earnings, and Wall Street analysts caused a stock market bubble that burst. That left millions of middle-class investors—even those who thought they were playing it safe with Fortune 500 stocks—stripped of the nest egg that was supposed to send their kids to college and provide a comfortable retirement. Research analysts have lied to brokers and brokers have lied to clients. Did you ever think you'd live to see the day when the chief executive officer of a major brokerage firm would publicly apologize for his firm's failing to live up to the standards clients, shareholders, and employees expected?* Or the day that *BusinessWeek* would run a cover story titled "How Corrupt Is Wall Street?"† Perfectly competent people have lost jobs with little warning as companies cut back and restructured. Consumers have been told to spend money to boost the economy, as if buying a new computer or a stylish wardrobe were practically a patriotic duty, and credit card issuers have made spending so easy we've ended up a nation in debt past our eyeballs. We could be just one major massive corporate layoff away from an exploding consumer credit problem all over the country.

---

* The Merrill Lynch chairman and CEO offered a public apology at the firm's annual shareholder meeting in 2002. See Chapter 5 for more details.
† May 13, 2002.

Through the years we have heard from listeners who made the mistake of trusting their employers and believing it was a good idea to keep *most* of their retirement bucks invested in the company's stock. It sounded good. Since they were on-scene every day, they could presumably keep an eye on the investment—except that only those who doctored the books knew when to pull out. For years, we warned against investing more than 5% or 10% of any retirement plan in the stock of the company for which you work. In recent years we've received many remorseful calls from people who wish they had listened to our advice.

An Enron employee named Diana, from Pennsylvania, called us in tears. Her 401(k), invested 100% in the company's stock, was at one point worth more than $300,000, and she was planning a comfortable retirement in six years. You don't need us to tell you what happened to the value of Enron stock because of its well-documented scandal. Diana said she would have to work full-time until at least the age of 70.

All you need to do is read the headlines to know that there are many more Enrons out there!

Well, the best revenge is still living well, and we will show you how to live well in spite of uncertain times, and sleep well, knowing that your finances aren't going to come crashing down like a house of Enron stock certificates.

> **A downturn is when your neighbor loses his job. A recession is when your wife loses her job. A depression is when you both lose your jobs.**

Are You Financially Fit Enough to Weather a Downturn?

Be honest! If you are, you're the exception.

Would you run a marathon without being sure you are fit enough to withstand it? This is that kind of checkup. It's preventive care, so that you won't lose your shirt.

Now, you will have to start saving. It probably won't come naturally to you; Americans have earned the distinction of being the worst savers in the industrialized world. Many Americans have no savings at all, or have negative savings—that is, nothing in the bank and a pile of debts. As of late 2001, American consumers were in debt to the tune of $19.9 billion.

Our drive to acquire "stuff" without saving sets a very poor example for the next generation, because our kids then try to acquire even more than we did, in an age when prices are getting out of hand. If not for your sake then for your children's sake, to instill in them realistic values, ask yourself some hard questions before you spend to the limit.

Money Doesn't Buy Happiness, But It Can Buy You a Second Chance!

If you're going to live well you must consider, before you do anything else, where you are in relation to where you'd *like* to be. Forget about the economy at large. Are you happy with your job? Is your spouse or partner happy, career-wise? Can you afford to pursue your dreams? We believe in having dreams, and in realizing them.

We know plenty of people who have walked away from jobs in the middle of a recession because they've realized, with all our country has been through, that life is too short to be stuck in a job that is just a daily grind, and bravely gone forth to reinvent themselves. We have a close friend who was a big muckety-muck in the retail business, with a *high* six-figure income; she specialized in reviving faltering retail companies for resale. A tough job, a real pressure cooker. In return for her fat paycheck, she became accustomed to sleepless nights and no time for a personal life—all in the name of fixing someone else's mistakes, as she began to see it. So what did our friend do, just when she was at the top and companies were tripping over themselves clamoring for her services? She saved her money until she could comfortably say, "*Sayonara*, corporate America!" She is now starting a new career as a sculptor. She has enough savings to get her through about five years if she cuts back fairly drastically on her lifestyle. Who knows, had she stayed with the job, she might have eventually found herself out of work *in spite of* the demand, because corporate directors don't know the meaning of loyalty—and she might have been caught unawares without a financial cushion.

We have another story of a couple who walked away from financial security together, a couple named Ken and Daria Dolan. The time was 1984. Ken was a managing director of an international brokerage firm, and Daria was happily raising their daughter, Meredith, and taking an occasional acting job. The whole country had become infatuated with Wall Street as people who'd never invested before caught their piece of the new bull market, and life was good for many Americans, including the Dolans.

But Ken had a dream. . . .

He wanted to host a radio program using all he'd learned about personal finance to help people in a very public way, instead of just working with private clients. His dream came true in October of that year, when he was offered an on-air job at WOR Radio in New York City, beginning in early 1985. He accepted, though it meant taking a pay cut of 70%.

When Ken told Daria about the new job, she was in shock.

"I'll never to this day know what made me say it, but I said, 'Well, then, I guess I'll become a stockbroker,'" Daria recalls. A voice inside told her she was going to have to make some big changes to compensate. As a part-time actress, she could never hope to make up the shortfall. So she announced that she was going to enter Ken's old business as a stockbroker—a pretty risky proposition, seeing that she had absolutely no experience.

Ken didn't think she would be able to pull it off, and Daria wasn't so sure herself. But whether through some latent innate ability or out-and-out terror of being in the poorhouse, Daria passed the New York Stock Exchange Series 7 test that is required of anyone who wishes to obtain a license to conduct securities business with the public—and she became a broker.

In fact, she enjoyed giving financial advice so much that in 1986 she teamed up with Ken to host a talk show on another New York City radio station, and *The Dolans* was born.

As 1987 began, they thought nothing could stop them. So they quit the smaller radio station to write their first book, thinking that being successful authors would bring them a fortune in radio and television opportunities. The timing couldn't have been worse. The stock market crashed in October of that year, ad sales were down, and not many programmers were willing to take a gamble on a couple of personalities without a long track record.

Well, they—we, actually—were out of work for a whopping 18 months, and it felt more like an eternity. But we were able to hang in and keep knocking on doors until WOR Radio called us and offered us a talk show, initially in an 8 P.M. to 10 P.M. slot. We didn't have to give up our dream and go looking for "real" jobs. Why? Because we had enough savings to carry us through what amounted to a serious recession of our own. We didn't have fights about it or get worried and waste time contemplating turning back, all because we had our cushion. Recession is in the eye of the receiver; you can experience your own recession at any time, even if the economy at large is doing fine. Recession can be the best thing that's ever happened to you—if you make it an opportunity to realize your dreams. You might have to take a lower-paying, lower-level job, or launch a risky entrepreneurial venture, or fork over tuition and go back to school, but you can make it if you're prepared.

You *could* buy lottery tickets. But a solid money-management plan will *guarantee* you a winning number.

Say you need a new car. Do you really need the top model? Is there something that will fill the bill that costs less? Can you get by with a late-model used car?

You Can Stamp Out Debt Contagion

Debt can pass from one person trying to keep up with friends, colleagues, family, and neighbors to another like a plague. But consider this: Chances are your next-door neighbor who's driving a brand-new SUV went into debt to buy it. He's making his debts look like assets, which is more or less what Enron did. We can't count on our net worth rising just because we make ourselves look richer than we are. If we all lived within our means we wouldn't have nearly so many neighbors to envy, and we'd have a lot more peace of mind.

The goal is to buy what you can without taking on unnecessary debt. The SUV might be really nice, but the VW might get you where you need to go when you need to get there. And if that's the case, take a look at what the one would cost versus the other. If you thought you could make the payments on the bigger purchase, take the difference, the money that you're not going to spend, and put it aside for that proverbial rainy day.

How do you get started saving on a regular basis? It all begins with what some people call a "budget." Ouch. We prefer to call it a "success plan."

Anyone Saving for Retirement Out There?

Americans are more likely to save money for vacations and to repay debt than they are to build their nest egg for retirement, according to a 2002 study conducted by the market research firm Goodmind LLC for the GE Center for Financial Learning. The study polled 1,000 U.S. households. Of those polled, a combined 64% said they saved money for vacations or to pay off debt, but only 48% were saving toward retirement. The research also found that 19% of the respondents weren't saving money on a regular basis, and a whopping 53% said they couldn't afford to save! However, the probability of saving increased with a person's salary level. Among those with a household income of $100,000, 97% said they expected to put away some money.

More than 33% of all respondents said they saved between 5% and 10% of their monthly income, while more than one-fifth saved less that 5% and nearly a third put away more than 10%.

You can find some useful tips for saving on the GE Center for Financial Learning Web site, at www.financiallearning.com.

The First Steps to Financial Fitness

All financial fitness begins with a "success plan" (the concept formerly known as "budgeting").

We've changed the name because we *hate* the word "budget." It sounds like a tight-sphinctered, chaste approach to money management that only our Puritan forebears could love. What we're talking about is a plan for prioritizing your needs and the way you spend so that you'll succeed in having money for the things that are most important. In short, a success plan.

> **If you're not serious about getting a firm financial footing by starting to calculate your "income" and "outgo," then this book is not for you!**

Begin your success plan in small steps.

Step 1: Follow the Money

Daria uses her T square to get a gauge on where your money is going. This is how it works:

On a piece of paper, draw a vertical line down the center. At the top, write "Income" to the left of the line and "Outgo" to the right, like this:

Income	Outgo

On the left side, list all of your sources of income over the course of a year, and the amount you actually net after taxes. Take the total and divide it by 12. That's the amount of money you have available each month.

On the right side, make a list of all your expenses over the course of a year. There are three categories of expenses: fixed, variable, and periodic or irregular. Fixed expenses are the things you know you have to pay each month. Some of these, of course, will be variable, depending on factors that influence the size of your telephone, utility, and other bills that aren't the same from month to month. Irregular expenses are items such as property taxes, insurance premiums, and tuition, which you might pay annually or quarterly. Take the total and divide it by 12. That is the amount you are actually spending every month, prorated.

Make sure you have this much in your checking account every month, but take those prorated sums that you don't have to pay out every month and put them in a separate savings account, so that you get a little interest and there will be something left over when the bill comes due.

Step 2: Fill Out the Worksheet

Follow our budget worksheet each month, recording your fixed expenses and nonfixed expenses, such as food and clothing, which vary from month to month. Add your own items to our list as necessary.

What we are going to suggest will take some time, and we know it's a pain, but it will be worth the effort.

Keep a log every day for a month, writing down every dime you spend. Fill in the lines for the bills you pay once a month or less often. Make a copy for every day of the month and sit down every night before you go to bed and fill out your daily expenses.

At the end of the month, subtract this figure from your income. Is it larger than your income? Uh-oh. The difference between your income and your expenses is your cash flow. The object, of course, is to achieve a positive cash flow by cutting your expenses wherever you can and putting the extra into a savings account.

Yes, we know you've heard all this before. What we want to encourage you to do is set a goal as an incentive to save. By setting a goal, you'll have some incentive to create savings. Want a new car, a fur coat, a home theater? You don't have to buy the most expensive one, but get the whole family working toward something you all want. Make a game out of it: We need $ _____ to buy a home theatre. Where can we find the money?

Once you figure out where the money is going, you'll be surprised at how easy it is to spend a little less each day. The objective of this game plan isn't to deny you a daily tall skim-milk latte if that's something you really enjoy, but you will have to make some choices about what is most important. The idea is to cut down some of the big costs so

The Budget Worksheet

	Daily	Monthly
HOME		
Housing (rent or mortgage)	$ _____	$ _____
Heating	$ _____	$ _____
Electric	$ _____	$ _____
Telephone	$ _____	$ _____
Internet service	$ _____	$ _____
Cable TV	$ _____	$ _____
Water/sewer/trash	$ _____	$ _____
Miscellaneous/maintenance	$ _____	$ _____
INSURANCE		
Life	$ _____	$ _____
Auto	$ _____	$ _____
Home	$ _____	$ _____
Health	$ _____	$ _____
FOOD/ENTERTAINMENT		
Groceries	$ _____	$ _____
Meals outside of home	$ _____	$ _____
Movies/theater/sports	$ _____	$ _____
TRANSPORTATION		
Auto (gasoline)	$ _____	$ _____
Auto (maintenance/repairs)	$ _____	$ _____
Public (subway, bus)	$ _____	$ _____
Taxis	$ _____	$ _____
Parking fees	$ _____	$ _____

	Daily	Monthly
INSTALLMENT DEBT		
Car payments	$ _____	$ _____
Student loans	$ _____	$ _____
Credit cards: AmEx	$ _____	$ _____
Visa	$ _____	$ _____
MasterCard	$ _____	$ _____
Other	$ _____	$ _____
OTHER		
Vacation	$ _____	$ _____
Education	$ _____	$ _____
Child care	$ _____	$ _____
Unreimbursed medical	$ _____	$ _____
Gifts, contributions	$ _____	$ _____
Clothing	$ _____	$ _____
Alimony, child support	$ _____	$ _____
Spending money	$ _____	$ _____
Unreimbursed business expenses	$ _____	$ _____
Retirement plan—IRA, 401(k)	$ _____	$ _____
Savings/investing	$ _____	$ _____
Miscellaneous	$ _____	$ _____

that you won't be saddled with debts—crisis or not—and will have a nest egg for emergencies. And really, nothing gives you greater peace of mind. The idea is to find "pluggable" holes.

Step 3: Downsize Your Debts

Seriously—you can't get into financial shape if you're deep in debt. It's like gorging on Twinkies while you're pounding a Stairmaster.

Take a complete inventory of what you have and what you owe. Sit down with your spouse or life partner and do a complete inventory of the debts and assets each of you holds, both individually and jointly. If you're not in a relationship, sit down with yourself. Either way, it's time to face up to reality.

Now, how can you get the debts down and the assets up? We can't tell you too many times how important it is to get rid of debts. You're paying as much as 20% a month on your credit card balances, while you might be getting only 1.2% on a savings account. So as long as you have heavy credit card debts, you're throwing money out the window.

See Chapter 4 for a rundown of how to pay off those pesky debts. To build up your savings, first you'll need to start a success plan for cutting expenses and use the money you save to pay off your debts. If you need to get rid of debts and start saving, contribute less—temporarily—to your 401(k) or college savings, and put the money where it is most needed now, just until you get to a secure place.

Step 4: Find One Big Thing You Can Live Without

Browse in a store, find something you might have bought yesterday—before you started reading this book—but you don't really need, and put the money into a savings account.

Check Out Microsoft Money 2004 Deluxe

Need some help getting started in organizing your money life?

You don't have to be a computer techie to get the hang of our favorite software product for managing your personal finances and investments—Microsoft "Money 2004 Deluxe." If you're serious about getting your day-to-day finances under control, tracking your investments, preparing for tax time, and starting to design a blueprint for your future, consider this $39.95 (with mail-in rebate) investment (or $29.95 for the "standard" version) that will yield big dividends.

Managing debt, balancing your checkbook, and even paying your bills are easy with this product. Check it out!

Get a Goal

It's a lot easier to save money if you have long-term goals for your savings. What are the things you need and want? Yes, you should have an emergency cushion that can carry you through at least six months. But beyond that, save some money for your dreams. Invest this money in safe vehicles, such as money market mutual funds, Treasury bills, or certificates of deposit (CDs). Check off as many of these goals as apply, and fill in your own:

___ New home
___ College education
___ Getting out of debt
___ Career change
___ Travel
___ Taking care of your parents
___ New car
___ Vacation home
___ Retirement
___ A major improvement to your home
___ Your own goals _____

We used to tell people to save just $10 a month, but that's not enough these days. Let's get serious: Most of us need to become committed born-again savers. Still, it's better to save in dribs and drabs than not to save at all. If you save $10 by *not* buying some little thing, put the money in savings before temptation strikes again. Do this every few days and your savings will add up! Be creative about cutting back, and make it fun. Here are some little ways you can do it:

Buy one less item of new clothing for everyone in the family. We know a young single woman who organizes clothing exchange parties with her friends every few months. Instead of going out shopping, a group of women bring the clothes and accessories they aren't wearing often. Usually each participant finds something new and wonderful from among a friend's castoffs, and it costs them nothing. Or take clothes you don't wear anymore to a consignment shop and let them earn you cash, instead of leaving them "consigned" to the back of the closet.

One Saturday night a month, cook a dinner of everybody's favorite dishes at home and rent a video instead of going out on the town.

Take a sandwich to work instead of eating lunch in restaurants.

Make saving money a family effort. We see corporations cutting corners nowadays, asking employees to think of ways to save money. Well, families can do that, too. We won't start trying to guess where the money that corporations save really goes, but in your household, it can go into the highest-interest-bearing money market account you can find.

Step 5: Go Where the Interest Is

That brings us to making decisions about where to stash your savings. In spite of the sorry state of interest rates on savings accounts and money market mutual funds these days, you should have enough money in a savings vehicle to cover your expenses for at least six months before you start making investments.

That's because investments by their very definition carry an element of risk. The money you keep in savings should be a sure thing, there for you even if everything else in life falls apart. A paltry 1% earned in a money market fund still beats 1% *lost* in a mutual fund. Remember, this is your emergency stash, so don't tie it all up in a six-month maturity. Emergencies don't stick to a schedule.

To find the best interest rates around the country, check "iMoneyNet" at www.ibcdata.com for money markets, and www.bankrate.com for CDs.

Think Like a Millionaire

Maybe you've read *The Millionaire Next Door*. Downturn or not, there are still about seven million Americans with a net worth of $1 million or more or half a million in investable assets. We've known a number of self-made millionaires, and none of them got there by spending their hard-earned money on status symbols.

Millionaires *invest* approximately 20% of their household incomes each year. Sure, it seems easier when your income is in the seven figures, but many of them started small. People who become rich put their money into ventures that will earn money. Instead of buying your dream house in a trendy neighborhood when you're starting out, buy a duplex in an up-and-coming part of town and rent out half, then sell when the market goes up.

Ordinary folks have done this. We received a call on our show once from a newly-wed couple in California who told us they'd taken our advice and, instead of buying a single-family home, purchased a triplex shortly after they returned home from their honeymoon. They used money given to them as wedding presents for the down payment. They moved into one unit and rented out the other two. The two rents almost covered their mortgage, so they were able to buy another rental property. Nothing like starting a marriage with plenty of investment income!

Money markets carry slightly higher interest rates than a bank savings account, but they aren't federally insured. Still, your money should be safe with an established money market fund. Vanguard, Fidelity, and T. Rowe Price, to name just a few, have been around for years, and their money market funds have never lost their clients a dime. (*Note:* We are not talking about stock and bond mutual funds, which *do* go up and down.)

It's always good to keep some of your savings in CDs or Treasury bills, because they come with maturity dates, so that you are forced to keep your money locked in for a designated period. We're all weak when money is right there, after all. They come with maturity dates of three months or six months from the date you open the account.

Step 6: Be Good to Yourself

Factor in a small splurge here and there; you need to be good to yourself in tough times, too.

When Things Go *Very* Wrong

Be prepared for anything and everything.

No one could have been prepared for that horrendous day of September 11, 2001.

Among the many poignant conversations we had on our show in the months that followed was one with a woman from Brooklyn whose husband, a waiter at Windows on the World, the restaurant at the top of the World Trade Center, left that morning to work the breakfast shift and never came back. Our caller told us she didn't even know how to write a check, and that if the American Red Cross didn't come to her rescue soon, she might not be able to keep feeding her children. Liz, whose husband, Robert, was a senior vice president at Fiduciary Trust, on the ninety-sixth floor of Tower 2, knew that her husband had a will, but the only copy had been in his desk drawer at the World Trade Center. (See Chapter 9 for more details.)

We've all learned the hard way that we must *be ready for the unthinkable.* If you have six months of expenses in savings, you're in better shape than 99% of the population. But as you're building your savings, think about what you'd do if something happened tomorrow and your emergency kitty wasn't full.

Do you have assets you could liquidate, such as stocks, bonds, or mutual funds? (If you don't have six months of expenses saved, you should not be invested at all.)

Do you have jewelry or heirlooms you could sell?

In times of crisis we need our friends and family. To whom could you turn for an emergency loan? Talk about it with that person in advance.

Evaluate your investments. Are you taking too many risks with your "emergency capital"? This is money that you might need to support you and your family after a layoff.

Keep your portfolio liquid enough that you could switch to income-oriented invest-ments—we don't recommend any risk during times of emergency—to tide you over if you lose your steady income and can't afford to wait out a dip in the stock market.

Whatever you do, *keep only a small percentage, 5% to 10% max, of your investments or retirement account in your company's stock.* Since the Enron debacle, when employee 401(k) assets were frozen as the stock began to deflate, too many people have learned the hard way that relying on your company for an income is risky enough; if your investments are also tied up in the company's fortunes, you might find yourself wiped out. We might see federal laws that will prevent companies from adopting 401(k) plans with major hold-ings in their own stock. But if the past is any indication of the future, changes in the law will probably create as many problems as they cure. Your best protection against govern-ment and corporate shenanigans is to keep your holdings well diversified. (See Chapter 5.)

Open up a home equity line of credit if you think a layoff might be coming. We don't usually recommend tapping into your home, but this is a line of credit *to fall back on if all else fails.* The issuer will give you a line of credit that works like a credit card, but with lower interest rates and interest payments that are usually tax-deductible. *Don't use this line of credit unless you have no other choice.* And we mean no choice; take a job bagging groceries before you use your home as income. It's an emergency card to keep around. The reason to do this now is that if you should happen to find yourself out of work, it will be harder to get credit, so take out the line of credit while you're working, then stash it far from temptation's way.

These are basic precautions that everyone should take. In Chapter 9 we'll discuss hor-ror scenarios no one likes to imagine, but we'll show you how planning ahead can cush-ion the financial and even the emotional blow of death, divorce, and job loss.

How Do the Dolans Manage Their Finances?

Just a few days before our wedding, Ken confessed that he had a credit card debt of $3,000. That was in 1970, when a new Volvo cost $3,300. I was working as a flight atten-dant and, like most young single women in those days, had no credit cards of my own, and I was horrified at the idea of beginning a life together in hock. So I asked my father to cosign a loan so that we could pay the credit cards off quickly. But then we had to pay off that loan, so I figured we would have to go on a rigorous spending diet.

Ken has always hated diets, but counting financial calories turned out to be good for us, as it will for anyone. We cut up Ken's credit cards, every single one of them. We didn't buy anything we couldn't pay off within 30 days. That's a good policy for everyone. When we had our first apartment, one of our first cash transactions was buying two five-dollar pillows. For a while we ate dinner sitting cross-legged on those pillows. We bought furniture as we could afford it, and in the meantime we had a lot of empty spaces. And we were blissfully free of the burden of debt. That was our own little piece of nirvana.

Daria Pays Our Bills, Even Now.
But We're Not Saying You Should Try This at Home. . . .

I pay the bills because I am the more organized one in this couple when it comes to gathering up the bills and paying them in a timely fashion. But if Ken had never been a stockbroker, had never hosted a personal finance talk show . . . if Ken had been staying home writing poetry all these years while I earned a living helping people with their finances, you can bet I would sit him down and say, "Look, here are our monthly bills. Here is what we spend each month. Here is our investment statement." I'd make sure he was money literate.

We are both money involved. So it's okay that I happen to be the party who writes the checks, because Ken knows just where we stand.

But for people not in the money business, I believe it's imperative that they sit together when the bills need to be paid and discuss how they're going to invest. These responsibilities have to be interchangeable in case one partner is not around.

And invest only in items that the two of you understand and are comfortable with. Because inevitably what happens is the partner charged with handling the money side of the relationship does all of these things, the other partner is in the dark, and in the case of an emergency, they know nothing. Generally it's the wife left holding the financial bag. Statistically wives outlive their husbands, and certainly a woman in any relationship, married or not, has the statistical possibility of outliving her partner. A wife who lets her husband take care of all the money can fall victim to all sorts of scams, bad advice, and opportunists from the financial services business.

We're continually amazed at the number of people (well, okay, it's mostly wives) who don't know how to write checks. We had a next-door neighbor in Florida, a woman in her sixties, whose husband died unexpectedly. She came over and said, "I need some help." Turned out that, like the wife of the Windows on the World waiter, she had never so much as written a check! The fact that one person pays the bills doesn't mean the other shouldn't know what's going on.

If you sit down together every month and evaluate where you are and where you're going, then you both know how you're doing in terms of spending and saving money. If you both understand the types of investments you've made, you know which could be liquidated immediately in case of an emergency. And it also forces you to sit down and talk about the people in your lives, financial and personal, who could be trusted in an emergency.

Ken Answers to the CFO

If one party in a couple is really guilty of spending frivolously, you should decide right now that the stronger manager is going to be in charge of finances. As discussed above, for us that is most definitely Daria. She's the chief financial officer (CFO) of Dolan Family, Inc. When our daughter, Meredith, was growing up, no one made a big purchase without authorization from Daria, and I still discuss major expenditures with her—except, of course, around our anniversary, her birthday, and Christmas. Gifts are always allowed; if there's one lesson we all learn from tragedy, it's that life is short and we should be appreciative of the people we love. Just keep gifts within your budget.

With a profligate spender in the family, you should definitely put most of both paychecks in a joint bank account, so that the spender has to answer to the CFO.

Could I do what Daria does as well as Daria? Maybe. Could I learn to do it? Yes. Do I have enough knowledge to step in if we had an emergency? Yes, I do. I don't want to do it, but I certainly know where the checkbook is, and what bills come in every month that need to be paid. I recommend that every couple, right now, stop here and make sure each of you knows where the checkbook is kept and where the bills are!

Settling the "Guess" Work

Like all kids, our daughter, Meredith, wanted to wear cool jeans. We understood, but we also wanted her to know what things were really worth.

Daria recalls a day when Meredith was 12:

We were shopping, and I had to put my foot down and tell her there was absolutely no way I was going to buy her the Guess jeans that cost $90. I told her, "I wouldn't spend $90 on jeans for myself, and I won't even outgrow them." I bought her $32 jeans, and I thought they looked terrific on her.

But rather than relying on Mom's opinion, here's what Meredith, who is now grown-up and married, said when I called her and asked her if she remembered the Guess incident: "I wouldn't buy my kid $90 jeans today, either. In fact, I'm wearing jeans I bought at a discount store right now."

She accepted our spending habits and nonspending habits because we were consistent. Mom never gave in. Dad never said yes after Mom said no. We told her it's what's in your head and heart that really counts; she has known since childhood that wearing clothes from Guess or Ralph Lauren doesn't make you a better person than wearing clothes from Target or Wal-Mart.

For Couples Only

If you are half of a couple, you probably won't be surprised to learn that money is the number-one reason that couples split up. We've had countless calls since we've been on the air from people who fight with their partners about money, even if they went into the relationship thinking they saw eye-to-eye on financial matters. A trivial argument over one partner wanting to spend money on something that isn't quite as important to the other partner can escalate into a major battle over the values you each hold dear. Before you know it, you are pointing fingers at each other over career choices, matters of taste ("Why would you spend all that money on that hideous chair?"), and how you're bringing up your children.

We've seen it and heard it all. A member of our family, who shall remain nameless for the sake of peace at the Thanksgiving table, bought a 40-foot boat without discussing it with his wife, who had an inordinate fear of water. Their marriage never recovered from this one impulsive purchase—granted, an extravagant one, made even more expensive by the fact that he never learned how to pilot the boat; to use it, he had to hire members of the Coast Guard on their days off! Though he finally sold the boat, they were divorced a few years later. Moral: Spend money unwisely and your partner might not forgive you.

Why do couples fight? The best explanation we've seen yet comes from our good friend Olivia Mellan. Olivia is a psychologist who specializes in counseling couples about money issues, and she is an author of many books, most recently *Money Shy to Money Sure*. Her experience with couples led her to a theory of relationship-itivity that she calls Mellan's Law.

Think of it: Money is at the root of every decision you make together, starting with your first date. Did you go to McDonald's or Le Cirque? It was all determined by money.

If you're committed to spending your lives together, you've got to respect each other's money needs.

Money Secrets = Relationship Secrets

From the first day we went on the air, we've had people calling asking about the merits of keeping finances separate in a relationship versus handling all of the money jointly.

Olivia Mellan always tells our listeners that a woman should have some money and a credit card that she keeps in her own name. Women generally outlive their husbands, she points out, and need to be prepared to take care of themselves if disaster should strike. We think this is sound advice. And if you're the nonbreadwinner in a couple, whether you're a man or a woman, you should have an account and credit card in your name just in case something you never wanted to think would happen happens. *But . . .*

Mellan's Law: Why Money Personalities *Always* Collide

Moving in with the person you love? Even if you think like clones when it comes to money matters now, you *will* fight about money.

That's because when two personalities occupy the same space, inevitably they succumb to Mellan's Law: "If opposites don't attract, the relationship will create two opposites."

Olivia Mellan has divided people into four different money personalities:

- The Worrier
- The Avoider
- The Hoarder
- The Spender

Often Hoarders are Worriers and Spenders are Avoiders.

But money personalities adapt to each other by turning into polar opposites. Even if you are a Worrier and you marry a Worrier, one of you is going to worry more. The one who worries less is going to become a Spender or Avoider by comparison. "The same qualities you admired in your partner in the beginning will drive you crazy later on," says Olivia.

What do you do about it? Olivia advises that each of you acknowledge what you appreciate and envy about the other's money style. Then "walk a mile in each other's moccasins." In other words, try changing roles, writing journal entries of how it feels to act like your partner. These exercises will help you understand each other's money needs.

Be grateful for your differences. They're a sort of natural shock therapy to keep the two of you from going overboard with hoarding or spending, worrying or avoiding.

For us, we're both Hoarders and savers, but Daria is more of a saver.

Ken was a "premarital spender," and he had to learn to control it in the early days of our marriage. Daria has some not-so-fond memories:

I used to keep a suitcase half-packed and stuffed under the bed, ready to make my escape home to Mom and Dad if Ken didn't stop spending. I sometimes think the only reason I didn't go was the fear of hearing my mother say, "I told you so!"

But Ken has now taken on the role of Hoarder. I'm the one who has to tell him it's okay to buy something he has his eye on.

We're all in agreement, when the three of us talk about this issue on our show, that there should be no money secrets in a good relationship. If you've suddenly found yourself with an abusive spouse, that's a different story; you don't want this partner to have access to your money. But in a *good* relationship, both parties should know what's coming in and what's going out. Because if you're spending money without the knowledge of your partner, you're creating a veil of secrecy. It's a form of cheating on your spouse, engaging in clandestine purchases or investments. Are you with each other or not? If you're going to have a relationship in which you communicate well with each other, you're going to have to be open about where your money goes.

Consequently, we think it is imperative that there be a general household account, with both parties as signatories. The household bills, including your personal expenditures, should go through this account. Otherwise how do you know your partner isn't overspending and killing your plan for success?

The Dolan Checklists in this chapter will help you manage the money that is "yours, mine, and ours" before and after you move in together.

It doesn't sound very romantic, but take our word: Money matters can make or break your romance. Money really does matter.

Before You Start Living Together

✓ Talk about money and be honest about your assets and liabilities, income and outflow. You may want to forget your past relationships and make a fresh start, but your relationship with money will follow you forever.

✓ Sit down together and add up your individual debts. Come up with a plan to pay them off as soon as possible.

✓ Decide how you are going to keep your bank accounts—joint or separate. If you decide to keep separate accounts, open a joint one for your household expenses.

✓ Plan your joint money goals and how you are going to reach them together.

After You've Moved In

✓ Discuss your goals regularly, preferably at a time when you're not under the gun to solve a money problem. Even when you keep separate accounts, you need to coordinate financial plans if you hope to retire together.

✓ Settle on who will be CFO of your two-person corporation and how you will delegate money duties. Who is going to pay the bills, balance the checkbook, and handle investments? The other party should get a full briefing of these activities, and

Money Matters You Must Settle *After* the Wedding

1. Estimate how much tax you'll owe as a couple next year by filling out an IRS Form 1040 for "married filing jointly." Ask your tax professional how many exemptions you should take on your W-4 form. (You can get a new W-4 form from your employer.) That way, you'll have the taxes deducted throughout the year, rather than getting a nasty surprise come tax time.

2. Change your beneficiary. If you have an employer pension plan or a life insurance policy, make your spouse your beneficiary.

3. Review your health coverage. Many times, it makes sense to combine your health insurance under one plan. Under most plans you have 30 days from your wedding day to add your spouse to your employer-paid health insurance plan without subjecting the new plan member to a medical exam.

4. Review your disability insurance. Now that someone else is depending on your income, it's doubly important that you have adequate coverage. The disability coverage you have through your employer may not be adequate; at best it may replace only 80% of your income. You'll have a lot at stake if one of you becomes temporarily disabled—especially once you and your spouse have a mortgage to pay.

5. Prepare your estate plan. First, both of you need a will. It's best to hold everything in joint ownership when you have limited assets—such as cars, your house, and bank accounts. With joint ownership, you avoid probate and, in most cases, estate taxes when the first spouse dies. As your estate grows over the years, you and your spouse may want to own some property individually so that you can take advantage of more complex estate-planning techniques.

6. Start funding your tax-deferred retirement plans. You and your spouse will be well on your way to an early retirement if you get started saving money in tax-deferred accounts. Take advantage of 401(k), 403(b), SEP-IRA, and Keogh plans and fully fund your IRAs (as long as your contributions are tax-deductible).

be senior VP of other household functions, such as shopping or home repairs. But remember: You each work for the other, and good executives delegate. So learn how to perform each other's duties.

✓ Now that you've set up a "corporate" structure, resolve to hold "board meetings" at least once a month. This is when you'll report to each other on where your money

The Dolans' MMD Quiz (Be Honest)

Are you in danger of coming down with MMD? That's Marital Money Discord. Take our quick quiz to find out:

1. Do you discuss money matters such as budgeting in a calm manner at least once a month?

   ____ Yes   ____ No

2. Do you feel that you and your spouse are money peers?

   ____ Yes   ____ No

3. Do you and your spouse use credit cards sparingly? Do you know, chapter and verse, how much you owe on your cards?

   ____ Yes   ____ No

4. Do you discuss purchases, both personal and household, with your spouse before you make them?

   ____ Yes   ____ No

5. Do you encourage and discuss money responsibility with your kids?

   ____ Yes   ____ No

If you answered Yes to every one of these questions, you are well on the way to marital money health. If not, it's time to pull up your bootstraps and get to work—together. Isn't your marriage worth it?

---

is going and vote yea or nay on purchases you're considering. Make a plan to consult with each other on any purchases that cost more than a pre-agreed-upon amount, maybe $200; pick a realistic amount that won't break the budget. Even if it's for something the household really needs, your partner deserves a say.

✓ Don't criticize your partner about money matters in front of others. Talk openly, but talk privately!

✓ Never go to bed mad—especially about a money matter. You'll start the next day on the wrong foot!

✓ Coordinate your responses when your kids ask for something, so they don't play one parent against the other. If Mom says "no," Dad says "no."

Bank Fees . . . You *Can* Fight Back!

This section is not going to win us any friends in the banking industry, but we don't care. We think it's crucial that you know how much money your bank could be making from you.

We've heard from listeners with some truly weird tales of what goes on at banks: ATM machines that screw up, incompetent financial planners sitting in some bank branches, a charge to talk to a teller, telephone lines with absolutely no access to a human.

Well, get ready for a trend you might turn out to like even less. We're starting to see banks try to "brand" themselves with new gimmicks, such as "greeters" who welcome you at the door, free magazine subscriptions, Sunday banking hours, and even game areas to keep your kids occupied. Why are they doing this? Because there are so many banks competing for customers for a high-stakes range of products, including investments, insurance, and credit cards in addition to traditional bank accounts. They want you to have *fun* on their premises, so that you'll open more kinds of accounts!

Be prepared for aggressive marketing when you step into a bank. More than ever, you have to be a savvy shopper. Keep an eye out, especially, for banks that keep adding on hefty fees along with their "customer-friendly" campaigns. One thing you can fight is "fee creep." You can look for a bank that keeps its fees down.

Since 1945, fees have risen from 35% to 50% of banks' income, according to R. K. Hammer Investment Bankers, a financial services consultant in Thousand Oaks, California . . . fees for cash transfers, bounced checks, balances below a certain level, ATM transactions, dormant accounts, money orders, stopped checks, lost safe-deposit keys . . . and more. Many bank clients (you!) are unaware of banks' fee creep.

What Is "Fee Creep"?

It's that sneaky practice of slipping in account fees this month that weren't there last month. Your bank will, as a display of good customer communication practices, send you a letter warning that it is introducing a new fee or raising an existing one, all as the price of "serving you better." These creeping fees can cut into your balance like crabgrass on your lawn. Watch out for these trends, all sure signs of fee creep:

Trend Your bank starts charging a dollar or so to deposit money into your account and another dollar or so to withdraw money. There might be a small fee for talking with a teller at the window. And you thought the teller was just doing her job! More widespread, however, is the fee for the convenience of using an ATM.

What to do If there is a bank in your area that doesn't impose ATM fees, take your business there. They do exist. Check www.bankrate.com for Bankrate's list of banks with surcharge-free ATMs around the country. And write a letter to the manager of the bank you're leaving explaining that the fees are what drove you away. We're not crazy about ATMs anyway. If you plan ahead and get to the bank when it's open, we think you tend to be a little more careful about financial matters.

But especially avoid using another bank's ATM. They'll "surcharge" you $2 or more per transaction. It's a convenience when you're traveling, but withdraw larger rather than smaller sums to get your money's worth, since each transaction will cost the same. Look at it this way: If you get into the habit of withdrawing $50 from the corner ATM twice a week and you pay a surcharge of $2 each time, you'll lose $208 a year in fees for this little convenience.

Read the ATM screen carefully. Banks are required to disclose their surcharges. And stay away from ATMs in high-traffic areas such as hotels, airports, or casinos. The surcharges there are often even higher than those at banks. A $3 or $4 charge on a transaction is not unheard of in some states.

Trend Your bank is eager to spare you the horror of bouncing a check, so it offers you overdraft checking privileges, a permanent line of credit. The bank will automatically cover your checks up to a certain amount even if you don't have the funds in your account. But wait: You'll have to pay back the "loan" with interest. Some banks charge $20 to $25 or even more for an overdraft check, which costs the bank only a dollar or two to process!

What to do Don't you think that a 2,000% profit is too much? We do. To avoid overdraft charges:

1. Know your bank's clearing schedule.
2. Never write a check for more than your balance.
3. If you're not sure a check will clear, check your balance first.
4. Just say "no" to overdraft protection.

Trend The bank charges you as much as $15 to $20 for every 200 new checks. Those nice checks with your name and address come in your choice of colors or, for a premium fee, an image of an idyllic landscape or Elvis in his prime. They're a major profit maker for the bank. But do you think your long-distance provider and the bank that receives your mortgage payments (maybe the same bank that issues the checks) appreciate the pretty pictures you send them each month?

What to do Save a few bucks, for heaven's sake. You don't have to buy your checks from the bank. Order personalized checks from Checks In The Mail (800-733-4443; www.citm.com), or from Checks Unlimited (800-426-0822). These companies issue personalized checks, with a choice of designs, at about half the price of most banks.

Trend Some banks offer overpriced products and services, such as the service that automatically debits your account for a biweekly mortgage payment rather than the standard monthly mortgage payment. Your bank may charge $300 to $500 per year for relieving you of the task of writing this monthly check.

Dolan Ah-Ha

What to do We do believe in paying off your mortgage as quickly as possible. But why pay the bank to do it for you? Instead, do this: Divide one month's mortgage payment by 12. Send an extra 1/12 each month toward your principle's balance. Voilà—you will have accomplished the same feat for no charge.

Trend When the prime lending rate goes down, the first thing to suffer is your savings account. Your bank will never tell you how thrilled they are that they can use your money and pay you such a low interest rate. Many banks keep the rate excessively low to "encourage" you to invest in annuities and mutual funds.

What to do Roll the money into a money market mutual fund. You'll nearly double the rate of return without sacrificing liquidity.

Trend Banks make a lot of money in penalties and fees if your checking account drops below the minimum amount that you must keep in the account. And they waive check charges only on accounts with large balances.

What to do Although few banks will volunteer this information, you can ask and see if your bank will allow you to combine your checking, savings, and money market balances to meet the required minimum. Ask!

If you have an interest-bearing account, ask your bank to calculate the interest in the way that is best for you—from day of deposit to day of withdrawal, compounded *daily*.

And find out if the interest is "tiered." Many banks offer a higher rate of interest if your balance goes above a certain floor. What, they didn't tell you?! Guess they were just too busy dreaming up new ways to serve you better at a price.

Trend Many banks don't adequately explain all the important details relating to their credit cards. Many use misleading advertising and complicated new account forms to confuse you.

What to do Ask these questions before you sign up:

- Is there a low introductory rate if I sign up? How long does it last? What is the rate after that?
- What is the grace period for my payments?
- Can I transfer balances from other cards?
- What services come with the card? Some services you might expect are car rental insurance; a free safe-deposit box; free checking if you are a senior citizen or disabled, or if you have a mortgage, car loan, or certificate of deposit at the same bank.
- What is my liability if the card is lost or stolen? Is there a toll-free emergency phone number to call? See "What Your Credit Card Company Doesn't Want You to Know" in Chapter 4.

At all times, however, open all of the mailings from your credit card company, and watch out for "Changes to our Agreement." Read all of the fine print. Credit card issuers have a nasty habit of getting you in, then shortening the grace period or upping the ante on late fees. Be prepared to look for a better deal if your issuer changes terms.

The Bottom Line

Decide what kinds of banking services you need and shop around for the banks that best suit those needs. You don't have to stick close to home anymore now that online banking has come of age. Go to Bankrate.com (www.bankrate.com) for comparisons of banks around the country. If you want to venture into a pure-play Internet bank, get comparisons from Gomez Advisors (www.gomezadvisors.com), an independent, consumer-oriented outgrowth of a research and consulting firm that studies many features of electronic commerce and is particularly good with banks.

If you are considering a new bank, ask for a list of all possible fees. Then see if you can negotiate to lower some of those fees. You may be surprised at how flexible a new bank can be. Until all banks merge into one global giant, there is still competition for new customers.

How Are You Doing?

We've adapted this rundown of financial vital signs from a list designed by Rutgers Cooperative Extension. Use this list to see where you need to build up financial strength.

1. **Financial Goals.** Set dates for realizing your goals and figure out how much money you will need. Your goals should be attainable and relevant to you personally. Goals have different time frames and should be considered when making investment decisions.

2. **Net Worth.** Your net worth is calculated by subtracting debts from assets. Ideally, net worth should increase by 5% or more each year as a result of increased savings and reduced debt.

3. **The "Wealth Test."** This is the formula from *The Millionaire Next Door* that tells you where your net worth should be at your particular age and income. To calculate this figure, multiply your age times your income and divide by ten.

4. **Income and Expense Statement.** Add up both each month, with the objective of achieving a positive cash flow.

5. **Financial Ratios.** Your liquid assets should be equal to three to six months of expenses, for emergencies. Total debts should be less than total assets, or a household is technically insolvent. In another ratio, annual debt payments, including a mortgage, should be 36% or less of annual gross income.

6. **Spending Plan/Budget.** Do you have a spending plan? This is another valuable checkup tool because you can see if you are earning and spending money as anticipated. A spending plan includes projected amounts for income and expenses. Ideally, income should equal expenses plus money placed in savings. Adjust your spending plan as needed. People get into unmanageable debt when they lose track of just how much they're spending.

7. **Credit Card Checkup.** See Chapter 4 to assess whether you have too many credit cards and are paying too much interest. Try negotiating a lower interest rate and check your credit file periodically for errors.

8. **Tax Checkup.** What is your marginal tax bracket and would you earn more in a taxable or tax-exempt investment? Consider funding a tax-deferred employer retirement savings plan, such as a 401(k), and making a traditional or Roth IRA contribution if you are eligible.

9. **Insurance Checkup.** Do you have all of the policies you need to insure your life, health, and possessions? Are you paying too much for life insurance policies that promise cash value and won't necessarily deliver? See Chapter 10.

10. **Retirement Checkup.** First, you estimate the amount of income required annually. Next, you subtract anticipated sources of income. Finally, you determine the amount of savings needed per year and per paycheck.

11. **Social Security and Pension Checkup.** As you consider the state of your retirement plans, be sure to check on your expected Social Security and/or pension benefit. Also be alert to pension plan changes such as a switch from a traditional defined benefit plan to a less favorable cash-balance plan.

12. **Investment Performance Checkup.** To do this calculation, you need to know your beginning and ending account balance and the amount of money deposited in the account throughout the year. Are the allocations of your portfolio in stocks, bonds, and cash balanced in the way that is best for you?

13. **Estate Planning Checkup.** Do you have a will and a living trust? Does your partner? Do you each have copies of the other's estate plan? See Chapter 12.

Source: Adapted from Rutgers Cooperative Extension

Helpful Web Sites and Books

General Financial Well-Being

www.moneycentral.msn.com: Microsoft's MoneyCentral portal

www.smartmoney.com

Rutgers Cooperative Extension: www.rce.rutgers.edu for more on financial basics. Click on RU-FIT, Rutgers University Financial Independence Training.

Creating a "Success Plan" (formerly known as a "budget")

The American Bankers Association Web site has a budgeting game, which you can play with ABA's "Penny Banks," whose mother used to tell her budgeting is like a scale, because it tells you what you don't want to know. Go to www.aba.com/Consumer+ Connection/cnc_games.htm and click on their "On the Money Budget Game." You will need to install Shockwave from their site.

Banking and Credit Cards

www.ibcdata.com has consumer information about money market mutual funds.

www.bankrate.com has information on credit card, savings, and CD interest rates, banks with surcharge-free ATMs, and other consumer banking information.

www.fdic.gov has a list of Internet banks that are federally insured.

Couples and Money

www.moneyharmony.com is Olivia Mellan's Web site. Her newsletter deals with money issues that affect couples.

Alternatives to Marriage Project: www.unmarried.org. Site with information on financial and legal issues for same-sex and opposite-sex cohabitating couples.

Money Shy to Money Sure: A Woman's Road Map to Financial Well-Being, by Olivia Mellan and Sherry Christie; Walker & Co., 2001. $25.00.

Bank Ratings and Comparisons

www.bankrate.com

www.gomez.com

Trouble with Your Bank

Federal Reserve Board: www.federalreserve.gov/pubs/complaints/

U.S. Public Interest Research Group: www.pirg.org/consumer/banks/debit/fact.htm

CHAPTER 3

Your Home: Look Out for Your Number-One Asset

HOUSING BOOM HITS ... mortgage rates the lowest in more than 30 years ... now's the time to buy. ... Buy, buy, buy!

Hold on a minute! Take a breath. Some time ago, *BusinessWeek* ran an incredible article titled "The Housing Boom's Dark Side," highlighting the fact that soaring home prices are making eager buyers easy prey for scamsters for such things as fee rip-offs, overpriced credit, overblown evaluation, insurance scams ... and more! This chapter will help you get the best deal when you buy or sell your home. We don't want you to be a "bad deal" statistic!

It's true that America loves real estate (so does most of the world, actually), and the Dolans are no exception. Between 2001 and 2002 we closed on, or helped close family members close on, five homes. Five! Needless to say, we empathize fully with our listeners who, whether their incomes are average, well above average, or below average, have one thing in common: homeownership, with all of its joys and expenses.

What other investment becomes the focal point of your life? When the home becomes a matter of contention between the two parties in a relationship, it leads to a life on edge. When people buy themselves the top-of-the-line home or vacation property they've always wanted, then lose income due to a layoff, divorce, or death, there is nothing more devastating than looking around their beautiful house and realizing it could all be gone tomorrow.

We get a constant stream of calls from people in search of the American dream, wanting to buy their first or second home and wondering why the price of a house is so far out of line with salaries in so many parts of the country, and why the real estate market has stayed close to the stratosphere in many parts of the country while the rest of the economy has tanked. Part of the reason may be low mortgage rates, which enticed many people to buy homes. Another contributing factor is the sorry state of the stock market, which has led high rollers to stay away from equities and put their money into real estate speculation. Between 1999 and 2002, existing-home values rose 16.7% while the S&P 500 Index declined 7.5%!*

If you're thinking about buying now, or selling your present house and relocating or upgrading, or buying a vacation house or investment property, you should pay close attention to the warning signs of a real estate market going into decline. The housing market as a rule doesn't move as fast as the rest of the economy. Sellers don't immediately lower their prices when demand slows; they just let their properties sit on the market longer. One indication that a real estate market is about to decline is properties that have been languishing on the listings page for several months. In many parts of the country properties are sitting, especially higher-end housing in places like Silicon Valley. Another sign is a glut of offerings from the mortgage industry. We are seeing mortgage lenders coming up with a plan to suit every home browser: interest-only loans, and smaller and smaller down payments, to name two. It could mean that lenders are nervous.

Unfortunately, you can't count on predictable market cycles, and you can't believe anyone who claims to have a crystal ball. You can assume that economic recovery will bring a certain amount of stability to the real estate market. But the lesson so many Americans have learned the hard way is that you can't be sure the cushy paycheck you have today will be there tomorrow. Never again will anyone be able to make financial decisions based on job security. The *very* first asset you want to protect from all forms of paycheck insecurity is the roof over your head, which also happens to be the biggest purchase most folks ever make. This is one investment that gives you no room for risk-taking.

Buying a Home

On the face of it, any time is a good time to buy a house if you do your homework, which means checking comparable values and realistically figuring out how much house you can afford. If you and your partner have been able to hang on to your jobs, low interest rates make a first home, a vacation house, or an investment property an attractive prospect. But go over your finances when you're wide awake. Ask yourself and your spouse or partner a really tough question: If one of you were out of the picture, or lost your job, could the remaining earner afford to keep up the mortgage and maintenance? It's not a

---

* *Source:* National Association of Realtors, released April 5, 2002.

good idea to buy a house based on the combined incomes of two wage earners. There are just too many uncertainties.

Take, for example, the problems our daughter's best friend and her husband are currently going through in the Boston area.

Sally and Joe were both working for dot.com companies. You can pretty much guess the rest. In 1999 they had combined incomes in the low six figures. It didn't dawn on Sally until later that the $50,000-a-year she was getting to be a proofreader, correcting typos on a Web site, might be out of line. Joe's job, although more technically oriented, also paid a salary that seems excessive in retrospect. Flush with their dot.com income, they bought a house just outside of Boston.

A mere four months after the closing, Sally lost her job when her company dot.bombed. Shortly after, Joe's company—and his job—met the same fate.

It took them months to find new jobs, with many anxious days and nights spent worrying about how they'd be able to keep the house. Their new jobs pay a lot less than the old ones, though they probably offer more stability.

They are still in the house, scrimping on just about everything to make the mortgage payments. No more eating in restaurants, no new clothes, no vacations, not much in the kitty to finance home repairs if they need them. They're getting by, but keeping their fingers crossed.

Consider a few other real estate realities before you make any formal offers:

- ✓ The prices of high-end houses rise and fall faster than those of more modest homes.
- ✓ In an area where the economy is tied to one industry, such as Silicon Valley, today's multimillion-dollar mansion could be tomorrow's white elephant, with no rebound in sight.
- ✓ Don't assume that a good school district guarantees price stability; if the number of school-age children in the neighborhood declines over time, the real estate market might drop in tandem.
- ✓ Condominiums are less expensive than houses, but the prices are much more volatile.

First-Time or Seasoned Buyer: How Much Home Can You *Really* Afford?

That's a question Socrates would be pondering if he were a twenty-first-century philosopher, considering every market variable. But most lenders will answer with a simple formula. Your mortgage payments—including principal, interest, taxes, and insurance, which is often abbreviated as PITI—should equal no more than 28% of your *gross* income. Not your net, but your income before taxes.

The Perils of Joint Ownership
When Your Love Nest Falls Apart

We hope you live happily ever after in your home together. But since couples *do* break up, consider what the consequences could be before it happens.

If you're officially married and you get a divorce, dividing the home will inevitably be a big issue in court. If you're a two-income couple and one spouse dies, can the surviving spouse keep up the mortgage payments? These are the nasty questions you have to consider.

If disaster hits home, can you afford to keep up the payments? Oftentimes you can't. If you know your finances can't maintain the house, as hard as it is, sell the house before it becomes a credit problem.

Did you know that most foreclosures on homes are due to divorce? A couple gets into a snit over who is responsible for the joint property, and they start missing payments. Or they can't afford to keep two homes going.

Often in a divorce, the settlement decrees that the wife can keep the house, but then she finds she can't pay for it. When in doubt about your ability to pay, it is far, far better to sell the house, get what you can out of it, split it as you have to according to your separation or divorce agreement, and move to something you can afford.

We know a woman who divorced her husband and they had to buy separate houses. She bought a fixer-upper because it was what she could afford and fell in love with the contractor who fixed it up for her. Now they're married and living happily in a renovated house. Okay, no guarantees of this, and we don't generally recommend buying a handyman's special unless you are a handyman. But sometimes it pays to make a fresh start in life, even if you have to scale down.

Sell your house before it becomes a credit problem, and before you have to worry about the bank foreclosing on it. Divorce is stressful enough all around without the worry that comes from a home you can't afford, no matter how much you love it.

If you're a cohabiting couple, our advice is *don't* buy a house together. If you should split up without that ball and chain of a legally binding marriage contract, the home you bought together is going to become an albatross around your necks. Here's what we recommend for **gay or heterosexual couples** who want to own property:

1. Qualify on one partner's income and make that person the owner. If the relationship goes south, at least you'll be clear on who owns the house and is going to continue paying for it. Still, you should sign an agreement stating who the owner

is. If the other partner puts money into repairs over the time you're together, your agreement should spell out some form of compensation. That could be money, or maybe furniture. And if the nonowner partner has provided furniture, silverware, or artwork, of course these items go when he or she does. Your agreement should list the pieces of value, whether monetary or sentimental, and who their rightful owner is.

2. This is an option whether you're about to buy a house together or are a cohabitating couple living in a house you own together now. You can still draw up a contract that turns your ownership into a business partnership. Structure the purchase the way you would a real estate transaction with a business partner, with a legally binding contract. If you split up, one party is obligated to buy the other out, or you will have to sell the house on the market and split the proceeds.

    This is also a good way to buy investment property together. If you own a piece of rental property together and are getting income from the tenants, how you handle the income should be based on whether you need it for the property or not. We suggest you either put that money into a joint account for maintenance of the property only—and sign an agreement to that effect—or divide it in half.

3. Instead of one big house, buy two smaller properties, one at the beach or in the countryside. Bob buys the main house, Sue buys the vacation house, or vice versa. Each of you owns one house free and clear.

Whether you're married or cohabitating, if you own property together and you decide to sell it, you will need that person's signature. We heard from a woman in California who, at the age of 79, was fed up with her "hardheaded" husband, as she called him. She wondered if she could get out of the marriage without the hassle of divorce proceedings. Not possible once you're entangled, and joint homeownership is one of the many reasons. He could take off for South America and leave her with a house she couldn't afford on her own yet couldn't sell without his consent, or she could do the same to him. Think of the nasty possibilities if you don't have the protection of a marriage contract! That's why we always view joint ownership as a business deal.

Dolan Bottom Line

If you don't have any long-term debt, your lender may offer to let you use more than 28% to qualify for a bigger mortgage. Some fast talkers are offering up to 40%. Stick to 28%. Remember: A bigger mortgage means a bigger payment.

Too many borrowers are being convinced by lenders that they are able to borrow more (sometimes *much* more!) than they can afford. Don't be a foreclosure statistic!

Don't let offers of lower down payments turn you into a homeowner who lives in fear of a downturn in your finances. A lot of home buyers are "qualifying" for mortgages they wouldn't have qualified for in the past—that is, mortgages with down payments of next to nothing. As of mid-2002, largely because of low- or no-down-payment deals, home mortgage payments as a percentage of disposable income were at their highest levels since the Federal Reserve began tracking that statistic in 1980. We've heard from countless listeners who are spending as much as 45% of their *gross* monthly income on their mortgages.

The chart on the next page shows the maximum monthly payment you can qualify for (using 28%), given your gross annual income. The chart also shows the maximum debt load (36%) a lender thinks you should carry.

Dolan Ah-Ha!

Has your lender tried to lure you into buying a more expensive house with an "interest-only" mortgage? It sounds like a deal and a half; you get a mortgage and pay nothing but the interest for the first 10 to 15 years, depending on the terms. This way your monthly payments are low and you get to take the mortgage-interest tax deduction on every bit of it—for the first phase of the mortgage. Now for the bad news. Most of these loans have adjustable rates, so your payments could skyrocket if interest rates rise. Furthermore, you'll have much higher payments when you switch to the conventional loan period.

Don't jump into this just to buy more house than you can afford up front. We are not fans of these mortgages for anyone, but *especially* don't do it if you'll be retiring in another 10 to 20 years and will have less income than you do now!

Do the Numbers

Gross Annual Income	Maximum Monthly PITI*	
	(28%)	(36%)
$25,000	$583	$750
$30,000	$700	$900
$35,000	$817	$1,050
$40,000	$933	$1,200
$45,000	$1,050	$1,350
$50,000	$1,167	$1,500
$55,000	$1,283	$1,650
$60,000	$1,400	$1,800
$65,000	$1,516	$1,980
$70,000	$1,633	$2,100
$75,000	$1,750	$2,250
$80,000	$1,867	$2,400
$85,000	$1,983	$2,550
$90,000	$2,100	$2,700
$95,000	$2,216	$2,850
$100,000	$2,333	$3,000
$125,000	$2,916	$3,750
$150,000	$3,500	$4,500
$175,000	$4,083	$5,250
$200,000	$4,666	$6,000
$225,000	$5,250	$6,750
$250,000	$5,833	$7,500

*PITI: Principal, Interest, Taxes, and Insurance.

When you're calculating your mortgage, you will have to factor in whether you have a fixed mortgage, in which the interest rate is set at the time of the loan for the life of the mortgage, or an adjustable rate mortgage, which is subject to changes in the interest rate. At a time when interest rates are low, it makes sense in most cases to get a fixed mortgage. See the section "Attention All Buyers: How to Get the *Best* of the Low Mortgage Rates."

Attention, First-Time Home Buyers

When we bought our first home, we were scared stiff wondering whether we really could afford it at all. The year was 1975 and our daughter hadn't had her third birthday yet. The house was selling for $51,000, and you could get a conventional mortgage with only 10% down, without paying private mortgage insurance. To be honest, neither of us remembers exactly how we found the $5,100 to put down, and the entire closing procedure has been erased from memory, much the way trauma victims suffer amnesia after a shocking event.

Young couples are always calling us now, shaking in their shoes about buying that first home, and who can blame them at a time when $299,000 isn't going to get them a hell of a lot, especially in a large metropolitan area. These prices make no sense, and if we could change the situation for you we would.

The Big Hurdle: Getting That First Down Payment

You and your significant other both have good jobs, or maybe you're single and starting out on the right track. You have a solid income and you'll have no problem making mortgage payments on a place of your own. . . . But first there's the down payment.

Lucky you if you've been saving your money since your first after-school job and now you have enough to make a down payment. If you're American and you've accomplished this amazing feat, you should be listed in *Ripley's Believe It or Not*.

The total amount of money that Americans have saved in recent years amounts to no more than 1% of total disposable income. Look back at Chapter 2 for some tips on creating a success plan (formerly known as a budget) that will help you save.

On the other hand, there are a few other ways of obtaining the money for a down payment. Some of these techniques are okay, some are not.

What's Okay

Your in-laws (or parents) are willing to make the down payment. Most likely you will set this up, then, as a "shared equity" transaction. If a relative puts up the money, he or she will most likely want to share equity in your house, taking a portion of the profit or loss when you sell the house. This partnership might be your ticket to a home of your own. But a business arrangement with close family members is a very tricky thing. Have a real estate lawyer handle the details and draw up a partnership agreement that all parties agree on.

Rent a house with an option to buy. Just as you can lease a car with the option to buy, a landlord might be willing to draw up a contract that gives you the right to buy the property during an agreed-upon period. In fact, this option makes more sense with a home than it does with a car, since cars depreciate the longer you own them. (See Chapter 6.) You agree up front to a purchase price. Part of your monthly payment is credited toward your down payment if you exercise your right to buy the home.

It's a win-win deal. You get to see if you like the house and the neighborhood. You get the benefits of appreciation if the value of the property rises during your tenancy, because the price that you'll pay is locked in. If the house depreciates during the term of the lease, you may elect not to buy. The seller gets income while you're renting. You should, however, prequalify for a mortgage before you enter into this kind of agreement. Again, consult a real estate attorney.

What's Not Okay

You're young (or not so young), healthy, and gainfully employed, and you know you could tap into your 401(k) or IRA. *Don't do it!*

Sure, it will be years until you retire and need the funds. But you may have to pay a 10% penalty on any withdrawals made before you're 59½, plus you'll always have to pay ordinary income tax on the amount you withdraw. If you hope to have funds for your retirement, you will have to pay back the account, in which case you will have two loans to pay off, the mortgage and the retirement savings loan.

If you *borrow* from your company's 401(k), it will be treated as a loan you have to pay back. But what if you were to quit or lose your job? Then you'll be up a creek: You'll have to repay the loan immediately, or it will be treated as a withdrawal, with all of the accompanying taxes and penalties. You could be unemployed for months, trying to pay your mortgage *and* saddled with this extra debt.

Here's a better idea for Generation Xers and Yers who have a home purchase in their sights. Pull back on your retirement funding, and put the money into a liquid savings account until you build up enough for the down payment, closing costs, and emergency fund. That should be a minimum of three months' income.

How Much Should You Put Down?

We used to think it was okay to buy a house with less than 20% down, but in uncertain times, that is a risk few people can afford. Say you buy with only 5% to 10% down. There are still plenty of lending institutions happy to finance this purchase for you. There's a reason your purchase will put a smile on their faces: The lender stands to make a ton of money from you. First of all, you'll have to purchase private mortgage insurance (PMI), the lender's insurance that you're going to pay off the mortgage. Don't confuse this with mortgage life insurance, which pays all or a portion of your mortgage in the event of your death. (See Chapter 10 for a litany of the many insurance policies we think are a scam; this is one of them.)

But about PMI. The average cost of PMI is about $80 a month, but it can go up to $100 or more. Figure that as an extra $960 to $1,200 a year that the insurer makes. This is the price you pay—one of them, anyway—for buying with a low down payment. There is a high rate of default among buyers who make low down payments, but lenders are willing to take the risk of financing mortgages with low down payments because of PMI. If it's a bearable sum for you, and worth the price of being a homeowner, that's fine. But keep reading.

Okay, so you can handle the insurance part of it. But we're not quite finished. Do you have enough money in liquid reserves to cover closing costs, and then several thousand dollars more in case your ceiling should just happen to spontaneously cave in one day?

These things happen all the time. We used all of our cash to buy our first house, and we were broke when we moved in, so we passed on a $200 inspection. Six months later, we were scrounging around to pay an exterminator $431 to save the house from termites! We cut back on everything and thought we were going to collapse from tuna casserole and Hamburger Helper fatigue, but better us than the beams!

And no fair taking this money out of your retirement savings. As we've already explained, you'll pay a 10% penalty plus taxes if you're under $59\frac{1}{2}$, and what's worse, if you start dipping into your IRA or 401(k) now, what will you live on when you retire?

Then there is the matter of your mortgage. The inverse ratio always applies: The lower your down payment, the higher your mortgage payments. You get the best mortgage rates when you make a down payment of at least 20%. If you buy a $300,000 house and make a 20% down payment, which is $60,000, then your mortgage amount is $240,000. Say

When Can You Cancel Your PMI?

The Federal Homeowners Protection Act, passed in 1999, requires lenders to cancel PMI when your home equity reaches 22% and gives you the right to request cancellation of PMI when your equity reaches 20%. However, lenders have rules of their own; some will require that you have a good payment record, and many will require that a new appraisal be completed at your expense. Most will require that your loan balance be below 75% to 80% of your property's value.

HSH Associates, the nation's largest publisher of consumer loan information, publishes "A Homeowner's Guide to Private Mortgage Insurance," which costs only $4. Send a money order to HSH Associates, Dept. PMI, 1200 Route 23, Butler, NJ 07405, or check their Web site at www.hsh.com/pmi-announce.html.

you get a 30-year fixed mortgage at a rate of 7%. Your payments will be approximately $1,400 a month the first year. Now, say you buy the same house with a down payment of only $15,000, or 5%. Your $285,000 30-year mortgage might come at a rate of 9% (for illustrative purposes; but your mortgage rate will most likely be higher than the going rate if you put less money down), which brings your first-year payments to $2,130 a month. Add to that a PMI of close to $100 each month. Then don't forget property taxes, which can range from several hundred dollars a year to several thousand, depending on where you live.

We know what you're thinking. We were renters the first three and a half years of our marriage. Like everyone who gets out of school, goes to work, then looks in the mirror one morning and thinks "Holy moly, I'm an adult," we were hit with that flash of adult insight: Why should I be paying good money to a landlord when I could be building equity?

No question, equity is a good thing to have. If you live in an expensive city—Boston or San Francisco, for example—and you're paying $1,500 or more a month in rent, who can blame you for thinking that you might as well just write your check every month, hold it up in the air, and let the four winds scatter your hard-earned money? If you live in New York City you're probably snickering right now, thinking $1500 is about enough to cover the rent on your closet, if you even *get* a closet for the king's ransom you pay.

Certainly, the money you are paying in rent could be going into a mortgage. Just be aware that you are going to have many other expenses, such as roof problems, leaks, extermination, property taxes, insurance against fire and flood, appliance repairs. . . . The list is endless when you own. Accidents and emergencies happen. Our advice is to have at least $5,000 in cash reserves before you make the leap.

The Bottom Line to This Question of the Ages?

Because we live in insecure times, you are much better off buying a house that costs less than your maximum "affordable" price. Don't buy as much house as you can possibly afford, because what if your financial situation changes for the worse? Buy the *smallest* house in the *best* neighborhood. This is no time to speculate on the *best* house in the *worst* neighborhood. If it's already up-and-coming, you might want to go ahead, but don't take chances on a blighted neighborhood becoming gentrified. We have a global economy to turn around before your part of town catches up.

What About the Tax Write-Off for Mortgage Interest?

Do you itemize your taxes? Then you will be able to deduct the interest on your mortgage from your income. But how much of a tax break is this going to give you? It's really just pennies that you're deducting. If you're in the 28% tax bracket, you are deducting only 28 cents for every dollar you pay out, and the impact of the deduction phases down once your income rises above $160,000 or so.

And if you're one of the 70% of all homeowners who don't itemize their taxes, you won't be able to take the deduction. For many homeowners, taking a standard deduction saves them more than itemizing to deduct mortgage interest.

So while you may have many good reasons for buying a home, don't be hoodwinked into thinking this is one of them.

Before You Shop for a House, Prequalify for a Mortgage

The best time to shop for a mortgage is *not* when your dream house (or the closest affordable version of it) is for sale. Visit several lenders and get a prequalification. Why? For several reasons:

1. You will get an exact calculation of the mortgage you can afford, so you can do your house hunting based on a realistic price.
2. You will be in a *much* stronger position to negotiate terms when you find the house you want. Prequalification is equivalent to "cash" in your pocket. Sellers' ears perk up when they hear the words "preapproved." They know it's a deal worth discussing, rather than a deal that could fall through because the buyer can't get financing.
3. The hunt for preapproval gives you a chance to find the best deal on a mortgage, as well as clean up your credit rating, if necessary, before you finalize the terms.

Approach at least two or three mortgage lenders. These might be credit unions, S&Ls, mortgage bankers, or mortgage brokers. You'll give the lender some financial information, such as your current salary, your debts, and other income, and the lender will use

Dolan Ah-Ha

Is there any possibility that you can buy a house based on one partner's income instead of two? That may be the best house to buy. Women *do* get pregnant and have to take time off work. Men *do* get fired. So do women, and either way, it always seems to happen at the worst possible time. Ergo . . . a mortgage that one spouse could handle on his or her income alone takes an awful lot of pressure off. Even if you plan on having no children, or continuing to work right after having your children, all couples have to consider what would happen if they suddenly found themselves living on one income, whether it's due to child-rearing, losing a job, divorce, or disaster. *Don't stretch your income to its limits.*

Dolan Tip

When you're looking for preapproval on a mortgage, be sure to get a "lock-in" on the interest rate your lender quotes of 60 days—or longer, but that's tough to get. A 30- or 45-day lock-in may not be enough if you're just beginning your house hunt. The woods are full of lenders that advertise a locked-in rate. You pay $400 to apply for a mortgage, and you go through the whole exhausting process only to find out that the rate the lender first quoted has gone up during your application process.

Get the lock-in before you apply and GET IT IN WRITING. If the lender won't give you a written document, save your money and drive on.

this information to present you with several mortgage options with various rates, points, and loan terms.

Smart Money Move

Before you visit lenders, get a copy of your credit report from the major credit reporting agencies. (See Chapter 4 for how to get a credit report.) Check the report for any errors or bad credit information. This way, when you sit down with a mortgage lender, you can be up front about any bad credit information that may appear on your report. You'll stand a better chance of qualifying for a mortgage if the lender knows where the bad credit information came from. Follow the credit bureau's instructions on how to fix any errors you find.

If You Rent Your Home

There are still some 30 million Americans who are renters rather than homeowners, whether out of choice or necessity. For people who are young, highly mobile, or both, renting might be the better choice. If you don't plan to stay in an area for more than two years, or are new in town and not sure if you're going to stay, renting while you test the terrain makes sense—especially now, because you don't know if high real estate prices are here to stay. You could buy a house at top dollar, then be unable to recoup your investment if you decide to sell in a couple of years.

At the same time, rental apartments and houses are no bargain in times of a strong real estate market, which makes things tough for those who want to save money to buy and pay minimal rent. It's *really* important to stick to a "success plan" (what some call a budget) when you're renting, since you aren't ever going to see a return on your money.

How much should you pay? Generally, your rent should be no more than one-third your gross monthly income. Don't go over that.

While we tell home buyers to buy the worst house in the best neighborhood, as a renter you might come out way ahead if you rent the best house or apartment in a so-so neighborhood, depending on how prices are structured in your area. Don't sign a long-term lease unless you have a GREAT deal; otherwise, as a renter you should always be keeping your eyes and ears open for a better deal than what you have.

The Apartment Renters Resource (www.aptrentersresource.com) has tons of information about the current state of rentals in many parts of the country, as well as renters' rights and a locator service. Here's some advice we particularly like from this valuable site:

- Don't move at the same time everyone else is moving. Many landlords, particularly the larger, professional management companies, price their apartments according to current demand, so that rents are higher during the busy season. That varies according to the area, of course: High season would be winter in Aspen, summer at the beach, September in a college town, the end of the school year in a family neighborhood. If you can move during the slow season, you might find a top deal.
- Ask for a lower price. Rental rates are not written in stone, and you may be able to negotiate—somewhat. You might be able to get some type of a rebate off your move-in costs or first month's rent, or get some up-front fees waived.

If You Wanna Be a Landlord

So you want to invest in rental property? We noted in the previous chapter that this can be a worthwhile investment. Still, no investment is without risks. Probably the least risky route is to buy a two-family or multifamily residence and live in one unit while renting the others out. That way you'll be able to keep an eye on your tenants, and tenants might even be less likely to damage the property if the landlord is a neighbor. Just as important, you'll be around to fix things. It pays to be a handyman if you're a landlord; otherwise, inevitably you'll have to shell out money for plumbers, electricians, and so forth, when you least expect it.

If you buy property that is not close to your home, be sure you have a reliable property manager near the premises, or at the very least a trusted friend or relative living nearby, as well as a superintendent whom tenants can reach quickly in an emergency. Even so, be prepared to get a call in the middle of the night sometime informing you that the toilet in your rental bathroom has backed up. Be prepared for tenants who bolt only six months into a three-year lease.

We recommend that anyone who is a landlord or is contemplating being a landlord read the book *Landlording: A Handy Manual for Scrupulous Landlords and Landladies Who Do It Themselves* by Leigh Robinson, available for $27.95 from www.landlording.com, a Web site you should also check out.

You should know that *mortgages for a second home are different*. Traditionally, the terms have been less favorable because lenders have viewed second-home purchases as risky. Although that idea is starting to change, you should seek out a lender familiar with the second-home market to get the best deal.

Taxes on rental income are tricky. While your mortgage interest and property taxes are deductible, the regulations around rental income are complex. The tax implications depend on how much of the time you use the property yourself versus how much of the time you rent it. Details are available on IRS Publication No. 527 at the IRS Web site: www.irs.gov.

Rental income may not recoup your costs. If the property is seasonal, rent might generate less than 10% of the property's value annually. If you rent it out year-round the income will help cover the costs, but small-scale landlords generally find that rental income doesn't go quite far enough once they factor in the mortgage, property taxes, insurance, and maintenance. The idea is to invest in property that pays off down the line, when you sell it.

Vacation property is hot, thanks in large part to the aging baby boomers looking for a more relaxed pace, and investment property seems like the only way to get a good return on your buck right now. If you already own at least one residence and are thinking about buying an additional one as a place to vacation or to rent out, just be sure you've considered some special intricacies before you leap.

Don't count on a quick resale. Beach communities come and go in popularity. A remote country house might be your ticket to serenity, but when you decide to sell, plan around a long wait, possibly with a lot of people coming by and just browsing. Depending on the location and the economy, a vacation property can sit on the market for months, even years, before a serious buyer comes along.

Maintenance will be expensive. If you aren't there to fix things, you'll have to find someone reliable in the area and be prepared to pay them anytime something goes wrong, especially if you have renters in the house.

Check out the site www.landlord.com for timely information on laws and issues affecting landlords, as well as an online forum of property investors and landlords.

Your Home Is Not a Piggy Bank!

Our parents, and yours too if you're over 45, thought $8,000 was a reasonable price to pay for a modest but comfortable three-bedroom home. Now many of those parents are selling the same home for $400,000. But the days of that kind of appreciation are gone forever. Say you buy a house today for $400,000 from a nice elderly couple who got it 40 years ago for $8,000 and are going to whoop it up all the way to Florida on your down pay-

TIMPANOGOS HIGH SCHOOL

ment alone. Let's assume that 40 years from now the value is not going to rise in a similar proportion; if it did you could sell it for $20 million. Sure, anything can happen, but as of now the average annual appreciation rate in the United States is between 4% and 7%, according to estimates from the National Association of Realtors and Freddie Mac, the mortgage securities packager.

There are many reasons for the slowdown in the appreciation explosion we saw in the twentieth century. The first wave of baby boomers is in, or close to, the "empty nest" phase of life and may be scaling back on the size of its homes. Boomers in their peak earning years are gravitating to the brand-spanking-new luxury houses known as "McMansions," which are edging out older and less state-of-the-art–equipped properties. The stock market bust is making an entire segment of the population too financially insecure to trade their houses up. And most significant of all, builders continue to build, increasing the available supply of housing at a rate that could outstrip demand in the first decade of the twenty-first century, causing housing prices to stall.

Attention, All Buyers: How to Get the *Best* of the Low Mortgage Rates

Read the real estate section of your local paper to see what the going rates are in your area. But also check our favorite sites for detailed information about local and national rates. In case you haven't heard, there has been a revolution. You don't have to get a mortgage at your neighborhood bank; you can work with a lender via the Internet.

- www.Bankrate.com gives mortgage rates state by state.
- www.cbs.marketwatch.com features a daily rundown of national average rates for mortgages, as well as auto loans, personal loans, and savings. Click on the "Research & Tools" tab.

Those friendly folks at HSH Associates have a Web site that's chock-a-block with information about mortgage rates and other consumer loans. Check them out at www.hsh.com. First-time home buyers should invest in their Homebuyers Mortgage Kit, which includes a list of the best mortgage rates in your area and costs $20 plus $3 for shipping and handling. Experienced buyers can send for their mortgage report alone, for $10 plus $1 for s/h, or their "How to Shop for Your Mortgage" booklet for $10 plus $3 for s/h. Check the site for a list of their entire series of $4 booklets on everything from qualifying to refinancing to identifying environmental hazards in your home. Order through their Web site or call 1-800-UPDATES.

Dolan Ah-Ha!

Buying a home or investment property in a neighborhood that *was* down and out but is now beginning to turn around? The federal government awards grants to states and local communities to help revitalize neighborhoods. To look for grants that might be available to you, go to www.homestore.com and click on "Finance & Insurance," then on "Government Freebies and Breaks." An article by Ben Johnson will link you to a state-by-state index of Housing and Community Development offices, mayor's offices, or county executive offices. You will have to contact these offices to find out if monies are available.

Sun Nations Mortgage, a commercial lender, has an excellent Web site that serves up free information on FHA loans and how to qualify. Go to www.fhalibrary.com.

The Federal Trade Commission publishes a free mortgage money guide that will help you find the right mortgage for your pocketbook.

All About Mortgages: Insider Tips for Financing and Refinancing Your Home, by Julie Garton-Good, and *Successful Real Estate Investing: A Practical Guide to Profits for the Small Investor,* by our good friend Peter G. Miller, are helpful books.

The Banker's Secret ($14.95), by Marc Eisenson, will show you how to prepay your mortgage so that you can own your home free and clear.

Now we come to three basic choices you will have to make in selecting a mortgage:

Basic Choice #1: Should You Pay Points?

Points are a small charge on the mortgage. (One point equals one percent of the loan amount; so 2½ points on a $100,000 mortgage comes to $2,500.) Points are due in full at closing.

If you pay points, your interest rate will generally be lower. Let's look at an example: a $100,000 mortgage with 2½ points at 8% vs. a mortgage with no points at 8.5%. The difference in monthly payments: $35. If you choose the 8% loan, the $35 monthly savings would go toward recouping the $2,500 you paid in points. You would make up for the

Dolan Bottom Line

At the closing, pay for your points with a separate check. That way it is considered a payment of interest, not a service fee. Interest is deductible—service fees are not.

points in 6 years—every month after that you'd be ahead of the game. If you choose the 8.5% loan, you'd be paying an extra $35 a month for the life of the loan. Over 30 years, you would pay about $10,000 extra! As you can see, the longer you plan to stay in the house, the more sense it makes to pay slightly higher points in exchange for a lower interest rate.

You'll find lenders that offer all sorts of variations on the point system: everything from low interest rates plus a few points, to a slightly higher interest rate and no points.

If you don't want to pay your points up front, you may be able to work out a deal with the seller of the home involved. If you agreed to buy the home for $140,000, ask the seller to bump the sale price to $142,500. Then have it written into the contract that the seller will pay the points with the extra $2,500. The seller still gets paid his money, you get to roll the points into your mortgage and pay them over the life of the loan, and—even better—you can deduct the seller-paid points on your tax return next year!

After you identify the best interest rate/point combination, talk turkey with the lenders. Ask these three questions (and get all answers in writing):

1. What is my interest rate, and how long will you guarantee or "lock in" that rate from the date of mortgage approval? If you've been preapproved but the lock-in period has lapsed, you'll have to go over this question once again. We recommend getting a 45- to 60-day lock-in period in case there's a delay in processing your application.
2. If interest rates fall during my lock-in period, will you give me the lower rate? Some lenders won't allow you to drop to the lower rate, but it never hurts to ask.
3. How long will it take to complete the entire application process? Your application should be processed at least 10 business days before your scheduled closing.

> **Read Chapter 4 for tips on improving your credit history. The better you look on your credit report, the better the deal you can make.**

Basic Choice #2: Should You Get a Fixed-Rate or an Adjustable-Rate Mortgage?

There is no "one-size-fits-all" mortgage. That being said, our first choice for most borrowers is still a 30-year conventional fixed-rate mortgage with no penalty of prepayment. That way, you may knock off extra principal anytime you have extra money. At the same time, you aren't tied into having to come up with a big payment every month, as you'd have to with a 15-year mortgage, which generally will cost about 20% more in monthly payments.

If you have a 30-year mortgage and find yourself seriously strapped for cash, you can hold off prepaying in any one month and not worry about defaulting on your loan. Why add the pressure of having to make larger monthly payments with a short-term mortgage when you can accomplish the same thing on your own by prepaying when you're able?

When mortgage interest rates are low, most home buyers should avoid an ARM—that's an adjustable-rate mortgage.

Mortgage lenders came up with ARMs to sell mortgages in the early 1980s, when we had double-digit interest rates. It is best for the lenders, and doesn't help the homeowner, because everyone qualifies under that first low teaser mortgage rate. After that the gloves are off. When rates go lower, the adjustable mortgage rate never seems to drop as low as prevailing rates. ARMs have created a new breed of homeowner: a person who's constantly looking to refinance at a better rate. The more often you refinance, the more often you'll pay fees to get a better rate. Most people would probably be better off paying down their mortgage balance rather than refinancing when rates drop because of the amount of money it takes to refinance.

On the other hand, an ARM *can* work in your favor. We like them *if* your situation meets all of the following conditions:

1. You are absolutely certain you're going to stay in your home *less than two or three years*.
2. Your ARM has a 2% annual interest cap and a total lifetime cap of 6%.
3. You can get an introductory interest rate that is at least 2% less than the 30-year fixed rate.

Why an ARM Can Be Dangerous

Here is what could happen to your mortgage payments with an ARM. Here is how much your monthly payments would rise if you took out a $150,000 ARM with an initial interest rate of 3%, but your interest rates went up two percentage points a year.

Year	Monthly Payment
1st year (3%)	$632
2nd year (5%)	$800
3rd year (7%)	$982

Source: HSH Associates

"With a short-term ARM under these conditions, you probably will pay less over the next three years with an ARM than with a fixed-rate mortgage, even if rates go up," notes our good friend Keith Gumbinger, a vice president at HSH Associates, a surveying firm that publishes guides to home buying.

Stay more than three years, though, and the "adjustments" could become painful.

Latest statistics on mortgage defaults show that almost twice as many homeowners head into foreclosure with an ARM than with a fixed-rate mortgage. Buyer beware.

Beware, however, of mortgage lenders offering *really* low-interest-rate ARMs, with come-on rates of around 3%. If it sounds too good to be true, the lenders may be engaging in tactics such as these:

- Annual caps of 2.5%–3%.
- Lifetime caps of 6.5%–7%.
- No first-anniversary annual cap, and a 2% cap that applies only in later years. At the end of the first year, if rates go higher, your interest rate could jump to whatever the lender can get away with before the 2% cap kicks in!

Read any ARM agreement carefully and completely before you sign it—don't skip a word. Make sure that you understand how often the ARM rate will change and to which "index" your ARM is tied.

In addition, if you choose an ARM, *make sure it lets you convert to a fixed rate during the term of the loan.* That way, if you do wind up staying longer than three years, you can limit your exposure to rising rates. Most ARMs convert to a higher-than-market-rate interest rate, which is a good reason to avoid them.

You can find the best ARM rates in your area through HSH Associates (www.hsh.com) or Bank Rate Monitor (www.bankrate.com).

Basic Choice #3: Should You Attempt to Get an FHA Loan Rather Than a Conventional Loan?

Often, the decision comes down to Federal Housing Administration (FHA) mortgages versus conventional mortgages. Though there are distinct advantages to FHA financing, sometimes conventional financing may be the better option.

The main advantage to an FHA home loan is that the credit qualifying criteria are not as strict as those with conventional financing. Since these loans are backed by the Federal Housing Authority (which means the government agrees to pay the lender if you default), they require as little as 3%–5% down payment. FHA will allow the borrower who has had a few "credit problems" or those without a credit history to buy a home.

FHA will require a reasonable explanation of your credit transgressions, but will approach your credit history with commonsense credit underwriting. Like the priest in the confession booth, FHA will forgive you if you own up. Conventional financing, on the other hand, relies heavily upon credit scoring. (See Chapter 4 to learn how credit bureaus watch you.)

HUD, which insures FHA loans, has created a list of allowable and non-allowable closing costs that can be assessed. You might be able to save hundreds of dollars this way.

Limitation 1: With an FHA loan, no more than 29% of your gross income can go to principal, interest, taxes, and insurance.

Limitation 2: The FHA sets ceilings on the loans it will grant. In 2002, the maximum for a one-family house in a high-cost area (as defined by the local HUD office) was $261,609, while the maximum in an area that HUD deems close to average was $144,336. If you're looking for a mortgage that exceeds the FHA loan limits for the area, you'll have to either put additional money down or finance under a conventional mortgage.

Go to HUD's Web site, www.hud.gov, for an update on FHA mortgage limits in your area, or call the HUD Home Buyers Hotline at 800-767-4483. HSH Associates also has

VA Loans: Let Your Country Serve *You*

Anthony Principi, the U.S. Secretary of Veterans Affairs, mentioned an interesting program when he appeared on our show.

If you served in the military, or are the unremarried spouse of a veteran who died in service or is missing in action, you may qualify for a Veterans' Administration loan. Like FHA loans, VA loans are backed by a federal agency that promises the lender the loan will be repaid. VA loans require *absolutely no* money down. Zero. Zilch. There are caps on the interest rate—that is, established maximum interest rates. The lender cannot add more than one point to the closing charges.

Now here's the catch. As with FHA loans, there is a limit to how much you can borrow. The home you wish to buy must be appraised by the FHA or VA, and you can borrow only up to the appraised value. For example, if a seller asks $80,000 for a home, but the VA appraises the home at $75,000, you can borrow only $75,000. You'll have to either pay the $5,000 difference on your own, or come up with a compromise with the seller.

If you can live with that, VA loans are a terrific deal. For more information, call the VA's nationwide toll-free number, 800-827-1000. General rules of eligibility and a summary of the program are available on the VA Web site: www.vba.va.gov.

info at their site, www.hsh.com. Call the FHA Mortgage Hotline at 800-CALLFHA for a list of approved lenders.

Sit down with your loan officer or financial adviser and look at not only the short-term impact of the decision but also at the long-term costs of each program.

You might, in the end, decide to use the lender that has been financing the house you buy. We'll explain in the next section why you would do that. But nevertheless, have some willing lenders in mind before you start, because it's always going to put you in the best bargaining position.

When You Apply for a Mortgage

Don't be a sap . . . take control of the shopping prices and the "lock the rate" process. Some of the questions to ask a lender are:

- Are you licensed in my state? (Check with your state Attorney General's office.)
- Are there any "pre-payment" penalties?
- If this mortgage (held by the seller) is assembled, under what condition may I assume it?
- What are the *total* monthly payments including "PITI" (principle, interest, taxes, and insurance)?
- Will I need to pay for PMI (private mortgage insurance)?
- What will the closing costs total?
- What are the exact fees for doing this mortgage with your company? (This should be about 1–2 % of the amount you borrow.)

Don't do the "slip, sliding away" dance when you try to lock in a mortgage interest rate prior to closing.

Because of historically low interest rates for first-time home buyers, and a spate of refinancing, many mortgage applications (maybe yours) are simply not getting the attention that they deserve . . . and some promised rates are getting "busted"! Don't let it happen to you.

Dolan Ah-Ha!

Get a 60-day, not a 30-day, "lock" on the agreed rate. It will likely cost you $1/8$% or $1/4$% on your interest rate, but it's worth knowing that you're protected. (You're going to pay off the mortgage early anyway, right?!) No "surprise" fees . . . thank you!

House Hunting

Now you're ready for the hard part. Where is the perfect house? Do you want to use a real estate agent? Or are you prepared to go house hunting alone?

Step 1: Find a "Buyer's Broker"

Don't forget that when you call the real estate agent whose name is on the For Sale sign, you are at the mercy of an agent who often is working for the seller. Traditional brokers earn their commissions based on what the seller gets for his home, which means the higher the sale price, the bigger their commission. So most brokers have an incentive to pass along to the seller any information you share about how much you're willing to pay.

A buyer's broker, on the other hand, works for you, the buyer, and puts muscle on *your* side. A recent study showed that no matter how good or bad the real estate market is, you'll pay 96% of the home's list price if you use a traditional broker, while if you use a buyer's broker you'll pay an average of only 91% of a home's listed price. That's 5% less. On a $150,000 house, that's a cool $7,500!

To find one of these brokers, call your local board of Realtors and ask for the names of buyer's brokers in your area. If you can't find one that way, call the Buyer's Broker Registry at 800-729-5147. The Registry currently has about 250 members in 36 states. (There aren't that many buyer's brokers in the country, but many traditional brokers will become your broker if you ask them to.) You can also contact Buyer's Resource at 800-4-BUYERS or www.buyersresource.com/brinfo, or the National Association of Real Estate Buyer's Brokers at 415-591-5446.

Selling and Buying on the Internet

We think the Internet serves one major purpose: sorting out the myriad choices. From a buyer's standpoint, being able to take some virtual tours is a terrific and time-saving idea. We have nothing against "forsalebyowner.com." It's fine to start your house hunt with a mouse. But when you see something with real potential, start dealing with a human broker.

Virtual house tours might be tempting if you're relocating, but don't you dare make an offer until you actually see the property. The photos you see on the Web can hide rotting staircases, mildewed roofs, nasty neighbors. . . . The Internet is a great place to shop if you can return the merchandise for a full refund, but a house is not a shirt!

Questions to Ask a Buyer's Broker

You're hiring a broker to work for you, so you want to be extra sure he or she is really on your side! Before you sign a contract with a buyer's broker, ask these three questions:

1. How are you compensated? In general, we recommend buyer's brokers who charge by the hour—especially if you need the broker only to help you negotiate and close the sale. If you can't find a broker in your area who charges by the hour, find one who charges a flat fee of 2%–3% of the purchase price you're willing to pay, rather than a 2%–3% commission on the sale price of the home. This forces the broker to steer you toward homes in your price range.
2. Do you accept any financial "incentives" from the seller's broker to help close the deal? You want a broker who says "no" to this question. A buyer's broker who can expect compensation from both sides of the table will not have any incentive to get you the best deal.
3. Will you get price information for me? A buyer's broker can and should be willing to find out what the seller paid for a house and when. A traditional broker is not allowed to tell you this information. But this important information will help you make a reasonable offer on a home.

Buyer's brokers usually charge by the hour or a flat fee of 2%–3% of the purchase price you're willing to pay. Before you sign a contract with one, make sure he or she doesn't accept any financial incentives from the seller's broker; you don't need someone who's playing both sides of the table. See our list of three important questions you should ask before you sign your name to *any* agreement.

Step 2: Think Location, Location, Location

You have a broker looking out for you, but you can still drive around the area and look for houses for sale, check classified ads, and spread the word within your network.

Remember what's most important in finding your dream house or almost dream house: location, location, location. It's the oldest real estate rule on the books, and it still applies.

Take out the map and narrow down the areas you want to look at. There are a lot of houses in a lot of neighborhoods out there, so if you don't focus your search, you could become a career house hunter. Consider how moving to each area would affect your commute, your taxes, your shopping, your kid's schooling, and so on.

A great Web site that will help you research the cost and availability of homes in a particular area, along with facts about the locale, is www.homeadvisor.msn.com.

Then, don't drive around—*walk*. Visit during the day so you can see everything. Are there enough kids? Are there too many kids? Do people take good care of their yards? Does the street have too much traffic? How is the trash pickup, the level of noise? Do people take good care of their houses and property? Strike up conversations and see if your soon-to-be-neighbors are people you'd want to see every day of your life. Look for flyers in the local stores about community events and political concerns; you don't want to be a conservative in the midst of a liberal hotbed or vice versa. No detail is too small. An ill-fitting home is harder to undo than a bad marriage! If you find a house that really excites you, go back to the neighborhood at night and on a weekend or two, and see if you feel the same way about it. And of course, have a look at the schools your kids would attend—during the schoolday. Make an appointment to chat with the principal.

Our #1 choice for information about your potential new school system is www.schoolmatch.com.

They have rated more than 15,000 public school systems in America. Their School-March report card compares a school system or private school with others in its region AND in the nation!!

Twenty-two factors are included for public school systems and 33 for private schools . . . (religion, uniforms, tuition, day/boarding, etc.).

Start a checklist. Once you've targeted some neighborhoods, it's time to start looking at houses. Before you start, jot down a list of your "must haves." If you absolutely can't live without a fireplace or garage or three bedrooms, you can save a lot of time and headache by making that known to your broker.

Most home buyers see dozens of homes during their search. After the fifth or sixth house, it can be hard to keep the details straight in your head. Take a notebook to make sketches or jot down details that will help you remember what you like and dislike about each house. Ask the real estate agent if there is any material about the house that you can take with you, or some photographs.

Before you make the final decision to buy a home in a particular area (after you've checked at SchoolMatch.com that the school system is a sound one), check out www.houseappreciation.com. Their residential real estate ratings system includes only neighborhoods they believe to be in the top 32 percent in the United States in projected appreciation value.

By utilizing those two Web sites, you'll have a good shot at picking a home *and* a good school system in the same area!!

Our advice is always **buy the *worst* home in a *good* neighborhood rather than the *best* home in a *bad* neighborhood.** Once upon a time—the 1980s and 1990s—city neighborhoods were getting gentrified overnight, and property values were rising even faster. We're in an economic slump right now, and prices are likely to flatten out or weaken before they go up. The baby boomers are settled down and the high-tech boom has gone bust. Unless there's something special going on in your area that might create a chic buzz in a downtrodden part of town, assume that in 10 years your neighborhood will look pretty much as it does now. If you're in a desirable part of town, you can be pretty sure that renovations or additions will boost the value of your home.

On the other hand, if you can find a foreclosed home, a quick estate sale, or a fixer-upper in a good area, this is a bargain you might want to grab, especially if you're handy enough with tools and have the time, money, and inclination to fix it up. You can still build equity fast if you give your house a complete makeover.

Okay, you've found a house you like. At this point you might even have two or three houses in mind. Move on to step 3.

Step 3: Find Out Where the Bodies Are Buried

We're speaking figuratively, we hope! However, you have a right to know all the secrets contained within the walls. Ask the broker, either yours or the seller's agent, anything you haven't been told about the house and its current or previous occupants. Play detective. You want satisfactory answers to the following questions:

- How long has the house been on the market? If comparable houses in the area get snapped up while this one has been sitting for six months, why? Most brokers have access to Multiple Listing Service (MLS), a computerized database that will tell them the listing date and the length of time it typically takes to a sell a home in that area.
- Is there any structural damage?
- Are there any problems in the neighborhood, such as crime, poor schools, barking dogs, feuds?
- If the present owner is there at all when you visit, are both spouses present? If not, why? Are they divorced or separated? Has one moved because of a job transfer? If the sellers are anxious to sell, they might accept a lower offer. (See step 4 for advice on making the offer.)

If your broker can't tell you the price the current owners paid for the house, you can find out yourself. You can look it up at the county land records/tax assessor's office. All you need to know is the year the seller bought the house. Ask either the seller or your broker for that piece of info. You can also try Domania (formerly Home Price Check) at www.domania.com, a free service that lets you check the sale price of properties in many, though not all, parts of the country. Make sure you're in the ballpark. No matter how

Dolan Ah-Ha!

If a deal on a house looks too good to be true, check out whether it's surrounded by environmental hazards. Don't trust the seller's or the broker's word about this. Check to see on the Environmental Protection Agency's Web site, www.epa.gov, if there are hazardous-waste sites in the area. Test for lead in the tap water; for information on how to test, call the National Lead Information Center at 800-424-5323 or www.epa.gov/lead/nlic.htm. Have a look at newspapers that cover the community, or ask current residents, to see if there are other concerns, such as electromagnetic radiation from power lines or cell phone sites.

much you love the house, you don't want to overpay. Never, ever buy the most expensive house in a neighborhood. It will be almost impossible to sell at a profit!

Finally, take a trip to the county recorder's office and ask to see a copy of the master plan for the area. This is an incredibly important and useful document. If the asking price seems too good to be true, it might be because the county has plans to expand roads or put a new expressway through your backyard. The master plan will tell you at a glance whether you should hit the road yourself and find another house.

Step 4: Make the Offer

Unless you're buying in a really hot seller's market and your main objective is to get the house before another eager bidder does, you should offer at least a few thousand dollars less than the asking price. That's what asking prices are for; they're a starting point. If comparable houses have sold for less lately, if the owners are trying to unload the house because of changes in their lives, if the house has been listed for several months, those are all negotiating points.

The offer must be in writing. Your broker will help you draw it up. In addition to the

Dolan Ah-Ha!

Keep an eye on your lawyer to make sure he or she does a thorough job, or you could end up like a caller named Jessie, who thought he was closing on a legally zoned two-family property, only to discover—after the closing—that he'd bought a one-family house with an illegal basement apartment!

price you offer, you should include a time limit for the response—48 hours is the norm. The seller will also require a time limit for you to obtain financing and for closing on the house. After both parties sign the contract offer, it is a legally binding document. You should have a lawyer look at it before you sign. In many states, you will have to put a percentage of the cost of the house into an escrow account, which you will forfeit if you break the contract.

Step 5: Have the House Inspected

You really *must* have an inspector look at any house that you're ready to buy. Most signed offers stipulate that the offer is valid pending an official inspection of the house. In some states, the seller has to complete a seller disclosure form to make you aware of any known problems, but you still have to hire your own inspector to see if there are other defects that the seller hasn't mentioned or somehow has managed to overlook. We don't know of any way around it. But if you're wondering whom you can trust in this crazy world, it isn't your friendly home inspector.

When we bought our first house in Maine, we got a completely clean bill of health from a home inspector, but during that first winter we had a leak in the ceiling the size of a football. It ruined a 3 ft. x 1 ft. piece of the wall-to-wall carpet. When we picked out our dream house in Florida, an inspector wrote up 15 pages of the most detailed, comprehensive home inspection report we'd ever received. We felt great about this guy. He even got the seller to make a couple of changes. So we moved in, and one month later, we found a big bubble on the side of the staircase against the outside wall. At first we thought it was just masking tape from the construction, but when we poked it we found a totally hollow spot; it was a leak from outside. You could not miss this bubble, but somehow the home inspector hadn't bothered to check it. Then, one month later, we were visited with the nightmare of every homeowner: a swarm of ants. These repairs cost us $492.

Sad to say, the Dolans, too, can be fooled. Think about it: It's in an inspector's interest that people put houses on the market. The more problems they bring up, the less likely you are to buy the house, and the more annoyed the real estate agents who recommend them are going to get. Inspectors get most of their referrals through brokers, and brokers might stay away from inspectors who muck up the sale too often.

Generally, you'll have to put a contract on the house and make a deposit into an escrow account before the seller will let you inspect the house. Make sure the contract includes a clause allowing you to get your deposit back if the inspector finds any major flaws. Figure if they're big enough to cite, they must be big flaws indeed.

The contract you sign with a home inspector often contains a lot of wiggle room for him should you later encounter an expensive problem that the inspector missed. Don't assume an inspection certifies an entirely clean bill of health for the property.

Still, it's better to have a half-baked inspection than none at all. Just don't be so naive as to think that if some major quarrel comes up after you buy the house, the seller will pay for it. You'll spend years in court. That is why we suggest having emergency funds for those moments such as the one when we discovered the hole in the staircase. You can rant and rave, but in the end you usually have to chalk it up to the cost of owning a home.

Who are these home inspectors we love and trust so much? Well, almost anyone can call him- or herself a "home inspector." Don't hire just anyone. Ask a knowledgeable friend for a referral. Real estate agents might be eager to give you names, but we don't recommend taking them up on the offer. It's too easy for an agent to suggest someone who'll give a superficial inspection, thereby encouraging you to grab the house. Check with your real estate lawyer if you have one.

Once you find a potential inspector, ask the $64,000 question: Are you certified by the American Society of Home Inspectors (ASHI)? If the answer is "no," say "no, thanks."

Dolan Ah-Ha!

Before you close on the home (when you do the "walk through"), have the home inspection report *in your hand* to ensure that the seller made all necessary repairs. On one occasion, we made the mistake of trusting the seller to make all the necessary repairs *before* the closing. Don't *you* make the same mistake. "TRUST" is not what buying real estate is all about.

The ASHI requires inspectors to pass two exams and perform 250 certified inspections. Plus they must take 40 hours of refresher courses every two years. These are the toughest criteria of any organization that certifies inspectors.

But don't just take the inspector's word. You can check whether he is in good standing by calling ASHI at 800-743-ASHI. If you don't already have the names of a few inspectors, ASHI will send you a list of certified inspectors in your area, absolutely free, by mail or fax. You can also get this information from ASHI's Web site at www.ashi.org.

How to Cut 10% or More off Your Closing Costs

Your mortgage closing costs are negotiable. Don't let any lender tell you otherwise. There are a number of ways that you can keep your closing costs to a minimum. One of the best

The American Homeowners Association's
10 Tips on Buying a Home

Read this tip sheet before you start looking for a house. This is not a paid ad. We think the American Homeowners Association (AHA) is a very helpful organization for homeowners. It offers more than 35 services and products, many directly related to buying and moving into a home, to help members save money and time. For $99 a year, you get access to discounts on a wide array of products and a prescreened network of home-repair specialists available 24/7.

To join, call AHA's hotline at 800-470-2242 or join online at www.ahahome.com.

Our thanks to AHA founder and president Richard Roll for allowing us to reprint these 10 important tips:

Tip #1. Research is the key to discovery. Only by reading available materials, talking to friends and experts, and spending time looking at different homes will most buyers end up with their American Dream.

Tip #2. Make a plan. Developing a home-buying plan can help you focus on the important factors and organize the entire process. You may even want to use a binder with sections on house hunting, home financing, service providers, and so on. It's always a negotiating advantage to conceal your enthusiasm or emotional attachment to a deal. Planning your actions and needs will keep you out of the panic mode and allow you to take advantage of opportunities.

Tip #3. Value, value, value: The days of 10%–30% annual appreciation are winding down in many parts of the country. Today's shopper is looking at slower growth while guarding against the possibilities of falling prices and corporate layoffs that can dramatically affect the value of your home. That's why the classic rule of buying the worst house in the best neighborhood still applies. If you buy with an eye toward improvement, you can customize the home to fit your needs. The saying "make money buying a home, not selling one" should keep home buyers focused on the long-term importance of the purchasing price. Low offers, from genuine buyers, result in better deals because the seller knows they will have to compromise.

Tip #4. Create your own top-10 list of amenities when shopping for a home: List the features (swimming pool, fireplace, fenced-in yard, new appliances, etc.) that are most important to you. Establishing "your criteria" early on will save time and may keep you from buying a home on a whim—say, because of a circular stairwell—that doesn't meet your fundamental requirements. Four of your top-10 amenities should logically be sacrificed if an incredible value is available.

Tip #5. Find the right Realtor. An experienced Realtor will have a solid understanding of the neighborhood you are buying in, a Rolodex full of agents to hear about good deals on marketable properties, and a working knowledge of the Multiple Listing Service, the newer Realtors Information Network, and other home-finding instruments. Find one who makes an effort to understand your needs.

Tip #6. Sign a contract that protects you. Make sure the contract you put on a house allows you to arrange financing, inspect the home, and negotiate any problems that you uncover.

Tip #7. Put yourself in the seller's shoes. If you take time to understand the reasons the seller bought the home, his reasons for selling, and the home improvements he has made (or not made), you'll be in a better position to evaluate the home and negotiate a better deal. In the end, the process excludes the professionals and comes down to the individuals buying and selling. A closer look at the seller may give you an edge in deciding whether to buy and how much to pay.

Tip #8. Develop a mortgage shopping chart. There are 10,000 lenders competing for your mortgage business. Create a chart that lists different types of loans, fees, and at least five mortgage providers.

Tip #9. Get a quality home inspection.

Tip #10. Hire a skilled settlement attorney: After you have jumped through the home shopping and finance hoops, the last difficult maneuver is at the closing table. You want an expert who will scrutinize all the documents you will sign and can be helpful in last-minute negotiations. By the time you get to settlement, you have already pictured where your furniture will go, the best place to drink coffee on weekends, and the spot where your newspaper will land each morning. Your lawyer may be the only person on your side who is unemotional and levelheaded when obstacles arise.

Dolan Ah-Ha!

Not all closings go smoothly. Sometimes the seller hasn't provided some vital piece of information, or your loan application gets held up because the processor needs something and doesn't tell you until the last minute.

To keep your stress to a minimum, we suggest getting started with your mortgage application the minute you and the seller have a signed contract. Give yourself 60 days to closing so you'll have plenty of time to head off any delays. Plus, you can use this 60-day window of opportunity to cut a deal on your closing costs!

ways to get a good deal on closing costs, interest rates, and points is to find out which mortgage lender the current owner uses. Call up his or her loan officer and mention that you're buying the house, you're shopping for financing, and you wanted to give them a crack at your business. It's a lot easier for the lender to keep you rather than find a way to replace your business, so they might make the deal. Yes, you've been prequalified elsewhere. Be sure and tell the loan officer about the mortgage you can get from another lender, and you'll be in the bargaining seat.

We checked with our mortgage expert, Paul Havemann, a vice president at HSH Associates, for more tips. Here's what he says:

- For starters, you can expect to pay between $3,000 and $10,000 in closing costs, depending on where you live and the size of your mortgage. To get a "good-faith estimate" of closing costs from a lender, ask them to give you a "preapplication disclosure" before you pay an application fee. This itemized list will contain some pretty interesting items. The box below shows you the average amount your lender will charge for negotiable closing costs—and the amount you can expect to save by negotiating.

Negotiable Closing Costs

Negotiable Item	Average Cost	You Can Save
Appraisal	$250	5%–10%
Attorney fee (for the lender's attorney)	$250	10%
Inspection	$350	10%–20%
Title search and title insurance	$500	5%–10%

- When you get your itemized estimate of closing costs, call any service providers that are listed, such as the termite inspection company or property surveyor. Ask them how much they charge for their service and note any difference between what they quote you and what the lender has listed. (Some lenders pad their profit by increasing these costs. Let your lender know you won't pay extra.) We recommend paying any of these charges you can separately, to avoid such hassles.
- Check the list of negotiable costs and see where you can cut your bill even further. Does your lender want you to pay their attorney's fees? Some do this as a policy, but you may be able to avoid it.
- There are the fees known in the industry as "garbage fees." These include notary fees, recording fees, and transfer fees. You can't negotiate these prices, because they're set by your local government. But when the real estate market is not "hot," you may be able to strike a deal with the seller to go "halvsies" on some fees, particularly recording and transfer fees. It never hurts to ask.

Should You Renovate or Sell?

We sold our first home in Florida after 15 months that seemed more like eternity. We had built the house 10 years before in an up-and-coming subdivision that remained, a decade later, heavy on the "coming" but short on the "up"! It's always tough to sell a "used" home in an area where there is constant construction, because buyers have their pick of brand-new houses. After that experience, we know just what kind of dedication, and even creativity, it can take to sell your home at a good price with a minimum of hassle. But wait: Are you sure you want to sell your house? If you've been offered a job in another city, of course you have to sell. But if your family is just outgrowing your present home, it might make more sense, money-wise, to do some renovations or build an addition.

> **Market value of a newly renovated house = the average price of comparable homes in the neighborhood + the cost of your improvements.**

Should you renovate or sell? This is a question that can be answered with mathematics. First, find out what the average selling prices of houses in your neighborhood are. If a renovation would raise the market value of your house so much that you'd exceed that average price by more than 10%, don't renovate—instead, sell and move. Because you'll find it's very hard to earn your investment back. You'll either keep your house on the market for months, maybe years, or you'll accept a lowball offer and take a loss. House hunters who come to your neighborhood will, if they've been following our advice, be reluctant to buy your house if it's the best house in an okay neighborhood.

On the other hand, suppose you find that adding a new bedroom and bath to your house will still keep your market value in the ballpark in your neighborhood. There are still two reasons to hesitate:

1. Think you're Tim Allen's long-lost twin, a handyman do-it-yourselfer? Have you ever built an addition before? If you try to take on the whole project yourself, and you're not 100% good at it, you can end up doing more damage to the property price-wise than helping it. Of course, if the job is big enough and you can afford that kind of investment, you can hire a contractor. See the following sections, "Home Improvement" and "What You Should Know Before You Contract With a Contractor."

2. Are you by chance living in a 100-year-old Federal-style house built with bricks that now have a charming look of gentle wear? Are you going to be able to replicate the existing aesthetic in an addition? If people are going to pass your house and say, "Oh look, they added on to that house," you're going to be stuck with a nice spacious lemon when it comes to building equity.

Your decision is likely to rest with the kind of improvement your home needs. An added-on garage that looks added-on will do nothing to boost the value of the home.

Home Improvement

The market for buying and selling may be uncertain, but to judge by our listeners—and by a recent survey from Champion Mortgage of Parsippany, New Jersey—Americans are pouring money into home improvements. With the stock market sinking, many of our listeners tell us they figure making capital improvements on property they already own seems like one of the few relatively safe investments left out there. It makes perfect sense.

If you're thinking of making improvements, you *might* want to start with the ones that add the most resale value. This isn't always the best strategy. But if you're considering selling in a few years, these are the improvements that will give you the most investment bang for your buck, according to data from *Remodeling* magazine:

1. **Minor kitchen repairs.** A minor kitchen remodel will give you back all of the money you put in plus about 87%. With a major kitchen you're going to get a bit less, because you'll have more expenses.

   What constitutes a "minor" repair as opposed to "major"? We consulted an expert on home repair, Lynda Lyday, a licensed carpenter and cohost of the Do It Yourself (DIY) Network's *Talk2diy* on cable channels.

"A minor repair is painting, wallpapering, tiling, putting up cabinets and countertops yourself," says Lyday. "Major is breaking out walls, putting in an island, anything that requires calling an electrician or plumber, or putting in major appliances."

2. **A two-story addition** earns back approximately 83% of your expenses.

3. **An additional bathroom** earns back about 81%.

4. **Major kitchen remodeling** earns back 80%.

> **Factor in the disruption-of-your-life index. The two most disruptive home remodels have to be the kitchen and a bathroom.**

How much do you anticipate spending? Whatever you estimate, double it—at least.

Homeowners tend to make their guesstimates based on what Daria calls the Ken Dolan School of Thinking—that you can still get a loaf of bread for 30 cents and a quart of milk for a quarter. The Champion Mortgage survey found that homeowners, on average, estimated a kitchen-remodeling project would cost $18,658. Actually the industry

Resale Value Isn't Everything—
Especially If You Aren't Selling!

A listener named Kenny and his wife bought a 65-year-old house that needed improvement in a very desirable neighborhood. We were so pleased to hear they'd taken our advice about buying the worst house in the best neighborhood. When it came time to begin making improvements, they were weighing the importance of renovating the kitchen versus replacing the old, drafty windows. We told Kenny to go for the windows even though the kitchen would provide a great return on their money. Why? Because they had just moved in. They weren't planning to sell anytime soon, but they were planning to run the heat for many winters and the air-conditioning for many summers. They could reduce their energy bills right away with new, well-insulated windows, and those savings were more important at this stage than resale value.

The first thing you want to do is maximize the bucks you're spending.

The Inside Scoop on What You Should Know

Here's a homeowner's guide to hiring a contractor for a new custom house construction or a renovation, courtesy of Peter Martin, a former contractor in New York City.

How Do You Find a Contractor?

Personal referrals are the best way. Ask around for referrals from professionals, such as bankers, Realtors, appraisers, and lawyers. You can look at Web sites such as www.build.com, which matches customers to contractors, but you should still ask for references. Responding to advertising is the least reliable method. It's okay for lower-ticket jobs, but not for a major project.

What Should You Ask When You Interview a Contractor?

Ask about his organization: how long he's been in business, a general history of what the company has done, and the size and scope of its last five projects.

Ask if the contractor offers design services, or works with designers and architects.

Ask how frequently he bills *after* completing a job and how quickly he expects to receive payment. Ask his policy on change orders.

Ask to see at least one of the contractor's big projects. Pictures and information on a Web site are helpful, but don't tell the whole story.

Ask if there will be a full-time supervisor working on your job. For major projects, this is crucial, and you should meet the supervisor in advance. Ask yourself how you feel about the person or the team who will be working on your house. If you don't feel comfortable with them, problems are sure to arise.

What Should You Ask When You Interview References?

First of all, be sure you get several references and call them. Too many customers don't actually call references. Ask the reference how the contractor responded to phone calls, and how well he handled supervision and paperwork. A contractor's human interaction is even more important than his prices in the view of most homeowners, according to surveys.

Also ask if the prices for extras and change orders were reasonable. Would the reference choose this contractor if he or she could do it all over again? Does the reference think the contractor will take responsibility for repairs or corrections if problems arise later?

How Do You Solicit Competitive Bids?

The typical practice is to ask for price proposals from three contractors, either to get the "best price" or to verify that your favorite contractor is not "out of line." But the project each bids on is not the same project, no matter how detailed the plans and specifications. Each contractor is pricing his conception according to how he operates. You won't get to compare the actual performance, since you get only one in the end. Consider weighing price as only one factor. A contractor's price level reflects a self-esteem level and often the level of service you'll get. Some people select the highest bidder for that reason.

The Contract

- It's best if you or the contractor fill out or write up the contract. Attorneys tend to complicate things if you bring them in too early. You can get sample standard contracts from the Web site of the American Institute of Architects through www.enterprisefoundation.org or Smart Consumer Services, a consumer education firm in Crystal City, Virginia, that has one that you can order for $19.95, online at www.sconsumer.com, or by calling them toll free at 877-662-8767. (Be prepared to be put on hold for a long time if you order by phone.) You add identifying data, starting date, overall price, itemized prices, and payment schedule.

- Time clauses are not practical or reasonable. Almost all projects are completed behind schedule. Rarely is this caused by blatant neglect; it's usually because the contractor puts his resources elsewhere. Wide time parameters will cover this eventuality. Delays can also result from changes initiated by the client or prompted by discovery of hidden conditions. Some owners try to protect themselves by writing penalty clauses using tight time schedules. It is very difficult to specify your performance parameters—that is, the time it takes you or a designer to respond. If a penalty is defined, the contractor is constricted by date. To extend the date, he is in the position of accusing you of delays, which is going to sour your relationship. In many states, a penalty is not enforceable unless the contract also contains a bonus agreement.

- Some homeowners try to get initial waivers of mechanics' liens. Don't bother. These are the only practical and affordable protection most contractors and subcontractors have from not being paid. Worries that contractors will file liens maliciously are not well founded; parties who file falsely face substantial financial penalties. There is an exception in states that have guidelines that require partial waivers as the project progresses. Consult a lawyer to verify the protocols in your state.

The Actual Project

- If you contemplate any changes, act as quickly as possible. It's easy when the trade contractors are still there, but gets difficult when they must be scheduled to come back for that one item.
- Establish routine contact times with your contact person. Some production managers phone each client every day. Some people talk once a week. Sit-down meetings may be needed on a complicated project.
- Put away the worries and have fun; it's your house. Let the pros do what they're good at. That's what you chose them for.

average for a major kitchen remodeling is $39,000. And survey respondents estimated that an additional room would cost $16,607, when in reality it can cost around $47,000.

What Kinds of Improvements Don't Add Much Value to Your Home When You Sell?

A home office will give you a mere 54% return on your investment, according to *Remodeling* magazine. If you work from home or use the home office to run a sideline business, however, you can take a tax deduction.

From Lynda Lyday: A swimming pool, fountains, and ponds don't enhance the value. You might love those luxuries, but the buyer might not want a bothersome body of water on the property. For one thing, the buyer might be worried about the lawsuit potential if some guest, or even some trespasser, drowns or is injured.

A fireplace doesn't give you a great return either.

But if these improvements will give *you and your family* enjoyment and you can afford them, that could be reason enough to proceed.

What You Should Know Before You Contract With a Contractor

Anytime you bring in a contractor, you need to select very carefully. The key word is "reliable."

We asked Lynda Lyday how to find a contractor you can trust. Her advice:

- *Good references are key.* Request references and a portfolio of previous work to verify the quality of craftsmanship. Check with the Better Business Bureau to see if there have been previous complaints.

- *Take a drive and look at some of the houses the contractor has built or redone.* If he is new to your area, that in itself might be a red flag. Was he fleeing from displeased clients?
- *Never make the final payment before the work is completed.* Contractors have a nasty habit of disappearing once they've been paid. Lyday says avoid anyone who asks for the entire fee in advance, insists on being paid in cash, or suggests you borrow money from a lender he knows. He might be getting a kickback.
- *Communication is everything.* We can't emphasize enough how important that fourth point is. We've heard horror story upon horror story about what can go wrong when some little detail isn't crystal clear. Before you sign the construction contract, make sure it specifies exactly what is to be done, how much it will cost, and how payment is to be made.

Never make changes to the contract by oral agreement. If you want to change something later, always get it in writing as part of a "change order." You and the contractor are likely to have entirely different recollections of the same conversation.

Helpful Web Sites for This Section

www.contractor.com

Find additional information about home improvement on the Do-It-Yourself Network's Web site, www.diynet.com.

www.build.com, a director of building and home-improvement resources and advice.

Selling Your Home

We have sold properties in various parts of America in recent years, so we know just what a tricky business it is to orchestrate the "process" so that you maximize your sale price. You can do it, but you have to be an active seller; you can't simply let the process take care of itself. Of course, if it's your primary home we're talking about, you will probably be looking for a new house while you're selling the old one. Don't put more pressure on yourself by buying house B before you sell house A. You don't need two mortgage payments at once, after all. If you buy a new place first, you might become desperate to unload the old one, which means you'll be willing to sell for less. If you sell your house first, then need a new home, you might be so eager to buy that you don't hold out for the best terms.

As you can see, when you're both a buyer and a seller, you're in a tug-of-war on both ends, trying to get the lowest price as buyer in one case and trying to get the top price from your own buyer on the other. Isn't that a comment on life: Eat or be eaten.

It's a stressful and time-consuming proposition, no doubt about it, but here's our step-by-step guide to getting a win-win deal all around:

Step 1: Find the Right Broker

Thinking of trying to sell your house yourself? Unless a serious buyer is standing on your front porch as you read this, or you live in a market so hot that houses are selling overnight, we have two words of advice: FORGET IT!

You won't have comparables—that is, records of other recent sale prices in your area—to show potential buyers. You'll get people knocking on your door at all hours, and you'll have no idea if those people who appear when you're in the middle of dinner (or even getting ready for bed) are deadbeats or worse.

The 6%–7% commission you pay a broker is well worth the expertise you get in return. If we'd been left to our own devices, we would have sold another condo we once owned for $50,000 less than we actually got for it, thanks to a real estate agent who happened to also be the building manager. When she heard we were planning to sell, she asked how much we wanted. When we told her, she was shocked. Only by talk-

For the sake of true disclosure, we must admit we did recently sell our golf condo in Florida without a real estate professional. It happened out of the blue. *Sometimes* this kind of deal works out.

Our plan was to upgrade to a house in the area. Through a real estate broker, we found the perfect home and signed a purchase-and-sale agreement for five months later to accommodate the seller.

Our next-door neighbors at the condo complex, Lenny and Danna, had just sold their unit, a mirror layout of ours, and, like us, were planning to upgrade.

Lenny mentioned to a golfing partner that our unit would soon be going on the market. The golf partner called and asked if we would show it to him and his wife. We, of course, said yes. We were dealing with a friend of a friend, after all.

Knowing what our friends had just received for their place, we quoted the same price. Two days later the whole deal was done, without any real estate commissions! If you can find a buyer in a similar way, through your personal network, and you have a firm idea of what you can get for your home, by all means go ahead.

Dolan Ah-Ha!

When you talk with the salespeople who earned the title "Sales Agent of the Year" or who became members of the "Million Dollar Club," ask what percentage of the sales were homes they actually sold themselves. Some of the top agents out there make a career of scoring the listings for properties, then sitting back waiting for another agent in the company, or even another company, to sell the house, then taking a piece of the commission.

ing to her did we learn that a condo similar to ours had sold two months before for $50,000 more than we were planning to ask. As soon as she told us that, we hired her as our agent!

Find an agent who has a track record for making sales in your area and knows the terrain inside out and backwards. Ask friends or neighbors who have recently sold their home for referrals. Call your local board of Realtors and ask for the names of "Salespeople of the Year" in your area. Also call local real estate firms and ask them for the names of any agents who belong to the "Million Dollar Club."

Interview agents before you settle on one. Personal chemistry is important, enthusiasm is important, and past performance is critical. It's a big bonus if the broker actually lives in the area. If he or she has kids or grandkids who attend nearby schools, if he or she has a personal stake in the community, you'll be working with someone who can be expected to have a good sense of how to match a buyer with your home.

If an agent meets these criteria, ask these questions and see if he or she passes the test with these answers:

1. How long have you worked in this area?
A: Knowledge of the community is crucial to a successful sale. The answer must be at least 18 months or say "*sayonara.*"

2. How many homes do you sell annually in my area?
A: A good figure depends on the number of houses in the area and the number that go on the market each year. But you want to know that the agent has a track record for selling a significant share of property in the area.

3. Are you licensed?

4. Do you work full-time as an agent?
A: You want someone whose own fortunes are tied to selling your house.

5. Can you refer me to some of your clients?

6. Will you update me once a week in writing about the progress?

7. Will you list my home on the Multiple Listing System (MLS)?

8. Will you provide a "comparable" home survey so that we may together determine a fair asking price for our home?

9. Do you have a well-thought-out plan to market our home? Any unusual ideas? Are you willing to commit to those ideas in a written marketing plan?
A: Absolutely, positively yes. You should always know just what the agent is doing for you.

10. What plans do you have for advertising our home?

If a potential agent makes it through these questions unscathed, it's time to take him or her over the next hurdle. You are not ready to stop firing questions. Don't be shy about this. Remember, you'll be paying this person for his or her expertise, so make sure you get your money's worth!

Here's what you want to ask now:

1. How many listings have you had in the past six months, and how many of them have sold or have sales pending? Who sold them, you or another agent?
A: In a tough market, you want to see sales on at least a third of the agent's listings sold or pending. If houses are going like hotcakes where you live, question any listing that has been on the market for three to six months. Ask why it has not been sold.

2. What is your commission?
A: 6%–7% is fair.

3. What problems, if any, do you anticipate in selling our house?
A: Your agent should be up front about the challenges. A dream agent will tell you honestly what the problems are and then explain how he can solve them.

4. How can we work together to sell our home for a fair price?
A: There is no pat answer here. You're just looking for some creative sparks and a gung-ho attitude.

5. How have you determined the selling price of our home?

Dolan Bottom Line

Don't try too hard to negotiate your broker's sales commission. Think of it from the broker's point of view: A broker has only a finite number of "selling" hours during the day. A broker isn't going to concentrate on selling your home for a cut-rate commission when he's got a listing book full of homes he can sell for full commission.

A: Don't just trust the broker's word. Do your research on the prices paid in the last year for similar houses in the neighborhood and see if the quote is on target.

Not all brokers are going to welcome your grilling. We had one who walked out when we asked what specific magazines and newspapers our home would be advertised in and how often. But if you don't get satisfactory answers at this stage, you have to wonder if you would be able to trust this person to do his best for you. There is no shortage of real estate agents in America, so find one who appreciates your important concerns.

Step 2: List Your Home

Once you find the best broker for your needs, you'll have to decide what type of listing agreement is best for you. A seller's work is never done.

Basically, there are three ways to list your home:

- exclusive right to sell
- exclusive agency
- open listing

We recommend using an exclusive-right-to-sell agreement, which—as you probably guessed—gives the agent the exclusive right to sell your home for a set amount of time—we recommend no longer than six months. Of the three listings, this one should give the agent the most incentive to work hard, because he is assured of earning a commission on the sale even if another agent provides the buyer during the term of the agreement.

Your agent will list the house through standard channels, which may include news-

Pssst. . . . Wanna make a fast sale? Offer a $1,000 bonus to your broker if he or she sells the house within 30 days.

paper classifieds, the agency's circulars, and a Web site. But you can help your broker make your house memorable. Here's what we did: We made about 25 brochures with interior and exterior photographs of our house—including special features, in our case a wine cellar and eat-in kitchen—plus a copy of the floor plan. This will help people remember a home among the houses they may have already seen.

Use the brochure to create a "selling kit," where you also list helpful tidbits such as utility costs and the names and numbers of local schools and organizations. After a house hunter spends a long day schlepping around, your house will be right before his eyes, long after the others have become dim memories.

For your own security, don't include interior pictures that show valuables or where your alarm control is located. Also, don't post these sheets in public places where anyone could pick one up.

Step 3: How About a Little Extra Sales Appeal?

If your broker is doing her job, you are about to have a parade of strangers coming through your home. When you meet someone for the first time, how long does it take you to form an opinion about that person? About 15 seconds, right? Well, the same is true for a house. That's as much time as you have to trigger a positive response from a potential buyer, and it starts as soon as the house hunters see your front door. So give your house all the sales appeal you can. Here are our dos and don'ts:

Do

- *Remember first impressions start with your exterior.* One person's pink flamingo is another person's junk, so remove distracting lawn ornaments. Arrange your lawn chairs, picnic table, and grill so buyers can imagine themselves relaxing in "their" yard. Move garbage cans, tools, hoses, and toys out of sight. Mow your lawn, rake leaves, shovel snow, do some landscaping. Make sure your house number is visible. Give the street side of the house, shutters, doors, and window frames a fresh coat of paint.
- *Make your home look as clean and modern as you can without putting in half the house price all over again.* Let there be light. Make the house as bright as you can.

Dolan Ah-Ha!

Here's a tip from one of our listeners: Change all of the interior doorknobs for a cheery entrance to each room.

This is one of the main things buyers look for (right behind the kitchen and the bathroom). If your house is being shown in the daytime, be sure the shades are up and curtains pulled back. If it's at night, flood the rooms with lighting. You might consider putting in higher-wattage bulbs.

- *Give your walls a fresh coat of paint, in white or cream only*. We knew a brave couple who got a deal on a house in a desirable New Jersey suburb because other buyers felt downright blinded by the circa-1975 Day-Glo orange walls and cabinetry.
- *Go for a spotless, uncluttered look*. A good rule of thumb is to clear out 25% of your "stuff" when you put your house on the market. Give it to charity or put it in storage. Either way, the less clutter, the bigger the house will look. Polish the doorknobs. Put up crown molding.
- *Create a homey atmosphere*. Play soothing background music, something classical but not Wagnerian. Have a fire roaring in the fireplace or a fresh pot of coffee brewing. Have cookies baking, but if that's too time-consuming or caloric, here's how to cheat: Fill a baking pan with water, add some cinnamon, and place in a warm oven. It will smell like something yummy baking.

Don't

- "Help" your broker show buyers around.
- Have pets in the house when buyers are around.
- Cook "smelly" meals before (or during) open houses.

For more help, we recommend *How to Sell Your Home Fast for the Highest Price in Any Market,* by Terry Eilers ($12.95). Also *Starting Out: The Complete Home Buyer's Guide,* by Dion Hymer (Newman Communications, 508-478-0900) and *Home Owner's Tax Guide,* by Julian Block (Ruizheimer International, 800-942-9949).

Step 4: Brush Up on "Win-Win" Negotiating Strategies

When you get your first nibble from a prospective buyer, it's time to start negotiating. You don't usually negotiate with the buyer yourself—but you should stay involved.

With the help of your agent/broker, find out as much as possible about a potential buyer.

- Has the buyer been transferred? People who have been transferred need to find a house quickly.
- Does the buyer have kids? If so, make sure your agent points out what a great

---

Dolan Bottom Line

"He who negotiates best ends up with the most favorable terms." If your prospective buyers are savvy, they'll be asking you a lot of questions, too. That means the less you reveal about yourself, the better. Make sure your broker understands this. For example, you don't want a prospective buyer to know that you have already purchased another house contingent on the sale of your home.

Don't be discouraged if it takes three to six months (or longer) for your home to sell. Your house will eventually sell, and that's when the really fun part begins—moving.

---

school system you have, how close the local Y is, and whether other kids around the same age live nearby.

- Does the buyer have to sell another house before buying? You might want to offer a delayed closing.
- What does the buyer need? By focusing on the buyer's "needs" rather than "wants," your agent can negotiate strongly by pointing out how your home satisfies all those needs.

All You Need to Know About Movers

The Interstate Commerce Commission used to employ 30 people just to deal with complaints involving shipment of household goods, but it was closed down in 1995. With no federal agency to oversee this area, a growing number of dishonest and slipshod movers have taken advantage of consumers at one of the most stressful times of their lives. The Council of Better Business Bureaus (BBB) rates moving and storage companies as one of the most troublesome businesses that they rank.

So how do you find a reliable mover?

The search begins. Use the Yellow Pages or the Internet to find large, established firms—and get bids from *three* different movers for comparison purposes.

Check www.moverquotes.com on the Internet. You plug in your destination and estimate of the size of your move, and out comes a list of movers, estimated cost, phone numbers, and insurance coverage.

When you find a few likely candidates, check them out with your local Better Business Bureau for any complaints and with the American Moving and Storage Association at 703-683-7410 or at www.moving.org. If the mover has a clean record so far, call them. Ask for referrals from people they have moved a similar distance, with a similar volume of "stuff." Also ask if the company operates under any other names so that you don't make unnecessary calls.

If everything checks out, call again. Make an appointment to have a representative come to your home and give you an estimate. Never take an estimate over the telephone! The mover has to see what you're moving to come up with a realistic figure. Meanwhile, you want to see what the people who will be responsible for your possessions are like before you make your final choice.

Meet with at least three moving companies to compare rates and services. We always get three quotes—in writing—and usually take the middle price. However, don't choose a mover solely on the basis of price. A good reputation and a business with a long track record are important, too. Incredibly low rates are usually "sucker" quotes: What you save now will be more than made up when you get stuck with having to repair your piano after the movers have dropped it and then disappeared, or at least drawn out the negotiations so long you get fed up. You don't want to trust your worldly possessions to Joe's Fly-By-Nite.

During your initial interview, ask the movers about any extra charges they impose for carrying things upstairs or on elevators, long walks, pianos, valuable antiques, or heavy items. If your movers do the packing, it will add about 30% to your bill, so we suggest you pack as much as you can yourself. However, ask the moving company if they insure only the items they pack. This is a policy with most movers. So they will have to pack your delicate things. You can pack some of the heavy things, such as fireplace pieces and books. Ask for a "book rate," which is generally lower than that of other boxes.

Be sure to alert the movers about any possible problems such as stairways at the destination, tight corners, long, steep driveways, and so forth.

Ask for a "best price" *binding* bid. That means you are charged either the price on the written estimate (usually plus or minus 10%) or the actual cost based on the exact weight of your possessions and the company's rate, *whichever is lower*.

Make sure that the mover is bonded and that you know the extent of the company's liability for loss and damage before you hire them. Ask to see a certificate from the bonding company, and call the company to verify.

Ask about insurance. Find out if your homeowner's insurance covers your belongings during the move. If not, while moving companies are not licensed to sell insurance per se, you can get a "transit protection" policy from your moving company, which is coverage for your belongings. Many companies will have a basic liability built into the moving contract. Beyond that, if you are moving from one state to another, expect to pay somewhere between $175 and $360 for $40,000 worth of replacement-value coverage, with rates varying according to the deductible amount you choose. An in-state move will be subject to the individual state's rules about transit protection pricing, but in most cases the rates will be close to those for interstate transport. You can keep your cost low by choosing the highest deductible. Be sure to ask your insurance company for a referral to a local agent.

Typically, movers pay about 60 cents per pound for damage. That is not nearly enough! Pay for greater coverage. That should cost you about $7 for each $1,000 of declared value. Ask about in-transit insurance that protects you if your goods are lost or stolen on the trip.

Important Tax Information: Let the IRS Help You Move!

Nothing about moving is painless, but Uncle Sam can ease the stress a little if you qualify for deductions on some of your costs.

The best thing about writing off your moving expenses is that the deduction is taken "above the line." That is, you don't have to worry about itemized phase-out rules that could cost you a tax refund. You do, however, have to file the itemized form.

"Simply" stated, you must pass two tests. If you are a married couple filing jointly, only *one spouse* needs to meet the criteria:

1. "The 50-mile test." This means that you have to be changing jobs, and the distance between your new primary job and your former home must be at least 50 miles greater than your old commute between work and home.

2. "The employment test." To prove that you're not just looking for a change of scenery, but that you moved for employment reasons, you must be employed *full-time* in the general area of your new job location for at least 39 weeks during the 12 months after you make the move. If your employer transfers you or even lays you off, the IRS won't hold it against you, and will waive the 39-week test.

One More Thing . . .

If you're reentering the full-time workforce, you can claim the deduction even if you don't have a job when you move. But your new job, when you find it, must qualify by passing the two tests as outlined above.

Bon Voyage!!!

Should You Refinance? Let the Numbers Tell You.

Forget the old 2% rule!

Many people who bought their homes in the 1980s or early 1990s with high-interest-rate mortgages are gnashing their teeth right now. But the mere fact that interest rates are close to rock bottom isn't *always* an indication that you should refinance your home mortgage. When does it make sense?

Use this easy formula.

Divide the cost of the refinancing (let's say, for example, that it's $2,400) by the amount you'll save every month by refinancing to a lower interest rate (say, $200/month saving). $2,400 ÷ 200 = 12—the minimum number of months that you'll have to stay in your home to justify the expense of refinancing. If you plan to stay put, do it.

Before you sign anything, check your possessions carefully, then write on the delivery papers that you are signing for your shipment "in apparent good condition." This will protect you if you later find that something was damaged and you need to file an insurance claim.

Get FIRM pickup and delivery dates in writing—with compensation to you for meals and housing if the date is not met and you have to hole the family up in a hotel. Be sure that the date is entered on the bill of lading and becomes part of your contract with the mover.

Before the movers arrive, have a floor plan handy so that you can instruct them where to place each item.

Never agree to pay a deposit before the move, but . . . you'll probably need to have a cer-

Dolan Ah-Ha!

When interest rates go down, a whole nation of homeowners scramble to refinance their mortgages at lower rates. The refinancing pipeline gets clogged, which can often cause a delay in closing your loan. With a delay, you might find that your rate lock period has expired before the refinanced loan comes through and you don't get the low, low rate you'd expected. To protect yourself when applying for refinancing, lock your rate for 60 days instead of 30. It will cost you a little more, but if interest rates go up even a little after you apply, your money will have been well spent.

tified check or cash ready to pay the mover upon delivery, or you may have to pay storage charges to ransom your furniture.

To tip or not to tip? What you're moving is valuable, so keep the movers happy. On our last move, we intimated the amount of the tip early in the moving process, as the moving crew was packing everything up. Depending on the complexity of the move, we believe that a tip of $25 for each mover and $50 for the crew chief is a good rule of thumb if they do a great job. (That means no breakage, and they set up the mattress frames.)

Helpful Web Sites for This Section

www.moverquotes.com

www.homeadvisor.msn.com

Some Taxing Matters

Challenging Your Property Tax Bill

You wouldn't allow the IRS to calculate your income tax bill . . . would you?

And you'd never pay an invoice without checking its accuracy, right?

Well, then, why assume that the property tax bill that you received is accurate?

We're always surprised to hear of how many homeowners never take the time to check, let alone *challenge*, how their local government calculates their bill.

Many American homeowners enjoyed handsome gains in their homes' value during 2001. That's the good news . . . the bad news is that means higher property taxes in many parts of America.

Guess what: You could be overpaying. About two-thirds of the time that people challenge their tax bill, there is a change in the bill, many times in the homeowner's favor. There are even companies that will make the calculations for you. They generally charge 50% of your first year's savings. Yes, it's steep, but if you hadn't had the company there at all, you wouldn't have had those savings. There is a Web site devoted to the issue of overpayment of property taxes, www.propertytaxax.com, that is full of information about property tax appeals and offers an electronic book called *Property Tax Appeals: How to Win Your Case*, by George W. Evers for $19.95. Order through the site.

You may not need to hire an expert. Read what propertytaxax.com has to say—and we guarantee it will get you riled up—and then consider conducting your own appeal process. Just be ready to appeal as soon as the assessment arrives, because many communities limit appeals to tight time frames, often as little as 30 days. Here is what you do:

Dolan Warning

There's always a chance that your tax appeal may reveal that your home is being *under-assessed*! Make sure that you have a good case *before* you initiate the appeals process.

1. Review the records. Ask your county assessor for a copy of your property record card, which contains important information about your home, including its location, size, age, and amenities. See if there are any clerical errors in the details, such as the number of rooms, square footage, number of bathrooms, saying it has a fireplace or siding when it doesn't, or any other inaccuracies.
2. Check the measurements listed on the card yourself. If you spot an error and you can substantiate your correction, you may get the assessment just by making an informal appeal at the assessor's office. You'll have to go back to the county assessor's office with a list of correct measurements or photos of your house to substantiate your claim.
3. Have an appraisal. If there are no glaring errors on your property record card, you'll have to have your home appraised to prove that it has been overvalued for property tax purposes. The appraisal could cost $250 or more, but don't forget, a tax savings lasts for years.
4. You can also do your own appraisal by checking the assessed value and actual property tax paid on comparable homes in your area. Many of these assessments are listed in your local public library. Also, your county tax assessor's office can be very helpful as you research "comparables" in providing a record of appraisals and taxes.

Sit down with your tax assessor and make your case. If that doesn't work, you may appeal to a higher authority. Tell the tax assessor you want to appeal, and ask him for

A Tax Tip for Sellers

When you sell your house, you may exempt $500,000 of capital gains on a joint tax return, or $250,000 on a single tax return. You qualify if the house was your primary residence for at least two of the last five years, and you may use the exclusion once every two years. If you have a second home that has appreciated significantly, consider making it your primary residence for two years, then selling it to get the tax break.

Is Your Home Your Workplace? Deduct It!

If you work from home full-time, or even run a sideline business from an office in your home, let the IRS subsidize some of your related expenses, including utilities, insurance, maintenance, your computer, telephone, office supplies, and even your cleaning service. We love it when the IRS does something generous!

If you use part of your home exclusively for business—not necessarily a whole room, but a designated area—you can qualify. If you have a separate structure on your property that you use as an office, or a converted garage, you can deduct it as a business property as long as it is the principal place from which you conduct the business, or you hold meetings there on a regular basis. And you can deduct the depreciation if you own your home.

details on when the next meeting of the board of review or board of equalization will take place. You may have to request that you be placed on the agenda at that meeting. If you lose at this local level, you may also appeal to the tax assessor at the state level, depending on your level of determination!

For further help, we recommend a very good book: *Save a Fortune on Your Homeowner's Property Tax*, by Harry Koenig and Bob Lafag, published by Real Estate Education Co., $17.95 in paperback.

Helpful Web Sites and Books

Mortgage Information and Current Mortgage Rates

www.bankrate.com

www.cbs.marketwatch.com

www.hsh.com or call 1-800-UPDATES

Mortgages Online

www.houseappreciation.com

Buying Property

www.homeadvisor.msn.com

www.hsh.com or call 1-800-UPDATES

www.freddiemac.com

All About Mortgages: Insider Tips for Financing and Refinancing Your Home, by Julie Garton-Good. Dearborn Publishing, 1999. $19.95.

Successful Real Estate Investing: A Practical Guide to Profits for the Small Investor, by Peter G. Miller. HarperCollins, 1995. $17.00.

The Banker's Secret, by Marc Eisenson. Villard Books, 1995. $14.95.

Helpful Information for Renters

The Apartment Renters Resource: http://aptrentersresource.com

Helpful Information for Landlords

www.landlords.com

Landlording: A Handy Manual for Scrupulous Landlords and Landladies Who Do It Themselves, by Leigh Robinson. Landlording, 9th edition, 2001. $27.95.

www.landlording.com

Government Assistance in Buying a Home

www.hud.gov

www.vba.va.gov (for veterans only)

Buyer's Brokers

www.buyersresource.com/brinfo

Real Estate Agents

www.agentscout.com

Real Estate Lawyers

www.lawyers.com

Comparing Prices of Houses in an Area

www.houseappreciation.com

Internet Listings of Property

www.realtor.com

www.era.com

Home Inspection

American Society of Home Inspectors' site, where you can enter your zip code to find a home inspector in the area: www.ashi.com

Relocating and Moving

www.moverquotes.com.

www.schoolmatch.com

Home Financing

www.houseappreciation.com

Home Improvement

Do It Yourself Network: www.diynet.com

www.build.com

Hiring a Contractor

American Institute of Architects: www.enterprisefoundation.org

Smart Consumer Services: www.sconsumer.com or 877-662-8767

www.build.com

www.jeb.net

Building You Own House

www.homeplanfinder.com has a customized feature that allows you to design single-family house and duplex blueprints online by size and architectural style.

www.realtytimes.com—real estate news and advice

Best Deals in Your Area on Energy and Long-Distance Calling Plans

www.homeenergysaver.lbl.gov—provides an estimate of your annual energy budget and how to save

Challenging Your Property Tax

"How to Fight Property Taxes," $6.95, guide from the National Taxpayers Union: www.ntu.org or 703-683-5700

Property Tax Appeals: How to Win Your Case. Electronic book, $19.95. Order at www.propertytaxax.com

Save a Fortune on Your Homeowner's Property Tax, by Harry Koenig and Bob Lafag, published by Real Estate Education Co. $17.95 in paperback.

Home-Related Taxes

IRS Publication 587, Business Use of Your Home

IRS Publication 523, Selling Your Home

www.irs.gov or call 800-TAX-FORM

Home Office

www.aahbb.org

www.ahahome.com

www.homeofficemag.com

www.sba.gov/sbdc

CHAPTER 4

How to Stop Financing
Your Lifestyle with Debt

MANY AMERICANS ARE up to their behinds in debt. While the news headlines bring us a steady barrage of stories about corporations in trouble for accounting irregularities, we also hear tales of woe from our listeners and viewers who also assumed things would just keep getting better—so they bought whatever they wanted and put it on credit cards. We don't mean to make all Americans sound cavalier about getting into debt. We also hear from people who went into debt because of an emergency, or who financed their business start-up by maxing out their own credit cards.

The fact is, middle-class Americans are drowning in debt. A study on consumer bankruptcy conducted at the height of the bull market was the basis for a book titled *The Fragile Middle Class.**

The researchers found that some 90% of the debtors filing for bankruptcy at the threshold of the new millennium were a cross section of middle-class America. More than half were homeowners. Their education was slightly higher than the national average. Job losses, medical problems, and divorce accounted for about 80% of the bankruptcy filings. Many American families that look prosperous have so many debts they are just one emergency away from financial disaster.

A woman in her sixties called *The Dolans* to say she wanted to retire and had $53,000 in her retirement account, but $45,000 in debt from credit cards and loans. Talk about a

---

* *The Fragile Middle Class*, by Teresa A. Sullivan, Elizabeth Warren and Jay L. Westbrook, published by Yale University Press, 2000. The authors are, respectively, vice president and graduate dean of sociology at the University of Texas, a law professor at Harvard, and a business law professor at the University of Texas.

big dose of reality. We told her, point blank, that she would probably have to keep working for years to come in order to pay off those debts.

A man in his seventies phoned in to our radio show and confessed he had a maxed-out credit card that his wife of almost 50 years knew nothing about. He was worried that if he died before paying it off, she would be saddled with a bill their meager pension and Social Security benefits could never pay.

We can't imagine anything worse than unexpectedly losing your spouse, at any age, except perhaps losing the family's main breadwinner and discovering that you've inherited a mountain of debts you can't afford to pay off. Just a notch or two down the scale is losing your job, especially when the economy is in the dumps and it's hard to find another one. Or losing your job just when you owe thousands of dollars to the friendly folks at Visa, MasterCard, and AmEx, who were so eager to win your business. A person's life changes suddenly because of losing a job or losing income from self-employment, or divorce or death—and in the wink of an eye, a credit card debt that was affordable becomes a lead weight pulling you down.

Even in a lousy economy, we have been conditioned to be optimistic about our own futures, even to justify our purchases as an investment in future wealth. You might rationalize that you need a BMW to make a good impression on a prospective employer, and what parent isn't willing to go into hock to send their children to prestigious colleges so that they can presumably get high-paying jobs in adulthood?

Well, personal income rose 72% between 1990 and 2000, but personal debt went up 123%. The bankruptcy statistics continue to rise, with approximately 1.5 million American consumers filing for bankruptcy between early 2001 and early 2002, according to the American Bankruptcy Institute. Some of the cases may have been people rushing to file before the President signed a bill that would make it harder to declare bankruptcy. As it turns out, many members of Congress and the Senate, which each passed different versions of the bill in the summer of 2001, felt that after the 9/11 attack they should not make life even harder for people in debt, so negotiations on the bill were postponed. That's one thin silver lining in a very dark cloud over the country.

Consider some other scary statistics from CardWeb.com: There are 1.4 billion payment cards in circulation in the United States today, including credit cards, debit cards, and store cards, which means an average of around 14 cards for every American household. American consumers currently owe nearly $700 billion on all credit cards. Americans carry, on average, just over $8,562 in credit card debt from month to month.

The actual stories we hear are a lot worse than these statistics. Through the years we have been forced to limit the number of credit-related calls we answer on the air each day.

If we didn't, our program would become wall-to-wall credit calls to the exclusion of other money issues.

All too often someone calls us saying they can no longer make the minimum payments on three, six, even 12 credit cards.

We'll try to sort out the caller's income and outflow. "How much money do you make?" we'll ask.

"Thirty-eight thousand dollars a year."

"How much do you owe?"

"I'm not sure" is invariably the response we get. Whaat?! But we're no longer surprised. It's a pretty sure bet that you're in trouble if you've lost track of how much you owe.

Card issuers make it sound like a divine romance when they solicit your business, but they never tell you how much it will cost you down the line, in dollars and tears. You'd never be naive enough to marry such a smooth talker . . . we hope!

We're under a lot of pressure from everywhere these days. Every day you can find a news story about how lack of consumer confidence is eroding the economy further still. Yet we're being told that it's downright patriotic to go out and spend to stimulate the economy.

Our polite response to this demand is: Baloney! (This is a family book, after all.)

We've already spent ourselves into a hole, and the wherewithal to keep spending just isn't there. Since Washington's economic-stimulus package gives huge retroactive tax breaks to major corporations, these companies should be the ones going into spending mode. Consumers, on the other hand, ought to take a lesson from the corporate

Study Shows Debt Can Kill You

If you need no other reason to get out of debt, hear this. In early 2000, Ohio State University* came out with a study that found that credit card debt can actually kill you. Researchers found that people with large amounts of their income tied up in credit card bills were more likely than other members of the population to suffer from heart attacks, insomnia, an inability to control emotions, and a loss of concentration.

* The study was the work of Paul J. Lavrakas, director of OSU's Center for Survey Research, and former colleague Patricia Drentea, now assistant professor of sociology at the University of Alabama–Birmingham, who conducted a random telephone survey of more than 1,000 Ohio residents in 1997 and followed up in 1999. The results were published in the February 2000 issue of Social Science & Medicine. An article about the survey can be found by clicking on the "Problem Credit" link at BankRate.com

world and get the whole family thinking about ways to make the household a leaner operation.

The best thing you can do for your peace of mind is minimize your debts before they get out of hand. Even better, before they start. And if you are already in heavy debt, it's more important than ever to come up with a plan for digging your way out. We'll show you how to get on the track to debt-free living with the Dolans' Debt Clinic.

The Dolans' Debt Clinic

To get out of debt, you have to start with an honest list of every single debt you owe. Use our list and add your own. Write down the numbers from the last bill you received for each item.

How Much Debt Do You Owe?

Debt	Amount and Interest rate
Primary Home Mortgage	_____
Vacation Home Mortgage	_____
Investment Property Mortgage	_____
Car	_____
Personal Loans	_____
Student Loans	_____
Taxes	_____
Credit Cards	_____
American Express	_____
Visa	_____
MasterCard	_____
Discover	_____
Department Store Cards	_____
Others	_____

Are you married? Living with a partner? Now that you've listed all of your debts, ask your partner or spouse to do the same and compare notes. Whatever you do, make sure you each know what the other's debts are, as well as what the joint debts are. We're going to tell you further on in this chapter which bills you would be responsible for if, God forbid, anything happened to your partner.

Now, how do you get those debts down? We've divided our advice into two parts. Debt Clinic Part I is debt management 101, for everybody. Debt Clinic Part II is for those whose debts are out of control. Read both sections even if you aren't in dire debt. Knowing what could happen might be enough to send you tearing up credit cards left and right. That, by the way, is a good thing.

Part I: Debt Management 101

✓ *Make more than the minimum payment.* An extra $10 a month can make a world of difference. To make sure you get the most bang for every extra buck you pay toward your balances, put the extra money toward the card with the highest interest rate first. (This will actually eliminate your debt faster than paying off the card with the highest balance.) *Yet 47% of credit card customers are making only minimum payments on their credit cards. Don't get caught in this trap.*

✓ *Pay off non-tax-deductible debt first.* If you're paying 18% interest on your credit card balance, you'll make a bigger dent in your debt by paying off that nondeductible credit card debt rather than prepaying your mortgage. The same holds true if you prepay—or pay off—a car loan or personal loan (both nondeductible) rather than your mortgage.

✓ *Prepay whenever possible.* To prepay, just send the extra money along with your regular payment and include a note saying the money is to go *toward your principal.* (Be sure your loan agreement says you can do so without penalty.)

Dolan Bottom Line

Speaking of tax implications, ignore the old argument that says you shouldn't prepay because you lose the tax deduction on the interest you save. Let's say you don't prepay, and spend $1,000 on interest. Sure, that $1,000 gives you a $280 tax deduction (if you are in the 28% tax bracket) . . . but you still spent another $720 on interest you could have saved by prepaying!

Don't pay credit card companies a penny more than you have to. Here are some ways to hold your own against the credit card companies:

✓ *Clean out your wallet.* Americans have gone credit crazy! Most people today have an average of 11 credit cards. You really need only two or three, so apply scissors liberally.

   Which cards should go first? Say goodbye to your department store cards. They usually charge outrageous interest rates—and almost any store today will accept MasterCard and Visa. Granted, sometimes the stores tempt you by offering all you can buy at 15% off on the day you start credit with them. If you're really a smart shopper, you'll do this only if you *can* pay off the debt at the end of the month.

   One gasoline card (for emergencies) and one or two major credit cards plus an American Express card is more than enough. If you're part of a couple, the two of you should have just three or four cards between you: one Visa, one MasterCard, one AmEx, maybe one extra in your own name. What else do you need?

   If you are overspending the limits on those three cards, you're probably headed for trouble if you aren't already there. Always think about how much the monthly payment could build up to over a couple of decades if it was going into your retirement account instead of the credit card company's profit account.

✓ *Ditch your gold and platinum cards.* The fees on these cards are outrageous. Unless you absolutely rely on the extra perks that come along with these cards, cut them up and pocket the $100–$200 (or more) you save in annual fees—or use it to pay off other debts.

✓ *Don't pay an annual fee.* Cards with annual fees are a prime candidate for the chop block. Listen carefully—you don't have to pay an annual fee. No ifs, ands, or buts about it. Just call your credit card company today and ask them to lower or eliminate your annual fee. Competition among credit cards is stiff; your company won't be willing to lose your business over $20 or $40 (which is small change to them). You can fatten your wallet easily—simply pick up the phone and ask. Isn't saving an extra 40 bucks every year worth a painless two-minute phone call?

✓ *You can also use this technique to lower your interest rate.* Tell your credit card company that you've just received a credit card offer from another company offering a lower interest rate. Ask, "Can you match a 14% (or whatever lower rate you may find available elsewhere) rate?" If they can't, take your business elsewhere. Now is an excellent time to comparison-shop for the lowest interest rates on credit cards. We have the lowest lending rates since the 1960s, but will it surprise you to hear that many of the same banks that are paying only 2% interest on your savings account are still charging you interest rates as high as 21% on your credit cards? Consumer credit is a great deal (for them!). *Don't let them get away with that! You can slash your payments dramatically by getting credit cards with lower interest rates.*

Part II: If Your Debts Are Out of Control . . .

How do you know when your debt is out of control?

- ✓ When you have too many days left with no money at the end of your paycheck.
- ✓ When your account is down to a negative balance before your next payday.
- ✓ When you are simply not able to pay your bills with current income.
- ✓ When you don't know how much you owe.
- ✓ When you are paying off/down one credit card bill by changing it to another card!

While following our advice will help you take control, if your debts are so large they've seized control of you, we recommend that you seek help from a consumer credit-counseling program, which will help you work out a repayment plan and act as intermediary between you and the credit card companies and collection agencies. Be aware that working with a credit-counseling program is one more piece of data that could wind up on your credit report, but it will also show that you're making a valiant effort to clean up your debts.

We get a lot of questions from people about for-profit credit-counseling centers. Some of these places will tell you, "For $2,500 we can get all the bad information off your credit report." A lot of people get scammed this way. You should know that even some of these

Use Credit to Buy with Muscle

To hear the way we tend to rail about credit cards, you might think we don't approve of them.

Not so!

Actually, there are times when the best way to protect yourself as a consumer is to pay with plastic.

Here's a problem you've probably had at one point or another: You charge something on your credit card, wait eagerly for the product or service to arrive, and oops. The product or service is not quite what you expected or hoped. You can get an instant refund for the full amount you paid by calling in the big guns—your credit card company.

If you have a beef with a product or a company's service, stand up for your rights! One of the reasons we encourage you to use credit cards is that federal law gives you more legal muscle if you have a dispute. *And it won't cost you a dime.*

legitimate counseling groups are actually funded by the credit card companies! Talk about the fox guarding the chicken coop! They may advise against filing for bankruptcy, even if that could be your best option, because it isn't in their best interest.

We often refer our listeners to a couple of sources for debt help. One is the National Foundation for Consumer Credit, an organization of nonprofit counseling agencies. It's on the Web at www. nfcc.org, or you can call their 24-hour hotline at 800-388-2227 (800-682-9832 for service in Spanish). The NFCC has 1,450 counseling centers around the country. Operators will find a member office in your area or, if there isn't one near you, will set you up with a telephone counselor. The initial consultation is free; after that, you will pay a monthly fee of up to $50 while you are in the program.

Also, get a copy of *Surviving Debt: A Guide for Consumers*, published by the consumer group the National Consumer Law Center (NCLC). The book is $17 in bookstores, or is available by calling NCLC at 617-523-8089, or on the Web at www.consumerlaw.org. A number of our listeners have also found help through the Debt Relief Clearinghouse, which can be reached through their hotline, 800-4DEBTHELP (you can dial the whole nine-digit name, but you will also get through by dialing 800-433-2843).

If you try to go it alone, you'll have to negotiate with the collection agencies. Have your credit report in hand and be honest. Tell them you have a problem, whatever it is that's preventing you from making the payments. You need to contact them; don't wait for them to contact you. Start paying *more than* the monthly minimums required on your cards. Otherwise, it could take you 35 years to get rid of the debt! Then, of course, you have to budget. A credit-counseling agency can help you do all of this.

Warning Signs of a Credit Repair Scam

These are warnings provided by the Federal Trade Commission. Don't trust a company that promises to restore your credit and then tells you:

"Don't worry, we'll fix it in no time." There is no quick fix for heavy debts. You need to pay your bills on time and stick to a "success plan" in your spending.

"Pay us $ _____ now and we'll get back to you." Federal law prohibits credit counselors from collecting money before they perform services.

"We can get you a new credit identity." It is illegal to make this claim, and illegal for you to change your identity with a new credit or tax ID or a new Social Security number.

"We can remove all the bad news from your credit report." They can't take information about bankruptcies, judgments, tax liens, or delinquencies off of your report. Anyone who claims to be able to do so is lying.

Here are some other steps you can consider if your debts are out of control, in descending order from most desirable strategy to least desirable.

A Consolidation Loan

We generally discourage taking on new debts to pay off old ones. However, if you're burdened with a lot of high-interest credit card bills, it is a good idea to go to a credit union or local bank and get a low-interest loan to pay off your other loans (in short, consolidate everything). This way you'll be spending less money in the long run because your monthly interest rates on the new loan should be lower. Whatever you do, don't start running up new charges, and don't let the low-interest loan lead you into the temptation of spending again. The purpose of this loan is to get you out of debt and improve your credit rating. Make this your mantra.

A Home Equity Loan

Using the roof over your head as a piggy bank to pay off other debts has become the most popular form of a consolidated loan. Equity is the difference between your home's appraised—or fair market—value and your outstanding mortgage balance. A home equity loan might be a good idea if you haven't tapped into your equity before and you're willing to lock up those cards and not use them again until the loan is paid off. But the odds are against you; statistically, one year later people who have used home equity loans to pay off credit card debts are back in plastic debt to the tune of as much as before or even more; plus they now have an extra home loan to contend with. This is a situation that can be costly if you're not careful. Once again, let it not lead you into temptation.

There are three basic types of equity loans. Here's a rundown:

A term, or closed-end, loan, or a line of credit on your equity is technically a second mortgage. They are usually for a shorter term than the mortgage you used to buy your home in the first place, typically with a life of five to 15 years.

A term loan is a one-time lump sum with a fixed interest rate and the same payments each month. Once you get the money, you cannot borrow further from the loan.

A home equity line of credit (HELOC) is more like a credit card—yet another one. You can borrow up to a certain amount for the life of the loan, and even withdraw money as you need it. We don't believe in using your home as a piggy bank. If you *must* borrow using your home as security, get a *fixed-rate* loan. That way there will be no interest-rate surprises for the life of the loan.

Your Retirement Account: Your IRAs, 401(k), 403(b), etc.

In eight little words: DO NOT USE THIS ACCOUNT TO PAY DEBTS. But if you're totally stuck, as a last-ditch effort before bankruptcy you might tap into a retirement account. Some people think, I've got this 401(k) at work and I'll use it to pay off my debts. Don't do it unless it's absolutely your only alternative to bankruptcy!

Your Toughest Credit Questions . . . and the Answers

The Questions

We had a guest on our show whose husband had been killed in the attack in the World Trade Center on 9/11, leaving her credit cards that they'd both used in his name. She wanted to know if she should let the credit card companies know he was dead, because she worried that she would lose the accounts and have no credit in her name. We've received many questions that are twists on this one. Here are the related questions we hear most often:

- Am I responsible for my partner's debts? Does one spouse's credit rating apply to the other?
- If the person with whom I cosigned on credit cards dies and I can't afford the monthly minimum on my own, what do I do?
- If my husband dies and I have no credit in my name, should I just continue using his credit cards or should I let the credit card companies know he is no longer around? How can I get credit in my own name?
- If my partner and I keep separate credit card accounts, am I responsible for the bills if something happens to him? What if the expenses were incurred before we were married?
- Why are my ex-wife's creditors trying to get me to pay her bills when we were divorced two years ago?
- If I have a credit card in my name only, would my partner be liable for my debts if I die?
- What if my partner has been running up bills and then doesn't come home one day?

The Answers

It saddens us to hear questions such as these, but we know the answers are critical. We put them to a couple of experts: Gerri Detweiler, author of *The Ultimate Credit Handbook*, and Karen McCall, founder of the Financial Recovery Counseling Institute, based in San Anselmo, California, one of the best of the for-profit debt-counseling services, with branches all over the country.

You are liable for cosigned debts, such as joint credit. The Federal Equal Credit Opportunity Act says if there were joint accounts and one spouse is no longer around, the credit issuer can't close the account. However, the creditor can ask the surviving spouse to reapply using his or her own information.

"If you had a joint account and can continue paying, just go ahead with it," says Detweiler. "You may not have any problems."

Nevertheless, you need to notify the credit card company of your spouse's death; the same applies if you're getting a divorce or your partner has skipped out. But McCall says the good news is that creditors are likely to be sympathetic to someone who has suffered a tragic loss. "Creditors can put a lot of pressure on people," she says. "But you have to look at the whole picture and see if you're going to be able to pay the monthly minimums, then let the credit card companies know. They will probably be willing to give you more time to repay if there's been a death in the family." This is also true if you've been a victim of abandonment. Steady payments will help you establish credit in your name.

When it's a matter of a death, you should run, not walk, to the phone and notify the three major credit bureaus—Equifax, Experian, and TransUnion. (More on these bureaus, including the phone numbers, a little later in this chapter.) Also call the TransUnion service Opt Out, which removes names from promotional mailings and other records, at 888-5OPTOUT (888-567-8688). It's important to get your deceased spouse's name off such lists so that credit card companies won't keep sending out offers that can easily be intercepted by those nefarious outlaws of modern times, identity thieves. The recently deceased are very fertile ground for identity theft. Someone might apply for a credit card in your dead spouse's name, then take off on a spending spree in Majorca.

You are not responsible for debts incurred before your marriage if you do not share the account. However, if you live in a community property state,* any debts that are incurred during the course of the marriage are considered joint property. Furthermore, you may be held responsible for your spouse's student loans or tax bills. "These aren't subject to the same consumer protection laws as credit cards," says McCall.

If you live in a state that doesn't have a community property law (and the majority of states fit into this category), you are not usually responsible for debts your spouse incurred in his or her own name, even while you were married. You should know this and stand up for your rights. "I have personally witnessed debt collectors telling people they were responsible for their spouses' debts when they legally were not," says Detweiler. But—yes, there's a substantial "but" coming. If your dead spouse has left an estate, creditors can go after it, especially if he's left a substantial debt. If the debt is small, they might not bother.

---

* Arizona, California, Idaho, Louisiana, Nevada, New Mexico, Texas, and Washington are community property states. Check out www.mycounsel.com/familylaw for information on community property versus common law states.

TIMPANOGOS HIGH SCHOOL

We always recommend that a wife, whether she's working or not, set up at least one credit account in her own name, as insurance against death or divorce. Nearly anyone can establish credit with a secured credit card account. This is "secured" by money you deposit into a bank account. You will deposit $500 or more into an interest-bearing account, paying a very modest return, and the amount you deposit becomes your line of credit, the maximum you can charge on the credit card.

As long as you make payments on time, you will establish a good credit history, whether you're starting out or trying to redeem an old bad credit rating. And no one can tell it's secured; it looks like any Visa or MasterCard. It isn't to be confused with a debit card, which we don't recommend because someone could steal your card and drain your account. Check out www.bankrate.com for the best rates on secured credit cards. One problem with a secured card, however, is that many do no reporting to the credit bureaus. If they aren't reporting it, no one knows how well you're doing and it won't help you establish a solid credit record. So it's imperative that you contact the issuer of the secured card and get in writing from them the declaration that they do in fact report your transactions to a credit bureau.

Need we explain why it's so imperative to know what sort of financial obligations you are marrying along with the wonderful person whom you love? You should know about each other's finances and payment plan. And have a fallback plan just in case disaster strikes. In normal times, maybe you could take on a second job or add new clients if you have a business of your own, but don't count on this as a solution if you become the victim of a recession, and if you're bereaved, you'll need to take time to heal rather than working longer hours. Consider taking out a larger life insurance policy to cover the debts in an emergency. It's best to look for solutions when you're calm. Take inventory of your possessions, and make a list of luxury items you could sell if you needed instant cash. If you have a large enough house, McCall suggests taking in a renter if the bottom is about to fall out.

Also, once a year check your credit rating (that is, *your* rating, your *spouse's*, and your *joint rating*) through one of the major credit-reporting agencies in the United States. Think of this as a checkup on your financial health so that you'll be fully informed as to your qualifications for loans on the big purchases, such as a house, car, or college tuition. By the way, as a couple who recently contacted our show learned the hard way, a credit record of slow payments hits you in all kinds of places. The couple's auto insurance company had just raised their premium for two cars by $200 a year, based on a credit record that put them in a high-risk bracket. They wanted to know what their credit record had to do with their auto premiums. Well, it might have very little, but it tells insurers and lenders that they are running a risk of getting late payments from you, so they charge you more to give themselves a hedge.

More Questions and Answers

Q: Where do I find the credit card companies with the lowest interest rates?

A: Take your question to the Web; www.bankrate.com and www.cardweb.com are loaded with information about current credit card rates, and will also tell you where to apply.

Q: Should I let my children have credit cards?

A: If they're under 16, the answer is No! No! No! A credit card is practically a lethal weapon in unskilled hands. However, your kids will be bombarded with offers from card companies starting in their freshman year of college, and to give them some practice for the responsibility, we suggest you let them have access to a credit card when they turn 16, with some very strict limitations. Keep the credit limit down to $500. Also, ask the credit card company to send duplicate bills: one to your teenager, so that he or she will get used to receiving the bills and paying them on time, and one to *you*, so that you can monitor every transaction. One of the best lessons you can teach your children is to pay within 30 days.

Q: How would we pay our debts if my husband (or wife), the family breadwinner, was laid off or died?

A: This is one more reason to reduce your debt and boost your savings. Be sure, also, that the family's chief breadwinner has a life insurance policy that will cover the debts. (See Chapter 10 for more about insurance.)

Arming yourself with a credit report is, in fact, part of the prequalifying process for such loans, and if you have a good rating you're in a position to negotiate for the best terms. And if a catastrophe should ever befall you and cause you to fall back on payments, a good prior credit rating will stand as evidence to creditors that you are reliable under normal circumstances and deserve a break. With these frequent checkups, you'll also find out if there are any mistakes on your report that need to be cleared up.

All You Should Know About Your Credit Rating

Individual and household credit ratings used to be kept secret, but now you can get easy access to profiles of your credit history that show whether you've met your credit obligations and how quickly you've paid back creditors. You can request a credit report directly from any of the three major credit-reporting agencies, Experian, TransUnion, and Equifax. We recommend, however, that you get your credit report through the online service called MyFICO.com, which is operated by Fair, Isaac and Co., creator of the FICO score, the credit scoring model that is most widely used to determine a person's credit risk. For $12.95, MyFICO gives you an analysis of your current score in plain English, based on your Equifax credit profile, as well as helpful tips on what specific factors most heavily affected your score and how you can improve your FICO score over time. While the credit-reporting agencies can take up to six weeks to send you a report, MyFICO's report is available to you online for 30 days following the order date.

The report will give you a credit score of 100 to 900. Most U.S. consumers score between 300 and 850. Generally, the higher your score, the more favorably a lender will view your application for credit. The MyFICO report will tell you where you fit in comparison to other consumers, and what this means to lenders.

Bankrate.com, an excellent Web site that offers credit advice in addition to surveys of good and bad credit card rates, recommends checking with all three of the major agencies, because each report will have different information. This is due to the fact that credit reporting is a voluntary system, and creditors subscribe to whichever agency they want. If you find that your credit report doesn't list creditors that you always pay on time, you can notify the creditor that you want your good record reported to the credit bureau. By law the credit issuer is required to respond within a "reasonable time." That's some lawspeak and it's the way the laws are written; in plain English a reasonable time should be about 30 days. Contact information for the credit-reporting agencies appears at the end of this section.

An agency credit report contains four sections: identifying information, credit history, public records, and inquiries.

Check the *credit history section* very carefully. It is supposed to list your credit accounts and how much you owe on each one, as well as your record for keeping up with payments. Experian's reports will state whether you have a record of paying on time, as well as whether a creditor has ever "charged off" the account; that is, given up on collecting.

You will also see payment codes that are the credit industry's long-used method of grading your payment patterns for credit card accounts, installment loans, mortgages, and lines of credit. Here is a sneak preview of what they might say about you:

The public records section is a place you want to keep blank. It lists finance-related matters such as bankruptcies, judgments, and tax liens. Most of these problems, however, do not stay on the report forever as long as you take care of them. A Chapter 7 bankruptcy, in which all of your debts are wiped out but your assets are sold and the proceeds distributed among your creditors, is supposed to be cleaned off your record 10 years after the filing date. A bankruptcy filed under Chapter 13, also known as "wage earner's bankruptcy," in which you set up a repayment plan, is usually deleted seven years after the filing date. Less onerous reports, such as late payments or nonpayments, settlements, and tax liens should be deleted seven years after you make good on the problem. An upaid tax lien can be reported forever, but the reporting agencies often delete them 15 years after the filing date.

The final section: inquiries, is a list of everyone who has asked to see your credit report. These are divided into two sections: "hard" inquiries, which you initiate by filling out a credit application, and "soft" inquiries, which come from companies that want to send out promotional information to a prequalified group or current creditors who are monitoring your account. Having a large number of hard inquiries as a result of your applying for credit can affect your rating, because lenders perceive consumers who are seeking several new credit accounts as riskier than those who aren't seeking additional credit. The good news about this, though, is that contrary to a widely held belief, the impact is not that large unless the rest of your credit history is problematic. Also, if you have been "rate shopping" for a mortgage or auto loan, this action should be counted as a single inquiry; contact the credit-rating bureau if you've been penalized for your thoroughness with a list of multiple inquiries. Typically, inquiries are purged from the credit bureau files after two years. You can call Opt Out (888-5OPT-OUT, or 888-567-8688), which tells the credit-reporting agencies that you don't want them to sell or rent your name to marketers. Here's one more great reason, as if you need one, to throw out—after shredding—all of those unsolicited credit card offers that clog your mailbox, and nowadays your e-mail box too. Americans get bombarded with more than 3.5 billion credit card offers a year. Don't succumb to temptation.

What If a Bad Report Is Undeserved or Contains Mistakes?

Brace yourself for a battle, because it is not uncommon for reports to have errors. Some lenders estimate that as many as 80 percent of all credit reports contain some kind of misinformation.

As you probably know, identity theft is a growing problem, and one of the reasons you should check your credit report is to make sure that you aren't taking the rap for someone who has snatched your credit card number and made charges on it. Nothing is more frustrating than cleaning up a credit card account, then getting billed for more charges that you didn't make. Clear that up with the credit card company right away and you won't have to pay anything when you prove that the charges are not yours, but you want to make sure it doesn't haunt you on a credit report. As if you need it, this is another good reason to winnow down your credit cards. Don't carry around credit cards that you rarely use, and if you ever use a credit card at an ATM machine, pick a personal identification number (PIN) that isn't an obvious set of digits, such as your birthday, that someone could find in your wallet. A PIN should reflect numbers that mean nothing to anyone but you—the date you fell in love with your high school sweetheart or something.

MyFICO's report comes with a form to fill out if your bad credit rating is attributed to an account that isn't yours or a disputed amount. You should also, however, contact the credit company that put the mistake up there and get them to correct it. If they don't correct it within 60 days, or if they disagree with you and won't change it, you have the right to put in an addendum of 100 words saying why that piece of information is incorrect.

The process takes time, because the creditors have 30 days to respond to a charge of a discrepancy. As long as a charge is in dispute, that dispute will show up on your report.

If you're sitting in front of a loan officer to discuss a car or mortgage loan, and you have a bad credit report due to a mistake, tell this person about the problem *before* you even begin to talk about the loan. Few reports are read by humans now; they're handled almost completely by computers, and computers can't interpret. So the burden falls upon you to show the loan officer exactly what went wrong and why the information is incorrect.

Know Your Rights

This is still America, and no one ever goes to debtors' prison. Even if you *are* in serious debt, it is illegal for a debt collector to inform your employer or neighbors about your debt, call you late at night or at work, or engage in any other form of unfair harassment. If someone does hound you, call and write to the Consumer Protection Office of the attorney general in your state and report the calls. This office should contact the outfits that are after you. At the very least, you can tell the next collector who calls that you know this is illegal harassment and you've reported it; then send them a copy of the letter you sent to the Consumer Protection Office.

All You Should Know About Credit Cards

We've been talking about the perils of a credit card with a high interest rate, and that is just the tip of the iceberg. We've done several entire television segments on CBS about

Dolan Ah-Ha!

You can "opt out" of direct mail offers by having your name and address removed from mailing lists obtained from the main consumer credit reporting agencies: TransUnion, Experian, Equifax, and Innovis.

Call 888-5-OPT-OUT (888-567-8688).

The Big Credit-Reporting Bureaus and How to Find Them

Fair, Isaac & Company

Locations around the world. Check Web site at www.fairisaac.com for nearest location, or call 800-999-2955 within U.S., 415-472-2211 outside U.S. For a credit report, go to www.MyFICO.com

Equifax

Report fraud: 800-525-6285. Or write: P.O. Box 740250, Atlanta, GA 30374-0250. Order copy of report ($8 in most states): P.O. Box 740241, Atlanta, GA 30374-0241. Or call: 800-685-1111. Dispute information in report: Call the phone number provided on your credit report. Opt out of preapproved offers of credit: 888-567-8688. Or write: Equifax Options, P.O. Box 740123, Atlanta, GA 30374-0123. Web site: www.equifax.com

Experian (formerly TRW)

Report fraud: (888) EXPERIAN, (888) 397-3742. By fax: 800-301-7196. Or write: P.O. Box 1017, Allen, TX 75013. Order copy of report ($8 in most states): P.O. Box 2104, Allen, TX 75013. Or call: 888-XPERIAN. Dispute information in report: Call the phone number provided on your credit report. Opt out of preapproved offers of credit and marketing lists. Write: P.O. Box 919, Allen, TX 75013. Web site: www.experian.com

TransUnion

Write to: P.O. Box 6790, Fullerton, CA 92634. Order copy of report ($8 in most states): P.O. Box 390, Springfield, PA 19064. Dispute information in report: Call the phone number provided on your credit report. Opt out of preapproved offers of credit and marketing lists: 800-680-7293 or 888- 5OPTOUT. Or write: P.O. Box 97328, Jackson, MS 39238. Web site: www.tuc.com

what your credit card company doesn't want you to know. If anything, things are getting worse in the economic crunch. When interest rates decline, credit card issuers try to cover their own derrieres.

Even if your card has a variable interest rate that you would expect to see go down with other lending rates, it is likely to have a floor on that rate. We heard recently of a Visa that advertised a variable APR of 20.99%, but it turns out that is the minimum APR, so you

Definition

APR = Annual Percentage Rate. The interest rate reflecting the total yearly cost of the interest on a loan, expressed as a percentage rate. Under the federal Truth in Lending Act, the APR must be calculated in a standard way to allow consumers to make "apples-to-apples" comparisons of lending terms.

Source: www.bankrate.com.

don't benefit from lowered interest rates. Even with the prime rate at 1%, you're still paying a high interest rate on your balance.

What kind of deal is that? Major issuers of bank credit cards are moving away from variable interest rates anyway.

Earlier this year, statistics showed the average American carried thousands of dollars on his/her credit card(s). Grace periods are shrinking steadily to an average of 20.6 days, from 27.8 days a decade ago.

Credit card issuers *still* make most of their money from interest income . . . but watch out for those sneaky fees! Income from late fees and penalties is likely to exceed $10 billion this year.

Don't be a statistic!

Furthermore, credit card companies are fiercely competing to lure you in, but often with some come-ons that are too good to be true. The come-ons only get worse in the attempt to hook consumers who have problem credit ratings and know it. BancOne had an offer for a card that allowed you to borrow against your retirement account. Very, very bad idea. Do you know how much money you lose when you draw from your retirement account before you are 59½ years old? Federal law allows you to start withdrawing from any tax-deferred retirement account, such as an IRA, 401(k), or 403(b), at that age, but if you take anything out before then, you generally pay a 10% penalty, in addition to income taxes. This is money that should, ultimately, be taxed at the rates you'll be paying as a retiree, which are likely to be lower than the tax bracket you're in when you're working. Just thinking about the way credit card companies offer you the "opportunity" to rob your own future makes us livid.

What Your Credit Card Company Doesn't Want You to Know

Here are eight things that you'll likely NEVER hear from your credit card company and our solutions:

1. "Our Low-Interest Introductory Rates Seldom Last Very Long."

The old bait-and-switch routine strikes again. Have you received any credit cards offers in the mail lately? Of course you have. We're getting at least five a week in the Dolan household . . . and every one of them has a low introductory rate splashed all over it: "4% [or less] for six months!"

The idea is that a lower rate—even for a few months—will be enough to entice you to get on board. And it may be—if you don't know the full story. In much, much smaller writing somewhere in the offer you'll find the "disclosure box." This is where they bury all the stuff they don't really want you to know.

One of the things they really don't want you to know is that the super-low introductory rate they lured you in with may go up before the six-month introductory period is over.

We found the following disclosures in the fine print of one offer:

If payment is received late once during the introductory period, the rate will readjust to 12.99%.

If, at any time, payment is received late twice in any six-month period, the rate will adjust to 19.99% or higher.

SOLUTION: Mark your calendar for the day that the low rates expire or the date that the new, less-attractive restrictions kick in. Then make sure you flag the day one week before to make your payment; pay the balance off if you can.

Read the current cardholder agreement and ALL inserts that accompany your monthly statement. DON'T BE TOO BUSY TO AVOID BEING RIPPED OFF!

2. "Applying for a Lot of Different Credit Cards May Injure Your Credit Rating."

Many companies won't quote you a rate until you actually apply for a card, so they may be able to charge you more if you're a bad credit risk—tricky business.

SOLUTION: Forget filling out all of those "preapproved" applications. Do your homework . . . check out the deals . . . carry only three or four cards.

3. "We Want You to Pay as Little as Possible Each Month."

Over the past five years, some companies have quietly lowered the typical minimum payment from 4% to 2% of the balance. If you pay just 2% on a $1,900 balance at 18%, it will take 23 years to pay off the balance . . . and you'll pay more than $4,000 in interest.

SOLUTION: Pay more than the minimum every month and save big $$$ in interest. Pay as much as you can possibly afford.

4. "Our Credit Card May Not Have Any Grace Period."

Most credit cards give you 25 days before charging you interest if you're not carrying any unpaid balance; some give you 30 days. But others have cut back to 20 or 15 days. A few have NO GRACE PERIOD at all, charging you interest all the time on anything that you buy. On most cards there is no grace period for cash advances or for new purchases if you're carrying forward a balance from the previous month.

SOLUTION: Check the small print and choose the longest grace period that you can find, typically 25 days.

5. "Our Late-Payment Fees Aren't the Only Fees That We Charge!"

Beware of fees for closing your account. Beware of inactivity fees for failing to use a card for a period of time such as six months or a year, a fee for not carrying a balance, over-limit fees if you charge more than your preset credit limit, and transaction fees each time that you use your card.

SOLUTION: Don't sign on with a card until you have a list in writing of all fees that the company charges.

6. "We'd Love You to Do Our 'Skip-a-Payment' Plan."

Credit card issuers have two tricks up their sleeve to jack up the interest you owe. The first trick usually comes around the holidays. The credit card company sends you a warm and fuzzy letter "offering" to let you skip making your next payment. Aw, geez, isn't that nice of them—so considerate.

But they're not letting you skip a payment because they like you. What they bury in that letter is that you'll still owe interest—every penny of it—on that money while you skip a payment.

SOLUTION: Say thanks, but no thanks to this "generous" offer.

7. "Our 'Convenience Checks' Aren't a Great Deal."

For starters, the interest rate on these checks may not be the same as with your credit card—it's probably higher! Besides the interest rate, there are transaction fees. Most cards charge a fee equal to 2%–3% of the amount you write the check for.

Also, most have no grace period, so the interest on a "convenience" check starts piling up as soon as you write it.

Ditto all of the above warnings when looking at using your credit card to take a cash advance.

SOLUTION: If you get convenience checks in the mail—RIP THEM UP! Then call the issuer and tell them to stop doing you the "favor" of sending them. Even worse than the rip-off factor, these checks leave you vulnerable to identity theft. Mail delivery being what it is, the checks on your account could end up in the wrong mailbox—and the wrong hands.

8. *"You Can Haggle for a Lower Interest Rate."*

Credit companies spend big bucks to find new customers . . . so good clients have considerable leverage.

SOLUTION: If you are in good standing, call your issuer and negotiate for a lower interest rate and waiver of annual fee. Be sure to mention any other business that you do with the bank that issues the card. We are constantly telling our listeners that if you've been paying bills on a credit card with a 19% to 20% interest rate, tell the issuer, "I want a lower rate or else I'm splitting." You can always transfer the balance to a card with a lower interest rate and tear up the card with the high rates. It costs credit card companies money to replace you as a customer. There are 6%, 7%, 8%, 9% credit cards, and if your credit is good you should be able to get one.

www.cardweb.com keeps an updated list of average credit card interest rates. The best credit card deal is one with no minimum APR and a low interest rate. Bankrate.com gives an excellent rundown of rates and terms being offered by specific issuers. Their information changes periodically, because companies come in and want to attract new business and are bound to come up with a better deal, so check often.

Look for alternative credit card providers, such as credit unions and community banks. There are 5,000 credit unions in the United States that have attractive pricing. The Credit Union National Association can help you find a credit union in your area. Local banks often have lower credit card rates than the big ones that keep sending you junk mailings.

We'll say it again: THROW THOSE UNSOLICITED OFFERS OUT (after you shred them). Sure you might be able to get a credit card with a $6,000 limit in a flash — enough to take the whole family on a great vacation. But it isn't free money, after all; it's more the modern equivalent of selling your soul for two weeks of fun.

Cards We Don't Like

Affinity Cards. If you like the idea of having a card that gives 10 cents of every dollar you charge to Save the Whales or your college or whatever, this is a nice idea, but affinity cards should be used only by people who don't carry balances. They usually have the highest interest rates of all cards.

Debit Cards. We are, to put it mildly, not fans of debit cards. They should be used only by people who are so undisciplined they can't possibly handle credit cards. When your credit card is lost or stolen, as long as you report the loss within one or two days, the maximum for which they'll hold you liable is $50; in fact, if you have a good credit record and call them right away, they will most likely waive that $50. But with a debit card, someone can steal it and debit your account down to zero before you even realize it's gone. Check the fees that your bank may be charging!

ATM Warning. The thing you have to be particularly careful of is all of those ATM "debit" cards that have Visa or MasterCard logos. Banks are sending them to customers without asking. These cards can be used with or without a personal identification number (PIN), just like credit cards, but the thief has his hands right on your bank account. You might be able to recover your money eventually, but you'll face a loooong fight with the bank.

Personally we've never used ATM cards. We know, they're convenient and a lot of people like them. If you must carry one around, employ our obscure-PIN strategy (never use your birthday or any obvious numbers as your PIN). And try to hover over your transaction like a human shield when you're at an ATM machine. Paranoia is appropriate here; ATM card thieves have been known to watch with binoculars.

The more plastic you have in your pocket that could be ripped off, the more you open yourself to identity theft, monetary theft, and all sorts of problems—another reason to keep your credit card inventory down to just a few really good low-interest cards.

Don't Just Tear Up Your Credit Cards—Cancel *Them!*

This is another **Dolan Bottom Line** alert. Cutting up your credit cards doesn't close the accounts—you actually have to let the credit bureaus know that you've closed the accounts. And if the accounts aren't closed, you may hurt your chances of getting credit in the future, because it will appear that you've got open credit lines from those old cards. To close a credit card account, simply send a letter with your name, address, and account number to the credit card company, asking them to close the account.

The point is to show credit rating agencies that you are canceling, not being canceled by the card company because you're a deadbeat.

To make your point clear, use our form letter on the next page.

Bankruptcy

If you owe anywhere near a year's worth of take-home pay, you're in bad shape and bankruptcy might be your best option.

No doubt you'll think it stinks to be in the position of considering any kind of bankruptcy. Yet being stuck with a lifetime's worth of bills is no way to live, and that is why we have laws that allow people to make a fresh start. Instead of feeling depressed, consider the "harder they fall the higher they bounce" school of failure and success. Many famous people have declared personal or business bankruptcy and emerged successful again. Here are some you'll recognize:

Credit Cancellation Letter

[Your Name]
[Your Address]

[Date]
Dear Sir or Madam:

Please let this letter serve as notice that I am terminating my credit card account effective immediately. Please close the following account:

Credit Card Company: _____
Account Number: _____

Please send me written confirmation that my account has been closed. Also, please confirm that you have notified all appropriate credit card bureaus that this account was closed at my request.

Thank you for your prompt attention to this matter.

Sincerely,
[Your Signature]

- Mark Twain
- P. T. Barnum
- former Texas governor John Connally
- Francis Ford Coppola
- Cathy Lee Crosby
- Walt Disney
- 20th Century Fox Studios cofounder William Fox
- former U.S. baseball commissioner Bowie Kuhn
- Golfing great Jack Nicklaus was on the verge of bankruptcy in the mid-1980s after investors pulled out of two golf-course developments his company started.
- Willie Nelson considered filing for bankruptcy after the IRS raided his Texas homestead on tax-evasion charges and confiscated everything in 1990. Only through the help of family and friends was he able to pull himself up.

Don't rush into it; talk with a credit counselor first and see if you can work something out. A credit counselor will also be able to refer you to a bankruptcy lawyer, who will show you the ropes and represent you in court.

There are two types of bankruptcies available to consumers: Chapter 7 and Chapter 13, both named for the bankruptcy code numbers that identify them. Chapter 7, as we mentioned before, is a straight bankruptcy. You dissolve your debts but you also have to sell off most of your assets, and any monies realized are distributed among your creditors. You are still liable for:

- credit card charges made within 20 days of filing
- personal loans and installment loans made within 40 days of filing
- alimony and child support
- certain back taxes
- money owed as reparation for intentional harm you caused someone
- debts resulting from fraud

If you have regular employment, you might be able to file for Chapter 13 bankruptcy. This type is somewhat less of a stigma on your credit report, because you do repay your debts through a court-ordered repayment plan that usually stretches over a three-year period. It also allows you to hang on to your assets. You will still be liable for:

How Do You Recover from Bankruptcy?

Without a doubt, your chances of eventually being able to get loans for a house, a car, tuition, or a small business are better if you had good credit in the past and were driven to dire straits by a single incident, such as the death of your spouse, divorce, or the loss of your job. But while you're reassessing your life and your spending habits, you can begin to restore your credit by getting a secured credit card. Almost any bank will give you one. And again, it goes without saying, pay all of your bills on time. We can't say this too many times.

A number of issuers are now offering nonsecured cards that cater to people who are trying to establish or restore credit. The Aspire Visa from Atlanta-based CompuCredit is one such card. Others are available through LendingTree Inc. (www.lendingtree.com), an online loan site, Capital One, Providian, and Merrick Bank in Salt Lake City. Check bankrate.com for the most recent deals. These cards will NOT give you the best interest rates. Most rates range from around 15% to 25%. Many come with annual fees, which often range from $15 to $50, and your credit lines may start as low as $500. The issuers have begun to smell a growing market in people without sterling credit, so you might even find your mailbox flooded with offers.

- alimony and child support
- long-term debts that were not fully repaid during the repayment period

Although the bankruptcy will be removed from your credit record after 10 years (seven if it's a Chapter 13), proof of it will remain on file for 25 years in a regional bankruptcy warehouse. For the rest of your life you will have to answer "Yes" to the question "Have you ever filed for bankruptcy?" or risk serious penalties. Even so, bankruptcy doesn't have to be the end of your credit life.

You can recover if you get back on a firm credit track, and by that we mean paying your bills within six to 12 months and making sure the creditors report it to the credit agency. You may also have to hound the credit-reporting agencies to make sure your positive strides are noted on your credit report.

Helpful Web Sites, Phone Numbers, and Books

Debt Help

CardTrack.com

Consumer Credit Counseling Services: 800-388-2227

www.creditinfocenter.com

Credit Federal: www.creditfederal.com has information about getting out of debt and securing credit, including information about auto, consolidation, and mortgage loans.

Debt Relief Clearinghouse: 800-433-2843

Federal Trade Commission "Back-In-The-Black" Campaign: www.ftc.gov/bcp/conline/edcams/repair

Financial Crisis and Treatment Center: www.myvesta.org

GO Network: www.activedecisions.com

Institute of Consumer Financial Education: www.financial-education-icfe.org/credit_card_spending_tips/ index.asp

Jump Start Coalition (for teenagers and young adults seeking a basic financial education): www.jumpstartcoalition.org/

National Foundation for Credit Counseling: www.nfcc.org

888-5OPTOUT

Credit Card Information

www.Bankrate.com

www.CardWeb.com

Credit Rating

www.myFICO.com

www.equifax.com

www.experian.com

www.tuc.com

Credit Unions

www.cuna.org

www.ncua.gov

Legal Information

www.mycounsel.com

National Consumer Law Center: www.consumerlaw.org

NOLO Press, Berkeley, CA: www.nolo.com

Bankruptcy

American Bankruptcy Institute: www.abiworld.org

CHAPTER 5

The Investment Survival Guide

The stock market is *still* a slippery slope!

REMEMBER THOSE HOT high-profile, must-own stocks that included WorldCom, Global Crossing, and Enron, and the glowing recommendations the companies got from Wall Street analysts? We'd mention more, but we'd hate to see these pages become stained with readers' tears.

The truly sad thing is that even after all the hot air was let out of the stock market bubble of the late 1990s, Wall Street continued to tout failing companies. We received an absolutely shocking report from Weiss Ratings, Inc., the firm that rates the brokerage firms, saying that in the first four months of 2002—well after the Enron story was out— among 50 brokerage firms covering companies that had gone bankrupt that year, 47 firms continued to recommend that investors buy or hold shares in the failing companies even *while those same companies were filing for Chapter 11!*

Among the culprits were some of the biggest names in the industry. It was reported that Lehman Brothers maintained six "buy" ratings on failing companies, while Salomon Smith Barney maintained eight "hold" ratings up through the date the companies filed for bankruptcy. Also sticking with "buy" ratings until the bitter end were Bank of America Securities, Bear Stearns, CIBC World Markets, Dresdner Kleinwort Wasserstein, Goldman Sachs, and Prudential Securities.

"This analysis shows that Wall Street's record is far worse than previously believed," Martin D. Weiss, chairman of Weiss Ratings, said.

It's hard to find accurate, trustworthy investment information. Just a few months before Enron's collapse in 2001, 16 of 17 analysts who followed the company had given it a "buy" rating.

Once and for all, we are going to give you the straight scoop on investing. The fact is, your broker won't tell you, your financial planner won't tell you, your insurance agent won't tell you, and your banker won't tell you what you really need to know about investing your hard-earned bucks. No one cares about your money the way you do.

But with not too much effort you can do better than many of the so-called "experts" and have a comfortable nest egg for your future.

There isn't an investor in America who hasn't lost money. Brokers have lost money, too. But guess what, your broker probably hasn't lost nearly as much as you have. Financial industry insiders know a lot of things that individual investors don't.

There's a trust rift as wide as the Grand Canyon between brokerage firms and clients, and there should be. Wall Street hasn't been straight with us.

David H. Komansky, the former chairman and CEO of Merrill Lynch, actually admitted as much at the firm's annual shareholder meeting on April 26, 2002, when he publicly stated: "We have failed to live up to the high standards that are our tradition, and I want to take this opportunity to publicly apologize to our clients, our shareholders, and our employees."* To be sure, after Komansky's comments, Merrill Lynch and Salomon Smith Barney both announced they would try to reform the system by starting a performance-based compensation system for research analysts, paying them bonuses based on how accurate they are and how their recommendations benefit investors instead of on how much investment banking business they help win for the firm. Merrill Lynch has also started a new stock-rating system in which the ratings are simply "buy," "neutral," and "sell" instead of their more ambivalent old ratings of "strong buy," "buy," "neutral," and "reduce/sell." The jury is still out, however, on how well this is going to work. Don't hold your breath.

Meanwhile, on *The Dolans* we've had so many calls and e-mails from people railing about their brokers being incompetent, and ill-informed by their own firms, that we've had to screen them out of the show because there are just too many to air! But here's the terrible truth: There are more than a few brokers out there who know *just* what they're doing. Their aim is not to make money for you, but to beat all their colleagues each month and earn the highest commissions; and they'll do anything to keep their commissions rolling in, *especially* if all they have to do is sell your life savings down the river.

---

* Quoted in *BusinessWeek* cover story: "How Corrupt Is Wall Street?" by Marcia Vickers and Mike France, with Emily Thornton, David Henry, and Heather Timmons in New York and Mike McNamee in Washington; May 13, 2002.

They do this because their jobs and perks depend on it. Generally, it's the constant turnover of portfolio transactions that make those commissions, not the growth in value of the portfolio. And when a broker is a superstar generating millions in commissions, the firm's managers may turn a blind eye to his or her activities. One such star at Merrill Lynch shrank million-dollar portfolios into hundred-thousand-dollar lumps, and is now facing lawsuits left and right.

Just because someone is the "best" broker in the firm doesn't mean he or she is going to be good for you.

One broker at UBS Paine Webber *did* send an e-mail to a group of Enron employees suggesting they unload their shares in the company, on the same day that Enron's then-chairman, Kenneth Lay, secretly shed $4 million from his own stake. But instead of becoming a hero, that broker was fired. Why? Enron's stock did become worthless just a few months later, and the clients were, to put it as delicately as we can, royally screwed. But Enron was a big corporate client of Paine Webber. The firm was managing Enron's stock option program for employees and brokerage accounts for many company executives, as well as doing a substantial amount of investment banking work for Enron.

Wall Street firms just care about pleasing their big corporate clients. They used to claim there were Chinese walls between the investment banking side of a firm, the research analysis division, and the brokerage division, so that analysts could recommend buying or selling independent of the firm's relationship with the company in question, and brokers could recommend stocks to clients based on the analysts' research. But as has been well documented since the dot.com crash, at many financial services firms, a number of different departments are often in cahoots to please the big corporate clients. Everyone else can go to hell, as far as they're concerned.

William Donaldson, the chairman of the SEC, has been working hard on eliminating these kinds of conflict. Following the Enron debacle, the New York state attorney general's office conducted an investigation of many of the most established and trusted securities firms, and turned up internal e-mails showing that analysts often recommended stocks that they privately thought were not attractive for purchase. Yet they issued research praising the company and recommending that investors "buy," or at least "hold" the stock, just to win or keep the company as an investment banking client. Don't let anyone try to tell you the equity and bond markets are level playing fields.

As a result, between the spring of 2000, when the dot.com crash sent us into the second-worst bear market since World War II, and early 2002, more than 100 million individual investors in the United States lost $7 trillion in stock value, or 30% of their total investment. Maybe you were one of those people, and maybe you were investing to send your kids to college, or to retire, or to realize a dream. In early 2001 a woman called our program to tell us that because she hadn't taken our advice in 1998 to put her 16-year-old daughter's stock gains into guaranteed investments, she had lost two years of college money. The bottom line of her call was to tell our listeners to follow the Dolans' advice! (See Chapter 7 for more on investment strategies for your children's education.)

According to surveys by the Pew Research Center for the People & the Press, most of those investors were middle-class people between the ages of 35 and 49. Most had college degrees, many had postgraduate degrees, and most earned more than $50,000 a year, although a majority of Americans in the $30,000-to-$50,000 income range were also investing.

In short, those who lost the most as a proportion of their assets weren't the people at the top end of the wealth spectrum, but those in the middle class. They were intelligent people, just as you are. They listened to the hundreds of investment "pros" who said buy stocks to keep your money earning above the inflation rate, then lost 50% or more in the market, which is far worse damage than an inflation rate of 2% or 3% or even 7% could ever have done. Some were day traders who threw all caution to the winds, but many thought it was a good idea to stick to what they knew how to do and let their brokers be the investment experts.

Daria Became an Expert. You Can, Too.

Does the thought of poring over a balance sheet fill you with terror? Daria used to feel the same way.

I never took a finance course. I never took an economics course. I was a theater arts major at Webster University. But then came the day when Ken made the decision to go into radio and take a huge pay cut.

What I didn't mention in Chapter 2 is that when I announced to Ken that I was going to take his place as the stockbroker in the family, he discouraged me by saying, "Don't do it! It's a rotten business."

I took his words as a challenge. Without any background in anything financial, I discovered that even a theater arts major can learn to make investment decisions. And so can you. But you need to learn the *underside,* because that's what's killing your portfolio.

The first place you start is by informing yourself. Then you have to do your own research. Once you understand just a little bit about how each of the investments works, you will find it less necessary to use financial pros and do it yourself. Remember that anytime you can cut the expenses out of acquiring and making investments—the commissions and fees you've been paying the broker or mutual fund manager—your investments will be working harder. And why should you pay someone to lose money for you, anyway?

Wrong!

Kiddo, when you're talking about investments, you're on your own. You can't even count on the government to protect your interests. Congress and the National Association of Securities Dealers (NASD) are looking at ways to address the broker/institution and the broker/client relationship, but we think any regulations that result will be incomplete or out-and-out dangerous. Our representatives in Congress don't understand the ins and outs of the business, and the NASD has a vested interest in pleasing its members—who are the securities companies throughout the country, large and small.

You must *empower yourself* by learning how to make your *own* investment decisions. True, learning about investing isn't the most exciting recreational activity one can think of, but it certainly is one of the most important ones. And it isn't nearly as complicated as some people—many of whom are the same people who take commissions for playing with your money—would like you to believe. Again, no one cares about your financial well-being the way you do.

At the end of this chapter we'll show you how to deal with brokers and their more amorphous counterparts, financial planners (see box). There are, after all, many competent and motivated financial advisers out there, and you may genuinely not have time to do all of your investing yourself. But the more you know, the more you will be able to determine who is trustworthy and who isn't. So we'll show you how to begin investing on your own. The choice is yours. We just want you to be able to take care of yourself in this insecure world.

> What is a financial planner? Sometimes he or she is an insurance sales rep or a CPA trying to drum up more business. Sometimes a financial planner is a person with bona fide useful knowledge that can help you invest, buy a home, save for college, retire, and plan your estate, but you have to be able to identify the good ones. Financial planning was invented by the insurance industry and thus relies all too often on insurance products as the answer to your investment questions. (See our chapter on insurance to see how we feel about that!)

The Investment Gospel According to the Dolans

In spite of the unpredictability of Wall Street and the markets, it's still important that you invest. Why? We can answer that in three little words: current interest rates.

Your money isn't going to be put to work for you if you park it in a savings account. When interest rates are running under 2%, even under 1%, you might as well put your money under the mattress. Yes, that sounds kind of tempting. But a diversified investment portfolio is the only way to earn enough money over time to beat inflation. You have financial objectives. These might include buying a first home, buying a second home, buying a car, college for your kids, a secure retirement—you fill in the blanks. To achieve these goals you have to put some of your money to work making more money.

Should You Invest in Individual Stocks or Mutual Funds?

There are many good reasons to pick your own stocks instead of putting money into an equity mutual fund. True, in a mutual fund you spread your risk somewhat, because the fund managers put your money into many different stocks. However, even in a no-load fund you pay fees that reduce your earning power, and what's more, you are, once again, trusting money professionals who have reasons to invest where they do that may have nothing to do with your best interests. (See our section on mutual funds on page 148 of this chapter.)

You can also trust a broker to help you pick your stocks, but if you suspect your broker isn't monitoring your portfolio with the diligence you'd like, you are probably 200% right. We believe that many individual investors, with some vigilance and homework, can become skilled at picking their own stocks. If you haven't tried this before and want to start, we have plenty of advice for you in this chapter. First rule of stock picking: Stick to stocks in industries you understand.

Generally, it's a good idea to keep a close watch on your own investments, and that means buying individual stocks that you've picked yourself, or at least bought after doing some of your own reading apart from your broker's recommendation. However, if you don't have time to research stocks yourself, a mutual fund with a good track record is the sounder alternative. You can also put your money into a combination of stocks and mutual funds. But read the mutual fund prospectus closely before you invest, and afterward read the quarterly statements, to make sure your money is well diversified and not going into stocks that you already own.

If You're Part of a Couple, Plan Your Investments Together.

We believe that married couples should hold joint accounts (see Chapter 2), and that applies to investment accounts as well. But there might be exceptional circumstances. A wife being supported by her husband should have some assets in her name as a cushion. If you're in a second marriage and have children from your first marriage, you'll need to keep their college savings and inheritances out of the common pile (see Chapter 7).

What about couples who are living together? Holding joint investments of any kind, whether it's real estate (as we discussed in Chapter 3) or an equity account, will be tricky. Worst-case scenario: You'd have little legal recourse if your partner cleans out the account and skips town. And if your partner should die without a will that specifies the money goes to you, a relative could claim it.

Nevertheless, if you're in a committed relationship, the way you invest is part of that commitment. Plan a strategy together. This doesn't mean that one of you takes all the risks while the other holds nothing but no-risk U.S. Treasuries; if you're investing separately, you should each have a diversified portfolio for your own safety. But don't make investments that would keep your partner awake at night worrying about the risk! Talk it over, and weigh your decisions together.

You may not always agree on where to put your money—if you disagree on vacation choices and what color to paint the den, there's no reason to believe you won't have some differences of opinion when it comes to selecting a stock. That might argue for each of you having a small portfolio to call your own. Of all the things a couple can fight about, one of the most easily avoidable subjects should be "Didn't I tell you we should have invested in XYZ when it was down at $7 a share!?" But listen to your partner's reasons for objecting. Talk before you rush into anything. And don't be reckless. We believe in a well-thought-out buy-and-hold investment style for *everyone*, and when you're a couple you owe that much responsibility to your spouse.

Be honest with each other about what you own and what you're thinking of buying. Whether your accounts are commingled or separate, you ought to be investing with the same goals in mind. If one of you is more risk averse than the other, let the conservative investor in your family keep a portfolio weighted more in that direction, with large-cap stocks, high-grade bonds, and Treasury securities, but review your collected investments frequently—once a week or so, to make sure you're not overly weighted in one direction.

Is There a Gender Gap When It Comes to Investing?

Some studies have shown that women are better investors than men. Usually the reasons cited have to do with women's innate focus on more than numbers. When questioned in surveys, women have indicated that they make their investment decisions based on such factors as the quality of the products and the company ethics. Women may be more cautious than men, particularly because women statistically live longer and spend fewer years in the workforce, so many do tend to feel that they can't afford to risk their retirement money. But if it's a female quality to look at what the company is actually doing before buying stock, and to research investment choices, then all investors should think like women!

Got a Goal and a Little Extra Money?

Follow our simple rules of investing and you'll come out ahead over the long term.

Rule 1. Know thy sleep quotient. There's an easy way to figure out how much risk you can tolerate. Just ask yourself: "Will I be able to sleep at night if I put my money into this investment?" Will your significant other be able to sleep? If there is any tossing and turning over an investment, get out of it immediately.

Rule 2. Join, or start, an investment club. We love the idea of plotting your investment strategies with like-minded friends or colleagues. You can bounce ideas off one another and divide the research duties, so that you won't be overwhelmed. It's also the best idea since Pop-Tarts for spouses or partners to join together, as ten heads are going to be better than two at hatching a portfolio plan, and probably more objective. See the section titled "Don't Go It Alone: Join an Investment Club."

Rule 3. Keep track of what you own, but take a long-term view. Forget trading day-to-day. Check your stocks on a regular basis, about once a week, but don't be one of those obsessive types who pull out a Blackberry to check stock quotes every half hour. The market moves, and you can't stop it. At the same time, "buy and hold" doesn't mean "walk away and forget it"! Holding for the long term is also a losing strategy if you bought a sow's ear. Time *will not* turn it into a silk purse.

Rule 4. Invest regularly. Set a plan to buy one or two stocks per month, if market conditions are right, and stick to it. Invest in small increments each month rather than lump sums. This way you'll achieve dollar-cost averaging in the prices you pay.

Rule 5. Rely on solid research—not "hot tips." We can't give you tips on hot stocks, because a book has a long shelf life, whereas a hot stock gets 15 minutes of fame. (Okay, sometimes 15 weeks, but not much longer!) Our rule of thumb is to avoid whatever stocks are the darlings of Wall Street. Yes, you might get in early enough to make a profit, but don't succumb to greed and assume it's going to keep going up.

Rule 6. Go with stocks that you *know*. How can you effectively evaluate a company involved in a business that you don't understand? Read and learn, yes, but if it's, say, a company that relies on the technology for the latest synthetic heart and it makes no sense to you because you're not a cardiac specialist, stay away. Be on the lookout for companies with new ideas that make sense to you, and new approaches to old ideas.

Rule 7. Balance risk in your portfolio. If you invest with lots of risk, you might suffer losses you can't afford. But if you invest with no risk, your investments won't grow to provide

Daria Says, Look at the P/E Ratio and Make Your Mantra "KISS"*

During the bull market of the late 1990s, Wall Street's best-loved stocks became much too expensive, with share prices their earnings couldn't support. Enron is the textbook example. About the time that everyone was saying buy it, I looked at Enron as a possible investment for our retirement plans. The price-to-earnings (P/E) ratio was at a lofty 70. That meant I would have to pay $70 to capture $1 of Enron earnings! Way too rich for my blood.

I didn't need to waste time doing any more research. That P/E ratio proved the stock was overhyped and doomed to fail. A healthy respect for P/E ratios can save you a lot of time and losses.

A high P/E ratio is supposed to mean high projected earnings in the future, which is why so many investors were gullible enough to stick with Enron. The average market P/E ratio is 15 to 25, but the average can be higher or lower depending on the industry. Large-cap stocks have lower P/Es; aggressive-growth small-caps have higher P/Es. Before you buy a stock, always check how the P/E ratio compares with others in the industry. If the P/E ratio is much higher than the market or industry average, then the company has to either grow like gangbusters over the next few months or years to live up to Wall Street's expectations . . . or somebody's been messing with the books again. Be suspicious. Be *very* suspicious!

When a stock suddenly gets "discovered" by Wall Street, the P/E will rise. Make that your cue to consider selling and locking in the profits.

Many Wall Street pros will cite you chapter and verse on why this theory is too simplistic. We say bravo for the old KISS theory:

*Keep It Simple, Stupid.

you with the *total return.* That's return on investment calculated as *both* the income from the investment and growth of the invested capital.

A successful portfolio is one that spreads the risk over a number of different kinds of investments: stocks for growth; bonds and CDs for income; municipal bonds and Treasuries for tax advantages and safety; money market mutual funds for liquidity.

Rule 8. Don't minimize the impact of compounding! A lot of people believe that it's impossible to achieve financial security without having a big pile of money to begin with. *Wrong!*

If you take just $1 per day and invest it at 8% compounded interest, on average, here's what you'd have:

After 5 years you'd have $2,245

After 10 years you'd have $5,595

After 20 years you'd have $18,045

After 30 years you'd have $45,751.

We know you're asking, "Where the heck can I get 8% interest at today's rates?" That's why we said *on average*. In a good year you should be able to get a 10% average annual return with stocks or a mutual fund. In bad years, you get less, and in an occasional whopper of a year you might get 15% to 20%, but that is *not* the norm. Averaged out, 8% is what you want to strive for over time. (See "Investing in Mutual Funds" to decide if mutual funds are right for you. We have mixed feelings about 'em.)

How to Avoid the Next Enron, Global Crossing, WorldCom, and _____ (fill in the blank)

It's impossible to foresee 100% of the time when a company is in trouble and its stock about to go down the tubes. But you *can* exercise due diligence to evaluate a stock before you buy it, and keep tabs on the stocks you own. That includes your stock in the company for which you work. We recommend keeping only a small portion of your company's stock in your investment portfolio, because you already have a huge stake just by working there, and we don't care how solid your company looks—if an ill wind blows, you could be wiped out. Just ask all those Enron employees who kept most of their 401(k)s invested in company stock!

In Debt, out of Work, or Generally Feeling Squeamish? If You REALLY Can't Afford to Lose Money Right Now, Don't Take Chances!

If you open a brokerage account, you'll be asked to review a form that has a little section on assessing your risk. It's a bunch of bull.

Absolutely *every* investment carries an element of risk, unless it's a government-guaranteed instrument, such as U.S. Treasuries or certificates of deposit (CDs). If you tell a broker, "I don't want to lose money," the meeting is over on the spot.

Wall Street insiders and the financial media have made it seem as if anyone who doesn't buy stocks or mutual funds is a fool. This kind of "advice" is the worst disservice that's been done to the average American.

IF YOU CAN'T AFFORD TO LOSE MONEY, DON'T INVEST. Investing 1.5% in a guaranteed investment is always better than a 1.5% loss in stocks or a mutual fund. If you're in debt, you are losing more money in interest than you could gain from almost any investment. (See Chapter 4.) If your marriage would suffer because your spouse is

Dolan Ah-Ha!

If you are a shareholder of a publicly listed company, you may exercise your "inspection" rights to review corporate books, expense reports, internal e-mail, minutes of board meetings, and other corporate documents. Not too exciting on the surface, but you never know what you'll find! Use these rights to conduct due diligence once you own the stock. This will help you spot warning signals such as these:

- There's a lot of public relations "sizzle" around the company and/or the CEO, but you can't find evidence of a strong business plan.
- Every Wall Street analyst loves the stock and is talking it up. As we've said many times, experience has made us suspicious of any Wall Street darling.
- Senior company executives are selling a lot of their stock in the company. Do they know something you don't know?
- The revenue growth from one quarter or one year to another is very strong, but there's no specific new product to explain the rapid growth. Growth figures can be nothing but an accounting sleight of hand.
- The company is buying up other companies left and right that aren't even related to its core business. Whatever happened to sticking to the businesses you know best? Duh!
- The company's cash flow (defined as cash on hand to pay bills, salaries, expenses, and general overhead) is anemic. Cash flow is cash that is already sitting there. It is *not* "accounts receivable." Nor is it "net income." An unscrupulous or overly aggressive accounting firm can use all kinds of tricks to make net income look large. Look for a company with a strong CASH FLOW.
- The company is carrying an excessive amount of debt or is significantly increasing its debt. Guess which investors are going to suffer the most if the company can't meet its obligations: the small ones who don't have the scoop on when to pull out.
- The company has a history of suspending or reducing its dividends, or has recently stopped paying dividends. *Something* is amiss!

worried about paying off debts while you're hot to invest, or vice versa, the cautious party wins this round. If putting money into the stock market would keep either of you from having the good night's sleep you need to get back on your feet, *don't do it!*

But if you can afford to invest just a little bit—say $50 to $100 each month—you can gradually build up an asset base. See our section titled "Investing on the Cheap."

Dolan Ah-Ha!

Here are three flawed assumptions about investing. Even many seasoned investors get it wrong. Don't you believe for a minute that:

1. "If you diversify your portfolio, you can't lose money." Yes, *you can*.
2. "The people who buy stocks based on what the market is doing at the moment are investors." Newspaper stories often get the term wrong, as when they say, "Investors scrambled to unload Cisco shares." These are not investors; they're traders. Investing means you put the money in, and let the share price rise over time. Investors don't buy today on good news and dump tomorrow on bad news; that's a trader's job.
3. "A wise investor buys and holds forever." Just as foolhardy as trading at every downturn is holding on to a stock that has lost its way. Your grandfather's belief in loyalty to a solid stock, such as AT&T, was considered sound back in the days when people called it Ma Bell. But in today's economy, new technologies can spring up overnight and make a company that is #1 in its field today obsolete tomorrow. Think of the old-fashioned wired-down telephone. If you were holding on to AT&T today, you'd be as shortsighted as the guy who, back in 1900, bought stock in the most successful buggy-whip-manufacturing company—and held it even after Henry Ford came along with the horseless carriage. "Buy and hold" *is a joke* unless you have the highest-quality stocks.

A Piece of a Little Emu Ranch? Maybe Invest in Alpacas? (An Actual TV Commercial Offer) . . . No Way!!

There are investors and then there are speculators. If your dad gave you several million bucks to keep you off the streets, and has promised several million more if you blow this stash, you are welcome to try speculating in any of the ventures listed here. Otherwise, steer clear of them; it's just too easy to lose your shirt. So don't invest in:

- Anything that you have to feed! If you love racehorses, go to the track, but don't buy a horse of your own unless you can afford to lose every dime. A Triple Crown comes along only once in a while—but vet bills and oats are a guaranteed expense.

We had a caller who wanted to know our opinion of putting some money into an emu ranch. Emu steaks are said to be nutritious and emu oil to make your skin youthfully soft, but too much can go wrong.

- Heating oil futures (see our definition of futures).
- Commodity funds/futures. Ninety-five percent of "investors" lose money in futures.
- Initial public offering (IPO) of stock from a "cold caller." Remember dot.com stars? Enough said.
- Rare coins. Good luck finding an "expert" to trust.
- CMOs—collateralized mortgage obligations. Collateralized "moron" obligations would be more apt. These are a complex form of mortgage-backed bonds, or bonds backed by a pool of mortgage loans. Evaluating the risk of CMOs requires very specialized skills.
- "900"-number offers. You want to pay for a call to a con artist?
- Vending machines. You'll end up with a garage full of worthless machines.
- Wireless cable/paging company investments. Are you expert enough to evaluate the technology that makes this company's technology "superior"?
- Most time shares. Before you consider buying one, think of the 600,000 people desperate to sell theirs.
- Any kind of limited partnership. Remember the late 1980s?

"HELP—A Loved One Has Died and Left Me a Lump Sum"

Over the years we've heard from countless widows whose spouses died in an untimely fashion, and the widowed spouse never had a chance to think about what she'd do with the life insurance payout as well as other financial decisions that must be made.

Never make an investment decision at an emotional time.

We are still hearing horror stories from the spouses of people who died in the September 11 attacks. One woman made the mistake of listening to a broker with a big scheme for the $100,000 life insurance payout she received after her husband died. The broker talked her into buying four $25,000 real estate limited partnerships. Each is now worth approximately . . . nothing.

What do you do with an insurance payout? Put it into a three- or six-month Treasury bill. It will earn a little bit in a 100% guaranteed instrument while you get your life back in order and look for investment alternatives.

On This Page: No Model Portfolios

You've heard the expression "never put all of your eggs in one casket"? (It will be a *casket* instead of a basket if you invest this way.) You balance risk by spreading your assets across a spectrum of high-risk (or at least moderately high, depending on your tolerance) to low-risk investments.

You've seen model portfolios for each stage of your life?

You're not going to see them here!

We HATE model-portfolio percentages. We believe they are what gets too many people in trouble in the first place. The standard model portfolio, devised by a broker or financial planner, will tell you that when you're young you can take plenty of risk and when you're close to retirement you can't.

Not so. Many young couples have mortgages, and children who will need secure funds for their education. Many young—and middle-aged—professionals have no job security. Many senior citizens have tons of disposable assets, the leisure time to pick stocks, and absolutely no worry about being downsized onto an unemployment line.

So how do you allocate your portfolio? By your specific goals as an individual or as a couple. If you're young, single, and just building a nest egg, put some money into growth stocks, but no more than half, and put the rest into something that will assure you of some savings for when you want to buy a house or have children, such as tax-free bonds, and some in a highly liquid money market account. (Actually, most people under the age of 25 don't invest, but if you can you should.)

What if you're a single parent? You can't afford to lose money, so put most of your money into Treasury securities, high-yield bonds, and money market funds, with a smaller portion in growth and income mutual funds or dividend-oriented stocks.

When your children are growing up, and even after they've left you with an empty nest, you should aim to preserve your wealth with conservative investments, but walk on the wild side with 5% to 20% in growth stocks or mutual funds.

But any strategy depends so much on your income, your dependents, and your commitments. The less you have, the less you can afford to lose.

One investment every individual and couple should have is a retirement account. If you have an employer who provides matching contributions to a 401(k), take advantage of this potentially profitable (remember Enron?) state of affairs and contribute—the maximum if you can. Matching contributions are like free money for your retirement if the stock goes up! If your income is below $110,000 for individuals or $160,000 for couples, you should be contributing as much as you possibly can to a Roth IRA, which shelters your investment earnings from taxes, although not your contributions. See Chapter 11 for the Dolan lowdown on retirement accounts, the investment for the Everyman and Everywoman.

Don't Go It Alone: Join an Investment Club

It's stressful and time-consuming to start investing your money on your own. But you don't have to do it all on your own. You may have more fun, and a chance to weigh your decisions, if you join or start an investment club. If you join with your significant other, it's like having a support group to keep the two of you from guessing in the dark and then blaming each other when a stock heads south.

If the idea makes you think of blue-haired ladies in Beardstown who can't get their return rate right, you should know that today's investment clubs are hipper, younger, more diverse, and more aggressive. And they've been more successful than many mutual funds. The National Association of Investors Corp. (NAIC), an investment-education group that has been a sort of clearinghouse for investment clubs since 1951, calculates an index for its members with the top 100 returns.

There are more than 32,000 investment clubs in the United States, and among them they invest some $190 million each month. The median age of members is 53. The average investment per member is $84 per month. The typical investment club has members whose main investment goals are retirement, financial security, and financing their children's education. By the way, far more women than men are joining clubs—NAIC membership is 69% female and 31% male, with 54% of the clubs for women only, 38% mixed, and only 8% exclusively male. But if you're a man, don't let the statistics stop you. To our minds, this is more proof that men aren't as brave as women when it comes to admitting they need support in making their big decisions, such as where to invest. In a rocky market, it's a smart man who forms a team to take on the market.

The NAIC says that clubs should seek stocks that will double in five years, shooting for returns of approximately 15% per year.

Your club should be composed of people who think like you, with similar investment goals. Don't join a club with financial planners or brokers in its ranks, because they might not stay objective. Don't fall in with people who are interested only in buying the latest hot pick on Wall Street.

We recommend starting a club from scratch with friends and friends of friends, rather than joining one that is already well established. Half of the reason for joining investment

Online Investing Is Here to Stay

In spite of all the people who got creamed trading stocks minute-by-minute online, we are moving slowly toward the day when most investing is done via the Internet.

But you have to be sober about the way you place your bets. The Internet is still the equivalent of the Wild West. There is no sheriff. Anyone can set up a Web site and make phenomenal claims, then disappear with a big pile of other people's money before any regulatory agencies catch up with what's going on.

We've had callers tell us they are really really tempted to put money into a CD or money market fund they've dug up by searching online. Some of these online banks are offering accounts that promise interest rates of as much as 3%, while the corner bank will give them no more than 1.3%. Who wouldn't be tempted? And it's a dandy way to get your money's worth from your savings, as long as you can be sure you're packing your money off and sending it to a bank that is federally insured. If you see a site for a bank you've never heard of, and it claims to be insured by the Federal Deposit Insurance Corporation (FDIC), don't take the bank's word for it. There are a number of online banks that claim to be FDIC-insured and are not. To find out if a bank is insured, contact the FDIC Central Call Center in Washington, D.C., at 877-ASKFDIC (877-275-4432) or search for the institution on the FDIC Web site, www.FDIC.gov.

When in doubt, or if it's a matter of just a fraction of a percentage point, we prefer that you go to the bricks-and-mortar bank in your neighborhood. At least you know where your money is.

But if it's an online investment account you're after, there is a well-respected independent consulting firm that can give you reliable ratings on Internet brokers, both full-service and discount. It's called Gomez Advisors, at www.gomez.com. Go to the "Scorecards" section of their site, and click on Brokers. They rate brokers every quarter, using as their main criteria ease of use, customer confidence, on-site resources, relationship services, and, for discount brokers, overall cost. Charles Schwab, Fidelity Investments, and E*Trade show up pretty consistently at the top of the list of discount brokers.

Do not choose an online broker based on commission costs alone. Some of the low-commission brokers aren't able to get you the best execution. If you haven't already learned this from a sad experience, being online is no reason to succumb to irrational exuberance. Do your own research before you buy, or work with an investment club. Do NOT rely on information posted on message boards. People can say anything on a message board, and they do!

clubs is the education you all get together. A club that has been up and running will have gone beyond the basics and may leave you lost in the dust.

Usually a club meets once a month. Members have assignments to research stocks, and present their research at the meetings. Then the club votes on where to put their money.

If you are interested in starting a club, the NAIC is a worthwhile source of advice. Here is how to contact the organization:

NAIC
P.O. Box 220
Royal Oak, MI 48068
Tel: 248-583-6242, or toll-free, 877-275-6242
www.new.better-investing.org

Your club can join the NAIC for $40 a year plus $14 for each member. Everyone receives a subscription to *Better Investing*, an NAIC magazine that provides stock research reports, and lists of regional conferences and seminars. The club also receives NAIC's guide, *Starting and Running a Profitable Investment Club*. Individuals can join for $39 a year. The NAIC also has approximately 50 regional councils that hold periodic investing seminars for beginners.

This is a club with a mission. Here are some of its guiding principles:

✓ Invest regularly, even when the stock market is weak. Don't try to time the market.
✓ Reinvest all earnings.
✓ Invest in growth companies. Look for companies with good prospects for sales and earnings.
✓ Reduce risk by diversifying your portfolio.

Sounds pretty sensible to us.
Also check out these two books for advice:

The Investment Club Book, by John Wasik; Warner Books, 1995, $13.95.
Starting and Running a Profitable Investment Club, by Thomas O'Hara and Kenneth Janke, Sr.; Times Business Books, 1998. $15.00.

How to Read the Stock Tables 101

Do you really really know what the numbers mean when you look through the stock market tables? Here's another basic tutorial, just to be sure you have it right. We won't tell *anyone* you're reading it!

Here are tables for three different types of stocks from hypothetical companies, and what the headings mean:

52-Week							Sales (daily)			
High	Low	Stock	Div	Yld	PE	Vol	High	Low	Last	Chg.
46.59	29.50	ABC	1.32	4.4	12	43364	30.90	29.01	30.25	−0.35
25.92	11.95	HITEC	—	—	72	1006	22.30	21.50	22.19	+0.77
35.70	25.80	SLPR	1.08	3.3	19	36	32.85	32.35	32.50	−0.50

52-Week High, Low: Highest and lowest price during preceding 52-week period.

Div: Annual dividend per share. HITEC is a small-cap stock that pays no dividends.

Yld: The dividend as a percentage of the stock price, computed daily.

PE: Price-to-earning ratio, derived from dividing the company's stock price per share by earnings per share. HITEC, with its stratospheric PE ratio, is going to have to show quick growth to meet analysts' expectations. Or it could be another Enron in the making. The other two are companies that are expected to grow at a snail's pace.

Vol: Number of shares sold during the day, in thousands. For example, 43364 in the table above stands for 43,364,000 shares traded. SLPR is a sleepy stock, with only 36,000 shares sold during the day.

Weekly High, Low, Last: Stock's highest, lowest, and final price per share for the trading day, shown in dollars and cents.

Change (Chg): The difference between the closing price at the end of the trading day and the closing price the day before.

Investing in Stocks

How do you get started finding companies that seem like worthy prospects?

Well, let's start with some advice from the pros. Here's some encouragement from none other than Ken's old classmate at Boston College, Peter Lynch, the legendary Fidelity Magellan mutual fund manager. One of Peter's rules in his book *One Up on Wall*

Street: How to Use What You Already Know to Make Money in the Market (Simon & Schuster, 2000) is "Stop listening to professionals!"

"Twenty years in this business," Peter writes, "convinces me that any normal person using the customary three percent of the brain can pick stocks just as well as, if not better than, the average Wall Street expert."

When it comes to picking stocks, Peter has found many "ten baggers" (stocks that appreciate tenfold or more) just by keeping his eyes, ears, and mouth open. For example:

- During a business trip to California, he got a great burrito at Taco Bell. Someone at the Holiday Inn told him about the L.A. burrito chain.
- His kids at home had an Apple Computer, and the systems manager at Fidelity had just purchased a number of Apple computers.
- Peter loves the coffee at Dunkin' Donuts.
- Peter's simple philosophy of looking for investment opportunities right under one's nose helped make Fidelity Magellan one of the most successful mutual funds in history.

We believe in looking for companies with unique new products or superior services. Go for the player that has more market share than any others in the field, or with little true competition. When stiff competition begins to emerge, it might be time for you to pull out of that stock while it's still ahead. But beware when some new company starts touting "revolutionary" technology. An investor who plays it safe seeks proof first. Look for quarterly earnings per share up at least 25% over the previous year. Look for six to 12 consecutive quarters of earnings increases.

It *might* be a good sign if the top mutual fund managers are buying the stock. You can find out what stocks a mutual fund is holding easily by calling the toll-free number and asking the rep on the other end to mail you a prospectus. But don't get too excited. We're nonplussed by what mutual fund managers are buying; most of these "experts" invest like lemmings, following the flock right over the cliff with the Amazons and Enrons of the world. We'll tell you what we really think of mutual funds managers a little later in this chapter.

Fortunately, these days you can find plenty of research data on your own. It's easily accessible online. Your aim is to track a stock's performance over the past year so that you can buy it low. At the same time, you need to set a realistic sell price when you make your purchase. So how do you find a realistic goal when it's so hard to trust what Wall Street analysts say until they prove themselves trustworthy? There is no formula. However, we have found over many years that the Value Line Investment Survey, which comes out once a week, with a survey of around 135 stocks in each issue, is an objective and reliable source for evaluations of companies and what to expect from the share price. You can get the Value Line Investment Survey free at most major libraries, or invest in a subscription, which costs $598 a year for either the print version or the electronic version online, but it's money well spent. We're subscribers. Information about Value Line and subscriptions can be found on the Web site, at www.valueline.com. You can start with a 13-week trial subscription for $65.

Once you hit your goal, *sell!* Remember, few companies stay on top forever.

Also check the news each day to keep abreast of comings and goings at a company. If you bought the stock because the company had a strong management team, but then the

Answer These Questions Before You Buy

If you make your own investment decisions, these are the questions you should ask yourself—and answer thoroughly—so that instead of gambling with your money, you'll be plotting an investment strategy. If you invest through a broker, you should ask your broker these questions before every stock purchase. This is one way to show a broker that you are a client who isn't going to let anyone pull the wool over your eyes!

1. Why does this stock qualify as an appropriate idea for me in light of the investment objectives that I listed on my new account form?
2. Is the company a leader in its field or does it have the potential to be one? (Why?)
3. How strong is this company's management team and how much stock do they own? (Why don't they own any/or much stock? Where's their commitment?)
4. Does the company have a *unique* product or service?
5. Is the company's debt low—or at least stable?
6. What's the "downside" to this company's supposedly bright future?
7. What will changes in the economy and consumer buying habits, and on the political scene, do to the price of the stock and the company's products?
8. How does this company's performance compare with that of its competitors?
9. On what assumptions are the projections you have presented based?
10. How did the company fare during the last recession?
11. When (and under what circumstances) do we sell? At what price?

Ask a broker this last question and you'll nail him to the wall! Too many brokers think only about buying, without a goal or a contingency plan in case the investment doesn't pan out.

board ousts the CEO, it *may be* time for you to consider selling. If the company was known for its successful research-and-development division, but it spins off that division to focus on a completely different line of business, you should sell. In short, if the reasons you bought the stock don't exist anymore, *sell!*

The other change to watch out for is downside. You should have a *stop* point if the share price begins a downward spiral. We think a 10% to 15% price decline is plenty. If your share price drops this much, don't wait for it to come back up. It might never happen. Cut your losses and move on.

Sites That Will Help You

There are Web sites galore that can help you find performance data, research, and advice to help you select stocks as potential investment candidates. Here we grade them, from the most elementary to the most advanced. If you haven't designed your own investment strategy before, start with the elementary-level sites, and work your way through to our "College Level" sites. If you're an old hand at this, go right to "College Level."

Investment Kindergarten

http://university.smartmoney.com. Don't let the name fool you. This site, run by *Smart Money* magazine, is great for Investing 101. It even has a link by that name. The site will tell you all of the basics about terms and strategies. Free.

Middle School Level

www.better-investing.org. The NAIC site, in addition to serving up information on investment clubs, offers educational programs, services, and tools for individual investors, as well as stock and mutual fund investing tools. Most of the information is free.

www.moneycentral.msn.com. Click on "Investing," then go to the Research Wizard. This section of the site gives you performance charts, news, earnings information, even access to the Securities and Exchange Commission (SEC) filings that are required of all companies listed in the United States. If you don't have specific companies in mind, browse through the site's industry lists. The site has similar information on mutual funds. Free.

Morningstar—www.morningstar.com. The Chicago-based investment information firm is traditionally associated with mutual fund rankings, but in 2001 the firm introduced a rating system for stocks. For a reasonable fee—$12.95/month, $115/yr., $199/two years—you can get a "premium membership," which will give you access to a rating designed to steer investors away from overvalued securities and toward undervalued ones.

The rating is based on the ratio between a stock's current price and its estimated "fair value." The fair value is determined by a discounted cash-flow analysis involving estimates of growth rate, profitability, and asset efficiency. The Morningstar Rating for stocks assigns one to five stars using the following scale:

5 stars = Fair value is 30% or more above the current market price
4 stars = Fair value is 10% to 30% above the current market price
3 stars = Fair value is 10% above or below the current market price
2 stars = Fair value is 10% to 30% below the current market price
1 star = Fair value is 30% or more below the current market price

Thus, five stars indicate a highly undervalued stock, while one star indicates a highly overvalued one.

College Level

Sites for sophisticated investors ready to pick stocks.

www.Dailygraphs.com This is the Investors Business Daily site, and it will give you access to information that investment professionals use. The service comes at a high price, but it's worthwhile if you are going to invest seriously. The complete equity research package costs $1,000 a year, or you can receive the stock research tool with access to stock charts, data, and proprietary ratings for $720 a year.

www.multexinvestor.com. This site has free daily briefings and analyst reports on most listed companies, including some foreign ones. Some of the reports are free, whereas others will run from $10 to $50 apiece.

www.money.net has real-time quotes from the New York Stock Exchange, the American Stock Exchange, and NASDAQ for $12.99 a month.

How to Get an Annual Report, Read It, and Understand It!

During these days of "creative" accounting, it's never been more important that you understand the "numbers" . . . hoping that they are accurate. Don't ever put your money into a stock without seeing the company's annual report.

Most listed companies now put their annual reports up on their Web sites. Go to the site and click on "Investor Relations." Then follow the instructions to download the annual report. Usually you will need to install Adobe Acrobat, which is free. You can also get free annual reports by calling the Public Register's Annual Report Service, a Connecticut firm that offers more than 3,600 annual reports, at 800-426-6825.

True, an annual report is not exactly a Grisham novel, but it's a clue to what goes on behind the scenes. *Be sure and read the CEO's message.* The tone of his or her comments are often enlightening. You *can* skip the pages with pretty pictures accompanying text that tells how dynamic and socially responsible the company is. They all pay public relations people handsomely to come up with that kind of spin.

What should concern you most is the financial pages. You'd be amazed at what can be found in the microscopic print. Look for the Management Discussion and Analysis, also known as MD&A, which should give you a description of the business, financial information about revenues and profits from different lines of business or geographic areas, as well as a rundown of sales and expenses. This is the part you want to examine with a microscope—almost literally. Below the balance sheet is often a gray mass of tiny but all-important footnotes. Read these even if you have to invest in magnifying glasses. This is the information the company is required by law to reveal, but some companies hope that if they make it small enough, investors—and the press—won't bother to read it.

A balance sheet is often overly complicated, and the footnotes even more so. Enron's was so complex, even accountants couldn't figure it out—and the obfuscation was deliberate, because the company was trying to hide its lack of income. Be wary of any company that makes its financial pages hard to comprehend.

There ought to be more adult-education classes on reading a balance sheet. If you can find one where you live, by all means enroll.

The footnotes have to mention such expenses as acquisitions and one-time charges that can bring profits down. They are supposed to mention accounts-receivable money that the company has given up on collecting, and money paid out in taxes and stock-option grants.

This is not to say that important dealings can't be hidden in the balance sheets that you find in annual reports. You might find even more disguised activities in quarterly earnings releases that are reported in the news before the company files the numbers with the SEC. You may remember that venerable IBM was found to have used $300 million from the sales of a business division to lower its operating costs and raise its profits for the fourth-quarter 2001 earnings figures the company gave analysts and investors in an initial conference call (the figures were later revised on the quarterly report), instead of accounting for the transaction as a one-time gain.* Although this practice is deceptive, it is not

* "As It Beat Profit Forecast, IBM Said Little About Sale of a Unit," by Gretchen Morgenson, *New York Times*, Friday, Feb. 15, 2002; p. A-1.

illegal, and companies will argue that they're partly in the business of buying and selling assets. Sure, and making computers on the side.

Moral: Be sure to scrutinize the footnotes when you see a remarkable leap in revenues or profits from one quarter to the next or even one year to the next.

Go for the Dividend

Dividends are a somewhat old-fashioned concept that is back in style. The aggressive-growth companies, dot.coms, and high-flying IPOs of the late 1990s didn't pay dividends. In the old days investors went into the market expecting a little extra income each quarter through dividends. In the so-called "new" economy, we were all supposed to invest a little today and quadruple our money tomorrow; investors didn't expect to stick around to see a full quarter. Considering what happened, doesn't a fairly reliable sum of money coming in every three months sound like the monetary equivalent of comfort food?

We believe in a steady diet of dividends. A company can lie like crazy on the balance sheet if it doesn't have to pony up a payout to investors every quarter, but when the company has a track record for paying dividends, the size and reliability are an indication of whether its finances are stable. You can't pay a dividend when the company is broke!

Here's what you should know about dividends:

- You won't get them from hot, young, untested companies. The companies that pay dividends tend to be Fortune 500 companies that are considered growth-and-income investments—that is, investors expect them to produce slow, steady growth rather than a quick return.
- The fact that a company has a history of paying dividends is not a foolproof guarantee that the stock will make money, or even that you'll keep getting dividends forever. The board of directors of a company decides if it will declare a dividend. It is usually paid out on a quarterly basis, but the board can elect to withhold or reduce the dividends if the company is facing a cash squeeze.
- Dividend-paying stocks are a defensive strategy for tough times. They're the same stocks that will look unappealing when the market is booming because they are mature companies that aren't growing rapidly when the upstarts are bragging about revenue growth of more than 100% a year. If you find yourself wanting to believe such claims the next time around, take a deep breath and remember the technology bubble of the nineties. Always keep some of your portfolio in dividend-paying stocks as a cushion against the risks you take with the portion that's in aggressive stocks.

A Hot Tip—Go for a DRIP

We suggest that instead of spending your dividend, you reinvest it through a dividend reinvestment plan (DRIP). That way you keep increasing your investment without paying commissions. More information on DRIPs can be found on an educational Web site called www.dripadvisor.com.

Investing on the Cheap

DRIPs

www.firstshare.com. For a $30 annual membership fee, plus a few extra dollars for referrals and handling fees, First Share allows you to buy stocks that offer DRIPs in small quantities—small meaning as little as one share at a time. The idea is that you build your portfolio through dividend reinvestments, which give you a built-in dollar-cost averaging.

www.sharebuilder.com. Sharebuilder will carry out investment transactions for a small fee, with three different plans available and no minimum investment required, so that you can buy just one or two shares at a time.

www.netstockdirect.com allows you to purchase shares directly in small increments so that you can dollar-cost average. You can even have a set amount of money automatically deducted from your bank account each month. There is no charge to join.

www.mfea.com. You can use dollar-cost averaging to invest in mutual funds, too. The Mutual Fund Investor's Center is an information site that will give you a list of mutual funds that waive the initial investment requirement if you commit to investing $50 a month.

Dollar-Cost Averaging

One of our favorite techniques for lowering your investment costs. You invest a set amount of money at regular intervals—most commonly, every month, or every quarter. The amount is the same, but the number of shares you buy varies based on the price. Your money gets you more shares when the market price is down and fewer when the price is up, but over time the average price per share will be less than the price you would have paid if you had purchased all of the shares at once.

The key to this simple strategy . . . picking good stocks!

Unfortunately, in bear markets, when this strategy really works (with good stocks), most people don't continue. So instead of getting many more shares at bargain-basement prices, they end up with fewer shares at higher prices.

If you are just starting out as an investor and don't have a lot of cash to play with, you can get into a DRIP plan very affordably. This is also a smart way to give a gift of stock to a child. (See more in Chapter 7.)

Investing in Fixed-Income Securities

We are firm believers that every investor's portfolio should contain a fixed-income component that pays a constant, fixed rate of return. That means fixed-income securities.

"Which ones?" you ask. Should you buy certificates of deposit, Treasury securities (investing with Uncle Sam), corporate (taxable) bonds, or municipal (tax-free) bonds? There is a lot to sort out here.

First a "Bonds 101" lesson.

Bonds 101

When you buy a bond, you are in essence lending money to an entity. It's the entity's debt. That entity promises to pay principal *and* interest back to you on a timely basis.

In our opinion, the point of bonds is to generate predictable income. So we believe in buying only the high-grades.

Here is how the bond-rating company Standard & Poor's (S&P) grades bonds:

AAA is the top grade, applied to the bonds pretty much certain to maintain their principal value.

AA is the next-highest rating. Next in order are:

A

BBB

BB At this point, the bond has a higher-than-average chance of defaulting. Bonds of this grade and below are known as "junk bonds."

B

CCC These bonds are extremely vulnerable to loss of principal value.

D Applied to a bond that has failed to maintain its principal value. The lowest grade.

G refers to U.S. government securities, the safest bonds of all.

We believe that most investors should not buy any bonds with less than a AA rating from S&P or Moody's. Don't chase yields, which means buying the bonds with the highest interest rate. Don't forget, the higher the interest rate, the higher the risk. "Total return" is the key.

Types of Bonds

Corporates

Corporate bonds are taxable and are traded on most major exchanges. They are not risk-free, but a high-grade corporate bond is safer than most stocks, though generally with less upside potential.

U.S. Treasuries

There's no such thing as a "zero-risk" investment, but U.S. Treasury securities have to be the closest thing to it! These bonds are backed by the "full faith and credit" of the United States government. This means that the government will always pay you—*no matter what*. They promise not to default on your investment. The income from U.S. Treasury securities is, generally, exempt from state and local taxes, but you'll still have to pay federal taxes on your income.

You can buy Treasury securities from a broker, through your bank, or directly from the Federal Reserve, at no commission, which is what we recommend. The maturities on Treasuries range from three months to 30 years. The longer the maturity, the higher the risk you take that inflation or changing interest rates will reduce the value of your investment. Long-term Treasuries usually offer higher interest rates, to reward you for taking more risk. Basically there are three types of Treasuries:

Treasury Bonds: You can buy U.S. Treasury bonds for as little as $1,000. Treasury bonds have maturity dates—meaning the date on which the principal amount becomes payable—of 10 to 30 years from the date of purchase. The interest you earn is paid semiannually.

Treasury Notes: Treasury notes have maturities of 2 to 10 years and are issued in $1,000 denominations. Like T-bonds, T-notes pay interest semiannually until maturity, when you receive your principal back. The newest twist to T-notes are *Treasury Inflation Protected Securities (TIPS)*, which are designed to keep pace with inflation. We're fans of TIPS. You get a government guarantee that the real purchasing power of the principal will keep pace with the rate of inflation. TIPS also pay interest semiannually until maturity. They are available in a variety of maturities, with a minimum denomination of $1,000.

Treasury Bills: T-bills have maturities of three months and six months. You'll need a minimum of $1,000 to invest in a T-bill. Unlike other Treasuries, T-bills don't pay you any current income. You buy T-bills at a discount to their face value and then you receive the full $1,000 when the bill matures. T-bills are like short-term CDs, guaranteed by the U.S. Treasury instead of the FDIC.

You can invest in T-bills and notes *online* through the Treasury Direct service. You can order the forms online at www.publicdebt.treas.gov or call 800-722-2678 for information on opening an account. For the address and phone number of the nearest local branch of the Federal Reserve Bank, go to www.bog.frb.fed.us/otherfrb.htm.

If the Treasury securities you want aren't coming up for auction when you want, buy through a major stockbroker instead. You'll pay a commission, but the government bond desk at most brokerage firms is friendly and consumer-oriented. They'll often bend over backward to help you get the best rate and maturity.

Treasury Zero Coupon Bonds: A Good Bet for College and Retirement Savings

Wouldn't it be wonderful if there were an investment that would let you plan ahead for fixed amounts of money that you'll need later—to pay college expenses, or fund your retirement, for instance? Say hello to zero coupon bonds!

With zero coupon bonds, you decide when you want them to mature by purchasing specific maturity dates. The price of zeros is extremely sensitive to changing interest rates. As a result, zeros are among the most volatile fixed income investments around. That's why we recommend buying zeros *only* as investments you will hold until maturity, when your return is guaranteed. If you buy zeros that mature in five years and you need to tap your money in three years, you could lose some of your investment.

Zero coupon bonds don't pay you any *current* income. You make money on zero coupon bonds by buying them from a broker at a deep discount (paying a *whole lot less* than the bond's $1,000 face value). You then get $1,000 when the bond matures. The difference between what you paid for the bond and its $1,000 face value is the amount of "interest" you earn. What's the catch?

Well, even though you don't get handed the interest each month—as you do at your bank—the interest is still taxable to you in the year it's earned. That's one reason we like zero coupon bonds as an investment for tax-deferred retirement accounts. In an IRA or Keogh, you don't have to pay yearly taxes and you get the full benefit of the long-term compounding of your zeros.

With zero coupon bonds, you don't receive any current interest, but the IRS taxes you as if you'd received it anyway.

The Costs of a $1,000 Zero Coupon Bond*

If you purchase a zero coupon bond with a $1,000 face value and the following years to maturity:	At these yields, your purchase price would be:			
	3% Yield	4% Yield	5% Yield	6% Yield
30 years	409	304	227	170
29 years	421	317	239	180
28 years	434	329	251	191
27 years	447	343	264	203
26 years	461	357	277	215
25 years	475	371	291	228
24 years	489	386	306	242
23 years	504	402	321	257
22 years	519	418	303	272
21 years	535	435	354	289
20 years	551	452	372	307
19 years	567	471	391	325
18 years	585	490	411	345
17 years	602	510	432	366
16 years	620	530	454	388
15 years	639	552	477	412
14 years	659	574	501	437
13 years	679	597	526	464
12 years	699	621	553	492
11 years	720	646	581	522
10 years	742	673	610	554

*Your cost for zeros based on years to maturity and interest rate paid

We also like using Treasury zeros to fund your child's college education, because you know exactly how much you will have and when. But don't forget the taxes that will come due each year. If taxes will be a big problem, buy highly rated municipal zeros. The best strategy for buying zeros for college? Buy zeros that will mature each year, just before your child's college tuition bill comes in!

Should You *Be Buying Municipal Bonds?*

"Munis" are debt obligations issued by a state or local municipal government or agency, often to support a specific public works project. You pay no federal taxes on the interest, and no state or local taxes if the bond was issued in the state where you reside.

It doesn't make sense to invest in munis if you're in the 15% tax bracket. Single or joint filers in a higher tax bracket, however, should seriously consider buying them.

Should you buy munis instead of taxable bonds? Your decision should be determined by the effective yield of the tax-free bond you're considering.

The yield on municipal bonds is usually less than the yield you would get from taxable bonds of the same maturities. However, because you don't pay tax on municipal bond income, your actual "net" yield would be higher than the taxable yield you receive from corresponding corporate bonds, depending on your tax bracket.

To calculate your taxable equivalent yield, divide the tax-exempt yield by 1, MINUS your tax bracket. For instance, if you want to buy a municipal bond yielding 4.5%, and you're in the 36% tax bracket, your effective yield would be 5.47%. Here's the math: 4.5 / (1 − 0.36), or 4.5 / 0.64 = 5.47%. So you would get the same amount of money in your pocket from both a high-quality municipal bond that is yielding 4.5% and a corporate bond that is yielding 5.47%.

As with all taxable versus tax-free decisions, we recommend that you check the taxable equivalent yield before you make your final decision. If munis do make good sense for you, invest in the highest-rated municipal bonds you can find, hold until maturity—and enjoy the tax-free income!

Two excellent Web sites: www.bondsonline.com and www.msrb.org.

Savings Bonds

We like savings bonds because they are affordable, tax-deferred, and absolutely safe from default. Any age group can benefit from their use.

We much prefer the Series I bonds, because they have almost consistently out-yielded the EE bonds and they have the inflation protection missing from EE bonds.

The Treasury Department's Education Bond Program allows you a federal tax exemption on the interest from Series EE and Series I bonds if you pay qualified higher-education expenses in the same calendar year that you redeem the bonds, with certain caveats. (See more on using savings bonds for your children's education and giving bonds to children as gifts in Chapter 7.) The Treasury Department has a Web site that will give you a complete rundown of the bonds available, along with purchasing information, at www.savingsbonds.gov.

Dolan Ah-Ha!

When you buy bonds, don't put all of your money into one bond basket. Buy a selection of bonds with staggering maturity dates. You will always have a bond that you can liquidate in an emergency, and money coming due in increments to capture higher interest rates when they're available.

Are "Junk Bonds" Worth the Risk?

NO! They're junk! In the 1990s, "junk," or high-yield, bonds were bringing in average annual returns as high as 24.2%, which was approximately twice the return on long-term government bonds. But for now, the upside seems to be history. Since 1999 the average annual return has been *negative*, at –2.3%. In shaky times, buying the lowest-grade investments is like digging through the bottom of the trash barrel. These bonds also carry a high possibility of default. Which means you could lose your entire investment!

Should You Buy Individual Bonds or a Bond Fund?

We're often asked whether it's better to invest in individual bonds or in diversified bond funds. Our answer is always the same for most investors: We prefer individual bonds to funds.

Some bond funds, contrary to their name, mirror stocks more than bonds. Because the portfolio never matures, you have no guarantee of getting your original investment back in full. If you shouldn't be taking any risks with your principal, stay away from bond funds. Since bonds are rated for safety or lack thereof, you are much safer buying individual bonds with high ratings.

Buy Individual Bonds If . . .

You have $50,000 or more to invest in individual bonds.

You are retired or close to retirement, and looking for predictability.

Once you know the percentage of your portfolio you want to put in fixed-income investments, you can determine if you have enough money to properly diversify your bond purchases. For corporate bonds, we recommend buying 10 to 12 different bonds; at $1,000 apiece, that would be $10,000 to $12,000. With municipals you'll need $50,000 or more to properly diversify. For smaller portfolios, the only individual bonds we recommend are Treasuries—T-bills, T-notes, or zero coupon bonds.

A Web site that we like a lot for up-to-date information about bonds is www.investing-inbonds.com.

And that brings us to the wide world of mutual funds. . . .

Investing in Mutual Funds

Many investors like mutual funds. You may like *some* of them less after you hear what we have to say.

Earlier this year you read that the SEC is investigating a number of mutual fund companies for trading improprieties . . . again. The little guy gets the short end of the stick!

The SEC claimed that these scandals may have hurt investors and inflicted long-term damage on the $7 billion mutual fund business.

Make sure you do your homework before you buy. Check which mutual funds the SEC is investigating!

THAT said . . .

Three Reasons Individual Investors Like Mutual Funds

First of all, let us say that there are some very well-managed mutual funds . . . and some major turkeys! According to an article by John Waggoner in *USA Today* just a few months ago, a record number of mutual funds are headed into oblivion.

Since the bear market began in March 2000, 414 stock mutual funds have been liquidated according to Morningstar, the mutual fund tracker. Morningstar also reports that some funds have been the victims of a new trend—mutual fund mergers. More than 584 bond funds have merged or liquidated since March 2000. That said, here's more of the "real story."

1. *Diversification.* Each dollar you invest buys you a share of the mutual fund's entire portfolio. That portfolio contains the stocks or bonds of many different companies. Fund managers may invest in hundreds of securities from different companies in order to reduce investment risk.

2. *Professional portfolio management.* A mutual fund gives you access to the expertise of professional money manager(s). These managers are often supported by a whole staff of investment analysts.

3. *Liquidity.* Mutual funds issue new shares and redeem existing shares on demand. You can buy or sell shares of a fund on any business day. The price you pay per share equals the current market value of the fund's investments, divided by the number of shares outstanding (the net asset value per share, or NAV), based on that

day's closing prices. If you buy a mutual fund that charges a sales commission (load), you pay the closing price per share (NAV) plus the sales charge.

So What's Our Beef About Some Mutual Funds?

What's not to love about an investment that gives you all of this built-in diversification and expertise? Here's what we *don't* like about them:

1. *Costs and fees.* You can end up paying fairly hefty fees for the services you get. The fees commonly range from 0.35% to 2% of assets per year, and are taken off the top of the fund's profits.

2. *Capital gains taxes.* Even if a fund loses money, you might find yourself saddled with a capital gains tax bill at the end of the year. Why? Because the manager is constantly selling holdings, and if he or she sells at a gain, you are taxed. The rate at which a fund manager buys and sells investments is known as the turnover ratio. The lower the turnover ratio, the better, since you may have to pay taxes on the capital gains from profitable investments that are sold by the fund. When you call to get information on a mutual fund, ask, "What's the fund's turnover ratio?" Stay away from funds with high turnover ratios (the closer to 100% a turnover ratio is, the more taxed you'll be).

3. *The portfolio manager is playing with other people's money.* Portfolio managers receive compensation, and retain their jobs, based on how well their fund performs in comparison to other funds in the same category. They take all kinds of risks to keep the returns stellar. They might do all kinds of buying and selling and hedging that they'd never do with their *personal* portfolio. When the market starts going against a fund, the managers tend to panic and dump stocks to keep rate of return from falling. They can exacerbate your losses because of their panic.

Professional management and diversification are not a guarantee that the portfolio will grow. Witness a prominent mutual fund family (you'd recognize the name—Putnam Investments, the fourth-largest mutual fund company in the United States) that discontinued 11 of its 66 funds back in March 2002, due to lack of performance.

4. *Popular stocks tend to get around in the mutual fund world.* If you own three mutual funds and you think you're diversified, don't be sure of it! Take a look at the 10 top holdings in all three of those funds. You may find they're exactly the same! Even if you are holding one maximum capital appreciation fund, one equity income fund, and one growth fund, the managers could be buying the darlings of Wall Street to keep their returns looking good.

TIMPANOGOS HIGH SCHOOL

Dolan Ah-Ha!

Some fund companies have become so desperate for new business they have offered brokers an extra commission to push their funds on you, the investor. Even major fund families have been known to do this.

Consider what happened to a friend of ours as he was retiring and ready to roll over his 401(k) plan to an IRA. He went to see his broker, who made a number of recommendations. Then he asked us to review those recommendations.

The broker had put together a brightly colored, eye-catching binder with a review of four recommended mutual funds, all of which were "growth and income." The top 10 holdings of all four funds were listed, and guess what? All four funds contained the *same 10 stocks* (in different amounts), most of which paid no dividends! These were supposed to be growth and INCOME funds, yet their top 10 holdings did not pay dividends. We might also add that this happened in 1998, and most of the stocks were tech companies! Enough said.

We urge you to make the effort and create your own diversified portfolio, sort of like your own mutual fund, without paying hefty fees and placing your money in the hands of a portfolio manager who really doesn't care if there's enough money there in 10 years for your daughter's wedding—he (or she) is interested only in covering his own you-know-what.

But if you really wish to put money into mutual funds, we're happy to show you how to cover your front and back end.

Mutual Funds 101: The Basics—No More, No Less

Mutual funds give you the same diversification that wealthy investors get from the stock and bond markets—without having to invest $100,000 or more. With a mutual fund, you can invest in hundreds of stocks or bonds without a lot of money.

A mutual fund is a pool of money managed by a professional money manager, known as the fund manager or portfolio manager, or by a team of portfolio managers. The fund manager invests your money—along with money from thousands of other investors—in stocks, bonds, and other securities, depending on the type of fund you choose.

The fund manager buys investments with a specific, stated objective in mind. Some mutual funds invest in stocks for dividends, capital appreciation, or both. Some funds

Dolan Ah-Ha!

More mutual fund firms are using the "team" portfolio management concept these days instead of one highly visible manager. Why? Because if a mutual fund becomes known mostly for the person at the helm, if that "star" portfolio manager leaves, investors just might get nervous and liquidate their holdings—and who can blame them?

invest in bonds for regular income, and some invest in a mixture of stocks and bonds for growth and income. See our glossary on p.152.

As a shareholder of the fund, you reap your proportionate share of any gains (or losses) on investments made by the fund. Every investor gets the same rate of return *per share*, whether they invest $1,000 or $100,000.

Most mutual funds are part of a "family" of funds—a group of funds that are owned by one management company. To encourage you to invest all your money with them, management companies create different funds with different investment goals.

Mutual funds try to make investing as easy as possible. Although we don't recommend that you give anyone access to your checking account, most funds have automatic investment plans so you can automatically make regular contributions to your mutual fund by having money withdrawn from your bank account and invested instead of having to bother with writing checks. They also offer automatic reinvestment programs so you can have your dividends and capital gain distributions poured right back into the fund and used to buy new shares of the fund. Most fund families also allow you to transfer your money into different mutual funds within its family with a simple phone call.

You can also easily withdraw money from your mutual fund account—usually with just a phone call. By law, open-end mutual funds must redeem any or all of your shares—at your request—on any business day, with the exception of "sector" funds.

Whenever you exchange shares of a fund, write a check from your money market fund, make an investment, or reinvest dividends, a statement will be sent to you to confirm your transaction. In addition to these confirmation statements, you'll also get monthly or quarterly account updates, depending on the fund.

But, remember, with both load *and* no-load funds, you *do* pay for the ease of investing (the portfolio manager does the work!) with different kinds of fees, taxes, and paperwork. In a bear market, as we have been recently experiencing, it may create worse losses than individual stocks.

Charles Jaffe, the mutual funds columnist with *The Boston Globe*, provides very interesting and helpful information. Not long ago, he wrote a column that really caught our eye titled, "Putting Your Funds to the Test." Charles states at the beginning of the article that if you can't answer the basic six questions, you should plow into a prospectus, head to your fund company's website, or revisit your portfolio-building strategy for a refresher course.

In brief (these questions are important whether you own or are thinking of purchasing a particular mutual fund!):

- What is the fund's investment strategy and market-capitalization or band-duration profile?
- Who is the manager and what is the investment style?
- What is the fund's expense ratio? (We talk about that, too, in this chapter.)
- How is the fund rated by independent experts (Morningstar, Hipper, ValueLine)?
- What is the fund's role in your portfolio?
- Does it match (or, if you own it, *still* match) your investment objectives?

He also makes some other good points in this particular column. Look for it. We'll recommend to Charles Jaffe that he run it again!

Types of General Stock Funds

Balanced (B) Object is to protect principal by investing in a balance of stocks and bonds.

Capital appreciation (CA) Also called "aggressive-growth funds." Generally risky, with higher turnover.

Equity income (EI) Seek income and growth by investing in stocks, especially those that pay high dividends, and bonds. The most conservative stock funds.

Growth (G) Invest in companies whose earnings are expected to grow faster than average. Moderate risk.

Growth and income (GI) Invest in companies expected to show average or better earnings growth and pay steady or rising dividends. More conservative than growth funds.

Index funds (IF) Mirror major market indices such as the S & P 100 and the S & P 500. A fund invests in stocks of a particular index only, and reflects market performance of that specific index.

Micro-cap (MR) Invest in tiny companies, those with market capitalizations (total market value of shares outstanding) of less than $300 million.

Small-cap (SG) Invest in small companies, those with market capitalizations of less than $1 billion.

Earning Money with Mutual Funds

There are three ways to make money with a mutual fund:

1. *Dividends or interest* earned from the investments that are owned by the fund.
2. *Distributions of capital gains* earned on investments that the fund manager sells at a profit.
3. *Increased share value* as the value of the investments that are held by the fund increases. This is known as the net asset value (NAV). The NAV represents the value of a single share of a mutual fund. Load funds charge you more than the NAV to buy a fund, because commissions are added in. When you sell your fund shares, you are paid the NAV.

Whenever an investment inside the mutual fund declares a dividend, you receive a pro-rata share of that dividend. You also receive your share of any net profits from the sale of investments. You can have the dividends and profits mailed to you, or have them automatically reinvested to buy more shares. These payouts, called distributions, may be paid monthly, quarterly, or annually. Fixed-income mutual funds may declare distributions daily, although they are paid out monthly or quarterly.

For tax purposes, you'll receive a year-end statement from the fund showing what part of the money you've earned represents ordinary income and what part represents long-term capital gains. The distinction between ordinary income and capital gains is important. Long-term capital gains are taxed at a maximum rate of 20%, while ordinary income can be taxed at up to 39.6% (depending on your tax bracket). In addition, you can offset your capital gains with any capital losses you have for the year (or that you carried from previous years).

The amount of dividends, interest, or capital gains distributions you get from a mutual fund depends on the kind of investments the fund owns. Funds invested in high-rated corporate bonds may pay you interest of 5% to 10%, based on the income from the bonds. A fund investing in small-growth companies will most likely have no income from dividends. Your profit from this fund would be due to any appreciation in the price of the stocks owned by the fund.

Checking a Fund's Performance

The best place to look for up-to-date information about a mutual fund's performance, as well as news and analysts' research, is the site run by Morningstar, www.morningstar.com.

Dolan Bottom Line

Anytime you withdraw money from a mutual fund, or transfer money from one fund to another fund, the sale of shares and/or subsequent purchase of new shares is a taxable event unless the funds are in an IRA or other tax-deferred retirement account. Remember to keep careful records of your transactions.

Most of the information on the site is free, but with a premium membership ($12.95 a month, $115 a year, or $199 for two years) you will get access to the most advanced research, news, and rankings of funds as well as individual stocks. Try the premium membership for 30 days free and see if it's worth the investment for you.

When you are checking a fund's performance, look at the tables that show how it has fared over the last one, three, five, and ten years. Look for steady performers that have consistently been among the top five funds in their category.

Reading the All-Important Mutual Fund Prospectus

Before you make a final decision to put money into a fund, call the toll-free number (quickest way to find this is on the fund family's own Web site) and ask them to mail you a prospectus. Think of this read as a trail of clues that will tell you what's *really* going on in those plush offices where the fund's managers make their decisions. There are two things you really need to look at in a prospectus:

1. *Investment Objective:* You'll find the investment objective listed in its own section of the prospectus. The investment objective explains the goal of the fund. The three most common goals are growth, income, and growth with income. If

In 2002, Morningstar Inc., the mutual fund–rating company, changed its system so that funds are rated not in the fund universe at large, but only against other funds with similar investment styles, based on more than 50 separate fund categories. While this system is designed to give each fund a better chance of showing how it compares to others in its particular investment category, it also means that some funds that have been terrible performers could rank at the top of a badly performing category.

Caveat emptor.

you're looking for more income from your investments and the fund's objective is growth, you're in the wrong ballpark. The objective also tells you how the fund manager proposes to meet that goal (aggressively, moderately, or with as little risk as possible).

2. *The Expense Ratio:* The expense ratio is listed in the fund's fee table, which shows you all the fees and expenses the fund subtracts from the fund's performance (and your investment) each year. The lower the expense ratio the better, because the more profits will go to you. In a diversified stock portfolio, we don't like *any* expense ratio that is over 1% (0.3% for an index stock fund, 0.5%–0.6% for a bond fund).

The prospectus will also tell you about the fund's management (Who are the advisers, and what is their background and track record?), the services provided (Does the fund offer an automatic investment plan or IRA accounts?), and tax consequences (What is the likely tax impact on an investor in your tax bracket?). See the section "Mutual Funds and Your Taxes."

Beyond the Prospectus — The Annual Report

Another important thing to look at before you buy a mutual fund is the annual report. When you request any prospectus, ask for a copy of the annual report as well (see page 138). The annual report tells you what the portfolio manager has invested in during the year.

Take a close look at the stocks and/or bonds that are listed. If the entire annual report lists companies you've never heard of, or companies whose business practices you dislike, this fund won't suit your needs. If most of the bonds listed in the portfolio have a Standard & Poor's rating of BB or below, don't buy that fund.

Mutual Funds and Your Taxes

Here's the part of the book we call the "insomnia cure." Mutual fund taxes are more complicated than those of just about any other investment around, so figuring them out can be one of the most tedious things you've ever done. Unfortunately, if you don't pay attention, getting something wrong could be the most costly investment mistake you ever make — so no fair skipping this section if you have mutual funds!

The main difference with taxes on mutual funds is that you pay taxes on your capital gains and dividends every year — whether or not you sold any of your shares — while with stocks, you don't pay taxes on your gains until you sell your shares.

There are three taxable events when it comes to mutual funds: selling your shares, receiving dividends, and receiving capital gains distributions.

There's no way to get around paying taxes every year on any capital gains distributions and dividends (even if you automatically reinvest them)—and you certainly don't want a fund that makes less money! At the end of the year, the mutual fund family will send you a Form 1099-DIV that lists the dividends, interest, or capital gains for the year—all the information you need for your taxes. But you can try to lower your taxes and prevent a migraine come tax time by following these rules of thumb:

1. **Before you buy a fund, consider the tax implications.** Every time the fund manager buys or sells stock within the fund, it creates a taxable event. The rate at which a fund manager buys and sells investments in the fund's portfolio is called the "portfolio turnover." The lower the turnover ratio, the lower your taxes. If taxes are a serious concern to you, stay away from funds with high turnover ratios (the closer to 100%, the higher your taxes).

    Certain types of funds tend to have a higher turnover than others. Aggressive-growth funds generally have a higher turnover than growth and income funds, for example.

2. **Buy a fund AFTER it has paid out its dividend.** Let's say a fund is going to pay its dividend on December 1. You invest $2,500 on November 30—which buys you 100 shares at $25 apiece. On December 1, you receive a $1.20 dividend per share. The share price drops to $23.80 to reflect the dividend payout, and you owe taxes on $1.20.

    Your friend, Bob, invests $2,500 in the fund on December 2 (*after* the dividend was paid) and gets 105 shares for $23.50. The difference: Bob doesn't owe taxes on the $1.20 dividend and you do!

3. **Remember that switching money between mutual funds—even within the same fund family—is a taxable event.** You may think of it as swapping funds, but you are actually selling shares of one fund to buy another. An exchange of shares from *any* mutual fund to another is considered a "sale" and subsequent purchase for tax purposes.

4. **Avoid the dreaded double dividend tax trap.** If you reinvest your dividends, you could get caught in the most common mutual fund tax trap we know of—paying taxes on those dividends twice.

    Here is an example: Say you buy 200 shares of Widget fund for $20 a share (a $4,000 investment). The fund pays you $460 in dividends, which you automatically reinvest for 20 more shares. The fund hits $24, so you decide to sell. Here's where most people make their mistake.

Your cost basis is *not* $20 a share. The shares you bought with the $460 had a cost basis of $23, not $20. So, you're selling 200 shares at $4 taxable profit (the current $24 price minus the $20 cost basis) and 20 shares at a $1 taxable profit ($24–$23). If you had lumped those 20 shares in at the same cost basis as your original 200, you would owe taxes on an extra $60!

5. **Keep very thorough records.** Besides keeping every darn piece of paper your mutual fund sends you, we suggest starting a logbook to track your transactions. Use any old spiral notebook to write down every purchase, sale, transfer, dividend, and distribution (and note whether you received it or automatically reinvested it). This log will become your best friend come tax time.

6. **Sell your funds with taxes in mind.** Probably the most complicated part about mutual fund taxes is figuring your cost basis when you sell. You actually have three different ways to figure your gains—and only you can decide which is best for you.

The magic two words when it comes to mutual fund taxes are "cost basis."

When you sell fund shares, your gain (or loss) is the difference between the sale price and an elusive figure known as your *cost basis*—essentially the price you paid for your shares, including any fees you paid when you bought them, plus any dividends and capital gains that you have reinvested in the fund. If you sell all your fund shares at one time, your tax calculation is pretty straightforward, since your cost basis is simply the total amount you invested over the years. But if you plan to unload only a portion of your shares, the tax code offers three ways to compute your cost basis:

Average share price method When you use the average share price method, you figure your cost basis simply by dividing the total dollar amount of shares you own by the number of shares. For example, if you own a total of $10,000, and you own 500 shares, your cost basis is $20 a share.

First in/first out method When you use the first in/first out method, it is assumed that the first shares you bought are the first shares you sold. Let's say you bought 100 shares at $20 a share, and then later bought 100 shares at $25 a share. Now you sell 100 shares. For tax purposes, it is assumed that the first 100 shares you bought are the ones you're selling now, so your cost basis is $20.

Specific share method The third option, the specific share method, lets you specify exactly which shares you are selling. Let's say you bought 100 shares at $20, 100 shares at

$22, and 100 shares at $25. Now you want to sell 100 shares. You can designate—*before* the transaction takes place—exactly which shares you are selling. In effect, you choose your own cost basis. One note: It is very important that you clearly specify to your broker (we recommend putting it in writing) which shares you are selling before the sale. You cannot designate the shares after the sale.

You should talk with your accountant to see which option works best for you and gives you the best tax results. But here are a few things to keep in mind. Once you choose a method for calculating your cost basis, you must stick to it. No switching methods mid-course. Second, you must keep very good records if you want to use the first in/first out or the specific share method.

Get a free copy of IRS Publication 564 (call 800-TAX-FORM). Believe it or not, this IRS booklet actually does a very good job of explaining these rules, complete with examples of how the rules work in different situations.

Open-End Funds vs. Closed-End Funds

There are two types of mutual funds: open-end funds and closed-end funds. Open-end funds are the traditional mutual funds we've been talking about up to now.

Open-End

The fund is called open-end because there is no fixed number of shares issued as there is for a stock (or for a closed-end fund).

The price you pay for a mutual fund share of an open-end mutual fund is based on the market value of all the fund's investments, minus costs, and then divided by the number of mutual fund shares owned by the fund's shareholders.

Like stocks and bonds, the price of an open-end mutual fund rises or falls every day, depending on what happens to the investments that are owned by the fund. Every time an investor buys shares, the mutual fund issues more shares. Higher demand for the fund doesn't mean a higher share price, as it does with stocks. Each day, a mutual fund must determine both the value of its portfolio and how many shares are outstanding.

When an open-end fund closes to new investors, it no longer accepts any money from new investors. Sometimes, the fund may no longer accept any more of existing shareholders' money either. As long as you own shares of the open-end fund before it closes, you still have all the investment and redemption privileges that you had when the fund was open to new investors.

Closed-End

A closed-end fund is more similar to a stock than to an open-end mutual fund. A closed-end mutual fund raises money by selling a fixed number of shares and investing the proceeds. The number of shares doesn't change. Like stocks, closed-end mutual funds are listed on a stock exchange. The only way to buy shares of a closed-end fund is through a stockbroker, where you'll pay brokerage commissions.

The value of a closed-end fund is not based on the net asset value, or NAV (the underlying value of the portfolio), but, rather, on the market's *perception* of how the fund is doing. When the market value of the fund's shares is less than the NAV of the investments that the fund owns, the fund is trading at a *discount*. This means you can buy the fund's share for less than its assets are worth. When the market value of the fund's shares is greater than the NAV of the investments, the fund is trading at a *premium*. This means you're paying more than the investments are worth on the open market. You want to buy closed-end funds at a discount.

You'll find a listing of discounts and premiums for closed-end stock funds in the Monday edition of *The Wall Street Journal*. Bond funds are listed on Wednesdays. Look for the heading "Publicly Traded Funds."

Making Sense of Mutual Fund Fees

Mutual fund fees have also come under *much* closer SEC scrutiny this year. Mutual fund companies charge management and administrative fees in return for their services. These fees, known as the *expense ratio*, commonly range from 0.35% to 2% of assets per year. The fees—which include 12b-1 fees, management expenses, and trading commissions—are taken off the top of the fund's profits. The remaining profits are then distributed to you.

If you're not careful, mutual funds can "fee" you to death. Hefty operating expenses are handicaps that a fund may not overcome for years. Before you invest in any fund, look carefully at its fees (these costs *must* appear in the fund's prospectus—usually on page 2 or 3—in a standard format that is dictated by the government). You should also check the prospectus about other charges the fund may have. For example, the fund may charge a load for reinvesting your dividends.

Annual expenses, in the form of management expenses and administrative costs, nibble away at your returns. All of these fees are assessed as a percentage of your total invested assets. The money comes out of the fund's profits before you are paid. Excessive mutual fund fees eat away at your initial investment and future profits. Here's what you need to know about fees before you invest:

Dolan Bottom Line

The lower the expense ratio the better. (Lower expenses means more profit for you.) In a diversified stock portfolio, we don't like *any* expense ratio that's over 1% (or index funds with annual expenses over 0.5%, or bond funds with expenses over 0.5%–0.6%).

Front-End Load vs. Back-End Load

Many mutual funds have loads (a sales charge—like commission). Most mutual funds that impose a sales charge, or load, do so up front, when you buy the fund. This front-end load can range from 2.5% to 8.5%, which is the maximum the National Association of Securities Dealers (NASD) allows and is not common. What exactly does a load mean? Well, if you send $10,000 to a fund, the amount of your money that will actually be invested to build your wealth will range from $9,150 to $9,750. The rest of your money goes to the salesman and the mutual fund company.

Another way funds hit you with a load is by charging a redemption fee—also known as a back-end load. This load is a commission that is charged against your account when you *sell* your fund. There are three ways funds can charge a back-end load: (1) as a set percentage of your original investment (not on the balance after it's grown), (2) as a set percentage of your fund's total value (including your investment and any growth), and (3) as a declining percentage that disappears over time (usually after five years).

You may already own a mutual fund that charges front-end or back-end loads. If you're happy with your fund's performance, you don't have to sell it just because of the load.

How to Choose the Right "Money Market" Mutual Fund

Money market mutual funds have become indispensable investment tools. They act like checking and savings accounts but usually pay higher interest rates than you can earn on your bank accounts. But there's one important difference: Money market funds are *not* insured like bank accounts.

Money market funds can invest only in the two highest grades of commercial paper and they must keep their maturities—the point at which the debts become due—at 120 days or less. Because the market price of short-term investments fluctuates much less than that of long-term investments (such as 30-year Treasury bonds), short-term debt is inherently safer. Money market funds issue and sell shares at $1 each and always stand ready to be redeemed at $1.

Dolan Bottom Line

In general, we recommend buying Treasury money market funds. The yield may be a wee bit lower than that on other money markets, but the safety and tax advantage can't be beat.

As safe as money markets sound, you should still be picky. In general, money market funds come in four varieties. In descending order of safety:

1. *U.S. Treasury funds.* These funds eliminate the risk of default by investing solely in short-term Treasury securities, which are guaranteed by the federal government. These funds are generally free of state and local taxes.
2. *U.S. government and agency funds.* These funds invest in bonds and notes of federal agencies whose credit is implicitly, but not explicitly, guaranteed by the Treasury and by Congress. This very slight extra risk (over U.S. Treasury funds) boosts the fund's yield. These funds are usually free of state and local taxes.
3. *Diversified taxable funds.* These funds keep the bulk of your money in the commercial paper of U.S. corporations. They may also own Treasury and agency paper and bank CDs.
4. *Tax-free funds.* These money market funds invest in short-term tax-exempt securities of state governments and municipalities, and they pay income that is free of

Dolan Ah-Ha!

A question that we have fielded any number of times over the years relates to "load" (sales commission) funds versus "no-load" (no sales commission) funds.

"Hey, Dolans," callers ask. "Doesn't it always make sense to buy a no-load fund instead of a load fund?"

If you are able to find a no-load fund with a good long-term track record that matches your investment objectives, sure, why pay a load? But be careful—"no load" doesn't mean "no fees"!

When comparing all of the costs of owning a particular mutual fund, be sure to research not only sales fees (if any) but also the cost of *continuing* management of both kinds of funds and how often the portfolio manager trades in and out of holdings. The more often the portfolio is turned over, the more taxes you'll pay.

You might be surprised when you do the math.

federal taxes. Some tax-free funds invest only in the securities of a single state. This income is then free from state and local taxes as well. But, because these funds are less diversified, they are also more risky.

Investing with a Broker or Financial Adviser

Once upon a time in a distant galaxy, people trusted their life savings to brokers and financial advisers who always made investments according to their clients' needs and wishes, never thinking of per-transaction fees. When people needed to plan for the future, they put their trust in financial planners who were highly competent and recommended only the most appropriate products no matter what rip-off insurance policies and other vehicles their companies were trying to push. But these people were definitely not living in the United States in the twenty-first century.

Now, ladies and gentlemen, back to reality. In this world, you have to be a highly informed consumer *before* you start seeking financial advice. So-called "experts" are hanging out shingles everywhere, some of them just to take advantage of people in trouble. The Web is full of advice, but which sites are worth your time?

When a financial professional is advising you, he or she is being remunerated by the amount of product sold and frequency of selling. Doing well for you is not necessarily this person's prime mission in life; the bottom line is. The smart pros don't want to burn you because they don't want to lose you as a client, but they have some powerful incentives—such as hanging on to their jobs—to sell you a lot of things that you might live very nicely without.

Such as? Here are a few products that you don't need:

- "Investment" insurance policies.
- Home equity lines of credit to get you out of some other form of debt.
- Adjustable-rate mortgages when you plan on being in a place for a long time, so you "can afford to buy" more house than you can really afford.
- Mutual funds, stocks, or bonds that a broker needs to sell because if he doesn't meet his quota of products sold for the month he'll be fired.

Believe it or not, there are brokers who regularly read the obituaries, looking for rich men who have died. Then they call the widow with some "trust me with your investments" spiel to get their hands on the money she has inherited. A savvy widow will find her own broker, or invest her husband's estate herself in investments that she understands. Handing your hard-earned money to a financial professional can be like lending someone your car and they return it with a huge dent, or like trusting your home to a house-sitter while you're away, and returning to a tank of dead tropical fish and beer-colored carpet stains. Nobody else takes care of your things with the loving care that you do, and that includes your money.

So how do you find financial pros whom you can trust? You can't unless you have some knowledge of the kind of investments that are right for you.

Let's make a distinction, so that you'll know where to start. What's the difference between a financial planner/adviser and a broker?

Either one could leave you "broke-er" if you don't select carefully. But a good financial planner helps you devise a complete life plan: vehicles for college savings, retirement savings, how much to spend when you buy property, even a plan for putting money aside. A broker, on the other hand, advises you on investments and executes the transactions for you from your account.

Do you need both? No. Either one will handle your investment transactions.

Whichever you choose, finding a broker or financial planner who knows what he or she is talking about, is more concerned about your financial well-being than about his or her commission, and helps you take control of your financial future is nirvana for any investor. But if you don't know anything about finances, you're going to be helpless in some financial adviser's hands, like a lamb at the slaughterhouse. Don't think we're exaggerating.

A lot of people call themselves "financial advisers." Some CPAs are now doing it to drum up year-round business. Many insurance brokers do financial planning. Duh—what do you think their agenda might be?

Any financial planner whose immediate fix for all your financial woes is an annuity or an insurance policy should send red flags up all over the place. The concept of financial planning was instituted by the insurance industry. It is heavily dependent on the selling of insurance products, most of which are totally inappropriate for growing your assets. The only assets that grow are those of the person who sells you the policy.

But there are some very good financial planners and some very good brokers. The best way to find either is by getting referrals from family members, friends, and business associates who have shown evidence of being intelligent enough to know good from bad. (A friend or relative with a track record of sound investments is showing reasonable evidence of such intelligence.)

It's imperative that you meet with the adviser face-to-face. You want to set up a good working relationship, and how are you going to do this with someone who won't even meet with you?

But before you meet, call the adviser and ask for his or her credentials. You want a financial planner who is a CFP (certified financial planner) or PFS (personal financial

Here Are the Questions to Ask a Broker and the Answers You Want to Hear

1. "How long have you been a broker?"

Answer: You want a minimum of five years' experience.

2. "What kind of products do you specialize in?"

Answer: Here's one more reason you should know what kind of investments will work best for you. (See Chapter 5.) If your goal is to build a portfolio of individual bonds, you don't want a broker who specializes in mutual funds.

3. "Where do you get *your* financial advice?"

Answer: This is a surprise question for most advisers and brokers. As a result, you'll probably get an unrehearsed and hopefully honest answer. You want to hear that he or she taps into a variety of resources, including professional publications, personal contacts in the industry, institutional research, and other material that would not be easily available to you. Otherwise, you might as well be making your own financial/investment decisions. And if he says the firm's investment research department is his source of stock recommendations, don't walk away, run! By now you must be aware, from all the exposés in the news, that equity research analysts are paid handsomely to recommend client companies, and often fired if they issue negative findings.

4. "Are your transaction costs (commissions) and fees competitive with those of other similar firms?"

Answer: Have the answer proven with real examples. Ask for a detailed list of all commissions, for recommended products and nonrecommended products.

And Watch Out for These Warning Signs

1. *Gobbledygook.* We don't care how good a track record an individual has; if you can't understand what he's trying to sell you, you're headed for trouble. If this professional can't adequately explain why a particular investment makes sense for you in *less than two minutes*, get out of Dodge!

2. *A financial pro who wants to meet you at your home.* Don't invite them in. Always go to the so-called "professional's" office. There are quite a few good reasons for this:

You can get up and walk out. People tend to act out of guilt, even if it isn't conscious: If you think *Oh, we made the salesperson come all the way over here,* you might feel inhospitable pushing him or her out the door.

You can see the environment in which your potential adviser works. Does it seem like a comfortable environment for your money? Does it look like the office of someone who is successful and knows what he or she is doing?

3. *Solicitation by phone.* It should go without saying—you don't want your money manager to pick you out of some phone list. Nothing makes the hairs on the back of our necks stand on end more than the person who calls people cold, announcing an important new "investment opportunity." Don't trust anyone who uses the word "opportunity" in connection with your money. This is the way most scams are sold. Hang up the phone!

Daria Dolan Ah-Ha!

Like many physicians, people in financial services love to confound you with jargon. It rocks you off-balance, so that you feel inadequate and ignorant, a walking target for whatever the "pro" is trying to push.

If the language is unintelligible, ask for clarification. If you still can't understand, get up and walk out. Feeling stupid is preferable to *being poor* because you lost money in investments you didn't comprehend.

I can't tell you how many men, in particular, just can't bring themselves to admit they don't understand what it means when a broker says something like "Let's do a butterfly spread" or "Go short against the box."

The guy sounds authoritative, and the client doesn't want to show his ignorance, so he buys into it. In my experience as a broker I've seen some incredibly astute businessmen make the stupidest investment decisions because they can't bring themselves to say those simple words, "I don't understand."

If a broker/financial planner can't adequately explain an investment idea in two minutes or less, tell him, in so many words, to cut the b.s. Say: "Just give me the facts that explain why this investment fits my investment objectives."

specialist). Don't go to a CPA who also "does" financial planning. Taxes are tough enough to understand without someone trying to also get a handle on investments. Both parts will suffer, because each part of the equation needs total concentration.

The CFP or PFS designation should give you assurance that this person has completed the educational requirements. Then check to see if any complaints have been lodged against this person by contacting the Certified Financial Planner Board of Standards (888-CFP-MARK, www.cfp-board.org), or if your planner is a CPA, the American Institute of CPAs, PFS Division (888-777-7077, www.cpapfs.org). For brokers, check for complaints by calling the National Association of Securities Dealers (800-289-9999) and your state securities commission. It's imperative that you check out the broker's record with the state and not the North American Securities Dealers (NASD), which has ways of covering up and hiding—not to mention losing—bad news on some brokers. So go directly to your state, because the states tend to keep more honest reports.

You may run a background check on an investment adviser at Investment Adviser Public Disclosure (adviserinfo.sec.gov), a database provided by the Securities and Exchange Commission. Lots of important info here . . . a financial planner's government filings, how much money the firm manages, its fee schedule . . . and more!

If you don't have a reference, you might schedule an appointment with the branch manager of any well-established brokerage firm with local offices. Discuss your background, investment expertise, and investment objectives, then ask the branch manager to introduce you to two or three brokers in the office who he believes can best help you, not the one who happens to be Broker of the Day. Whatever you do, don't walk into a brokerage firm off the street hoping that the broker who happens to have time to see you that day will be your Prince Charming. You're probably talking to a rookie, or the firm's resident has-been who is desperate to drum up new business.

Once you've found the names of at least three financial pros, set up interviews in their offices. Remember, you're interviewing them—they're not interviewing you! And never, ever, let them come to your home. You want to see where they work.

Trouble with Your Broker?

The National Association of Securities Dealers sets rules but doesn't crack down the way it should. If you think your broker has cheated you, the better regulatory body to contact is the North American Securities Administration Association (NASAA), which is devoted to investor protection and can advise you on a course of action. NASAA has administrators in each state and the District of Columbia, as well as Puerto Rico, Canada, and Mexico. The Web site www.nasaa.org has a list of regulators in every area, or you can call the corporate office in Washington at 202-737-0900 for information.

An excellent book on this subject is *Investor Beware: How to Protect Your Money From Wall Street's Dirty Tricks* (paperback, John Wiley and Sons, 1993), by our friend, prominent securities litigation attorney, John Allen. Go to his Web site, too: www.investorbeware.com.

Helpful Web Sites, Software, and Books

Investment Basics

Microsoft Money 2004 Deluxe. An easy-to-use program that helps you track your investments and act as your own portfolio manager. In computer stores or order at www.microsoft.com/money.

www.moneycentral.msn.com News that affects your investments. Click on "Investing," then go to the Research Wizard. This section of the site gives you performance charts, news, earnings information, even access to the Securities and Exchange Commission (SEC) filings.

http://university.smartmoney.com The site will tell you all of the basics about terms and strategies. Free.

www.ahorrando.org The Spanish-language site of the Bond Market Association's educational arm. The site offers information about stocks, bonds, and mutual funds, as well as advice on saving for retirement and handling financial emergencies.

Investment Strategizing

Treasuries
Buying Treasury Securities (write to the Federal Reserve Bank of Richmond, Public Affairs Office, P.O. Box 27471, Richmond, VA 23261; $4.50).

Stocks
One Up on Wall Street: How to Use What You Already Know to Make Money in the Market, by Fidelity Magellan's legendary portfolio manager (now retired), Peter Lynch. Simon & Schuster, 2000. Paperback, $14.00.

Bonds

Most books about bonds are a little too scholarly. For an easy, understandable guide, we recommend our book, *Smart Money: How to Be Your Own Financial Manager.* ($8.95)

www.investinginbonds.com The Bond Market Association's Web site features news and a comprehensive guide to bonds. Includes a link to the Spanish-language investing site www.ahorrando.org.

www.savingsbonds.gov The government site for information on U.S. savings bonds

www.dailygraphs.com This is the Investors Business Daily site, and it will give you access to information that investment professionals use. The complete equity research package costs $1,000 a year, or you can receive the stock research tool with access to stock charts, data, and proprietary ratings for $720 a year.

The Value Line Investment Online Survey. You can get a 13-week trial subscription for $65. www.valueline.com

www.vanguard.com
www.quicken.com
Both sites have interactive calculators that can help you plan an asset-allocation strategy.

Magic Numbers: The 33 Key Ratios That Every Investor Should Know, by Peter Temple. Temple, a former financial analyst, explains the stock-picking criteria you should use in easy-to-understand terms. John Wiley & Sons, 2002. $29.95.

Online Banks and Brokers

www.FDIC.gov—to check if a bank is FDIC-insured

www.gomez.com—to check broker ratings

Annual Reports

Public Register's Annual Report Service: 800-426-6825, www.prars.com

Buying Stocks in Small Lots Using Dividend Reinvestment Plans (DRIPs)

www.firstshare.com.

Money Market Funds

www.reservefunds.com

www.sharebuilder.com

www.netstockdirect.com

www.mfea.com

Investment Clubs

The Investment Club Book, by John Wasik, Warner, $13.95

Starting and Running a Profitable Investment Club, by Thomas O'Hara and Kenneth Janke, Sr., Times Business. $23.00.

www.better-investing.org. The NAIC site, in addition to serving up information on investment clubs, offers educational programs, services, and tools for individual investors, as well as stock and mutual fund investing tools. Most of the information is free.

Mutual Funds

www.morningstar.net, Morningstar

www.fundalarm.com

Winning in Mutual Funds, by Jay Schabacker (800-879-2988; $18.95)

If You're Clueless About Mutual Funds and Want to Know More, by Seth Godin ($15.95, Dearborn)

Avoiding Trouble with Brokers and Fighting Back

www.investorbeware.org. Site run by securities litigation attorney John Allen, with up-to-date information on investor recourses against brokers and a claim you can file online.

Finding a Broker or Financial Planner

Fee-only financial planners www.napfa.org, or call 800-366-2732

Institute of Certified Financial Planners, 800-282-7526

International Association for Financial Planning, 800-930-4511

American Institute of Certified Public Accountants Personal Financial Planning Division, 800-862-4272

CFP Board of Standards: to confirm if a planner is certified and if he or she has ever been disciplined, 888-237-6275, www.cfp-board.org

National Association of Insurance Commissioners: Get the number for your state insurance commissioner to check licenses and rules violations, 816-842-3600, www.naic.org

American Society of CLU & ChFC (insurance agents), 800-392-6900

National Association of Personal Financial Advisors, 888-333-6659

North American Securities Administration Association: Get the number of your state securities commissioner, check a planner's licenses, and ask about disciplinary actions, 202-737-0900, www.nasaa.org

Securities and Exchange Commission: Check whether the planner is a registered investment adviser and get any other information available, 800-732-0330, www.sec.gov

National Fraud Exchange Mortgage Asset Research Institute: A one-step background check on stockbrokers, financial planners and advisers, real estate agents, trust advisers, and mortgage officers. Cost: $39 for one name; $20 per person after that, 800-822-0416.

Mutual Fund Glossary

The Main Types of Mutual Funds

Aggressive-Growth Funds (also called capital appreciation). The goal is maximum growth of your principal or capital. These funds usually pay little or nothing in dividends and have lots of turnover, buying and selling investment holdings frequently. Aggressive-growth funds are the most volatile. Such funds may specialize in fledgling companies or in larger firms with fast-rising profits.

Asset Management Funds. The goal is to make money by anticipating or responding to economic changes. These funds may be 100% invested in stocks or bonds or cash (money market securities) or a combination, depending on how the fund manager views the market conditions. The idea behind these funds is that the portfolio manager will do the switching and timing for you—so you (theoretically) never have to sell your shares and switch to a different fund.

Balanced Funds. The goal is to conserve principal by investing in a mix of stocks and bonds, while paying current income and promoting long-term growth. These funds traditionally hold 60% stocks and 40% bonds.

Corporate Bond Funds. The goal is to seek a high level of current income. These funds achieve their goal by buying corporate bonds and utility bonds. Some funds may also hold U.S. Treasury bonds or bonds issued by a federal agency.

Equity Income Funds. The goal is to combine long-term capital growth with a steady income stream. These funds seek companies that pay steady and rising dividends and also have growth prospects. Since rising dividends tend to lift stock prices, growth and income are likely to go hand in hand. Another possible advantage is that you would see smaller price declines with these funds when the overall stock market falls.

Flexible Bond Funds. The goal is to provide current income. These funds invest in combinations of high-grade corporate bonds, higher-yielding junk bonds, tax-free muni bonds, government-backed mortgage certificates, government bonds and notes, money market securities, and zero coupon bonds.

Ginnie Mae (GNMA) Funds. The goal is to provide current income. These funds invest in mortgage securities backed by the Government National Mortgage Association (GNMA).

Global Bond Funds. The goal is to provide broader diversification than you'd get from a U.S.-only bond fund. These funds invest in the bonds of companies and countries worldwide.

Global Equity Funds. The goal here is to provide more diversification than you'd get from a U.S.-only fund and to take advantage of opportunities worldwide. Global funds invest in securities traded worldwide, including the United States. The funds' managers handle trading and record-keeping details, and deal with differences in currencies, languages, time zones, laws and regulations, and business customs and practices. However, global funds add another layer of risk—exchange-rate risk. Your foreign investments may be worth more or less than the actual U.S. dollars you paid for them, depending on the value of other countries' currencies versus the U.S. dollar.

Gold Funds. The goal is to provide you with a hedge against inflation. These funds keep most of their assets in the stocks of gold-mining companies, gold coins, and gold bullion. Some gold portfolios may also hold silver, platinum, and other precious metals.

Growth Funds. The goal is maximum capital gains. Growth funds are generally more patient than their aggressive-growth counterparts and seek long-term appreciation of investments. They may buy blue-chip companies whose profits are expected to grow, or companies whose stock is selling for significantly less than (at a discount to) what the fund manager thinks it's worth. These funds usually have less volatility than aggressive-growth funds.

Growth and Income Funds. These can be the same as equity income funds (see above), but may include bonds in the portfolio.

High-Yield Bond Funds. The goal is to provide high current income. These funds must keep at least two-thirds of their portfolios in lower-rated corporate bonds (BA or lower by Moody's rating service and BB or lower by Standard & Poor's rating service). These funds generally give you a higher yield, but there is much greater risk of the bonds defaulting than with higher-rated bonds.

Index Funds. The goal is to provide growth that matches major market indexes. These funds invest in many of the securities of a given index. For example, the Vanguard Index 500 fund invests in the stock of a large number of the 500 companies on the S&P 500.

International Funds. The goal is to profit from investing in foreign stock markets (which may behave differently from U.S. markets), and by converting your investment into foreign currencies (which are worth more in U.S. dollars when the dollar's exchange rate is falling, but less when the dollar is rising). These funds invest in the securities of corporations outside the United States. Closely related are global funds (see p. 171), which can mix U.S. and foreign holdings.

Money Market Funds. The goal is to preserve your principal and provide current income with high liquidity. These funds invest in extremely short-term fixed-income investments and maintain a constant $1-per-share value.

Municipal Bond Funds. The goal is to provide income free of federal taxes. These funds invest in bonds issued by states and municipalities to finance schools, highways, hospitals, airports, bridges, water and sewer works, and other public projects. In most cases, income earned on these investments is not taxed by the federal government, but may be taxed under state and local laws.

Sector Funds. The goal is to invest in one particular industry area or "sector." These funds buy stocks in a particular industry such as utilities, technology, health care, or financial services.

Single-State Municipal Bond Funds. The goal is to provide income free of state, local, and federal taxes. These funds buy bonds issued by one state. As a state resident, you receive income that is free of federal, state, and local taxes.

CHAPTER 6

Don't Buy Another Car Until You Read This

A BRAND-NEW, ZERO-MILEAGE, shiny automobile could be the third-largest purchase of your life, after your home and your children's education. Do you think you have what it takes to go into battle with the dealer and get the best deal for yourself? If your answer is "yes," you're the exception!

We've all been to car showrooms, so we hardly need to tell you what happens there. First there's the smell of new cars. How is it that they all smell like luxurious leather even if the upholstery is vinyl? And those shiny new bodies in colors that somehow seem to match your personality, and the smooth way the ignition turns over . . . and the options . . .

Whoaaa. . . . Remember, the car salesperson's job is to get as much for the car as possible ("model price may vary from dealer to dealer"), while your goal is to pay the least amount. You should be getting ready for war. Rule #1 of the game plan is: Don't let on that you've fallen head-over-heels for a car. That's an invitation to an unscrupulous salesman (we'll say "salesman" for convenience, but women are salespeople, too!) to take advantage of you.

Car salesmen have known for years how to push the buttons that will make you want the car so badly you'll be ready to drive it home that very day. They still know how to get the best of a consumer if the consumer lets his guard down. You heard, as we all did, that the Internet was going to cause a consumer revolution; that all of the consumer-oriented sites that let us know the prices dealers pay the manufacturers would force the dealers to be more transparent in their price quotes. (See the end of this chapter for a list of our top picks among the auto information sites.) But it hasn't been that simple. The dealers now know that you've already looked up the invoice price before you visit the showroom. So,

Socially Responsible Funds. The goal is the same as with a growth fund, but these funds invest only in companies that exhibit a social conscience. Companies that take care of the environment and are aware of the rights and needs of their workers are "in." Firms that pollute, create weapons of war, or sell cigarettes or alcohol are "out."

U.S. Government Income Funds. The goal is to provide current income. These funds invest in a variety of government securities, including U.S. Treasury bonds, federally guaranteed mortgage-backed (GNMA) securities, and other government notes.

like irritating insects that develop immunities to every advance in pesticides, car dealers seem to keep finding new ways to arm themselves against the new "informed" consumer by adding new hidden costs.

Don't you think it's time you learned the rules of *their* game?

The Art of the Deal

You know what the dealer paid for the car, but in most cases *the lowest profit a dealership makes is on the car itself.* Surprised?

The big money is in *back-end charges.* In the hands of a slick salesperson, you can find yourself paying for extras that you may or may not really need, such as an extended warranty, an antitheft system, rustproofing, undercoating, paint sealant, a power sun roof, or servicing and parts sales. When a particular model is very popular, the dealer will add labels such as "market availability" and "acquisition fee"—charges an eager customer will pay all too eagerly even if they add up to thousands of additional dollars. The spread between what a dealer pays for a car and the "suggested" price slapped on the window by the manufacturer runs from a low of 6% for an economy model all the way up to 18% for a luxury car. That sticker price (MSRP) on the window is total fantasyland!

Another common trick: A dealer might leave out options on the list price and make you think the price includes a fully equipped car, then surprise you with the extras only after you've made it clear that this is the car of your dreams.

The invoice price overstates the true dealer's cost. It doesn't account for the "hold-backs" that dealers often get from the manufacturer. These payments that manufacturers give dealers to cover the costs of selling, usually equal to 2% to 3% of the cost of the car and refunded after the sale—the word in any other business would be "kickbacks," are no secret from consumers, thanks to *Consumer Reports* and the many sites that are constantly attempting to expose the car industry's backroom dealings. Consumer information online will also tell you about the incentives that manufacturers pay to move certain models. But even if you tell a car salesperson you know the dealership is getting a profit above and beyond the invoice price, the dealer will just deny it. There isn't much you can do about it; dealers will not shave the hold-backs from your price. But you can at least let them know you're wise to this practice.

The dealer *might* be offering customer rebates for certain people (recent college graduates or loyal customers, for example) and on certain models. But most incentive programs are designed for maximum inconsistency and confusion, intended to attract potential customers while still ensuring that manufacturers can get full retail price on many of the cars.

Trade-ins

The dealers know that practically everyone who has a used car to trade in also does research nowadays. But remember, while you may have found a great price for your old car on the Internet, the dealer will often find flaws in your car to try to knock down the trade-in value.

A frequent guest on our show, Kurt Allen Weiss, was in the automotive sales industry for 20 years. To quote him, he "got tired of taking advantage of consumers." His help with this chapter was invaluable to us.

> Kurt Allen Weiss's book, *Have I Got a Deal for You! How to Buy or Lease Any Car Without Getting Run Over,* is a hard-hitting exposé on how car dealers take advantage of consumers and how consumers can fight back. Read it before you make your next trip to a car dealership.

Kurt recently discussed with us the come-ons you see in 30-second spots on local TV stations throughout the country. Basically, if the deals sound too good to be true, they are, as you would know if you could read the fine print at the bottom of the screen, which tells you this applies only if you just finished college or if you're a loyal customer or renewing a lease. On a TV commercial the dealer might use type that is 6.5 points—that's the smallest print they're allowed to use by law, and it's this small! They can roll 400 words across the screen every four seconds. Just try keeping up. Moreover, monthly payment quotes exclude taxes, luxury taxes in the case of a car that costs more than $40,000, and what is called the acquisition fee. Ever try to understand the fast-talker on a radio commercial when he reads the disclaimer?

For that matter, Weiss claims he knows car dealers that routinely use illegal advertising come-ons. How do they get away with it? Because the fines the dealer pays as a matter of course are a small inconvenience compared to the profits they earn from unsuspecting consumers who see the ads and come in ready to swallow the bait.

That's only the beginning. You often don't even know when you're being had. Weiss estimates that 90% of the consumers who have been deceived walk away believing they got a good deal, and never realize in retrospect what happened.

For example, a salesman might tell you the monthly payment on your car is $250 when it should be $220. He may then try to sell you undercoating, rustproofing, and an alarm system, which would normally be $30 a month extra, but "because you're my friend," he will throw them in for only $10 a month. You walk out happy—with a payment of $260, $10 more than the total package would have cost.

Another scam: In undercover investigations Weiss has conducted for television news, he has found dealers packing life and disability insurance into the monthly car payments. You should buy life and disability insurance on your own to make sure you get the best price. (See Chapter 10 for good sources of inexpensive insurance.)

"Quote It Clean"

These are three magic words to use before you even start serious negotiations with a car dealer. When the salesman starts talking about the price and the payment terms, whether you're looking at a loan or a lease, you say:

"Quote it clean!"

Weiss says this will floor him (or her). "I've almost never seen a salesman quote a clean payment without being urged," Weiss says.

"Clean" means the monthly payments without all of the built-ins. With a clean quote you can begin your negotiations from the dealer invoice up, not from the list price down.

"With this one sentence, customers could cost car dealers $5 billion a year," says Weiss.

Don't let the dealer add unwanted things to the price. A listener named John called our radio show one day when we had Weiss in the studio. John told us about his experience buying a Chevy Impala with a sticker price that included $200 for an etching in the windshield to identify the car in case of theft. John didn't think it was worth the extra money. But since the etching was already there, John started to walk out the door. At that point, the salesman called him back and said if he still wanted the car he could have it without paying the extra money for the etching.

Why will salespeople suddenly become flexible if you stick to your guns and head for the door? Because the cost of acquiring you is expensive. It's best to make these demands when you're in the "boiler room" behind the showroom, because the salesman has put out some effort to get you that far and doesn't want to lose you. He or she knows that if you leave without purchasing a car on the spot, the chances of your returning are slim to none.

That's if you are dealing with an honest and reasonable operation. Weiss has seen salesmen rip up the contract and tell a customer who refuses the extras: "We don't want to sell you this car!" Some dealers claim you can't have the standard warranty if you won't pay for built-in extras such as an etching.

If that happens to you, take our advice—take your business elsewhere.

The Limits of an Extended Warranty

Car dealers love to sell extended warranties. Yet many standard warranties are good for as long as 10 years. If you plan to trade your car in when it's two or three years old, the standard warranty is absolutely all you need. If you're leasing a car for three years (the average lease period), you already have a warranty that covers the period of the contract.

Here's why we think that in many cases a buyer should just say no to an extended warranty. All too often, the dealer uses an extended warranty to lure you in, promising a lower financing rate in exchange for the purchase of the warranty, or telling people with marginal credit ratings that they can't get the loan unless they buy the warranty the bank requires.

Don't take this bait unless you intend to either:

1. Keep the car until its dying day, or
2. Sell your vehicle privately rather than trade it in.

An extended warranty can be useful in these two cases. It will increase your resale value in a private sale, because it will be the only way you can offer the potential buyer any form of warranty.

HOWEVER, make sure the extended warranty is transferable *and* offered by the manufacturer rather than an outside warranty company. Outside warranty companies often require that you lay out repair costs up front, then wait for their reimbursement, and they might refuse to pay unless you take your car to one of "their" authorized dealers for repairs. A manufacturer's warranty should be good throughout the country at any authorized dealer.

How to Get a "Clean" Quote When You're Shopping for a Lease

Most states in the United States have lease disclosure laws requiring that the selling price show up in the lease contract, so always ask to see the complete contract. Look at the actual selling price of the vehicle and make sure it is the same price you are getting.

Why It May Pay to Lease Your Car

We think leasing a car may beat buying one if you negotiate a good deal. Why sink tens of thousands of dollars into a purchase that is guaranteed to depreciate in value? A car

Dolan Ah-Ha!

From time to time 0% financing is offered to new car buyers. Don't be naive and *not* negotiate the price that you'll pay for the car thinking that the dealer is so wonderful for offering finance notes (0%) lower than you could get at a bank. It's the *manufacturer* offering the rebate, not the dealership. Negotiate *hard* . . . even if you're getting a sweet financing deal!

isn't an investment. The average consumer spends $125 a month in routine maintenance, not counting repairs, once a car reaches the ripe old age of three years, which not coincidentally is the term of most leases. The idea behind leasing is that you never plan to pay full price for the car; you just keep trading in your leased vehicle every three years (or less).

When you lease you are paying the bank's estimate of how much the car will depreciate by the end of the term. The residual value—the amount the bank anticipates the car will be worth when your lease expires—is the part you *don't* have to pay. The more the bank expects the car to be worth, the lower your monthly payments will be on the lease. As a result, you may be able to drive around in a more expensive car than you might be able to afford if you bought one. The bottom line is that when you lease, you put the burden of the future value of the vehicle on the bank instead of on yourself.

For this reason you should shop for a lease based on the **residual value** of the car. It changes four to five times during the model year of the car. **This is why it's better to lease a vehicle at the beginning of a model year, rather than toward its end.** As the year goes on, the banks lower their residual percentages because the vehicle is getting older, even if it has never been driven.

For current models, look in the Black Book, which comes out quarterly and is available in the auto loan departments of many banks, or go to the Automotive Leasing Guide online: www.alg.com, click on "Custom Residuals," and follow the directions for e-mailing the products department to request advance residual forecasts.

How Do You Know If You're Getting a Good Lease Deal?

"A good lease deal is like any other good deal, just with a few extra things to consider," says Weiss. Those "extra things" are:

1. *Remember what we talked about regarding residual value.* The more the bank guesses the vehicle will be worth at the end of the lease, the lower your payments are going to be. (Example: a $20,000 vehicle with a 50% residual value means your

When Should You Buy and When Should You Lease?

Listeners often ask us this question. The only rule of thumb is that there is no exact rule of thumb; it depends on your needs. Generally, however, if you can afford a new car, buying makes more sense. With a used car, you'll get a better deal by buying although it's worth researching leasing a used car. (See the section "How to Buy a Used Car Without Ending Up in the Scrap Heap.")

Buying used to be a better deal for people with shaky credit ratings. But in recent years it has become just as easy—if not easier—for nearly anyone to get financing for a lease, regardless of credit history.

However, if you can afford a new car and intend to keep it a long time, you will probably want to buy it. You can buy your leased car when the leasing period ends, but we don't recommend it in most cases.

One other reason to buy a new car might be that for a particular model from a particular dealer, you might get a better deal. This is by no means always the case; in fact, often leasing costs less. If you have a particular car in mind and you're torn, make these calculations to compare the costs:

1. Calculate the cost of buying a car: the down payment + monthly payments. This is Figure A.
2. Calculate the cost of leasing the same car: the down payment (if any) + monthly payments + purchase option (you can make a rough estimate of this based on the current price of three-year-old models of that car). This is Figure B.

Which figure is lower? That's the choice to go with. Remember, leasing is really just another form of financing. Either way, as long as you are paying for a car in monthly installments, the bank is the *real* owner!

payments will be based on $10,000. If another $20,000 vehicle had a 55% residual, then your payments would be based on only $9,000.)

2. *MILEAGE!* Make sure you lease a vehicle based on the actual mileage you are going to drive. Typically, you would get 10,000 to 15,000 miles a year without extra charges; that's somewhere around 36,000 allowed miles in a three-year lease. Yes, if you ask for extra mileage your payments are going to be higher, but only because your driving is depreciating the vehicle faster. Mileage charges are almost always cheaper when you buy them "up front" rather than paying for excess mileage at the end.

3. *Know the financial source!* Many dealers will use an institution other than the financial arm of the manufacturer (such as Ford Motor Credit, GMAC, etc.). Some of these "outside" banks are willing to gamble with higher residual values, which will result in lower payments. But do you really think banks are in the gambling business? Of course not. Many of these banks will beat you up at the end of a lease by charging you for every scratch, ding, and dent they can find! This is how they make up for what they lost in their "supposed" lower monthly payments . . . and often more! *Go with the manufacturer's financial source.* They are in the business of helping to sell cars. They know if they beat you up you'll never buy another car from their company again, so they always allow a more customer-friendly "normal depreciation" clause—a clause that is in every lease contract.

Should You Take Advantage of the Option to Buy When Your Lease Period Is Up?

NO, in most cases. Here's why:

Remember, the bank has already determined your payments based on what they guessed the residual (future) value of the vehicle would be. This is not a negotiable price, but a price set by the terms of the lease. However, that is part of what makes leasing a good deal. Start thinking about what you're going to do at least three months before your

What If Disaster Hits While You're Leasing?

Many of our listeners have called us asking if a lease is still valid if the lease holder dies. Can his survivors cancel the lease or are they responsible for it? Others have asked what to do when they lose a job and can't afford the payments. Is it possible to cancel the lease in dire circumstances?

The answer: You have to check the lease contract carefully *before* you sign it to see what (if any) circumstances would allow you to be released from the obligations. A lease, like any other financial contract, cannot be canceled. However, some financial institutions do offer a "death cancellation clause," which simply terminates the lease. Others, including outside companies, offer insurance for the same thing.

You can also sell off a lease. You might or might not be able to get a payoff amount comparable to the current value of the vehicle, but you might be better off selling at a loss than ruining your credit through a repossession.

Accept a lease only if the monthly payments are low enough that you can handle them if life should throw you a curveball. Check out www.leasetrader.com.

lease expires. Don't get caught being forced to make a last-minute decision! You can go to Kelley Blue Book (www.KBB.com) and www.autotrader.com to check out the car's value and begin to get an idea of whether the bank's guesstimate was on target or not.

If the bank was wrong and the vehicle is worth less than they predicted, you can, and certainly should, simply walk away from it.

If, on the other hand, you discover the vehicle is worth more than the bank anticipated, you could walk away the owner of a luxury car bought at a deep discount. Weiss suggests, however, that you consider *selling* the car instead of buying—and pocketing the profit. (You can sell a leased vehicle just like any other vehicle that has been financed. Some dealers will even use this as a selling point if the residual value is low.)

The consideration here is the wear and tear you'll have put on it. If the car is three years old, it might start to become a money pit—you know, one of those cars that might as well have a hole in the floor that you toss dollars down. The odds are that within the first year or two of owning the car you are going to have to start spending money on tires, brakes, and other maintenance measures, plus possible repairs.

Sometimes a manufacturer will come up with an inflated figure for the estimated residual value. It's called a subvented lease, and it moves slow-selling cars by making the monthly lease payments artificially low. If you find this is true of your contract, definitely turn in the car when the lease expires, or you'll be paying a lot more than the car is worth. If you really like the model, you'll be better off leasing a new model or buying an identical one at a used-car lot!

Our 10 Rules of Car Buying or Leasing

1. **Go into a showroom with an attitude.** Don't express enthusiasm about any vehicle; instead, challenge the salesman to prove to you why you should buy something on his floor.

2. **Never give a dealer your Social Security number or fill out any kind of application until you're ready to commit.** Once a dealer has information that they can use to check your payment history, credit rating, and so on, they *can and will* use it to negotiate with you. If you were late once with the payment on your last car, that might be ammunition in the car salesman's hands to say you don't qualify for the best of all possible terms.

    Naturally, you will have to produce your driver's license if you ask to take a test drive. But to keep the dealer from conducting a check on you based on your license number, insist that you sign a statement saying you are not authorizing a credit check.

3. **Shop at the right time**. The best time to buy or lease a car is at the end of the month or midweek, when business is typically slow. Other good shopping times include Christmastime and rainy days—whenever people would usually avoid visiting dealerships.

   You may have also heard that shopping at the end of the model year (June and July) is a good time to buy a car. That's true if you are *buying*. The dealer may be trying to unload leftover cars. However, when you are leasing, the best time to look for a new model is at the *beginning* of the model year, generally September. That's because the bank will have just estimated the residual value—the portion of the cost that you aren't paying for in your lease. You want the residual value to be high, because that will make the lease price lower, and the highest residual value is usually at the beginning of the model year. New residual guides come out at the start of every quarter of the year (January, April, June, and September). Often, if you wait three months, the residual value will have gone down and your lease will be more expensive. If you see a TV commercial announcing "blowout" prices for leases on models that have been out awhile, it may be a come-on!

4. **Find out how long the car has been sitting on the lot.** If a model's "days supply" exceeds 60 days, the dealer will be anxious to sell it. But remember, a vehicle is usually a slow mover because it is not well rated by consumer rating services. You can find out how long the model has been out in *Automotive News*, a trade publication that is available on some newsstands and in large public libraries. You can also find cars that a dealer is anxious to move by checking the white label on the driver's-side door or doorpost. It shows the month and year the car was made. The older it is, the longer the dealer has been paying to keep it on the lot. If your goal is to get the lowest price, keep an eye out for models the manufacturer is phasing out.

5. **Don't go it alone**. Always shop with a friend. It's harder for the salesmen to outnumber you, plus you'll have someone to help you negotiate. But pick a friend who isn't an impulsive shopper (and therefore likely to be a bad influence) and is willing to play "bad cop." A negative comment from your friend will drive the salesperson crazy! Script your shopping buddy, if necessary, to keep the salesmen off balance.

6. **Place an order**. You *may* get a better deal if you order a car rather than buying out of dealer inventory, which the dealer must finance. But remember, there's no financing for orders!

7. **Sell your "trade-in" elsewhere**. You'll get more money for your trade-in if you sell it privately or to a used-car dealer. Shop around. Trade-in $$$ at the dealership is sometimes smoke and mirrors! Also, keep in mind that a "like" dealer is often

going to offer you more. What do we mean by like? Well, if you were looking to trade in a Ford for a Honda (or vice versa), certainly a Honda dealer knows they are not going to get many used-vehicle shoppers looking for a Ford and are not going to be willing to go the "extra mile" on your trade to make a deal. However, if you visit a Ford dealer with a Ford vehicle and simply offer to sell it to them, they are more than likely going to offer you more than what the Honda dealer would.

8. **Don't buy high-profit items from the dealer.** That means most of the extras the dealer is chomping at the bit to sell you. Don't buy any of the following from the dealer:
   - rustproofing
   - glazing
   - undercoating
   - extended or service warranties
   - alarm/security system (buy these elsewhere—you'll save 50% or more off the dealer's price)

9. **Beware of low-interest-rate financing**. Many of those 1.9% and 2.9% deals are for two years only, after which you'll be making much higher payments than with a higher rate over a longer period. We're not saying don't finance with one of these deals, just be aware of the higher payments with the shorter-term loans.

10. **Remember: The MOST powerful negotiating tool any car buyer has is your ability to turn around and walk out of the showroom!** There are hundreds of dealerships with lots of cars for sale. Keep that positive attitude. Don't let them wear you down. Feel confident that you've done your homework and take control of the sales process.

How to Buy a Used Car Without Ending Up in the Scrap Heap

We've noticed a trend over the last few years: more and more people opting to buy used cars instead of new. And with record-high new-car prices, we can see why!

Aren't Used Cars a Risky Venture?

Not anymore. The quality and reliability of cars has generally improved since the late 1980s. A used car can be a good way to economize. The increasing popularity of leasing has filled used-car lots all over America with two- to three-year-old cars as leases expire. Previously leased cars entering the market sometimes offer as much or even better quality than a new model purchased several years ago. Granted, these cars are just entering the

Should You Pay a "Shopper" to Make a Deal for You?

If you're not comfortable negotiating, there are buying services that help, such as Car-Bargains, run by the Center for the Study of Services, in Washington, D.C. Contact Car-Bargains at 800-475-7283 or www.checkbook.org. For $190, the center's shoppers will do the legwork for you, gathering competitive bids from five dealers in your area.

If you're planning to lease a car, for $335 the center's LeaseWise service will get you bids on leases.

However, these services do not take into consideration the reliability and reputation of the dealer. "It's about the same as needing brain surgery and opening up the Yellow Pages to 'doctors,' closing your eyes, and letting your finger pick someone to perform the operation," says Weiss.

Well, we can't argue with that. We'd rather you get used to doing the legwork yourself. But if you do hire a "shopper," don't just assume that the lowest price they get is going to be the best deal. Before you buy, you should visit the dealers yourself and check out the terms thoroughly.

stage at which they begin to need maintenance and repairs, so look for a car that's still covered by a manufacturer's warranty (original or extended).

Where Can You Find the Best Deals?

Dealerships In spite of the hard sell and the polished techniques the salesmen use to lure you in, we think the most reliable source for used cars are new-car dealerships, provided, of course, that you read the preceding section of this chapter and go in with your "bull" detector on full alert. If you go to a new-car dealership that also sells used cars, chances are they are reselling their trade-ins. That may work to your advantage if the car has been checked out and repaired in the dealer's own service department before being offered for sale. They may also offer limited warranties. A reliable dealer will want to make you happy so that you'll bring repeat business—if you're really satisfied, maybe you'll buy your next new car there.

Used-car dealerships, on the other hand, tend to sell cars with higher mileage and more wear and tear than the trade-ins on the new-car dealer lots. The pricing in used-car superstores like CarMax and AutoNation USA can be nearly one percent higher than prices at franchised dealers. The cars tend to be rental and corporate fleet vehicles, which may have taken a beating at the hands of multiple drivers. It's fine to visit the superstores and take a printout, but then head over to your local dealer and see if you can cut a better deal.

Leasing Companies A recent major glut of used cars has made things very tough for many leasing companies when leased cars are returned to them. If the lessor doesn't buy that car at the end of the lease (and a lot of people don't) that leaves some nice bargains for the savvy buyer.

Car Rental Agencies Car rental agencies often sell older cars that have been with them around six months and have between 8,000 and 15,000 miles. Rental cars are notoriously abused by drivers, but this fact is also reflected in the price. You may be able to get an excellent deal. In fact one of the things to consider is that fleets of any kind generally maintain a vehicle more conscientiously than the average consumer does.

Newspaper classifieds are an iffy source. You might get a good price in a private sale, but if something goes wrong with the car you won't have much recourse. As with buying any used car, make sure you have the car checked out by a reputable mechanic whom you trust! Talk with your mechanic in advance. Usually a mechanic will check out the car for a fee of $100 or so, and report any repairs that might be needed. You can then either buy the car at a reduced price that takes into account the cost of the repairs, or walk away if the car doesn't seem to be in good shape.

How to Avoid Buying a Lemon

Wherever you take a serious look at a used car, follow these steps *before* you commit to buying:

- Test-drive the car and take it to a professional mechanic who is familiar with used-vehicle inspections. Be sure your mechanic lists the items he or she checks and get his or her opinion on the overall condition of the car.

    Ask the seller for the car's maintenance records. A person who kept good maintenance records probably took good care of the car.

Warranty Warning

If you are looking at a late-model used car, the odds are it will still be covered by the original factory warranty. But dealers make money from selling used-vehicle warranties, so they often don't bother to tell you that the used car has a balance left on the factory warranty.

Says Weiss: "Ask!"

But also ask exactly what the warranty covers. The emissions-control system is usually covered under the original warranty longer than the rest of the vehicle.

Get proof of past ownership. Many dealers will provide a vehicle history cost at no or low cost. A car's title history can be tracked with a single phone call.

- You can get a vehicle history report on any car registered anywhere in the United States or Canada through CARFAX, Inc. Call them during business hours at 800-444-0145, or check out a car online at www.CARFAX.com. You can get a report on one car for approximately $14.99 or unlimited reports for $19.99. CARFAX can also help verify that the odometer reading on the car you want to buy is accurate. CARFAX reports that of the cars they report on, 1 in 10 show a mileage discrepancy.
- Keep in mind that if the report turns up some problems, these problems become negotiating tools. You should either ask the dealer to have the problems fixed—without increasing the cost, of course—or insist on a lower price so that you can use the difference to have your own mechanic do the work that's needed.
- Check out www.autotrader.com to compare prices on used cars.

Buying and Leasing on the Internet

We are all for researching on the Internet and comparing features, prices, and options when you're considering what model might be right for you. But buying something as personal as a car is as risky as buying a house you've seen only in a picture on the Web: You're getting into a relationship, after all. (Would you marry by mail order?) It's important to sit in the car and test-drive it to see if it feels right. It's also important to see what you think of the dealer.

Yet there are now over 100 online car-buying services. See our list at the end of this chapter. If you are interested in a particular model but don't know much about it, you can post questions on the forum at *Car and Driver*'s site (www.caranddriver.com) and get feedback. Use the sites to search for the best prices, and use this information to bargain when you go to a dealership.

Best Strategies for Financing

The very best way to pay for a car is with cash *up front*. We're fans of this if you are going to buy a car, because it keeps you out of debt. And if you can live with a used car, it's far more affordable. When making an offer on a new car, offer the invoice minus manufacturer incentives. And remember, even 0% financing is usually just an illusion.

If you really *need* a big loan, we see that as one more reason to consider leasing instead of buying. You won't have to make a large down payment—so you can put the money that would have gone into a down payment into a real investment that will appreciate instead of depreciate.

Often, banks offer an almost no-interest (or in this case, lease-rate) loan on a lease if all the payments are made up front. Weiss told us a story about how his own step-father, who had always been a devout payer of cash for everything, got a better deal by leasing this way.

"He was buying my mom a $20,000 vehicle that happened to have a 50% residual value on a two-year lease," says Weiss. "The bank was offering 1.5% if the lease was paid up front."

The choice, then, was a simple one. He could give the dealer $10,300 right away and keep his other $10,000 for the next two years. Or he could pay a dealer $20,000 to buy the car. Figuring he could exceed that $300 by investing the extra $10,000 for two years, he leased for the first time!

But if you insist on buying a car with a loan, check out terms from many different sources before you accept dealer financing. At the very least, if you know a bank, a credit union, or an online lender is ready to give you a lower rate than the dealer, you might be able to talk the dealer into meeting the same terms—or offering you some special incentive such as zero down or no payments for a year.

As part of your new car financing process, you should check out online sources. At the end of this chapter, we list several sites worth the effort.

Start with the largest online vehicle lender, www.peoplefirst.com. It has a number of helpful features including the Interest Rate Tracker, free car and motorcycle insurance quotes from Progressive, free auto quotes from a dealer near you, and a $100 Loan Experience Guarantee.

Dolan Ah-Ha!

Speaking of auto financing . . . don't get overly excited by the prospect of "0% financing" ads that spring up when some auto manufacturers need to move unsold new car inventory.

The ad may draw you into the new car showroom (that's the idea, right?), but only those applicants with the best credit ratings (we estimate far less than 25% of applicants) will likely get those loans, or you may find that if you qualify, the loans may be of such a short duration that you can't afford the monthly payments.

Don't be so excited by the rate that you forget to negotiate a favorable price for the car. *Negotiate hard first* . . . then talk financing!!

In some cases, you may be better off taking a rebate rather than low-interest financing!

Go to www.edmunds.com, which has a calculator to help buyers compare no-interest and rebate offers.

How to Resolve Problems with Your New Car

Got a lemon on your hands? A lemon, according to the laws in most states, is defined as a new car in constant need of repair. "New" might mean anywhere from the first 12,000 to 24,000 miles of operation, or the first one to two years after the date of delivery to the original purchaser, usually specified as whichever comes first. If you suspect that your car is defective, or in some states that the seller monkeyed around with the odometer setting, you may be able to demand a refund or replacement from the dealer or manufacturer under your state's lemon laws. The dealer or manufacturer might be required to make anywhere from one to four attempts to fix the problem before you can demand action. Most often, the state law requires four attempts.

The laws vary greatly from state to state, however. Check out the coverage period and number of required repair attempts and days out of service for your state at www.autopedia.com. Get a summary of your state's laws and listings of lawyers prepared to go to bat for you at Lemon Law America, www.lemonlawamerica.com, which has links for every state. Most states make the manufacturer pay the legal fees if your car qualifies as a lemon. Also check out www.lemonaidcars.com.

We also recommend the Center for Auto Safety's Web site, www.autosafety.org, which has news of defects and recalls, information about lemon laws, lawyer referral links, and an online complaint form.

Keep copies of every receipt or document you get each time you attempt to have your car fixed. And if you believe you're entitled to a refund or replacement as discussed above, put your request in writing and send it to the dealer or manufacturer. You should also point out your state's lemon laws and explain why you think the problem is a violation.

Shopping for Car Insurance

If you have recently paid the latest premium of your car insurance, you won't mind a few ideas on how to save a few bucks, will you? Didn't think so. In addition to recommending a few good Web sites at the end of this chapter . . . a few ideas . . .

Your insurance agent may not tell you, but you, or a member of your family, may qualify for a discount if you:

- have a clear driving record for three years
- buy other types of insurance through the same company (home, life, etc.)
- have an anti-theft device/alarm in your car
- have more than one insured vehicle in your family

- increase your deductible (as we did) to $500 or $1,000 if you could afford to pay for that amount of damage.
- have a clunker. Does collision coverage still make sense?
- are already a member of a roadside assistance organization such as AAA. Do you need to pay for that kind of coverage from your insurance company?

And lastly, *shop around*. Get a bunch of quotes *before* you buy.

Selling Your Car for the Highest Profit

The Internet has made it easy to find out how much you should be able to charge when you're the seller. Of course, the buyer will try to negotiate with you, whether you're trading your old car in through a dealer or selling it privately. So here are some tips for getting a deal that will make you and your customer happy.

Start by checking out the market value of your car on a couple of sites. At www.Edmunds.com, the page marked True Market Value will give you pricing guidelines and an appraisal. On such sites as Edmunds or www.AutoTrader.com, you can conduct a search to see the asking prices for other cars of the same model and make as yours. Of course, the selling price will vary according to such factors as condition, mileage, and location.

*Resale Tips from Kurt Allen Weiss**

✓ If you have more than 15,000 miles per model year, you could lose dollars unless you sell it privately, in which case you may be able to tell prospective customers about your driving habits and how well you maintained your vehicle.

✓ Get the car in tiptop condition before you try to sell it, both inside and outside. Windshield damage, minor dents, little flaws in the interior, or dirt will almost always cost *you* far less to fix than the amount the dealer is going to want to subtract from your trade-in value.

✓ You get the best price from an automatic transmission; it can add $700 to $1,200 to your resale price, which is often less than the option cost to start with.

✓ A car without air-conditioning will lose an average of $1,000 to $2,500.

✓ Consumers who shop for luxury cars, even a used one, consider power windows and door locks a must.

✓ If the car isn't running well, have it checked out by an independent mechanic and get a written estimate of what is actually wrong and the cost to repair it. This will

---

* *Have I Got a Deal For You!*, pp. 34–35 and 42–44.

give you a good guideline to compare what the dealer or customer claims needs fixing and how much he'll want to deduct for those problems.

Negotiating With a Buyer

Now you're faced with a dealer who wants to pay as little as possible for your car, or a private customer who wonders if you're trustworthy. You have to be prepared to use that oldest sales technique in the books: overcoming all objections. Be honest and trustworthy, but be prepared to prove that your car is worth buying at the price you want.

Your best defense is to have a car that's in good shape and be ready to prove it. Pull out all of your old maintenance and repair records and offer to show them to anyone who is interested. Get a checkup from your mechanic and ask him to give you a report summarizing the car's condition. Let prospective buyers see the report; that way no one can walk away from the deal on the grounds that "I'm not sure about the condition of the car."

Never throw out the records and receipts for maintenance and repairs on your car, or for parts you've bought. Keep all of these papers in a file—one for each car if you own more than one—and be prepared to show them to any prospective buyers. We think the best way to short-circuit any concerns the buyer might have about trusting you is to have the car inspected by a certified mechanic and have the valuation report ready for the potential buyer to see.

Let the buyer test-drive your car. You should also let the buyer have the car inspected by his or her mechanic to prove you have nothing to hide.

Have a contract ready so that you can sign it as soon as someone makes an offer that you accept.

What If You Run Into Complications?

Many things can and do go wrong when someone buys a car from you.

You do have to be firm about your terms. A buyer might, for example, agree to meet your price only if you will take care of some needed repairs first. This sort of agreement can lead to misunderstandings that may haunt you for months, so it's best not to accept this offer. Sell your car when it's in good running order, but if it does need repairs, say so in your ad and let the prospective buyer have a list of the problems that need attention. Your ad should say—in readable print—that you are selling the car "as is." Remind the buyer of this before you close the deal.

On the other hand, what if the prospective buyer's mechanic finds a flaw that your mechanic overlooked? That can be tricky. The older the car, the more problems a mechanic is likely to find. Depending on how valid you think the repair is, you could do one of the following:

1. Propose to reduce the price by the amount needed for the repair.
2. Propose that you pay for half the repair and the buyer pays for the other half.
3. Take the car back to your mechanic—or to a third mechanic—for more evaluation.

You will have to be the one to decide the terms and stand by them. If the problem isn't a safety concern and the car drives well, you might have to point out that an old car is rarely in perfect condition, and this is your price, take it or leave it.

Car Repair Rip-Offs to Avoid Like the Plague

We've heard of mechanics switching spark plug wire connections to prevent a car from starting so that the car owner will pay for an engine overhaul. Sure, there are honest mechanics, but unless you know a repair shop well, be suspicious of anything they tell you there.

Take matters into your own hands from the day you bring your new (or new-used) car home with a careful reading of the owner's manual. If you follow the information about such factors as type and weight of oil to use in various seasons, proper maintenance intervals, maximum load you can carry, proper shift points if the transmission is manual, you'll be able to avoid many problems in the first place. Also follow the warranty requirements for maintenance and change your oil every 3,000 to 5,000 miles (sooner if you drive in heavy city traffic).

No matter how well you know your car, however, unscrupulous or incompetent mechanics sneak into nearly every car owner's life at least once. You can find a mechanic who gives you excellent service for a year or more just to win your trust, then hits you with an expensive repair that doesn't solve the car's problem. We have a friend whose trusted mechanic told him the right front wheel was vibrating because it needed a new hub and ball bearings, to the tune of $350. Our friend decided to get a second opinion and took the car to a service station, where the attendant filled the tire with air and stopped the vibrating on the spot! Or you can find yourself stranded out of town with a car problem, and at the mercy of a mechanic who figures he might as well take you for all he can because he'll never see you again.

Wherever you are, before you agree to any repairs, put everything in writing, including the problem you've experienced, the mechanic's diagnosis, and the estimated cost of fixing it.

Ask to see all replaced parts, along with the box the new part came in. You want to be sure the new part is the same quality as the old one. As long as you have name-brand parts in your car, your auto company cannot refuse to honor the warranty.

The best way to avoid getting ripped off, however, is to go in armed. You can travel prepared so that you can come across as an informed consumer even if you've broken down in the middle of the Texas panhandle on a 102-degree day and you don't know a soul for miles around. Ask your mechanic, and look on car Web sites, for the going rates for common repair jobs. Keep a list of these prices in your glove compartment. While prices can vary, and will be more in a big city than a small town, your knowledge will let every service manager know that you are playing hardball.

Never, never, never utter any of these sentences when you're in a repair shop:

- "I don't know anything about cars."
- "I don't care how much it costs, just fix it."
- "I have no idea what's wrong—it just wouldn't start." Take a guess, just to show you know car terminology.

Helpful Web Sites and Books

Negotiating With a Car Dealer

Have I Got a Deal for You! How to Buy or Lease Any Car Without Getting Run Over, by Kurt Allen Weiss. Order through www.kwproductions.com; $12.99.

Women: Learn "Garagese" and Fight Back

If you're a woman with a car, you probably feel that you haven't come that far, baby, when you enter a service garage. You might be the chief executive of a corporation, but mechanics still think they can take advantage of women in ways they would never dare try with men. Isn't it outrageous that so many otherwise high-powered women are afraid to take their own cars to a service station without bringing along a man to do the talking?

An automotive consultant named Mary Jackson runs a Web site designed to keep women informed about cars and how to deal with repairs, including a glossary of "garagese" terms everyone should know and a schedule of empowerment seminars around the country. Check out the site at www.womenatthewheel.com.

**Consumer Information on Dealer Invoices;
Buying, Leasing, and Selling New and Used Cars**

www.autobytel.com

www.autotrader.com

www.autoweb.com

Car and Driver—www.caranddriver.com

www.carbuyingtips.com

www.CARFAX.com

Microsoft Carpoint—http://carpoint.msn.com

www.cars.com

www.Edmunds.com (has an alliance with General Motors)

www.fightingchance.com

Kelley Blue Book—www.kbb.com

Guides to buying and leasing cars are available at the Federal Consumer Information Center Web site: www.pueblo.gsa.gov

Leasing

www.bankrate.com

www.intellichoice.com

www.leaseguide.com

Selling a Lease

www.leasetrader.com

www.leaseterminate.com

Online Sales

www.autosite.com

http://dealernet.com

The Auto Dealer's Point of View

www.autotown.com

Car Research and Roadside Assistance for Members

www.autovantage.com

Research and Ratings on Models

Consumer Reports Cars and Trucks—http://www.consumerreports.org/Categories/CarsTrucks/

Research on specific cars by title

www.CARFAX.com

Financing

www.peoplefirst.com
www.eloan.com
www.lendingtree.com

Excessive Car Trouble

The Center for Auto Safety—www.autosafety.org

http://autopedia.com/#LemonLaw

www.carlemon.com has links to "lemon laws" in each state

www.lemonaidcars.com

To Check the History of Safety Recalls on a Particular Make

Call the U.S. Department of Transportation Safety Hotline at 800-424-9393, or go to the Web site at www.nhtsa.dot.gov.

You can also check safety history on www.autosafety.org and www.lemonaidcars.com.

Women and Cars

www.womenatthewheel.com

Car Rentals

www.bankrate.com

www.hotwire.com

www.bestfares.com

www.travelocity.com

www.expedia.com

Auto Insurance

www.bankrate.com

www.Insweb.com

www.Insurance.com

www.Insure.com

www.quotesmith.com

SECTION II

Finance and Family Life

CHAPTER 7

Family Finances

LET'S GET ONE THING STRAIGHT before you read this chapter: We're not out to tell you how to bring up your kids. But a healthy example of sound money management is one of the most important gifts you can give them. "Managing" a child's money smarts through elementary school, adolescence, college, and early adulthood takes vast reserves of energy, but the rewards are priceless.

When our daughter, Meredith, was growing up, we were determined to teach her more about money matters and responsibility than our parents had taught us. (Sound familiar?) Still, we'll never forget when she got her first paycheck from a part-time job. She stared in horror at the net sum, then said, "Why is so much taken out for taxes? There's practically nothing left!" Welcome to reality, kid!

Let's start at *our* beginning. . . .

We were pressed for money when our daughter was on the way. The centerpiece of our living room—we were still in our bare-bones first apartment—was a big promotional Cinzano bottle that Daria put in a prominent spot on the floor, and we started throwing all of our spare change into that bottle. We managed to amass $400 toward the cost of Meredith's delivery.

That was in 1972. Today we can't imagine a bottle large enough to hold the thousands of dollars in spare change you'd need to go to the hospital and deliver a baby. We hope *you* have health insurance to cover it.

Then there are those prospective parents who go through heroic measures to have a baby. We get calls from people who want to adopt children—a $20,000-and-up proposition.

TIMPANOGOS HIGH SCHOOL

Why Johnny Can't Save

Jean Sherman Chatzky, in her column "Money Talk" in the July 2002 issue of *Money* magazine, reported that 85% of high school students aren't getting any school-based personal finance information. The JumpStart Coalition for Personal Financial Literacy (www.jumpstart.org), a group founded in 1997 in Washington, D.C., to promote personal finance education, administers a test to high school seniors that, over the years, has found that on average students get no more than 57% of the questions right, indicating a fairly abysmal lack of understanding of such subjects as saving, spending, insurance, investing, and credit.

We hear of couples who can't conceive without tens of thousands of dollars in fertility treatments, single women and lesbian couples pondering the costs of artificial insemination, women over 45 considering donor eggs, gay male couples looking into having a child by surrogate. We hear from people on their second marriage who already have children from first marriages but want to have another baby or two to cement this new "blended" family.

Any way you look at it, Kids = Expenses. The American family survives, and even thrives, against all possible odds, but it takes *mucho moolah* to start and maintain a family. The U.S. government has calculated the cost of raising a child from birth to the age of 18 as a whopping $160,140 for a middle-income family. Talk about sticker shock! Consider that this is the cost before you even begin to touch college tuition. We felt better about the cost, however, when we broke it down. It translates to $8,896.66 a year, $741.38 a month, $171.08 a week, or just $24.24 a day. You can manage that, can't you, in return for having your heart swell with pride and love every time you hold your child's hand?

If we were talking about anything else, we'd say wait until you can afford it. But you can't always postpone the arrival of a baby. And let's be realistic—who is going to let a little thing like money get in the way?

What we will say, though, is that if you want to start a family or add to an existing one, all of our advice about living on a budget (or, rather, a success plan)—steering clear of debt; avoiding getting overextended with too many houses, cars, and other grown-up toys—all of this advice applies, quadrupled.

By the way, whatever your income level, it still isn't a bad idea to find some large vessel and throw spare change in whenever you can. Make it a little secret stash. You'll be surprised at how it will add up. We *still* keep a stash!

When Meredith was a child, we started putting some money into mutual funds for her. We didn't think she was particularly concerned about the value of her investments . . . until the morning after October 19, 1987. Remember that day known as "Black Monday," when the Dow Jones Industrial Average plunged by 22.6% and a five-year bull market came to a screeching crash? Meredith, who had just turned 15, walked into the kitchen, where we were preparing breakfast, and asked us, "So how much money did I lose yesterday?"

Children and adolescents hear about bad news in the world and carry all of the weight on their fragile shoulders. More children than adults suffered post-traumatic stress syndrome in the year following the September 11 terrorist attacks. We wish we had a prescription for all of the world's ills. But we *can* tell you how to help your children feel more secure in insecure times by showing them that you are in control of your finances and teaching them how to be money-savvy.

Kids who learn early on how to properly manage their money have greater self-esteem and a sense of independence. Bad money habits may lead to problems in other parts of their lives later.

It's never too early to talk to your kids about financial responsibility. Just how early? You can start talking to kids about money as soon as they understand the concept. For example, when they reach age five or six, you can say to them, "This toy or candy bar costs so much money." You can use Monopoly or real money.

But this above all: Kids are copycats, so parents had better practice what they preach. Show them how to be money-savvy by spending and investing wisely *yourself* and by saying no both to yourself and to them when something is too expensive.

Money Moves When You "Blend" Families

More than 40% of all weddings today involve a bride or bridegroom (or both) who has been married before. If remarriage is in the cards for you, and you have children from

These Kids See Where the Money Goes

A listener from Wisconsin called us one day with a wonderful story. She and her husband cash their paychecks every two weeks and bring the cash home. Then, with their two kids, they sit at the kitchen table and reduce their pile of "pay cash" each time they write out a check to pay a bill. The kids' allowances are subtracted from the pile, as are grocery tabs and their other living expenses.

This is an excellent lesson for the kids. Mom and Dad are working hard, as indicated by the stack of cash. The kids feel financially secure, but they also see exactly where the money is going, and the importance of budgeting and planning.

TIMPANOGOS HIGH SCHOOL

your first marriage, or your new mate does, or both of you do, don't let your joy at finding a fresh start in life be tempered by worries about how to juggle the finances of two half-families and merge them into a new entity. (Yes, it's a little like launching a new corporation through a merger.) Our advice applies to all blended families, whether you're getting married or simply moving in together, whether you're a straight couple or a gay couple. (See Chapter 9 for more advice about handling your finances during and after a divorce.)

Whatever your situation, get your financial house in order from the start. Sit down with your future partner and discuss your present and prospective financial obligations, your assets, and your debts. This isn't a conversation any couple looks forward to. Talking about the potential death of a spouse before the marriage even begins, as well as what you'd do if you and your new spouse ever split up, is no fun. But as unpleasant as all of this might seem, it's absolutely necessary. To help you get started, here are the questions you should discuss *before* you move your blended family under one roof:

- ✓ What assets and debts do each of you bring to the marriage? Don't hold anything back from each other! If you don't feel comfortable telling this person about your money secrets, why are you with him/her? And be sure to discuss any ongoing support you're giving to (or receiving from) a former spouse or children from a former marriage.
- ✓ How will you treat property that each of you already owns? Will this property be held in your name, your spouse's name, or jointly?
- ✓ How will you treat property acquired during your marriage—including any increase in the value of property you each already own?
- ✓ How will you divide up the value of your pensions and Social Security? Will you each keep your own pension or be entitled to a share of your spouse's account?
- ✓ What claim will a former spouse or children from a prior marriage have on your assets, assets held jointly, and any assets acquired during your new marriage? If you are concerned, sit down with a lawyer and discuss the issue.
- ✓ How will each of you revise your wills? Work out a new estate plan (see p. 204) that addresses the needs of your new spouse, your children, other family members, and, if either of you is paying alimony or child support, the needs of the ex-spouse. If you have minor children, you should will your assets to them either through a trust or an annuity. Don't take a chance of willing it to them through their other parent. Even though it's legal to do that, and even though you might trust your ex-spouse, think of what could happen if he or she remarries and the new spouse, who might also have children from a previous marriage, gets hold of your estate. If your children are over 18, you can name them outright as the beneficiaries of your estate.

✓ Does either of you have an inheritance? Are you going to share this with the new family? You could be punished for your generosity if your new spouse is paying alimony and his ex finds out about this increase in assets! If that is the case, consider putting the money into a trust. That way your new spouse can access the interest, but the principal will go to your children. Or you could ask your spouse to waive any rights to the money.

✓ Ditto a business. If you run your own business, is your new spouse going to work with you as a partner or an investor? If not, you should purchase business continuation insurance.

Dolan Bottom Line

Federal law says your spouse is the sole beneficiary of your pension or profit-sharing plan (which probably makes up a big chunk of your estate), unless he or she waives those rights in writing after you are married.

✓ How will you handle your home in your will? If you have children from your first marriage, you probably want them to inherit your home ultimately, yet if your second spouse (their stepparent) survives you, he or she might want to remain in the house. A "life estate" (see next page) may be the best way to ensure that your spouse has a home for the rest of his or her life, and then, once your spouse dies, your home goes to your children. This is not to say it ensures harmony in every blended family, but if you don't set up a trust, your home may automatically go to your surviving spouse upon your death, and then to your spouse's heirs.

✓ How should your life insurance proceeds and pension be distributed? Do you want your children to get your life insurance and your spouse to get everything else? Or will the proceeds be divvied up? If you are paying alimony or child support, your life insurance could replace that money if you should die.

The Prenuptial Agreement

Did you guess what was coming? If either you or your future spouse has children from a previous marriage, we urge you to sign a prenuptial agreement that spells out all of your property, insurance, and inheritance agreements. The agreement should specify how your separate and marital property will be handled should you divorce.

You'll first need to gather together the following documents:

What Is a Life Estate?

It's a gift of your principal residence to your next of kin, usually your children. You deed the house to your children but continue to live on the property. You become eligible for an income tax deduction for the value of the property. You can elect to spread the deduction over a period of up to six years, and you pay no capital gains tax on any appreciation of the property. When your spouse dies, or if you outlive your spouse, your home goes to all of your children. The children cannot sell the house as long as you or your spouse are living there.

Legally speaking, a life estate is an efficient transfer of property. Emotionally, however, it may be a different story. You have to examine your case and consider the repercussions. Do your children get along with their stepparent? If you died and your new spouse occupied the house—possibly with his or her own children, and possibly with a new partner—would your children be furious? It's important to discuss the situation with your entire family. See an estate-planning attorney to work out this and other aspects of your estate.

- Deeds for any property you own
- Statements from all checking and savings accounts
- Statements from brokerage accounts and mutual fund families
- Statements from pension plans and IRA accounts
- Statements from credit card accounts
- Outstanding mortgage or consumer loan notes

Draw up your prenuptial agreement at least 2–3 months before your wedding so that no one can say that either of you signed the agreement under duress. In addition, make sure that both you and your future spouse have your own attorneys. To find an attorney near you who handles prenuptial agreements, contact your state bar association's referral service. You can get the number for your state bar through the American Bar Association at 312-988-5000, or go to the ABA's Web site, www.abanet.org. Or go to www.lawyers.com.

Your Estate Plan

As with any new marriage, we think it's important to review your estate plan and make provisions for your children—and your stepchildren if you have any. In addition to a prenuptial agreement and a will, we suggest you consider a trust, because it is more detailed and therefore harder to contest than a will. (See Chapter 12.) You may change investments, terms, or beneficiaries at any time. A revocable living trust is best if you want to pass your estate on to your heirs quickly and in the way you wish. You choose a trustee who, when you die, will distribute your estate exactly as you wish.

If you want your spouse to receive financial support from your trust and then have your assets distributed after you're both gone, a qualified terminable interest property trust (QTIP) is a possible solution. The trust is managed by the surviving spouse and a co-trustee. The survivor gets income from the trust and may even take some of the principal (with the co-trustee's approval). But the surviving spouse can't change the beneficiaries, who will receive the full assets of the trust, often free of federal estate taxes, after the second spouse dies. By making your children the beneficiaries, you protect them from being disinherited by a stepparent in the event that your widowed spouse remarries someone with gold-digging inclinations.

When Baby Makes Three

Lots of things change when you have a baby. Here are seven Smart Money Moves to make now to take care of your growing family:

1. *Review your life insurance.* Make sure you both have enough insurance so you or your surviving spouse can continue making mortgage payments, fund your child's education, and meet other household expenses in case one of you dies. Buy coverage equal to at least five times your current salary. Term insurance is likely to be your best buy. (See Chapter 10.)
2. *Review your beneficiaries.* Consider naming your child as a contingent beneficiary on any life insurance or pension plan in case you and your spouse die at the same time.

Dolan Bottom Line

Update your trust whenever there is a life-changing event, such as a remarriage or a birth of a grandchild or, God forbid, a divorce. Otherwise, revisit your trust every five years or so to make sure it's up-to-date. This is tricky stuff, so don't go it alone—and no "do-it-yourself" kits. It's well worth the money to have an experienced estate-planning attorney help you set up an estate plan that is best for you and your family.

Dolan Bottom Line

Don't let any fast-talking insurance agent talk you into buying life insurance on your child's life. We can think of only two situations in which we'd make an exception:

1. If your child has a physical or mental condition that *might* make it difficult for him to qualify for insurance later in life, buying a policy now might make sense.
2. If you have a child who is the star of a hot new sitcom and the whole family's fortunes would take a nosedive if something happened to your most precious of Hollywood properties. We have had calls from many parents who are hopeful that their child will "make it" as a model or actor. In our opinion, that's not sufficient reason to insure a child's life.

3. *Add your baby to your health coverage.* You usually have 30 days from your child's date of birth to add your child to your policy without having a medical exam. If you and your spouse have insurance plans at work, go with the policy that offers the broadest benefits, even if it's more expensive.

4. *Review your estate plans.* Both you and your spouse should update your wills so that you may name a guardian for your child. This is also a good time to double-check how you want to distribute your assets. You should also consider creating a trust. Should you and your spouse both die, the trust would be funded using assets from your estates. The trust would then pay your child's guardian money to cover the expense of continued care. (See Chapter 12.)

5. *Consider the tax consequences, which for once will be in your favor.* You get a deduction for every child you claim as a dependent. The child must be under 19, related to you by birth or adoption, unmarried (let's hope so!), and a U.S. citizen or a resident of the United States, Canada, or Mexico for some part of the year. Also you must have provided more than half of your child's total support for the year.

Depending on your income, you may also be able to claim a child tax credit on your federal return for every dependent child who is a U.S. citizen or resident. The amount of the credit will rise from $600 through 2004 to $700 from 2005 to 2008, $800 in 2009 and $1,000 in 2010. What happens after that depends on whether the President and Congress vote to renew this provision of the Tax Relief Act of 2001.

But to reap the tax advantages, you have to be prepared *before* you file. Apply for a Social Security number as soon as possible after your baby is born. The IRS has to have a record of his or her identity. To apply, file form SS-5 with the Social Security

Administration. You can get the form online at www.ssa.gov/online/forms.html, or find the office nearest you online at www.ssa.gov/reach.htm or by calling 800-772-1213 (800-325-0778 for the hearing-impaired). Security rules implemented last year will delay the card by up to 3 months if you wait until after the child's first birthday.

6. *Take advantage of a flexible spending account (FSA)* if your employer provides this very helpful shelter for some of your most crucial expenses. This account lets you set aside money before taxes are taken out to pay for doctors' and hospital bills not picked up by your insurance, plus day-care expenses.

7. *Our only other advice in this area is to enjoy every minute you can with your children.* They grow up so fast. It seems like yesterday that Meredith was riding her tricycle in front of our house, and now she's married.

Taxes and Children 101

- Divorce breeds complications when it comes to taking the tax deduction for dependents. Generally, the custodial parent gets to claim the children as dependents. If you're a single or divorced parent and did not live with the other parent at all during the last half of the year, you will have to prove that you qualify as the head of household. This means you must have paid more than half the household expenses for yourself and your child, and generally, the child must have lived with you for more than half the year. If your ex-partner or a relative pays a portion of your child's support, calculate whether you paid more than half the support. Special rules apply in a divorce or separation, however, so ask your accountant about the best way to proceed.

- If your adjusted gross income is $155,860 or less, if you adopt a child you receive a tax credit of up to $10,930 per child for the expenses associated with the adoption, such as court costs, adoption fees, and travel. If your income for the year falls within the eligibility phase-out range of $155,860 to $195,860, you may still receive some tax credits that can be applied to your expenses. If you adopt a special-needs child, you are entitled to the tax credit whether or not you have qualified adoption expenses.

- If both parents work, or one parent works and the other is either disabled or a full-time student, you can claim a percentage of the first $3,000 you spend on child care for one child or $6,000 if you are paying for care for two or more children, depending on your income. The income threshold is low but will rise gradually. A family with two children and an income of more than $43,001 in 2004 will be able to claim a tax credit of $1,200, or 20% of the first $6,000 spent on child care.

- You can shelter college savings from taxes by contributing to a "529" account or a Coverdell Education Savings Account. See the "Saving for College" section. Heed our warning, Mom and Dad (and grandparents)—start investing for college *early*! We can't tell you how many times a parent has called our show asking how to invest for college for their 16- or 17-year-old child. It's too late! (At least for the first tuition payment.)

The Mommy and Daddy Track

A common dilemma our listeners face these days is: "to work or not to work." A recent caller regaled us with a complicated assessment of whether it made sense, tax-wise, to return to work after the birth of her twins. "If I go back to work, I'll make X," she said. "But with heavy taxes and the cost of day care, I'll net so little, maybe it makes more sense, for my children's benefit, to just stay home until they're in preschool."

Once your first baby arrives, you, too, may find yourselves facing an emotion-wrought decision about whether you're both going to keep working. That's about as gender-neutral as we can get, but in reality, it's usually the new mom who has to make that decision, not that there's any reason a new dad can't stay home and take care of the baby. If Mom happens to be on a high-powered career track and bringing home most of the bacon, that may be the case.

Either way, many financial considerations come into play here. Can you afford to have one parent stay home with the children for a few years? Can you afford not to?

Consider the long-term consequences of quitting work:

- ✓ You will put a dent in your Social Security and retirement benefits down the road.
- ✓ The corporate world still doesn't quite get it: Women who leave a high-paying job to raise children often have trouble regaining ground. You might have to return to the workforce with a loss of job status and a lower salary. There are solutions to this problem, of course, such as starting your own business. But if your career is really important to you, the hiatus might be a tough blow—unless, of course, you discover that being with your children is a far more rewarding experience than any corner office.
- ✓ All kinds of studies have shown that the dynamics of a marriage can change when a wife stops earning money. She might feel that she's turned all of the decision-making power over to her husband.

On the other hand, lots of mothers find it hard to leave a small child alone with a care-taker. If you have a child who cries and can't understand why you're abandoning him every morning *and* you're paying out the nose for the whole painful experience—sit down and assess the whole situation. Add up all of the costs, monetary and emotional, long-term and short-term, and make your decision based on what works for your career goals and your family.

By the way, for resources that will help you find child care, and a wealth of information that will help you evaluate what kind of child-care services are best for you, from community day-care centers to live-in nannies, we *love* the site www.edaycare.com.

How to Bring Up Money-Savvy Kids

We saw our own contemporaries bring up their children with some pretty unrealistic ideas about money—for the most part, our generation thought money was a grown-up matter, and their little darlings should be denied nothing. Wonder why so many kids now in their twenties and thirties are living on credit cards? We were the exception, and we still believe it's never—we repeat, never—too early to teach your children about money. And so much to teach them: how to spend it wisely, how to save it, how to invest it, how to earn it, how to keep out of debt.

About spending and saving. You can lecture a child on thrift and responsibility until you're blue in the face, but children learn money skills strictly by the example their parents set for them. So if you're buying anything and everything and wondering how you're going to make the next credit card payment while at the same time telling your children to save a little out of their allowance, it isn't going to work.

If you have been overspending, it's time for some soul-searching. Is the high-definition TV that the kids want going to cut into money that you could be saving toward college? Why are you giving in? Many parents spend out of guilt. Both parents are working, or the parents are divorced, and because time with the kids is in short supply, they try to compensate with things. Isn't it better to spend a little high-quality time with them imparting high-quality lessons in how to be financially secure in this crazy world? You bet it is!

Even if you *are* able to give your kids the moon, it's important that they learn money skills themselves. The only way to do this is to give them realistic amounts of their own money to handle. That usually comes in the form of a weekly allowance. Insist that they spend their own allowance on some items, so that they'll understand the value of money. Encourage them to save a portion of it. Don't tie an allowance to chores, but allow the children to perform some jobs and pay them extra for that. And if the child decides to rake

The best word you can use with your child when it comes to purchases is a good old-fashioned "NO."

Going into debt for the immediate gratification of buying things today kills off future dreams and goals, especially for your children—and to say the least, presents a bad money lesson for them.

leaves for some extra cash and he strews them throughout the yard, don't pay him. This is another lesson—in doing a job and doing it properly.

Here is the Dolan plan for teaching money smarts at each stage of development, in a nutshell:

Ages 4–5 Start giving them pocket change. Let them spend their own money on gum or candy. Explain to them that if you buy the candy bar with this dollar, you will get back this amount!

Ages 6–8 On day one of first grade, establish an allowance so that you may begin to teach the concepts of savings, budgeting, and spending skills—the basics of sound money management. Give a weekly unconditional allowance. The main purpose here is to learn how to manage money, so don't withhold the allowance as a punishment.

Don't give extra allowance in exchange for chores. You can, however, assign tasks to your children and pay them extra if they complete the task to your satisfaction.

By all means, let them spend their money for those extra items they want.

When your child reaches the age of eight, we recommend buying her one share of stock in a highly visible company, such as a toy company or brand-name manufacturer. You can then show your child how to follow the stock in the newspaper. Plus she gets to see how supply and demand can boost share prices.

Ages 9–10 Teach kids about advertising. Teach them about marketing ploys and pricing premiums. Tell them that if you get one "free" when you buy one extra, it isn't necessarily the best deal.

Talk to them about paying bills for the house. Let them spend time with you while you are writing out the checks. Reinforce the notion that the bills must be paid on time and that there is a penalty involved if you are late.

It's also important to learn to say "No." Just because Sally next door has this doll or pair of shoes, it doesn't mean your children have a right to them as well.

These are the ages when your children should set up their own savings accounts with the money they are, ideally, putting aside. This is easy if you live in a small town or city. If you live in a big city, check to see what the minimum deposit is. You might need to go to one of the smaller banks. This is a good time to explain to them how interest works by showing them the banking statement. One good lesson to teach is that "interest" is your friend. If they want the Air Jordan sneakers, and it's more than you wanted to spend, then give them the amount you were prepared to spend, put it in the savings account, and let them earn enough interest until they can afford the Air Jordans! (Whatever happened to 1995 high-tops—the last of the reasonably priced sneakers?)

Ages 12–13 Teach them about "risk and reward." This is a good time to teach them about the stock market. Pick a stock in a company they like—for example, Nike, Toys "R" Us, or the Gap. Tell them that by owning shares of stock, you own a piece of the company. Track the stock with them every week in the newspaper so that you can teach them about the ups and downs of the market. Point out that by owning more, you can make more if the company does well, but also lose more if the company does poorly.

Ages 14–15 This is a good time for them to get a part-time job, a new responsibility.

Ages 16–18 Get them a credit card. Make sure there is a $500 limit. Tell them they have to get authorization from you before they make charges. Have the credit card issuer send duplicate bills, one copy to your teenager and one copy to you, so that you can keep track of the charges and payments. Have your teenager sit down with you as you write the check to pay off the balance.

A Great Credit Card for College Students

You want your 18-year-old to learn how to handle a credit card responsibly, but you don't want this lesson to be learned the hard way, with heavy debts. Try the MasterCard offered through College Parents of America (www.collegeparents.org), a resource and advocacy organization for parents of college students. With this card, you can set the credit limit (as mentioned above, we recommend a maximum of $500) and monitor the way your child is using the card through a Web site or toll-free phone number. The card has no annual fee and an interest rate of 12% to 15%.

Now, About That Allowance . . .

How much allowance should you give a child? That depends on how much you can afford and what things cost where you live. A good rule of thumb: Give enough allowance for your child to be able to buy a few candy bars or a toy without having to hoard for weeks, but not so much that they're able to buy every Sega Genesis cartridge the minute it hits the store.

Here is our **Suggested Weekly Allowance** according to your child's age. (Don't you wish you could get a raise just for getting older?)

6–8-year-old	$3
9–11-year-old	$4
12–13-year-old	$8
14–15-year-old	$15
16–19-year-old	$30

Talk with your child about how much allowance you'll be paying—and what that money must cover. It's okay to include enough money so your child pays for school lunches and Scout dues from his or her allowance, but be sure to include a discretionary sum, too. Cash that she can use any way she wants is the real learning tool.

Review your child's allowance once a year to keep it in line with changing needs and costs. (Meanwhile, don't bail her out if she overspends.) Gradually give your child a larger allowance and a freer rein on spending.

The early teens are a good time to switch from a weekly allowance to a monthly one so your teen will learn to budget money over longer periods of time. You should also increase the allowance to allow him to cover most, or all, of his clothing costs and entertainment expenses.

Above all else, don't set narrow rules on how your child should spend his allowance. Let your child make the decisions—and the mistakes. Your child's early experience with managing money will teach unforgettable lessons.

But how does a kid keep track of where the money goes? We recommend the Parent-Banc Checkbook for Children, for ages six and up. It's a kit that includes a novel kind of checkbook in which you're the banker and your child is the customer. You credit your child's allowance as a "direct deposit" in your child's account. (Your wallet stands in for the bank's vault.) When your child needs money, he or she writes you a check. Every time you accept a deposit or "cash" a check, use the opportunity to talk with your child about money, including the relationship between income and spending. It retails for about $14.95. For a list of stores in your area that carry it, call ParentBanc at 800-373-3333 or go to the Web site, www.parentbanc.com.

Help your child save a portion of his or her allowance. Start by opening a bank account in your child's name. Ask your bank about special accounts for young savers. These accounts usually waive fees and minimum-balance requirements. Watching interest build up on his or her savings is a great way to learn the power of compounding. You will probably have to cosign to open the account.

Dolan Bottom Line

Make sure your child's Social Security number is used as the account's tax identification number. That way, as long as your child is under age 14, interest earned will be taxed at your child's lower tax rate, not at your tax rate. This rule holds true as long as your child earns less than $1,400 a year in interest.

Teaching Your Child About Investing

Here's a legacy they will use their whole lives.

In Chapter 5 we talked about some online investment plans that allow you to buy just one stock at a time and reinvest the dividends through a dividend reinvestment plan (DRIP). This is a *great* way to make an investment for a child. As Internet-savvy as today's children are, they'll probably want to complete the transaction themselves.

Check out either of these sites:

www.firstshare.com For a $30 annual membership fee, plus a few extra dollars for referrals and handling fees, First Share allows you to buy stocks that offer DRIPs in quantities as small as one share at a time.

www.sharebuilder.com Sharebuilder will carry out investment transactions for a small fee, with three different plans available and no minimum investment required, so that you can buy just one or two shares at a time.

We also recommend:

Kids' Money

www.kidsmoney.org This is a no-nonsense multilingual site that sells money games and gives advice. The simple graphics and articles about teaching money management are geared more to parents, but kids over 10 will enjoy going through the lists of moneymaking ideas, some of which are quite creative. (Take other kids' pictures. Take pet pictures. Make greeting cards.)

KidStock

www.kidstock.com A lively site for parents and kids that covers the basics of investing and how to buy stocks and bonds. We like the inspiring facts and figures: "Did you know that if you had put $1,000 into a stock of a company when you were born and kept it there with earnings reinvested, but never put any more money into it, by the time you retired you would have $727,000?"

SmartStart

www.cibc.com/smartstart The site is run by CIBC, an investment firm, but the advertising is minimal. We had fun clicking on the colorful cartoon icons to play The Great Treasure Hunt Game and enter The Allowance Room, and the advice to parents is neatly organized according to your child's age.

Saving for College

Up until this section we've talked mostly about handling finances when your kids are under 18. Then there is college, which has become such a major big-bucks proposition, guess what business is increasingly getting into the act. Could it be financial advisers?

Since the Tax Relief Act of 2001 was passed, the financial planning industry has begun to sniff out opportunities helping parents sort out the new and expanded tax-sheltered college saving plans, and are marketing their services aggressively to middle- and upper-income parents. There's a new National Institute of Certified College Planners that is offering certification programs to tax and financial planning professionals to help them appeal to this growing market.

We smell commissions.

No doubt there are good college planners. But when it comes to helping you invest money for the day your kids go off to college, it's just another fancy way of coming up with investment advice that may or may not be based on your best interests. There are a number of specialized plans for college money, but you can figure them out yourself rather than wasting portions of your child's nest egg on commissions.

As we write this book, the average price for a year of tuition at a private college is more than $12,000. The top schools cost closer to $30,000 a year, which means an undergraduate degree at an Ivy League school will cost well over $100,000—and that's just for tuition, not including room and board. The cost of tuition at a state university rose by 107% between 1980 and 2000, to an average of $3,512, according to a recent study by the National Center for Higher Education in San Jose, California. Nonstate residents pay much more; a four-year undergraduate education at a top state school such as the University of Michigan will cost an out-of-stater around $30,000. The study found that for a poor family, sending a child to a public university takes about 25% of the family's annual income. For the middle class it takes about 7%, but if you have more than one child in college, figure on another 7% or so, and it's much more for private colleges.

Unless you're among the wealthiest 5%, college is going to be a squee-ee-ze on your finances. You need a strong defensive strategy to meet those costs.

The financial services industry uses projections based on present annual increases to tell you that you'll need, say, $250,000 to send little Johnny to Harvard, and the number is designed to propel you into such a state of catatonic horror that you'll sign over a huge check *now* for an investment that you haven't had a chance to examine from all sides. It's the "scare 'em" school of sweet-talking people into an investment product that earns the seller big commissions.

Particularly, parents of young children should watch out for the aggressive onslaught of advertising from financial firms that manage "529" plan funds. We'll explain how these plans work and how to get the best deal in the next section.

A further word of caution from our good friend Kalman Chany, who is president of Campus Consultants, Inc. (www.campusconsultants.com) and author of a book that every parent should read, *Paying for College Without Going Broke*—don't put yourselves in the poorhouse in order to invest for your children's education. They *can* get loans to go to college, but you can't get loans to finance your retirement. Older parents are especially vulnerable to this syndrome.

Those Wonderful Tax-Deferred College Plans

We do love the new provisions of the tax code that expanded both the allowable contributions and the uses of tax-advantaged education savings plans. The two plans you should be considering are:

- The 529 Plan, an investment account that lets your earnings grow tax-deferred, with withdrawals for qualified college expenses exempt from federal taxes, and in some states from state taxes as well. Your original contributions are NOT exempt from federal income taxes, but some states allow a state income tax deduction. It's named after Section 529 of the federal tax code.

Starting a Family at 35-Plus?

If you start having children in your late thirties or in your forties, you won't have that much time until your retirement when your kids are in college. So make sure you start putting away money for your retirement first, especially if your company offers a 401(k) with employer-matched contributions. That's free money that you don't get from any college investment account.

If you're putting money into a 401(k) or 403(b), or IRAs or a combination, it's all tax-deferred until you start making withdrawals. But these days many people start their families late enough that they still have kids in college when they reach the age of 59½, which is when you can start withdrawing from a tax-deferred retirement account. If that's the case, you can dip into your account for college costs. And if you have been socking away employer-matched contributions to a 401(k), you'll have been getting added principal for nothing. No story thrills us more than those from listeners who call and relate how pleased (and sometimes surprised) they are about how their contributions and their employers' contributions have compounded over the years.

Dolan Ah-Ha!

Just starting the search for a college for your teenager? Are you shuddering at the thought of paying for airfare, rental cars, and motels in umpteen different college towns? We have a solution.

Over the years on our radio show, we have often recommended Collegiate Choice Walking Tour Videos as a way of prescreening colleges. They're an advisory company that offers video campus tours of schools all over the United States, as well as universities in Canada, the United Kingdom, and Ireland. Unlike the promotional videos you'll get from the college recruiting office, these videos will show a genuine "day in the life" of the campus with typical sights and sounds. The idea is that you can view their videos first (at $15 per campus "tour" plus shipping charges, it's a lot less than hopping on a plane), then begin a weeding-out process, and devote your traveling time and dollars to the schools that are your top picks. Plus they offer tips for visiting colleges, college planning links, and magazine ratings of colleges. Contact Collegiate Choice at:

Collegiate Choice
41 Surrey Lane
Tenafly, NJ 07670
201-871-0098
www.collegiatechoice.com

But let's get one thing straight before we become too effusive about 529 Plans. They're worth considering for many people, but, of course, you need to know the facts before going forward with one.

Earlier this year, the National Association of Securities Dealers was investigating (they may still be investigating!) six brokerage firms that offer 529 plans, with other investigations likely to follow. The NASD was looking into whether some firms are failing to tell their customers about the benefits of investing in *their own state's* 529 Plans—many state 529 Plans offer tax reductions to state residents.

The NASD found that more than 90% of the money in the 529 Plans sold by certain

**You can compare 529s and Coverdells, and find a
529 consultant at www.savingforcollege.com.**

brokerage firms came from *out-of-state* investors, with some of those out-of-state plans not offering tax benefits unless you lived in that state! And deciphering 529 fees is getting harder! BE CAREFUL!

- The Coverdell Education Savings Account (ESA), named after the late Georgia Republican senator Paul Coverdell, who fought tirelessly for this measure. Formerly known as an Education IRA, a Coverdell is indeed much like an IRA in that you invest money that grows tax-deferred, but as with a 529, the withdrawals are tax-free if you use the money for the educational expenses defined in the plan.

If you have your retirement house in order, or can afford to make contributions to both efforts simultaneously, by all means take advantage of these tax-deferred college investment plans.

Still, we have a Dolan caveat: There is at this writing a sunset provision in the Tax Relief Act of 2001, meaning that unless the President and Congress vote to continue this particular provision, the tax laws affecting these accounts might expire in the 2010 tax year. So if your children are very young, don't count on having a tax-deferred account available right up until the day you start shelling out tuition money. Write to your congressional representative to say you like the provision. With any luck the law will stay in place, and at the very least the money you contribute up until 2010 will be grandfathered in.

The Coverdell Education Savings Account

A Coverdell has a couple of advantages over a 529. With a Coverdell you are able to choose your own investments, while 529s have more-limited choices. Also, you can make tax-free withdrawals from a Coverdell to pay for elementary and high school expenses—tuition, room and board, uniforms, tutoring, computer equipment, and almost anything else you can name—while 529s are designed to be used only for college expenses.

The maximum annual contribution to a Coverdell is $2,000, however, whereas with a 529 you can contribute much more.

There is also an income ceiling on the Coverdell. You are ineligible if you are a single filer earning over $110,000 a year or a married couple with an annual income over $220,000.

The 529 Account

These accounts are state-sponsored, and every state is authorized to offer them. The maximum you can contribute per child per account, over time or in a lump sum, is determined by each state's plan, ranging from $146,000 in Iowa to $305,000 in South Dakota.

If that doesn't seem like enough (perish the thought!), you can open a second account for a child. You can even start the account before a child is born—so that you can start investing really early.

Much of the money in 529s is invested in mutual funds. As with any mutual fund, there are load funds and no-load funds available in most states. Go for a no-load 529 if you can in your state. Sales commissions on load funds will run as high as 4.25%—that's enough for a lot of books and pizzas down the line.

If you thought we were tough on brokers in Chapter 5, hear this: *The Wall Street Journal** did an investigation and found that 70% of the people in Rhode Island participating in the state's college tuition savings program were buying an Alliance Capital plan through a broker and paying sales fees—while they could have bought an almost identical college fund directly from Alliance Capital with no load. Why did they let themselves get taken advantage of? Because they were comfortable buying through a professional.

Turns out that once 529s became popular because of the new 2001 law, brokers launched a full-scale marketing blitz, with some plans that are far more complicated than they need to be. Some of these plans are designed to make you scratch your head and cry out for advice from a professional. Major firms have gotten into the 529 act—the largest manager in terms of assets under management is Merrill Lynch, followed by Putnam Investments, Alliance Capital, and Teachers Insurance and Annuity Association College Retirement Equities Fund (TIAA-CREF).

We believe that TIAA-CREF offers a particularly attractive 529 product because of its low minimums, low fees and above-average returns. For more information, go to www.tiaacref.com/tuition/index.html.

One of the biggest attractions of 529s is that the earnings grow tax-sheltered—but you need to know what the **state income tax consequences** will be *before* you decide upon a particular plan.

At the **federal** level, everyone is covered. Earnings are not subject to federal taxes as long as you keep the money in the account, and withdrawals are exempt as long as you use the money for qualified educational expenses.

State laws about tax exemption vary from one state to another, however. Here's the potential horror tale: If you live in a state that doesn't tax the earnings, and buy a national plan from a well-known financial firm, you may be buying a plan that is administered in another state and doesn't give you the favorable state tax treatment you should be getting—meaning you're losing dollars that could be earning compounded returns while

---

* "Hefty Fees Can Crimp Your College Savings," by Lynn Asinof; *The Wall Street Journal*, Wed., April 17, 2002, page D2.

your child is growing up. You might choose the plan offered by a firm, but it's actually sponsored by a particular state, with investments that may generate tax deductions only for residents of that state. More information is available in a guide to college plans from the National Association of Securities Dealers (NASD). You can download the guide from the NASD Web site at no charge. Go to www.nasdr.com/529_saving.asp.

On the other hand, if you live in a state that allows state income tax exemptions for withdrawals from both in-state and out-of-state plans and doesn't allow a deduction for the contributions, you can invest in any plan and still get all of the favorable tax treatment allowable. For details on each state plan and updates, check www.savingforcollege.com.

Do you still think you need a broker to manage your 529 Plan? Even brokers get misinformation sometimes from firms that manage these plans. Learn your state laws, then choose your plan yourself and make your own cautious investment decisions. Want to teach your kids to be self-reliant? Here's one way you can show them investment-management skills.

Here's Our Guide to Where Your 529 or Coverdell Money Should Go as Your Child Grows Up

Up to age 13: You have time to ride out market downturns, so you should go for aggressive growth. But watch the market, and don't stake your child's future to a "hot" sector, such as high tech, that could fall through the floor in a few years. If putting 100% in stocks makes you nervous—and it makes just about everyone nervous in a bear market—put up to half in fixed-income investments: bonds or bond funds.

Ages 14–17: Fourteen should be the watershed age for reassessing what you're doing with your college funds. If you've been extremely aggressive right up until then, it's time to start going into much safer investments. Each year increase the bond funds with the best

---

Dolan Ah-Ha!

A number of states currently allow your child's 529 Plan to be owned by a trust. This makes sense, in many cases. The trust owns the 529. You, as the donor, have control over the timing and distribution of the funds in the plan even if you pass away. If you set it up so that the trust doesn't own the 529 and instead the assets pass to a successor owner who has the right to withdraw funds at any time for this purpose, someone responsible still maintains control.

Q: What if I fund a 529 for my child and he ends up not going to college?

A. You can change the beneficiary to another family member. You can even use it to go to college or graduate school yourself, or you can pass it along to a grandchild, in which case the transfer is treated for tax purposes as a gift from the first beneficiary to the second. Saving the account for someone in the family who will appreciate it makes the most sense, because any withdrawals that aren't used for college expenses will incur taxes and penalties.

Q: Can I transfer assets from a college savings plan in one state to a similar plan in another state?

A: You can roll over the balance in most states. However, contact the plan sponsor to find out how each state's laws will treat the tax deductions and exemptions in rollovers.

Q: Do I need to open separate accounts for each of my children?

A: Yes. Each account may have only one beneficiary, but you can open accounts for as many beneficiaries as you like.

Q: Can more than one person make contributions to an account?

A: Yes. However, only the account owner has control over the way the assets are invested. A person who wishes to make a sizable contribution may want to consider opening a separate account for the same beneficiary.

Q: Will a 529 affect my child's eligibility for financial aid?

A: Currently it is considered a parental asset, so the impact is minimal (see Dolan Bottom Line, p. 221). If it is funded by grandparents, it will not, because none of the grandparents' assets are counted toward the expected family contribution (EFC) that colleges use in determining aid eligibility. However, once the child starts college and you start taking out distributions to pay for tuition and expenses, the school counts the distributions as income to the student when determining financial aid eligibility in subsequent years.

Q: Are there any gift or estate tax benefits?

A: Yes. Contributions are eligible for the $11,000 gift tax exclusion and the generation-skipping tax exemption. Generally, you can contribute up to $55,000 ($110,000 per married couple) for each beneficiary in a single year without federal gift-tax consequences. A one-time $55,000 gift may be prorated over five years. All contributions are removed from your taxable estate. However, if a contributor dies prior to the fifth year, a portion of the contribution will be returned to the contributor's estate for determining taxes.

track record and underweight stock funds. Don't do what one of our listeners did. Back in 2000 she called and said she wished she had listened to us when we said the market was overextended and people should start getting out of equities. She left her child's entire college fund invested in equity mutual funds, and lost two years of tuition money.

Age 18: Play it safe from here on, with 100% of the fund in fixed-income investments. That's money market funds, CDs, short-term bond funds, or a combination of the three.

State Prepaid Tuition Plans

Another savings option to consider is a state-sponsored prepaid plan. These plans had fallen from grace because their returns were modest, but in the bear market they have been beating many mutual funds with an average return of about 5% a year. They're meant to rise in value at approximately the same rate as state university tuition.

The way a prepaid plan works is this: You make payments based on your child's age, and the state invests the money. The money and earnings grow tax-deferred at the feder-

---

Dolan Bottom Line

Here's a question that keeps parents awake at night: Will a college savings plan make your kids ineligible for financial aid?

Unfortunately, it will.

A 529 is considered a parental asset at this writing, which means that no more than 5.6% of the value is counted in the formula when a college calculates a student's financial needs. This may change, however, and the money might be counted as student income, which reduces aid by 50 cents for every dollar after an exemption for the first $2,330.

A Coverdell ESA is considered a student asset and reduces aid eligibility by 35% of the balance in the account each year. With a state prepaid tuition plan, you disqualify yourself for financial aid.

If you can afford to give a child money through the Uniform Gift to Minors Act (UGMA), you probably don't need financial aid. UGMA accounts are considered an asset of the child and reduce eligibility by 35%.

Rules change, however. Check the Princeton Review site at www.review.com/college for late-breaking news of how these plans will affect the financial aid package.

al level, although state laws vary as to whether the earnings are taxed. When it comes time to go to college, the state covers your tuition bill up to the average tuition price at a state public college.

You are not locked into going to a state school, but if your son or daughter goes to a private college, you'll have to find a way to foot the bill for the difference. If you have one of these plans, you can't get financial aid. You can invest only until your child reaches the ninth grade. But some plans allow you to switch to a 529 Plan.

Here's a strategy to consider: If your state offers it, start a prepaid plan now. When the market rises switch to a 529 savings plan. Or if it looks as if you're going to need financial aid, you can roll the prepaid plan over into a 529.

For a list of prepaid plans in each state, go to the National Association of Student Financial Aid Administration Web site, at www.nasfaa.org. Many links to information about plans are available on the Mapping Your Future Web site, www.mapping-your-future.org/features/SavingsPrograms.htm or www.collegesavings.org.

Finding the $$$

Before you know it, little Johnny will be 16. There'll be a pile of college catalogs in his room, and your free time will be taken up with campus visits. This one is the best school in the world to study government policy and bio-tech all in one; this one has a three-time champion rowing team; this one has the ratio of male to female students that any girl would love.

It sounds great, but are you ready to pay for the attractions your college-bound teenager wants?

A college education is the second-largest purchase you are ever going to make, after your home. And if you have two or more kids headed for college, we could be talking well into six-figure amounts. Certainly, education is an investment with returns you can't measure in anything so trivial as dollar figures, though hopefully it will launch your young students into careers that are both rewarding and remunerative.

That being said, you should still shop for a college as shrewdly as you'd shop for a stock, a house, a car, or anything else that someone is trying to sell you. Because campus recruiters, like brokers and sales reps from any industry, are in the business of *selling this particular college*. The idea is to get the *kid* hooked on the idea that this is the school for me—then, *if* he or she is accepted, the haggling over financial aid and scholarships begins.

If you can shell out the bucks for four years at Harvard, no problem, read no further. But all other parents know this: It may be possible to get financial aid even if your family income and assets place you above what appears to be the qualifying range.

Rather than list all the kinds of federal education loans available, the most popular

Financial Aid 101

Aid comes in three forms. The best kind, of course, is grants and scholarships, which don't have to be paid back. Chany encourages students to seek grants, which are fairly plentiful and are need-based. And grant money is almost always tax-free. Scholarships are great if you can get them. They're usually awarded by the schools themselves, based on merit. Federal work-study is also need-based, as are student loans.

being the Stafford and Plus loans, here is a list of our favorite Web sites that list these loans and how to qualify for them:

www.collegeboard.com
www.ed.gov
www.finaid.com
www.petersons.com
www.SallieMae.com
www.slccloans.com

Also, don't forget the book we recommended earlier in this chapter, Kalman Chany's *Paying for College Without Going Broke.*

Chany says most parents have serious misconceptions about financial aid for college. Here, from the horse's mouth (actually from Chany, and the way he helps college-bound kids get where they want to go reminds us more of an eagle than a horse!) are the top mis-beliefs parents and kids harbor when it comes to financial aid:

The Five Top College-Aid Myths

1. *My kids won't qualify for financial aid unless our household income fall belows a specific cutoff amount.*
   A number of factors influence your status in qualifying for aid. What schools take into consideration are:
   ✓ Cost of the school
   ✓ Whether it's a one-parent or two-parent household
   ✓ Whether both parents are working and earning income
   ✓ Number of children and other dependents in the family (so if you are supporting your aging parents, they will be factored in)
   ✓ Number of family members currently paying tuition (so if you're thinking of

going to school yourself, you might actually enhance your child's chances of getting aid)

✓ High medical expenses in the family (again, if you are supporting aging parents and they require a great deal of medical care, that will be part of the picture)

✓ Total value of the family's assets

The amount of aid you can get is in part determined by the cost of the school. That's why parents with an income of under $40,000 might find that it costs them less to send a child to a top private university than to a state university!

Virtually every family can receive a low-rate Stafford loan ($2,625 a year for freshmen and sophomores, $5,500 for juniors and seniors) and a PLUS loan, which covers the total college cost. (Apply at your local bank or credit union.) They don't lessen the load, but they do spread it out.

2. *If we own our home, we won't qualify.*

Under federal guidelines, your home equity isn't considered an asset. What is important, however, is that you find out how each of the colleges on your list calculates the amount they assume you can pay: Do they use the federal or the College Scholarship Service (CSS) method? Under the CSS method, your home equity does count. If you have lots of equity built up and lots of consumer debt, you'll get less aid. But, if you pay off your consumer debt with a home equity loan, your net worth decreases and the amount of aid you're eligible for increases dramatically.

Colleges are interested mostly in your income, whether it's from salaries or investments. If you own rental property and make a profit from your renters, that counts for more than the value of your home does. On the other hand, it's a very bad idea to sell stock or property and put the money into a bank account in the year before you apply for aid. In the application process, the college will calculate your "expected family contribution" (EFC), which is determined by factoring in your income, including income from investments and other assets, minus your financial obligations. The college subtracts your EFC from the total costs of a typical year—factoring in tuition, living expenses, books, and room and board. Then they decide whether they want to help you with the difference.

Families with incomes in the $125,000 to $150,000 range can demonstrate need at private colleges, and families with incomes up to $90,000 can qualify at state colleges.

3. *The school itself is the best source for information on aid.*

"That's like saying the IRS is the best place to go for advice on tax savings," says Chany. The financial aid officer, known as the FAO, works for the financial department, not for you. He or she is trying to get as much money from each student as possible. Meanwhile, you're trying to spend as little of your own money as possible.

Recent studies have found that as many as 65% of private colleges and 27% of public universities engage in what is known as financial aid leveraging. This is a process used to determine how little aid the school can award per student and still get the student to enroll.

How do schools get away with this practice? By simply not telling you the many ways that you can manipulate your assets to show need. Is that dishonest? We're not saying hide your assets in a Swiss bank account. We're saying take advantage of the strategies available to you. Many of these are outlined below, in the section titled "How to Qualify for Financial Aid," and you will find more strategies in Chany's book.

The FAO will make you an aid offer and tell you that federal regulations prevent the school from giving you any more. Chany says that is, at least in some instances, a bald-faced lie.

This is not to say that negotiating for more aid will get you what you want. You might have some clout if, say, you have a daughter who has been accepted at two schools with comparable academic standards and reputation, and School B has offered a larger financial aid package, but she really wants to attend School A. Then you can go to the FAO at School A and explain that your daughter would really prefer to accept their offer, but you just can't afford to turn down School B. It will help a *lot* if your daughter is a highly desirable student to School A. Excellent grades and achievements go a long way in giving you the upper hand.

4. *Financial aid goes to the students who need it most.*
   "Money goes to people who know how the system operates and how to answer the questions on the applications to their best advantage," says Chany.
   Take advantage of the strategies.

5. *Scholarships are where the real money is.*
   Scholarships represent less than 5% of all the available aid, says Chany.

Chany Ah-Ha!

An uneducated consumer is a college's best customer!
  We couldn't have said it better.

You might have heard that billions of dollars in scholarship monies go unused every year. Chany says these claims are out of date, and based on tuition money that companies and nonprofits, including universities themselves, made available to their employees—not necessarily to 18- to 21-year-old undergraduates.

Advance Planning for Financial Aid

If you think you are going to need aid, start early—begin your strategy as soon as your child enters high school. Here is the Dolans' Guide to Qualifying, stage by stage:

Three to Four Years Before College

- Put assets into your retirement accounts.
- Keep assets in your name if you think you'll be eligible for financial aid. Financial aid formulas assume that you, as parents, can tap as much as 47% of your after-tax income to pay for college expenses. But the formula assumes that a maximum of only 5.6% of your assets are actually available. Your child, on the other hand, will be expected to contribute 35% of his or her assets to college bills. So don't set up a Coverdell or 529 in your child's name unless you're sure you can get by without financial aid.
- You might consider returning to college or graduate school yourself. The expected family contribution is divided by the number of people in school. So you can nearly double your aid eligibility this way. But be aware of this caveat: Many private colleges consider only the number of *dependents* in school when distributing their own funds, so you won't count.

Two Years Before College

- College financial aid formulas use "base year" income as well as assets you own as of the date you complete the forms. You'll get more financial aid if you can make

---

Dolan Ah-Ha!

There are a couple of ways you may be able to get a discount of up to 1¼% on already historically low student-loan interest rates:
- If you make your payments by electronic funds transfer.
- If you make on-time monthly payments for a required number of months (usually 48) to the lender or Sallie Mae.

your base year income look as small as possible. Before December 31 of your child's junior year in high school, do the following:

- Sell appreciated assets and take your capital gains.
- Cash in Series EE U.S. Savings Bonds to pay for college expenses.
- Take your employee bonus now rather than in January.
- Invest as much as you can afford in your tax-sheltered retirement plans.
- Defer bonuses and pay increases after January 1 of your child's junior year of high school. Take as many tax deductions as possible. If you own a business, it's a good year to take losses. Your after-tax income this year will determine how much aid you are likely to qualify for.
- Pay off your credit card debts. This debt doesn't exist as far as FAOs are concerned. When is an asset not an asset? When you have $10,000 in savings but $8,000 in debts, and you're trying to qualify for financial aid. What number do you think the financial officer is going to use in adding up your worth? The amount that's in your savings account, of course! If you pay off your debts, you just might qualify for aid.

One Year Before College

- Don't sell any appreciated investments. Instead, borrow against your countable assets, such as savings accounts, stocks, bonds, and real estate, and use the borrowed money to continue paying debts.
- Submit the Free Application for Federal Student Aid (FAFSA) before January 1. You can get a copy of the form from the high school guidance office. Aid is a first-come, first-served business, and the FAFSA form will be the basis for most of your aid. Fill it out and mail it as soon as possible after January 1. The form will ask for your after-tax income, but don't worry if your taxes aren't done in time to provide exact income amounts. Just give your best estimate and get the application in the mail right away. In addition to the deadline for the FAFSA, be sure to meet each school's deadlines and filing requirements. You may have to fill out other forms as well for each school your child is interested in, so check the application materials at each school for more details. The sooner you file, the more financial aid you're likely to receive.

Apply for student loans in the right order.

- Have your child apply for a Stafford loan first (these are from $2,625 to $5,500 per year). If you still need funds, apply for a PLUS loan for the balance. PLUS loans,

Kids and Parents Read This:
Checklist for Getting Financial Aid

✓ *Assume you're eligible.* Don't rule yourself out because of income or academics. And don't rule out a college because you think it's too expensive. The higher the cost, the more aid you may receive.

✓ *Don't wait to be accepted to a college to apply for aid.* The coffers may be empty by spring.

✓ *Get application forms as soon as possible in your senior year of high school.* You'll need the FAFSA form for the upcoming school year, which is available in December at high schools, colleges, and libraries. You may also need the CSS/Financial Aid Profile form, state aid forms, and forms provided by the college.

✓ *Check the deadlines and be sure to meet each one.* Many colleges have different deadlines for different forms. Some may be due in December, though most are due in February or March.

✓ *Figure out your "expected family contribution."* Use worksheets in financial aid guidebooks to calculate—before you apply—what the colleges will estimate you can afford to pay. Be sure to get up-to-date information, as formulas can change year to year.

✓ *Before December 31 of your senior year of high school, maximize your aid eligibility.* College freshman year aid awards are based in part on income for the year ending December 31 of the student's senior year in high school. Consider making appropriate adjustments to your assets, debts, and retirement provisions.

✓ *Parents: Do your income tax forms early.* To meet early aid application deadlines, you'll need to do a draft version of your income tax return for the year before your teenager starts college. Many schools will require a copy of your actual return in the spring to verify your information.

✓ *Follow instructions carefully on application forms.* Common mistakes that can disqualify your applications are: forgetting to sign them, leaving lines blank, or using the wrong writing implement (some forms require pen, some pencil).

From *Paying for College Without Going Broke,* by Kalman A. Chany with Geoff Martz, Princeton Review Books. Reprinted with permission.

which are limited to the cost of college minus other financial aid, are a loan given to parents. The interest rate is usually lower than that of other personal loans; by law it cannot exceed 9%. However, you will be required to start paying it back within 60 days after the final loan disbursement. Check this excellent Web site: www.finaid.com.

Blended Families Beware the Stepparent Trap

When you apply for federal financial aid, the government demands that you include a stepparent's salary on the forms, even though stepparents have no legal responsibility to their stepchildren. Thinking of remarrying while your kids are thinking about college? They could gain a wonderful stepparent but lose aid eligibility.

What if you just move in together? What if you're a gay couple and struggling to have your union officially sanctioned as a marriage? Well, this time regulations just might work in your favor. The aid forms ask the student about the income and assets of the custodial parent, if the parent is married, and if so it asks about the spouse's financial picture. If you live in a common law state and you have been living together long enough for your relationship to qualify as a common law marriage, your significant other WILL be counted as a stepparent. The other area that gets tricky is your housing arrangement. If, say, you're the mother of the student, and your boyfriend moved in with you and pays half the mortgage or rent, his contribution is counted as part of your income. Otherwise, the policy seems to be "don't ask, don't tell."

Scholarships

Yes, there are some available, but most are reserved for students with something extra special to offer. A true budding genius should have no problem. And if your child has any special academic, athletic, or artistic talent, it is worth looking into. There are also awards for students interested in particular fields of study, or who are members of underrepresented groups. "Underrepresented" at a particular college can apply to certain ethnic backgrounds, or to certain special needs, or it can be a part of the country that seems like a distant planet to most of the students.

But as Chany has pointed out, scholarships aren't nearly as plentiful as students. Searching for scholarships takes some detective work.

Avoid the "search firms" that offer to find the money for you. These are companies that charge you money, with promises of finding money for you, and most of them are run

Is Tuition Reimbursement Insurance a Good Deal? Only If . . .

. . . only if your child is an athlete and therefore vulnerable to getting an injury that will keep him out of school for several months, or has a serious health condition and therefore might have to take a medical leave. Here's another add-on that some salesperson somewhere might try to sell you. Tuition reimbursement insurance, designed to refund the money you'd lose if your child drops out of college before the end of a semester, is fairly inexpensive. It can run as low as $30 or as high as $150, depending on the price of the college, but it's usually closer to the high end. Anyway, it's useless if your child drops out of school for any of the reasons that most college students drop out: financial problems, bad grades, substance abuse, pregnancy—basically all the stuff of your nightmares. You get only 60% of the costs back if your child drops out due to mental health problems, and you get the refund only if he or she has been hospitalized at least seven days. Illnesses with a physical *and* psychological base, such as anorexia or bulimia, are usually taken case by case. You know your own child, and you have to be the judge of whether this kind of policy is worth buying.

by scam artists who know how to make their business sound legit by injecting the name with words like "National," "Federal," "Foundation," or "Administration." Every year, overly eager families lose over $100 million to these operators. You'll find valuable advice about how to protect yourself on the Web through the National Association of Student Financial Aid Administrators, www.finaid.org/scholarships/scams. FinAid says be suspicious of any company that charges an application fee, guarantees success, or tries to pitch its own services at an event disguised as a financial aid "seminar."

Instead, spend your money on one or two reference books. Our favorites are *The Scholarship Advisor* by Christopher Vuturo (Random House/Princeton Review books; $26 paperback), who managed to get more than $885,000 in college aid offers himself, plus post-college travel and graduate school scholarship awards, and *How to Go to College Almost for Free* by Ben Kaplan (HarperCollins; $22).

You'll also find some terrific scholarship resources online. We heartily recommend the site mentioned previously, the National Association of Student Financial Aid Administrators at www.finaid.org. They have everything there—including links to sites that will match you with a database of awards that fit your profile, as well as ordering information for many of our favorite books, government and private sources for financial aid, scam alerts, and information on admission testing.

For an even more comprehensive series of links to scholarship databases, check out www.college-scholarships.com.

Other good sites:

www.wiredscholar.com, operated by Sallie Mae, the education loan provider

www.collegeboard.com, with information from the College Board's annual survey of financial aid programs

www.scholarships.com, which has a database of some 500,000 scholarships and grants

www.FastWeb.com, another database of scholarships

www.petersons.com

Summer Jobs

Every kid is looking forward to those wonderful summer months that offer lots of free time to hang out with their friends, swim, bike, and generally have a good time. But it won't be long before many kids get bored with doing nothing other than hitting up Mom or Dad for a few bucks to pay for all that fun.

With that in mind, parents are now starting to search for positive ways to avoid the summer "blahs," to help their kids to make a few much-needed bucks *and* maybe pick up some valuable real-life business experience.

The U.S. Department of Labor conducted a survey that revealed that 30% to 50% of young people who left school had little or no knowledge or foundational skills required to hold a good job. At the same time, paradoxically, more than 50% of U.S. employers reported that they cannot find qualified applicants for their most basic entry-level positions. Students surveyed said that very little of what they learn in high school is helpful when they enter the workplace after graduation.

Summer jobs and entrepreneurship give young people the chance to develop skills, learn how to work with others, and explore the world of business. If summer jobs are scarce in your area—even after you and your kids have looked where we recommended—why not help your kids start their own business. Talk about real-world experience!

Here are some of the best sources of job information:

1. Check out www.coolworks.com. It's a comprehensive source of interesting summer jobs.

We found that www.coolworks.com lists more than 35,000 jobs in interesting places, in the United States and overseas. All jobs are listed by state and region, and by job category.

2. Call your local chamber of commerce and ask if any members may need some summer help, or if you or your parents are or know a member, get a list of members and send each a notice of your availability for the summer.
3. Check out www.family.com for more summer job information.
4. Visit the Federal Job Center online at www.fedworld.com. Or you can check your local directory for the office nearest you.

Helpful Web Sites and Books

TROUBLE WITH THE IRS???
Nationally respected tax litigation consultant, Dan Pilla, has joined us many times on our television and radio shows.

Dan's "must have" tax materials include his books *The IRS Problem Solver* and *How to Get Tax Amnesty,* and his monthly newsletter, Dan Pilla's "Confidential Tax Bulletin." All are available at www.taxhelponline.com or by calling 800-34-NO TAX.

Family Finances

www.abanet.org

Adoption

www.adopting.org

www.adoption.com

www.adopt.org

Day Care

www.Careguide.com

www.edaycare.com

Bringing Up Money-Savvy Children

www.coolworks.com

www.family.com

www.fedworld.com

www.firstshare.com

www.kidsmoney.org

www.kidstock.com

www.MSN.com

www.Moneycentral.com

www.parentbanc.com

www.sharebuilder.com

The National Endowment for Financial Education has information on its Web site about starting a high school financial planning program. Go to www.nefe.org/pages/education. html. To request information kits, contact:
NEFE High School Financial Planning Program
National Endowment for Financial Education
5299 DTC Boulevard, Suite 1300
Greenwood Village, CO 80111
Phone: 303-224-3510

Kids' Allowance: How Much, How Often, and How Come? by David McCurrach. Kids' Money Press, $8.95.

College Parents of America (CPA), a national membership association dedicated to helping parents prepare for and put their children through college. 8300 Boone Boulevard, Suite 500, Vienna, VA 22182; 703-761-6702. www.collegeparents.org

Prescreening Colleges

Collegiate Choice's videos. Order at www.collegiatechoice.com

Financing College

www.collegeboard.org

www.college-scholarships.com

www.collegiatechoice.com

www.ed.gov

www.fastweb.com

www.finaid.org

The Wrenn Ferguson Group at U.S. Bancorp Piper Jaffray's Web site, www.lucky529.com

The NASD Guide to College Saving Plans: www.nasdr.com/529_saving.asp

www.petersons.com

Princeton Review: www.review.com/college

www.salliemae.com

www.savingforcollege.com

www.scholarships.com

www.slccloans.com

www.studentadvantage.com

www.wiredscholar.com

Our first choice: *Paying for College Without Going Broke,* by Kalman Chany with Geoff Martz (Princeton Review), $14 on Amazon.com.

The Best Way to Save for College: A Complete Guide to "529" Plans, by Joseph F. Hurley, CPA. Published by www.savingforcollege.com, $26.95. Order through site.

The Scholarship Advisor, by Christopher Vuturo (Random House/Princeton Review books; $26 paperback). A catalog of scholarships, plus advice on getting one.

Peterson's College Money Handbook, Peterson's, $26.95. Outlines aid offerings at 1,700 colleges and universities. One chart compares each school's average aid package for freshmen. Comes with software (for computers running Windows) that helps estimate costs and payment options.

School Loan Consolidation

U.S. Department of Education Direct Consolidation program: www.loanconsolidation. ed.gov or 800-557-7392.

Summer and Part-Time Jobs

www.coolworks.com

www.family.com

Federal Job Center—www.fedworld.com

Fast Cash for Kids (2nd edition), by Bonnie and Noel Drew (Career Press; $13.99). An overview of 101 projects for kids from ages 10 to 18, including start-up instructions, creative marketing ideas, and how to write a business plan.

The Lemonade Stand, by Emmanuel Modu (Gateway Publishers; $19.95 plus $4 shipping; 800-438-8336).

Entrepreneur? (full- or part-time?)

go to www.entrepreneur.com for lots of helpful information . . . and consider subscribing to the monthly ENTREPRENEUR magazine for $19.97, by calling (800) 274-6229 (actually, it's *cheaper* on their Web site!).

CHAPTER 8

Talking Money with Your Parents

DARIA'S GRANDFATHER USED TO SAY it was improper for grown-up children to talk about finances with their aging parents because, as he put it, "You don't pluck a chicken before it's dead."

He paid the price for staying "unplucked." We had no idea what was in his estate until after he died. But his biggest mistake was making the assumption that he was going to die before his wife, my grandmother, who was six years younger. In those days—we're talking late 1960s—there was a cap on how much money could pass to the spouse without incurring estate taxes. That is no longer the case. But at the time, he tried to protect his wife from estate taxes by putting all of his assets in her name. As it turned out, she died *first*—which meant he inherited an estate that paid taxes on *his own money!*

You, as an adult child (let's hope more adult than child) need to know what your parents have done *vis-à-vis* their estate planning, as well as the state of their finances and insurance. Why? Because you never know what might happen tomorrow.

Some trillions of dollars in assets are going to pass from retirees to baby boomers over

If you don't mind seeing your parents go through their life savings to take care of themselves, or *your* life savings after *theirs* are gone, don't bother reading this chapter.

the next generation. You should know if your parents have their estate plans in order, so that the IRS won't get its hands on the bulk of your legacy and your family won't have to spend unnecessary time and money in probate court.

Then, too, your parents may end up in your care. If you don't know the key details of their finances when life is coasting along at status quo, how can you possibly expect to help them in an emergency, when emotions are running amok and, sad to say, you might suddenly find yourself taking care of a parent who no longer has the mental or physical ability to reason and communicate?

If your parents should become ill or incapacitated, or unexpectedly die, you should be able to step in and quickly make arrangements. That's the grim face of reality. You should also know whether your parents could potentially outlive their life savings. If that happens, how will they get by? They need to have a plan. YOU may have to help them make that plan.

Who would take care of your parents if you were not around? In cases of long-term care, it's important to understand that although it's a problem for the parent in the long-term-care situation, it's a worse problem for the caregiver. The caregivers are the ones who burn out first.

Your parents could go through *your* money to pay for their long-term care. Even though, legally, our parents aren't our responsibility, states are now going after the kids to pay for their parents' health care because the costs of Medicaid, which is basically welfare, are out of control.

Medical science has enabled us to live *longer* but not always *better*. If your parents are like most senior citizens, they're terrified of losing their independence and their ability to make their own decisions and get around without help. Furthermore, senior citizens who have even a little bit of money are prey to con artists and unscrupulous sorts with big plans to invest their life savings in stocks of companies that don't exist (or shouldn't exist), or insurance policies that don't deliver on promises. It's important that you be there to see if your parents need a guiding hand in their financial strategies so that their golden years can be a time of quality living.

Dolan Bottom Line

Because people are living well into their eighties and nineties, you may have to take care of aging parents *longer* than they took care of you.

Learn by Our Mistakes

Daria's family is full of stories. Here's what happened most recently:

I'll never forget that awful phone call on Thanksgiving morning of 2001. We had just seen my parents the day before, and my dad had been O.K., though he was a bit forgetful. We'd been aware that his mental health was gradually degenerating, but we'd expected it to be months, maybe even years, before his condition worsened to the state of needing professional help. Certainly, none of us had expected it to happen overnight! But there it was; on Thanksgiving morning my mother called and said he had suddenly lost control. It was as if he'd fallen off a cliff. My loving mother, Norma, could no longer take care of him at home. He was beyond the help of an assisted-living facility. We had to take him straight to a nursing home. I still find it hard to believe that my dad, who was so vital and alert just a few years before, is now a patient in a Florida nursing home.

We've got another question that plagues us: Who is going to pay the $5,000-plus bill every month?

My parents didn't have long-term-care insurance to pay for nursing home care in the event of catastrophic illness. They couldn't afford the policy. Medicare Hospital Insurance pays for a maximum of 100 days in a nursing facility, and the average stay is about 24 days. When the Medicare payments ran out for my father, my mother had no choice but to start dipping into her savings. Once she spends down enough, and has so few resources left she is near the poverty level, she can apply for Medicaid, which is defined as a state welfare program and has strict limitations on your income and the amount of assets you may own.

My parents are not exceptions to the rule. There are many senior citizens depleting their life savings to get down to what the government allows them to retain before Medicaid kicks in, which is not a lot of dough.

The saddest part is that it all could have been avoided if only we'd talked about potential medical disasters with my parents and devised a plan in advance. Ken and I could have purchased a long-term-care policy for my folks. The gifts that we bought them over the years could have easily paid for the premiums.

I would urge anyone who can afford it, instead of giving your parents big holiday gifts, get together with your siblings, have everyone chip in, and buy them long-term-care insurance. Don't wait until a crisis hits before you hold a family financial powwow! That's much too late. Believe us, we know what we're talking about.

What to Ask and How to Ask It

We've known aging parents who have their affairs in order and feel perfectly comfortable telling their children, and even their grandchildren, all about it. We have a friend whose grandfather had a plan mapped out to *disinherit* his profligate-spending son-in-law, our friend's father, and the grandfather told the whole family about it a decade before he died. The revelation created a lot of family disharmony, but at least there were no deathbed or post-deathbed surprises!

But for most families "money" and "old age" and "wills and trusts" are among the toughest subjects you might try to broach. Our parents (like most of us) were raised not to talk about their money. Add to that the complications you might have if your parents are divorced, your own kids live with your ex, your parents have far more money than you have or vice versa, you are supporting your parents, your parents disapprove of your lifestyle or your partner—or any combination of such factors. You'll need to build a bond of "money trust" between you and your parents before they'll feel comfortable having you know everything about their finances.

Some parents still look at their 30-, 40-, 50-, and 60-year-old children as "kids," and can't imagine having a weighty discussion about money matters with someone who is "just a kid." Needless to say, if your parents, like most parents, fit into the difficult-to-talk-to category, you will have to employ some high-level diplomacy. Your discussions should focus around three main objectives: to **maximize** their available cash, to **protect** the assets they have amassed over many hard years of work, and to **maintain their independence.**

Some tips from us:

- To broach the subject, look for the cues that your parents drop. They might make references to "when I'm gone," or to the financial condition of friends, particularly those who have recently gone through a change in health or lost a spouse. Squelch your instinct to reassure your parents that "you'll live forever." Reality-check time! No one lives forever; one of the reasons we have children is to preserve a little bit of ourselves through our lineage. Instead, use their opening gambit to start a meaningful conversation about money.
- Find a reason to begin talking about money issues. Mention a relevant article from a newspaper/magazine, or a topic you recently discussed with a friend. For openers, how about the importance of having a will or trust and long-term-care insur-

ance? Offer a rationale for the conversation: "Everything is going so fast these days, we should start planning for the future as a *family*!"

Here's an easy conversation starter: "Need any help with bills? Bookkeeping? Tracking bank fees? Brokerage account/commissions?" One way you can get involved is by offering to be your parents' "financial secretary." You can handle their correspondence, phone calls, paperwork, and investment details. It's the best way to learn the most about their situation. But remember, as you take on new responsibilities for your parents, always double-check their comfort level.

- Introduce a possible scenario and discuss different situations, beginning with the *least* threatening, such as understanding a pension payout, surviving spouse alternatives, and how and if your parents' savings and investments will provide for them during the next 10, 20, 30 years. Ask them questions they have about their financial security.

- If your parents don't bring up the topic of money during the next month or so, show them this chapter and ask what they think. If all else fails, ask one of your parents' peers to broach the subject with them.

- When you're talking about money, stress to your parents that you are not interested in taking over their bank accounts or their lives, and that no decision will ever be made without them. Remember how it felt when you were a kid and your parents "decided" your future without asking you first? That's the image we want you to keep in mind.

- Tell your parents you're thinking of revising your own will and want *their* advice. That might open up dialog about their own estate provisions.

- Does your employer offer long-term-care insurance to employees at a discount? Often other family members are eligible for coverage. If you have this benefit, take advantage of it, and ask your parents if they are interested in getting coverage, too.

- If the initial conversation becomes uncomfortable, postpone further discussion until another time. You might try bringing in a trusted family financial adviser to back you up. Sometimes the presence of an "outsider" can be helpful.

CAUTION: When you ask questions, you should be prepared for answers that may not be what you want to hear. Be ready for a discussion about such matters as who would be the best executor(s). Be ready to hear that one child might be receiving more than the others because of special circumstances.

If you ask the right questions the right way, talking about money with your parents becomes a win-win situation. Your comfort level will rise once you know how your parents want important decisions handled and where they keep important papers. Your parents, meanwhile, will be reassured that you're not taking over the helm of their finances;

you're merely helping them steer along the financial waterways—and getting the training you need to take over completely if it ever becomes necessary.

Ask Your Parents These Questions

Ultimately, you should hold a family powwow to talk about your parents' finances. Choose at least one adult child to be the note taker of the meeting. This way you have a record of the discussion and a list of items that require follow-up. Act promptly on any decisions that are made at the meeting. If you're missing any of the important estate planning documents we've listed on the next page, agree on a date by which you'll have these documents.

Here's your agenda:

1. *Are your insurance needs being met?* Once your parents have no one depending on them for income, and no mortgage or other large debts to pay off, they may no longer need life insurance. They will never hear this from a life insurance agent; in fact, there is a segment of the life insurance industry that preys on senior citizens, talking them into buying expensive policies and annuities that are completely inappropriate. (See Chapter 10.) At this stage your parents may be *much* better off using their disposable cash to buy long-term-care insurance. Sit down with your parents and a trusted insurance adviser to review their insurance needs.

2. *Do you have wills and when did you last review them?* Remind your parents that a will is the only way for each of them to make sure that their assets are handled according to their wishes. We recommend that your parents review their wills at least every five years. Encourage your parents to make an appointment with an estate-planning attorney to have a will drawn up or revised, if necessary. Ask if they would like you to come with them—and respect their wishes if the answer is "no."

3. *While your parents are at the lawyer's office (if you can get them there!), they should also consider having a durable power of attorney drawn up.* A durable power of attorney remains valid once your parents are incapacitated. If your parents are reluctant to give you power of attorney, have their lawyer hold the power of attorney until it's needed. If your parents don't have a trusted estate-planning attorney, you may call your local bar association for a referral.

4. *What kind of health care will you need if you become incapacitated?* Your parents may have a firm preference for receiving home health care, moving in with family members, or living in a nursing center. Knowing your parents' wishes in this area will make things easier for everyone, should the need for ongoing care arise. If your

Dolan Bottom Line

Help your parents locate the documents you'd need if you suddenly had to run their affairs. Find all of these documents. Make copies for yourself. Make extra copies and put them in a file that you can always locate. Make MORE copies and keep them in a fireproof file cabinet with a lock. You can get these at any office-supply store. You may have papers of your own to add, but here is our list of vital documents you should have:

- Bank account numbers/brokerage statements
- Names, addresses, and phone numbers of their physicians
- Names, addresses, and phone numbers of their lawyer, broker, and insurance agents
- Names, addresses, and phone numbers of their closest friends and relatives
- Names, addresses, and phone numbers of the handymen your parents call if they have household emergencies
- Social Security ID cards
- Pension plan information from their employers
- Tax returns for the past 3–5 years
- Deed to the house
- A list of debts (loans, etc.)
- Medicare and Medicaid information
- Copies of all insurance policies
- Copies of their birth certificates
- Copies of their wills
- Living will
- Copies of all power-of-attorney documents and trusts
- Prepaid funeral contract
- Funeral instructions (i.e., do they wish to be buried, cremated, or whatever)
- Instructions for pet care, and even garden care
- Add your own

Don't want to go through all of that now? Okay, wait until you have to hunt for these documents on your own. Here's an exercise to practice for the day you have to start your search. Some evening, turn your back and have someone hide a quarter in your living room. Turn off all the lights.

Now find the quarter in the dark.

Get the point?

parents prefer a continuing care center, help them research different centers now until they find one or two they like.

5. *Where do you keep your important papers and checkbook?* Emphasize that you aren't interested in how much money your parents have, you just want to make sure nothing gets overlooked if they have a sudden illness and can't handle their finances. You must know enough to make sure that all ongoing expenses get paid (mortgage, loans, bills, charitable contributions) and all income is received (dividends, interest, and pension and Social Security checks). We have had *dozens* of calls over the years from frustrated "kids" who are unable to find a suddenly deceased parent's will, insurance policy, bank statements, and so forth. It's a *big* problem if you aren't prepared.

6. *What investments have you made?* After you understand what investments your parents currently own, evaluate those investments to make sure that they match the investment objectives of most people their age. Aren't you glad you read our chapter on investing? Etch those objectives in stone—*safety* and *income*. Don't offer investment advice unless you're knowledgable and comfortable with the various choices available.

7. *How much money do you have in savings, investments, and retirement accounts? How much will your parents receive each month from pensions and Social Security?* You need to gauge whether they will be able to support themselves if they should live to be 100.

Managing Your Parents' Investments

How should your parents' money be invested once the nest is empty and they are retired or facing retirement? Never, never in anything risky! These are the years when blood-sucking brokers and salesmen come knocking at their door, using all manner of persuasive tactics to put your parents' money into investments that will be good for no one but the person who is selling them. Annuities for 90-year-olds, swampland real estate, "rare"

Dolan Bottom Line

No matter how much you disagree with your parents' financial decisions, remember that while they are healthy and capable, your participation in their money matters is "by invitation only."

coins, junk mail that "guarantees" a 21% return on your investments—we've seen and heard it all. The calls we've had from senior citizens (and their kids) reporting outlandish schemes quadrupled between the late 1990s and the start of the new millennium.

We're always amazed that people who would complain about being charged $2 for a cup of coffee in their local diner will turn around and drain their life savings buying stupid stuff from strangers on the phone, but it happens all the time. One of the saddest reasons that so many senior citizen scams exist is that lonely elderly people, lacking anyone else to talk with, will stay on the phone with a "nice young man" who chats them up until they're hooked. Take the elderly gentleman who called us, almost in tears, to tell us about the "rare" coins he had purchased for $5,500 from a "very polite, low-pressure" salesman who called him and chatted him up on the phone. The man had the coins appraised; turned out they were worth only $900. By then his money was gone. Remind your parents to hang up when strangers call.

These are the investments that are appropriate for this stage of their lives. If they have money in *anything* that doesn't appear on this list, it's time to sell!

- ✓ Large-cap, dividend-paying stocks—as a *small* percentage of their portfolio
- ✓ CDs (if FDIC-insured)
- ✓ U.S. Treasury bills/notes/bonds (if held to maturity)
- ✓ Money market funds—for liquidity and emergency savings
- ✓ Cash
- ✓ Fixed annuities—only if illiquid holdings aren't a problem
- ✓ Municipal Bonds—if their tax bracket is 28% or higher

How Do You Find a Good Elder-Care Attorney?

There is no substitute, including reading this chapter, for sitting down with a qualified elder-law attorney. How do you find one?

Ask friends for references.

Consult the Lawyer Referral Department of your local chapter of the American Bar Association. Their Web site—www.abanet.org—has a directory.

Go to these two lawyer locating sites, which have state-by-state listings:

www.lawyers.com

The Martindale-Hubbell Legal Network—www.martindale.com

Protecting Your Parents' Assets

This is complicated stuff! The bottom line, *before* we begin, is this: Consult an elder-law attorney to help you and your parents through the maze of health care planning for their senior years. It's *well* worth the money.

What follows is general information to get you started. Individual circumstances may dictate alternate strategies.

There are an awful lot of do-it-yourself plans to try to protect the family estate from unscrupulous lawyers as well as estate taxes. Parents, particularly when there is a widowed parent, often try to avoid having wills because they don't want to deal with lawyers. Some have an aversion to talking about wills, as if talking about death will bring it on. It's extremely important to not try to do estate planning yourself. Your parents could be setting themselves up for gift tax problems—and they've now gifted you their cost basis.

One of your parents'—and your—biggest concerns could be their health care in their senior years, particularly if one or both of your parents need long-term care. Medicare offers nowhere near enough coverage for nursing home stays. It will pay, on average, for up to 27 days of nursing home care after three consecutive days in the hospital. So there are only three ways to pay for catastrophic long-term care, which usually means a stay in a nursing home (see p. 253 for alternatives). A nursing home stay can be financed with:

1. Cash
2. Medicaid
3. Long-term-care insurance

Long-term-care insurance is discussed in depth in the next section. But first, let's take a look at Medicaid. Since Medicaid is essentially welfare payments for health care, the government demands that your assets be close to the poverty level before you can qualify to have long-term health care financed by Medicaid. As a result, many senior citizens are forced to "spend down" until they qualify. In most states a Medicaid recipient can have no more than about $1,000 in bank accounts, stocks, and other liquid assets, plus money put aside for a prepaid funeral. Personal property, such as jewelry, furniture, artworks, and antiques, are not counted unless the state or county social service agency has an assessment that says they are of great value. The value of a home that is still occupied, whether by the recipient or by a spouse, is not counted in the formula, but if you have a widowed parent who is in a nursing home, the house will have to be put on the market within several months. A home that is not a principal residence may have to go. (See Chapter 12, where we talk about protecting your own assets, for a list of Medicaid's countable and noncountable assets.) So your parents could be left with nothing for themselves if they are able to leave the nursing home, let alone for their heirs.

However, there may be a way around this dire scenario. Your parents may be candidates for a four-year long-term-care policy—or you may buy it for them. With a four-year policy, you may transfer your assets to your heirs or put them into trust when you go into a nursing home, and still qualify for Medicaid before your long-term-care coverage expires. The caveat is that if you try to transfer your assets within three years (36 months) of your Medicaid application, or if you transfer your assets into a trust within five years of your application, Medicaid will most likely disqualify the transfers, and you will be forced to spend most of your life savings, and sell your home and most of your possessions before Medicaid will pay for long-term care. For example, if you are admitted to a nursing home on November 1, 2003, and you transfer your home to your children on that same day, you can apply for Medicaid after November 1, 2006, and your home's value is protected. Meanwhile, you have your long-term-care insurance policy covering costs until November 2007.

A young man called us with a gut-wrenching story that should teach all of us a valuable lesson. Both of his parents had entered a nursing home within 30 days of each other, and the $10,000-per-month charge (for both parents) would wipe out their life savings in less than six months! He had to sell the family business to pay for his parents' nursing home care. A little preplanning would have saved the fruits of a lifetime's work.

If your parents need long-term care now and Medicare doesn't cover it, here are two alternatives. Neither of these options is cheap, painless, or risk-free—but neither is watching your parents impoverish themselves.

Help with Selecting a Reverse Mortgage

AARP, which runs a large site devoted to information about reverse mortgages at www.reverse.org, says the bottom line in selecting a lender is simply this: "how much total cash you will get versus how much you will pay." The site has some 30 pages of information explaining what you should know before you select a reverse mortgage.

Show the contract offered by lenders to a lawyer before you decide on anything. You can find a HUD-approved counselor, who will review your contract free, through the National Reverse Mortgage Association in Washington. Phone them at 202-939-1760 or check out their information online at www.reversemortgage.org.

The National Reverse Mortgage Association's Web site also has an important reference tool: a state-by-state listing of approved reverse mortgage lenders.

1. Consider a reverse mortgage on their house. The lender pays them a percentage of the value of their home, with a guarantee that your parents may live there for the rest of their lives. There are good reverse mortgages and then there are some bogus ones, but fortunately there are good sources of information and help.
2. Sell your parents' house and put the proceeds in a money market fund that offers check-writing privileges.

Once your parents' savings run out—which means they are now practically broke!—Medicaid will start paying for their care, and they can't be kicked out of the facility once they're in.

What to Do When the Senior Citizen
Health Care Crisis Hits Home

With the costs of health care for everyone spiraling way out of control, senior citizens are the hardest hit because they're the group that needs the most health care and the most expensive treatments. Many HMOs are pulling out of senior citizen health care left, right, and sideways. Physicians are refusing to take new Medicare patients because they say the government pays them too little to cover the costs.

We don't know where this is going to end, but something has to be done. Are we going to have to go the Canadian route of socialized medicine? (There are problems with that system, too!) Are we going to see more and more senior citizens hopping on buses to Canada for their pharmaceutical needs?

How much is it going to cost your parents (and maybe you) if they end up in a nursing home? A truckload. A nursing home in some parts of the United States costs as much as $100,000 per year. Costs are expected to be as much as $300,000 a year by 2020. And you thought college was expensive!

If the premiums are affordable for your family, a long-term-care insurance policy (LTC) may be the best solution. The bible of long-term-care advice, *Planning for Long-Term Care* (available for $14.95; www.books.mcgraw-hill.com), published by the United Seniors Health Council, recommends buying long-term-care insurance only if your parents:

- Own assets of at least $75,000 (excluding home and automobile)
- Have annual retirement income of at least $25,000–$35,000
- Can pay premiums without adversely affecting their lifestyle (or you can pay the premiums without feeling the pinch)
- Can absorb possible premium increases without financial difficulty

Although the cost of such protection may be more than $3,000 per person per year, the price pales in comparison with the cost of long-term care. The number of policies has more than doubled since 1990, thanks to the growth in the market for such policies as America grows grayer. Over 120 insurance companies offer them. Check out www.longtermcareinsurance.org, a buyer's advocacy site that will give you detailed information about long-term-care insurance and policy rate comparisons. The best policies include a comprehensive mix of coverage for nursing home stays, home care, and assisted living.

How Much LTC Coverage Do You Need?

For most buyers, the policies should cover 80% to 100% of the cost of long-term care in their region. An important question to ask yourself when investigating the cost of an LTC policy is to determine what percent of the cost you may comfortably self-insure. It should be somewhat less than what you currently spend on keeping yourself healthy, going on vacations, etc. The theory being that nursing home residents don't have to maintain a household.

If you pick an amount of self-insurance, e.g., $100 a day, ask yourself, "If your spouse had to write a check to a nursing home every month for $3,000 for your care, would your spouse be able to maintain his or her current standard of living?" If the answer is "yes," that's the amount of self-insurance vs. the daily benefit paid by insurance.

In addition, some states set minimum amounts of daily benefit that must be included in your policy, such as $50 or $100 a day. Minimum coverage should be $100 per day for nursing home and $50 for home care. Assisted living daily benefits should be somewhere between those two figures. Ideally, you should purchase a policy with a daily benefit that can be applied freely among all types of care.

There is no easy answer as to "when" you should purchase LTC insurance. Some professionals say "in your 50s," "wait until you're in your mid-60s," etc. About 40% of all persons admitted to nursing homes are under age 65. While the vast majority of those "younger" admissions will recover, their disability may prevent them from getting insurance later. In addition, the "statistically unwise" argument is simply not correct. The only issue is whether over your lifetime, you want to spend $40,000, $50,000, or $80,000 for the *same* coverage.

When Does an LTC Policy Kick In?

Medicare offers limited coverage for nursing home stays. It will pay, on average, for up to 27 days of nursing home care after three consecutive days in the hospital.

You're Not Getting Any Younger Yourself, So Do You Need an LTC Policy?

Once you hit the age of 50, you might hear from insurance agents trying to sell a policy for *your* old age. Should you buy? Only if you can afford it. The average person who buys an LTC policy is 67 years old. Owning it before that age is statistically not money well spent, because you probably won't need it before then. Unless you have assets of $250,000 or more, including your home, an LTC policy may be too expensive for the coverage that it would provide. If it costs more than 6% to 8% of your annual income in premiums, it's too expensive for you.

However, be aware that the cost goes up as you get older. A policy purchased at age 50, with $150-per-day coverage for life with the coverage beginning 90 days after you are eligible, would cost between $2,500 and $3,000 per person per year. At age 60 the same coverage would cost between $3,000 and $4,000, and at age 70 it would cost around $5,000 per year. Yet once you reach age 65, there is a 40% chance that you will need long-term care at some point.

Don't despair! There are ways to lower the cost. You can look for a policy with a limit on the number of years for which it would pay. This could be enough, because statistics show that most people stay in nursing homes no longer than three years. They are either cured or—here's the bad news—they go out feet first. We recommend that you consider buying a long-term-care insurance policy that gives you four years of benefits.

If your parent is homebound and needs nursing services on an intermittent basis, Medicare will pay up to 35 hours of home health visits. Once your parent's condition improves, he or she may be ineligible for coverage.

If you can afford to pay some of the care costs after your Medicare coverage is exhausted, consider buying a long-term-care policy with a 90-day or a 100-day waiting period rather than a 30-day waiting period. You'll save about 10% in premiums.

How Long Will You Need Coverage?

The period in which your parents are covered is called the benefit period. You can buy a "lifetime" policy if you believe that they might spend more than five years in a nursing home. But that's very expensive—and usually unnecessary. Again, the average nursing home stay is three years; the likelihood of staying longer than that is just over 10%. Most nursing home admissions are for relatively short periods of time—less than three months.

TIMPANOGOS HIGH SCHOOL

Buying a policy with a four-year benefit period that covers nursing homes, home care, and assisted living is generally adequate.

Don't buy a shorter benefit for home care, because home care is seen as an alternative to taking people out of their homes and placing them in nursing homes.

Will the Policy Keep Up with Rising Costs?

It will if you buy a policy set up to keep pace with rising health care costs, with an inflation-protection rider that increases the daily benefit amount. The best rider is one that promises 5% more per year compounded beginning the year after you buy the policy.

If your parents are in their seventies, a simple 5% inflation adjustment is sufficient because they'll likely need the benefit payout sooner.

If your parents are in their eighties, they should probably forego inflation protection, because they won't likely live long enough to justify the extra expense for inflation protection.

If you currently have serious medical problems, but are insurable and think you might need care sooner rather than later, consider buying a very high daily benefit with no inflation protection. That way, you'll have more insurance coverage up front, and that's better than waiting 14 years to have your daily benefit double, with 5% compound inflation.

When Should Benefits Begin?

In determining when benefits should begin, insurance companies look at your ability to perform typical activities of daily living, or ADLs, also known as "benefit triggers."

Policies pay out benefits when you are unable to perform at least two of these ADLs, such as inability to bathe. These policies have a list of five or six Activities of Daily Living of which you must trigger two. (You cannot choose which Activities of Daily Living will trigger your policy.)

Will the Policy Lapse If You Can't Pay Premiums?

You may choose nonforfeiture protection that provides some LTC coverage even if no one in the family can pay the premiums. The shortened benefit period option allows you to receive benefits if you pay premiums for a certain number of years, usually five to seven years.

Policies also pay benefits when your doctor has determined that you are "cognitively impaired," meaning your short-term memory is failing and it is necessary to have someone supervise you for your own protection.

You can read all about long-term health care insurance in a very good book from the United Seniors Health Council in Washington, D.C: *Long-term Care Planning: A Dollar and Sense Guide.* $19.50; 800-637-2604; www.unitedseniorshealth.org.

For more information about financing long-term-care alternatives, contact:

The Eldercare Locator Service, run by the the U.S. Administration on Aging
800-677-1116
www.eldercare.gov

The "Best" Long-Term-Care Policy

There's no easy "one-size-fits-all" long-term-care policy. Ask your insurance salesperson to provide you with an Outline of Coverage and a Policy Brochure for several companies. Good salespeople for these policies will have C.I.T.C. (Certified in Long-Term Care), C.S.A. (Certified Senior Advisor), or C.F.P. (Certified Financial Planner) designations, and will have sold a minimum of 50 of these policies. Don't rush. Comparison-shop, then pick the policy that fits your needs and pocketbook. Shop around and compare policy benefits. If you change your mind after buying the policy, in many states you have 30 days to cancel. One of the best sources for policy rate comparisons we've found is the buyer's advocacy site www.longtermcareinsurance.org.

We recommend that your policy include:

- "Level Premiums"—At the present time, no company guarantees they will never raise your rates. Some major companies have never raised their rates, and some will guarantee no rate increases for up to ten years. But all long-term-care insurance companies currently reserve the right to raise their rates in your state on a class (not individual) basis. That means they can raise the rates on all policyholders with your policy form, if your state insurance department approves the increase.
- Skilled nursing care (which is prescribed by a doctor and provided by skilled medical personnel) and custodial care (which can be provided by people without professional skills) in a nursing home, or at home, without any restrictions on previous care. This last point is important. You don't want a policy that requires, for example, your aging parent to be hospitalized before the insurer will cover nursing home stays, or prior skilled nursing-home care before they'll pay for custodial care.
- Assistance with as few as two "activities of daily living" (ADLs). These include

needing help with bathing, dressing, eating, toileting, transferring, or because of incontinence. (Walking around is not an activity of daily living.)

- A daily benefit amount that's lower than the daily cost of nursing-home care in your parents' area. For instance, if the average nursing home costs $150/day, purchase a $125/day benefit and make up the $25/day difference yourself. You'll save $275–$300/year in premiums.
- Inflation protection that automatically increases your initial benefit level annually at least 5%.
- A four- to six-year cumulative benefit period rather than lifetime benefits. This saves you $600–$1,000 a year.
- A 90-day-or-more "elimination" period (which is the waiting period between when you enter a nursing home and when your benefits begin) shaves another $300–$450 off your annual premiums.

Your total premium savings following our advice on these policies is a whopping $1,175–$1,750 per year! Your parents should invest these savings so they can use this money to offset the cost of the first 100 days of long-term care. In less than nine years of paying premiums, they'll have saved enough on premiums to offset any up-front costs.

Finding the Best Long-Term-Care Facility

Thinking about your parent moving into a nursing home is an emotional event that raises many questions, not the least of which is: How do you know for sure whether a nursing home is the best option? We put together this easy checklist that will help you decide what's best for your loved one:

- ✓ Can your loved one no longer live independently even with assistance?
- ✓ Does your loved one require round-the-clock skilled supervision?
- ✓ Does your loved one need help with two or more of these activities: bathing, dressing, eating, walking, or going to the bathroom?
- ✓ Is your loved one placing difficult demands on your emotional and physical health and on your finances?

If you answer "yes" to at least three of these four questions, your loved one will be better off living in a more controlled environment.

Nursing Home Alternatives

There are many options available besides a nursing home. Which one is right for your situation depends on the type of care your loved one needs. We've listed seven nursing home alternatives that provide quality care in a more "homey" environment.

1. **Home Health Care: Your Loved One Stays in Familiar Surroundings**

   Look for a home health care agency that offers a wide variety of care, including nursing care, in-home doctor and therapist visits, medical equipment delivery, and assistance with daily activities. There are also other home-care agencies that will do housecleaning and shopping, and deliver ready-to-eat meals (Meals on Wheels).

   Make a list of the types of care your loved one needs and which services you or other friends and family can provide. Remember: The more services that are needed, the more the home health care will cost. At the same time, don't be penny-wise and pound-foolish—you can't take care of everything yourself; you need to have some help.

   Medicare, long-term-care insurance, and veterans benefits may cover some of the costs for home health care. Also, call your health insurance provider and ask what specific coverage you have.

   To narrow down your search for a qualified home health care agency, we recommend contacting your local branch of the National Association of Area Agencies on Aging (1112 16th St. NW, Suite 100, Washington, DC 20036; 202-296-8130) and the Foundation for Hospice and Home Care (320 A St. NE, Washington, DC 20002; 202-547-6586).

2. **Combine Home Health Care with Adult Day Care**

   These centers combine medical, nursing, therapeutic, and psychiatric services with recreational activities and meal services. You drop off your loved one in the morning and pick him or her up in the evening. You can use these centers daily if you have an outside job or occasionally if you're caring for someone at home but need a day off now and then. Your loved one would still spend nights at home, but would be in a stimulating, protected environment during the day.

3. **Take Your Loved One to an Independent Living Center**

   These centers are similar to adult day-care centers, but they provide intensive physical therapy sessions so your loved ones can relearn or improve the skills they use

Dolan Bottom Line

A state-by-state listing of nursing homes and other related services can be at your fingertips in a snap. Send $50 to the American Association of Homes for the Aging (901 E St. NW, Ste. 500, Washington, DC 20004; 202-783-2242) and ask for a copy of *The AAHA Directory of Members*. Also ask for their free brochure "Choosing a Nursing Home: A Guide to Quality Care."

in everyday life—skills they might have lost due to a stroke, for instance. Your loved one still lives at home but receives ongoing therapy every day, as opposed to only two or three times a week.

4. **Take Advantage of Adult Foster Care Homes**
   Much like foster care for children, this option is for loved ones who are in fairly good health but prefer not to live at home or with relatives. The foster families receive a small stipend in return for their services and at least one adult in the foster family will have undergone elder-care training.
   To find a foster care program near you, contact your local Area Agency on Aging, Department of Social Services, or Family Service America Information Center (11700 W. Lake Park Dr., Milwaukee, WI 53224).

5. **Create Your Own Shared Housing Arrangement**
   Your loved one can share a house with a more mobile peer, a younger person, a couple, or with other members of a shared group home where five to 15 older folks share a house that they (or their local aging agency) have purchased or leased.
   The best source of information on setting up or joining an established shared home is the National Shared Housing Resource Center (321 E. 25 St., Baltimore, MD 21218; 410-235-4454, www.nationalsharedhousing.org).

6. **Invest in a Continuing-Care Residential Community**
   Here your loved one will receive lifetime housing, and nursing care when necessary. You'll usually pay a lump-sum entrance fee or "endowment" of anywhere from $35,000 to $300,000, plus a monthly service fee of $200 to $1,000. Make sure that the contract includes a clause that allows you to get a refund if your loved one decides to leave the community and that the community provides alternate arrangements in the unlikely event that the community dissolves or goes bankrupt.

The American Association of Homes and Services for the Aging (AAHSA) puts out several good brochures, including "The Continuing Care Retirement Community: A Guidebook for Consumers" ($9.95, postpaid). Order through their Web site at www.aahsa.org.

7. **Move Your Loved One to a Retirement Apartment Facility**
   Rooms, meals, housekeeping, personal care, and social activities are all contained in one area at a retirement apartment. Your loved one can live in his or her own apartment and can either cook meals, have them delivered "room service" style, or eat in a common dining room with other residents. Monthly costs for this care range from $200 to $1,000.

   For more details, get a copy of these free brochures from the AAHSA: "Nonprofit Housing and Care Options for Older People" and "Living Independently: Housing Choices for Older People."

Footing the Bills for Your Parents? Don't Forget the Tax Deduction

If you provide more than half of an aging parent's support, you can declare your parent a dependent even if he or she is not living in your home. In addition to getting the dependent deduction, you can take a tax deduction for your parent's medical expenses. To prove you pay the expenses, pay your parent's bills directly, rather than giving them the money.

Senior Citizen Scam Alert

If you are near aging parents who are starting to have moments of forgetfulness, look for warning signs that are an indication they need your help.

Bills that are accumulating on the counter are one warning sign; you may need to take over the bill paying.

Try and get a peek at the mail and see if there are a lot of solicitations for contests. Get your parents on the "do not call" lists that are available in most state attorney generals' offices. It doesn't mean everyone is going to abide by that, but it could keep some of those horrible abuses of seniors—phone callers with contests and such—from making those calls.

Beware of "senior" scams—such as sweepstakes entries and insurance policy pitches. Consumers lose more than $40 billion a year to telemarketing fraud. People over 50 years of age are especially vulnerable and account for about 56% of all victims, according to a recent study by the American Association of Retired Persons. Scam artists often target older people, knowing they tend to be trusting and polite toward strangers and are likely to be home and have time to talk with callers.

Here are the places you can contact with complaints if your parents are bombarded with calls and mailings from scam artists:

Consumer Response Center
Federal Trade Commission
Washington, DC 20580
202-FTC-HELP (382-4357); TDD: 202-326-2502
You can file a complaint with the commission by contacting the CRC by phone, by mail, or online.

National Consumers League
1701 K Street, NW
Washington, DC 20006
202-835-3323
The National Consumers League and the American Association of Retired Persons conducted research on telemarketing fraud targeting the elderly and offer suggestions for older people and their families in a brochure, "They Can't Hang Up," available from the National Consumers League.

One last word: If your parents are mules about the subject of finances—when it's your turn, don't do the same thing to your children!

Helpful Web Sites and Books

Long-Term Care, Long-Term Care Insurance, and Financing Alternatives

The Eldercare Locator Service: 800-677-1116; www.eldercare.gov

Insurance Information Institute: www.iii.org. Information about all kinds of insurance.

www.insure.com: The Insurance Guide, a consumer site with articles and research about all kinds of insurance. Click on "Long-term Care" for many links to other reports with information and advice about caring for aging parents.

www.aarp.org: One of the best organized and informative sites for seniors.

www.longtermcareinsurance.org: A buyer's advocate for long-term-care insurance and policy rate comparisons.

Long-term Care Planning: A Dollar and Sense Guide, published by the United Seniors Health Council. $19.50. Order, using a Visa or MasterCard, from their Web site, www.unitedseniorshealth.org, by phone at: 800-637-2604, or mail a check to USHC, 409 Third Street, S. W., Suite #200, Washington, DC 20024.

How to Protect Your Life Savings from Catastrophic Illness, by Harley Gordon. Financial Strategies Press, 2002. $19.95 + shipping. To order, call 877-771-2582.

Elder Care

www.caregiver.org

www.careguide.com

www.elderweb.com. Full of up-to-date information about studies and legislation, as well as a state-by-state guide to senior citizen programs, laws, insurance, and how to locate records.

The Handholder's Handbook: A Guide for Caregivers of People With Alzheimer's or Other Dementias, by Rosette Teitel and Marc L. Gordon; Rutgers University Press, 2001. Hardcover $40.00; paperback $17.00.

Elder Care Law and Lawyers

American Bar Association—www.abanet.org

www.lawyers.com

The Martindale-Hubbell Legal Network—www.martindale.com

www.seniorlaw.com: The Web site run by the New York law firm Goldfarb & Abrandt. This is a Web site where senior citizens, their families, attorneys, social workers, and financial planners can access information about elder law, Medicare, Medicaid, estate planning, trusts, and the rights of the elderly and disabled.

The Senior Survival Guide, by Peter J. Strauss and Nancy M. Lederman. Facts on File, Inc., 2003. $35.

Assisted Living

Consumer Consortium on Assisted Living—www.ccal.org

Government Sources

U.S. Administration on Aging—www.aoa.gov

www.eldercare.gov

www.medicare.gov

www.seniors.gov

CHAPTER 9

Preparing for the Unexpected

MOST OF US LIVE in our own little worlds. We get up, go to work, love our families, do our best to stay out of trouble, financial and otherwise. . . . We don't realize how fragile our lives are until a crisis hits, or we hear of a tragedy a little too close to home.

In 2002, we were closing on a piece of property, when our lawyer phoned, apologizing for being so late in returning our last call to him, but his receptionist's sister had been killed just the day before. She was only 42 years old. A good friend of ours, a woman in her forties who worked at our country club in Florida, went to the doctor for her annual physical, feeling fine, but found out she had liver cancer. Two weeks later she was dead, leaving a husband and two small children.

You never know what it might be, but *the* most unexpected event, possibly in all of American history, was September 11, 2001. Who could ever have been prepared for that catastrophe?! Ever since then, the calls are still coming in from people who want to know how The Dolans can help them get a grip on their fears of financial—as well as emotional—devastation. We've all learned that we can't afford to get fat and happy and complacent.

Our mission, with this book and our national radio show, is to at least help you withstand a crisis financially, which in itself gives you a certain measure of peace of mind.

The September 11 attack, and the economic crisis and life changes that came in its wake, serves to underscore the importance of being prepared so that you and every member of your household know what's going on vis-à-vis where important papers are, what the bill-paying strategies are, and how the household runs in general. Can we help you sit down with your significant other, look him or her in the eye, and ask: "Where would our finances be if you left me or were killed in a terrorist attack tomorrow?" You bet we can! Call it tough love.

Suddenly Single

Nothing wreaks havoc with your finances faster than finding yourself suddenly on your own again, unexpectedly, through divorce or death. The consequence of both situations is often a sharp drop in a woman's standard of living in the transition from two incomes to one—or, in the case of homemakers, one income to NONE!!

A few important "widow/divorce" statistics to consider:

- The average age for a widow in the United States is 55 years.
- Women live an average of seven years longer than men.
- One-half of the women married in the past 20 years will eventually divorce.
- Ninety percent of women will be on their own sometime in their lives and will have to "go solo" to manage their finances.
- Only 15% of divorcing women receive any form of spousal support. Fewer than one-half of women awarded child support ever get the full amount that they are due.
- Two-thirds of divorced women can't afford to keep their homes.
- Eighty-five percent of divorced women in one survey got nothing from their husband's pension or health benefits.
- The typical woman's standard of living drops 45% in the first year of divorce, whereas the average man's jumps 15%.

To be sure, the numbers in that last item can vary greatly depending on many different factors. One recent survey found that among men over 50, incomes dropped 14% following a divorce—though women of the same age were found to suffer a 39% plunge in their income.

We have heard from plenty of men who are exceptions to the statistic and have cut back their lifestyles drastically after a divorce so that they can support their children and maintain two homes. If a couple has been living beyond their means to begin with, then they split up and have to maintain two households . . . well, men can find themselves forced to cut way back, too. That's why it is not at all uncommon to find a divorced man living in a rented hovel; he might have a state-of-the-art entertainment system that he got in the settlement, but he's keeping his own overhead minimal so that he can help his ex-wife keep up the mortgage payments and pay child support.

In short, becoming suddenly, unexpectedly single is a concern for both men and women. It's also an important scenario to consider for people who are cohabiting. If you don't have the benefit of a marriage contract, in fact, you *really* need to think about how you'd get by without your partner and put things in writing.

We don't like to think about such things, either, but we're here to help you out if either of the two worst things that can happen happen.

Part I: Our D-I-V-O-R-C-E

Our phone lines are jammed with calls when we have as a guest on *The Dolans* our friend Jacalyn Barnett, a marital lawyer in New York City. Here are some of the no-holds-barred questions and answers heard on a recent Dolans hour dedicated to the nasty subject of divorce. These questions are some of the most common ones that we field:

Q: My sister has just filed divorce papers. Our mother is elderly. If she should die before the divorce is final, would my sister's husband be entitled to any part of the inheritance?

Barnett: When a potential heir has a divorce pending, the will should be rewritten so that it's specific. In this case, it should say that money is to go to your sister only.

That's the easy part. The big question is whether there is going to be a support obligation in this divorce. If the inheritance is substantial, it could not only reduce her ex's support obligation to her and to her children, but it could also lead a judge to rule that she has a support obligation to him. It might be a good idea for your mother to put the money into a trust for your sister, so that there won't be a large lump sum that factors into the equation. Your sister would not receive any benefits from the trust, however, which might hurt her or the children. But if the trust benefits the children, it could reduce their father's support obligation.

Q: I'm 79 and married to a hardheaded man. I don't really want to go through a divorce, and I don't want money from him; I just think we need to go our separate ways. Can we live apart without getting a divorce?

Barnett: A marriage is a legally binding partnership, and you can't dissolve it simply on a handshake. If you don't file for a divorce, you are married for all purposes. He could run up debts and you could be held responsible for them even if the debts aren't in your name. What if your estranged husband were to become sick and have to be put into a nursing home? If he needs money to pay the bills, the state would look to *your* assets as well as his before it would step in to take care of him with Medicaid.

Q: **I'm divorced and getting child support from my ex-husband, in an amount based on the fact that his annual income is about $100,000 while I'm making only $26,000 a year. Now my ex wants to change careers, to do something that will pay much less. I don't understand how a person in the peak of his earnings potential can do this when he has a child!**

Barnett: You need to see a lawyer again and you might have to take your ex to court. A court is likely to rule that if a person chooses to lower his income, his assets should become available for support. It is critical that you show in court that his loss of income was voluntary.

Q: **I'm a 78-year-old widower and have a 42-year-old son who's having marital problems. I have a feeling his wife is hanging on until I die so that she can get the inheritance. How can I protect my son in my will?**

Barnett: There is no way to guard your assets 100%. If they stay married, she will be entitled to a certain portion of his estate if she outlives him and he has the assets in his name at death. If they get a divorce, the assets might be used for her support. However, the best protection is to place the money in a trust and attach restrictions. If your son has children, you could create educational trusts for them that would bypass their parents.

Q: **I'm getting a divorce and will receive child support for my son, but he has Down syndrome and will be dependent all of his life. How can I make sure he's taken care of?**

Barnett: You should use some of the proceeds from your child support, or settlement if you have one, to set up a **supplemental needs trust.** This will provide for your son when you're no longer around without disqualifying him for government benefits. (See Chapter 12 for an explanation of how a supplemental needs trust works.)

Q: **I'm self-employed in an industry that is slipping big-time. Now I'm getting a divorce. Will the small profit I expect to earn this year be counted as a personal asset in determining the settlement?**

Barnett: Title to an asset in most states doesn't mean it belongs only to you in a divorce. A marriage is an economic partnership, and your wife will be allowed to participate in her share of the assets you acquired jointly. The only reason your business assets wouldn't be counted as an asset would be if you had started the business before you got married and both of you signed a prenuptial agreement stating that the business assets, income, *and* appreciation were yours alone.

Breaking Up When You Weren't Married

Here's a question from a woman who decided it was time for Splitsville *before* the wedding:

Q: If I break off my engagement, do I have to return the ring?
A: Some states now have laws requiring that you give back the ring even if you were the one who was dumped. New York is one of these states. There have been a few lawsuits that resulted in a ruling that an engagement ring isn't an unconditional gift. If the ring is an heirloom from the man's family, from a moral point of view it seems fair that he gets it back.

On the other hand, if the bride-not-to-be or her parents have already doled out big bucks for the wedding that aren't refundable and the man breaks off the engagement, the *decent* thing might be to let her keep the ring as a kind of "settlement." She could sell the ring and keep the money to make up for the lost deposits.

As the questions we've received on our show indicate, a breakup brings out the greediest and most vindictive side of human nature. If you're dissolving a marriage, at least you should have a clear-cut legal partnership that, like any other contractual partnership, can be terminated with a legally binding court order that attempts to reach a settlement that's financially fair to both parties (even if the warring parties don't think so). But when it comes to couples who weren't yet married, or were cohabiting, the laws are less fully defined, although that is gradually changing. The law has even come up with its own term for opposite and same-sex nonmarried partnerships: a de facto relationship.

Barnett cautions that when you're breaking up it's important to see a *family lawyer*—not just any lawyer—who keeps up with the laws in your state about divorce, living together, and other aspects of coupling and uncoupling. The laws change from year to year, and each state has its own set of guiding principles.

If You Are Moving in Together

The advent of same sex "marriages" or civil unions and the surrounding controversy that will likely continue for years serves to highlight the need for smart financial planning for both heterosexual and gay partners who choose to blend their lives.

A legal "marriage" status is important because it generally provides a package of economic protections for the couple (and children)—such as Social Security retirement and survivor benefits, workplace health and benefits coverage, automatic inheritance rights, preferential estate tax treatment . . . and others!

So if you *don't* have marriage status, you should protect yourself BEFORE you begin a de facto relationship unpleasant though it may sound.

Draw up a "Living Together" agreement. The agreement should state clearly what is "yours, mine, and ours." Plan what you would do with joint property if you were to split up, or if one of you dies. We have said before that we don't think unmarried couples should buy houses together or hold other big assets jointly, but if you're together many years, inevitably you will acquire some things together—furniture, artwork, a television, a computer, souvenirs from your travels. If you also have children together, or adopt children together, you should sign an agreement working out how you would handle child support, especially if one of you is the main breadwinner and the other has little or no income.

For a look at the laws that govern cohabiting, we recommend the book *Living Together: A Legal Guide for Unmarried Couples,* from the publishing house NOLO Press. The list price is $34.99, but you can order it at a discount through NOLO: www.nolo.com/lawstore/products, or call 800-728-3555.

Throughout this chapter, we'll explain the special considerations for de facto breakup and widowhood when it comes to settling financial affairs.

If the End of Your Marriage or Relationship Seems Nigh

Don't ignore the warning signals. You may be trying to work it out, but if you are able to get your own financial arrangements in order, that will be one less problem to plague you. Draw up a master plan for yourself and your children so that you will have the money you need.

- If you don't work, consider getting a part-time job now, especially if your spouse is overextended financially and isn't wealthy. When you have an income, your spouse's support obligation will be lower, or even nonexistent. However, if you need a cushion in case one of you walks, it's best to have your own money. You might also be needing money of your own to pay for a lawyer.
- If the credit cards are all in your spouse's name, it's time to get one or two in your name. It will be easier to establish your own credit while you still have combined assets.
- Make a list of your assets. Look for the following:
  tax returns for all years of marriage
  pension plan statements
  the most recent audit of a family-owned business
  all insurance policies
  latest pension/profit-sharing statement

list of safe-deposit box contents
bank/investment firm statements listing all assets
mortgage loan papers

If you think your spouse may be hiding assets, hire a private investigator to search for hidden assets. It sounds mercenary, but the $50 or $75 per hour could be money well spent. A "private eye" of our acquaintance tells us he's seen high-net-worth spouses park assets in everything from dummy corporations (in one case, with a dog named as CEO— seriously!) to offshore accounts in the Cayman Islands. Even people of modest means have been known to conceal their real worth by liquidating accounts and hiding the cash in a safe, or transferring assets to relatives.

Hire the investigator through your lawyer for two important reasons:

1. Your lawyer will recommend an experienced, trusted investigator.
2. Your lawyer can establish client-attorney privileges with the investigator. This way, you cannot be ordered by the court to give your spouse's lawyer any information the investigator uncovers.

Illiquid Assets

In most divorces, the largest assets tend to be your home(s), insurance policies, and pension plan, and for some couples, a business. All of these are relatively illiquid assets. The biggest financial mistake you can make in a divorce is failing to take into account the tax implications of dividing or liquidating assets such as these. Lawyers don't always know what your tax liabilities will be. Talk to an accountant about your divorce as well.

The House

We'll never forget a call from a woman in Wisconsin who was awarded the house in a divorce settlement because she had three kids under the age of 18. She was *so* proud that she was able to preserve a home life for her children. But she missed one important consideration—she didn't take a good look at her finances to see if she could keep up with the mortgage payments. There are a couple of lessons for everyone in her story.

First, we've seen all too many wives get the home, then find they can't keep up with the mortgage, property taxes, maintenance, or all of the above. Two-thirds of all divorced women can't afford to keep their homes after the divorce.

Second, in this particular case, the husband had covered his you-know-what. The couple had agreed to terminate the jointly held mortgage, so that he had been absolved of responsibility for payments. He wanted protection from his ex-wife's financial obligations.

We felt for her. But divorce is a messy business, and our job is to tell you how to protect yourself from being liable for mortgage payments if your spouse remains in the house but defaults.

A divorce decree doesn't automatically absolve you of responsibility for a jointly held debt. The creditor still has a contract signed by you and your ex, and has the right to pursue both of you. But if you're the party who is worried about protecting your credit rating, you have to terminate your jointly held mortgage. There are three ways you can do this:

If you can qualify, *substitute a new debt for the old one*. This is called **novation.** The creditor agrees to remove the name of one person as an obligated party. However, the practice is usually available only to people of means; the party who stays on as signatory to the debt must have a high income and an excellent credit rating.

Refinance the mortgage. If you are awarded the house and don't qualify for novation, you should refinance in exchange for the title transfer. The secured debt should be in a sum sufficient to provide a cash buyout of your share if that is part of your settlement.

Sell the house: It may break your hearts, but if your mortgage payments are high, the most sensible strategy may be to sell the house and make a fresh start, in a place where the upkeep will be less expensive. However, it's not the solution for everyone. If you bought your house at a great price and have low mortgage payments in a city where the real estate market is booming, it might be difficult for each of you to keep up with the payments on two new homes in the area, even with the proceeds from the sale of your old one. If you're going to need major improvements to make the house salable, consider whether the cost of the work is something you can afford at this difficult time.

Talk to your accountant before you decide what to do with property.

The Retirement Assets

All of the money that you and your spouse hold in retirement plans, which include pension plans, 401(k) plans, IRAs, and all other tax-deferred retirement assets, will be included in the property settlement. We'll show you how the court usually divides these assets, then we'll show you the Dolan Alternative for keeping the current value intact for both parties instead of dividing it in half.

The Conventional Way Retirement Assets Are Divided In most cases the judge will try to divide the value in the plans equitably, but "equitably" can be a very loaded word when it comes to calculating the value of an asset designed for future use rather than the present, often financed by one spouse with matched contributions from an employer. The valuation of a defined-contribution plan is usually determined by multiplying the account balance by the percentage of vesting. A defined-benefit plan may be divided according to calculations of the future stream of income. However the valuation is determined, you need a court order to specify how the joint interest in your retirement accounts is to be divided. The court will do this by issuing what is known as a **Qualified Domestic Relations Order (QDRO)**, which the plan administrators have to approve. Without a QDRO, you have no guarantee of how the plan will be divided, and you could end up with an incorrect division and a whopping tax bill. Each order has its own terms regarding *when* the plan will be divided, too. Sometimes you have to wait until retirement; sometimes it is rolled over into separate IRAs. In addition, you may have no control over the way the plan is invested.

Some divorcing couples settle the retirement asset question by agreeing that one spouse will keep the retirement account but award the other something of equal value in return.

If you're the nonworking spouse, do you get your share of the pension retirement plan now, or do you have to wait until your ex retires? In most cases, you can get your share right away. But we advise that you roll it over into an IRA—and get a QDRO that specifies these terms. If you take your share in cash, you will pay income taxes on the entire amount and penalties if you're under 59½.

We hate to see divorcing couples liquidate these important assets when they're still young and may be subject to penalties for withdrawals, not to mention taxes. But all too often people find themselves strapped for cash with no other cushion. We've also seen the nasty scenario that occurs when a working spouse is ordered to transfer all or most of the retirement assets to the ex, and the ex makes withdrawals, leaving the original owner liable for the taxes and early-withdrawal penalties.

The Dolan Alternative The trouble with the division of retirement assets by QDRO is that each one of you will have to live on reduced benefits. Here's what we suggest that you consider:

Offer to waive your claim to your ex-spouse's pension in return for your ex-spouse buying you a **fixed annuity** of equal value, with you as the owner and beneficiary of the plan. If you've listened to our show, you may have heard us bad-mouth some kinds of annuities left and right (stay tuned for Chapter 10), but annuities are an investment vehicle with a limited number of highly useful applications, and this is one of them. Your ex-spouse could use tax-deductible alimony to buy an annuity that would pay you the same amount as your ex-spouse's pension. This way, both of you get 100% of the pension value—giving you more income and more goodwill toward each other! You can also do this if you were a long-term cohabiting couple, in which case it will be difficult in most states to get a share of the retirement plan.

The tricky aspect of this plan, naturally, will be making sure the annuity retains a value similar to that of the pension plan. Don't try to play catch-up with a variable annuity. The expenses will eat up far too much of your investment. As we'll explain in Chapter 10, the only kind of annuity we ever recommend is a "fixed" one, which gives you a fixed interest rate.

What if your ex-spouse dies before retirement? Know your rights. Make sure any court order you get includes payment of a survivor's benefit. If this isn't part of the court order and your spouse dies before retirement, you won't receive any of the benefits from a retirement plan. If you use the annuity alternative, you will get the value of your annuity and won't have to worry about the provision to the pension plan.

There is another way to protect yourself in this scenario. Buy a life insurance policy—a standard inexpensive term policy—on your ex-spouse's life and have your lawyer get your ex-spouse to pay the premiums in lieu of part of his or her alimony. As long as the premium payments are considered "alimony," your ex-spouse can deduct them. However, you should protect yourself just in case your ex fails to keep up the payments. You can do this by requesting that the insurer send out **duplicate notices** of every premium payment and/or nonpayment. If your ex should happen to default, you can make the payment, then file a suit to get reimbursed. The alternative is that if your ex, unbeknownst to you, stopped paying premiums, you could lose the death benefit and not even know that you've lost it until it's much too late.

How the pension is divided, and how you receive payment, varies from state to state. For a detailed look at pension rights, we recommend these two books:

Your Pension Rights at Divorce: What Women Need to Know ($24.95). It explains what a wife facing divorce should know about her rights under six different retirement systems, but it's a good book for men to read, too. Order from the Pension Rights Center, 1140 19th St., NW, Suite 602, Washington, DC 20036-6608; 202-296-3776; e-mail PnsnRights@aol.com; www.pensionrights.org.

Pension Issues & Divorce ($29.95). Order from divorcesource.com, 800-680-9052, www.divorcesource.com. The site also has a wealth of information about divorce issues and a summary of divorce laws in each state.

The Business

If either you or your spouse runs a business of your own that you acquired, improved upon, or financed during the marriage, the value of the business, another highly illiquid asset, is going to be a factor in the divorce settlement, even if the ownership interest is in the name of only one of you. Remember that question about this from our show. A person who owns a business could, conceivably, arrange in a prenuptial agreement that everything from the business—assets, income, *and* appreciation—are his and his alone, so that even if a garage operation grows to a multimillion-dollar corporation, the ex-spouse gets nothing. We say *don't marry* anyone capable of being that greedy.

More often, however, both parties will be entitled to a share of the business, but the spouse who owns it will try to underestimate the value in divorce proceedings. If you're the other party, don't rely on your spouse's estimate! You have a right to seek an independent appraisal, so do it.

You can hire a joint appraiser, which will cost less, but only if your present relationship with your spouse is civilized enough that you can agree to it, and agree that neither of you will contest the appraisal. Needless to say, the appraiser should be someone who is completely objective, as well as experienced in the intricacies of joint appraisals and the attending tax consequences. Don't hire an accountant who has done work for the business before.

If you have been living together for many years and your ex-partner's business has been successful, you may be able to seek a settlement if you can show that you were helpful in getting the business going. If you earned money to keep the household afloat while your partner was starting the business or experiencing a downturn; if you lent money; if you helped out by, say, minding the store or providing consultation gratis; if you can prove that your moral support or professional contacts helped make the business possible, you should hire an independent appraiser to assess the current value, then talk to a lawyer about whether the laws in your state allow you to sue for compensation. The thing is, you have to prove that you had an agreement—either that you'd help out in the business, or that your partner would support you. A written agreement signed by both parties early on in your relationship is VERY important; it doesn't sound very romantic, but it could save you. You won't get compensation simply based on the fact that you cohabited. That sort of deal—financial support in return for a sexual relationship outside of marriage—will sound in court like an illegal trade commonly known as the "world's oldest profession"!

Tax-Wise Moves

If you have not lived with your spouse for the last six months of the year, and you claim any children as dependents, you may be able to file a "head of household" tax return and take advantage of the lower tax rate. Consult an accountant.

If you pay a property settlement, you will not be hit with a gift tax.

If your retirement account assets are being split up, you can roll your share into an IRA without paying a 10% penalty—even if you're under age 59½. You can also use your alimony (which is considered earned income) to fund your IRA.

You can deduct any legal fees that relate to tax advice or investment advice, to the extent your miscellaneous deductions exceed 2% of your adjusted gross income. Ask your lawyer for an itemized bill that details the specific cost for these matters.

Child Support and Alimony

Another way to take advantage of tax deductions concerns child support and alimony. Alimony is tax-deductible. Child support is not. So if one spouse earns significantly more than the other, and is therefore in a much higher tax bracket, it makes sense to pay more alimony than child support because alimony is tax-deductible, leaving more money to go around.

The collection of both alimony and child support is still a women's issue. We've heard stories of high-earning women with stay-at-home male partners who end up paying alimony to a man who's been taking care of the kids, but by and large, most of the recipients of alimony are women, and in these days of two-career couples, only about 15% of divorcing women are awarded any form of spousal support. Of those who do receive an award, only about a third receive the whole amount. Fewer than half of the women awarded child support receive the full amount due.

The women who are awarded alimony tend to fall at one end of the economic spectrum or the other. Either they were married to very rich husbands and can prove they deserve support because they were assets to their husbands' career ascent, or they have been stay-at-home moms with few skills that would translate into the job market.

Alimony is usually a temporary award—money to help you go back to school and acquire new job skills, or to help you get back on your feet. Often women who are awarded alimony are advised by their lawyers to negotiate for a lump sum, to avoid a monthly battle for the money. A lump sum has the advantage of being something you can take care of in one quick swoop, then never have to call and beg your ex to comply with the agreement. The disadvantage is that you will pay taxes on the entire sum in the year you receive it. Remember, also, that if you remarry, and according to some settlements even if you move in with a new partner, you will lose your alimony. All the more reason you should sign a prenuptial (or pre–moving in) agreement with Partner #2, stipulating that you will receive some compensation if this relationship doesn't work out.

Monthly child support payments should be very reliable, as long as you know where you ex is and he has a steady job. All child support orders issued since 1994 have an automatic wage-withholding provision, so that the money goes directly to you without your ex ever getting his hands on it. Overdue child support payments can be deducted from any tax refund your ex is due, and Social Security or pension plan payouts can be sent to you.

It's probably no surprise to anyone that we get lots of calls from divorced women who have been relying on alimony and child support—then one day the ex-husband quits his job, skips town, and is nowhere to be found. We counsel these callers to contact their state's Department of Human Services for assistance in tracking down deadbeat dads. Some states are actually getting pretty good at it!

Health Insurance in a Divorce

If you are covered under your ex-spouse's health insurance plan, you can continue to get coverage under the Consolidated Omnibus Budget Reconciliation Act of 1985 (known as COBRA) if the company has at least 25 employees. But this coverage costs an arm and a leg and lasts for only 36 months after your divorce—and you're covered only if the company is notified within 30 days following your divorce. See the Health Insurance section of Chapter 10 for information about purchasing your own policy if necessary. If you're the custodial parent and your ex is the one with the group policy through his employer, the children can be covered by the group policy. Children of unwed parents will be covered if the company has a policy of covering dependents in a cohabiting family. However, there is a sticking point if the children are covered by an HMO. Most HMOs are regional providers, not national. If you and the children move out of the service area, they'll be insured only for emergency care. In that case, you might have to put the children on your policy.

Social Security Benefits

Divorce has a number of Social Security ramifications. If you have been married for 10 years, you may be entitled to half of your spouse's Social Security payouts. So if you are close to reaching that threshold, it might be worth hanging in there for a few more months. Otherwise you will receive no spousal or survivor benefits.

You may be able to get Social Security benefits based on your ex-spouse's work if you:

1. Are at least 62 years of age
2. Did not remarry before you were 60 years old, and
3. Were married to your ex-spouse for at least 10 years.

Along with these three requirements, in order for you to start collecting Social Security benefits, your ex-spouse must be collecting Social Security benefits, OR must be at least 62 years old and have worked long enough (40 quarters) to have the right to collect Social Security.

To get specific information on your ex-spouse's work record, call the Social Security Administration, 800-772-1213.

What to Ask Your Lawyer

Since divorce laws vary from state to state, it's important to discover everything you can about your financial rights. There's no such thing as a dumb question, so ask any question that comes to mind. No matter what, though, make sure you ask all these questions:

✓ How does your state divide marital property? If you are splitting up with a de facto partner, how does your state divide property acquired together?

✓ How likely is it that your home will have to be sold (and is it in your best interest to keep the home or not)? Some states say you must sell your home immediately and divide the profit; other states let you stay in the home until your children reach age 18.

✓ Which is better for you, assuming you're eligible for both—alimony or child support?

✓ Would you receive alimony in a large sum, partial payments, or not at all?

✓ How is child support determined, and who pays?

✓ If you supported your spouse or partner while he or she was going to college or graduate school, can you get reimbursed for the actual tuition you paid? As an alternative, are you entitled to a percentage of your ex's future earnings?

✓ What are your rights to your spouse's pension benefits? Make sure any court order you get includes payment of a *survivor's benefit,* or you won't get any of your ex-spouse's pension benefits if he dies before retirement.

If You're Contemplating a Divorce, Be Sure You . . .

✓ Find a good support system. You need friends and family around you. There are many online chat rooms and bulletin boards that offer support; two we especially like are Divorce Plus at www.pages.prodigy.com/divorceplus/div00.htm, and www.fathersdivorceline.com. However, ask around about community-based support groups, too, so that you can meet with people in a similar situation face-to-face.

✓ Construct a "success plan" (formerly known as budget) that reflects your post-divorce standard of living.

✓ Update your benefits and insurance. Change the beneficiaries on your insurance policies and retirement plans.

✓ Revise your will, especially if you have children. You want to be sure that your assets get to your children.

✓ Draw up a durable power of attorney to make sure you have someone available to make financial/medical decisions for you if you are unable to do so yourself.

✓ Start saving. For most people, the urge to console yourself with a splurge is something you'll have to overcome so that you can accumulate cash to tide you over until the divorce settlement becomes effective.

✓ If you don't already have one, you need a disability insurance policy to make sure that you'd have income if you were unable to work.

You'll find a wonderful 26-item checklist at www.divorce-online.com. The checklist covers everything from determining who pays for your kids' college education to how to find hidden assets. This site also offers free articles and information that you can download.

We hope these tips help you and those you love cope with a difficult situation. Unfortunately, divorce isn't the only time you may find yourself without your spouse. We hope you have a long and harmonious marriage, but part of our job is to show couples how to be prepared for the final act.

Part II: Till Death Do Us Part

The death of a spouse or long-term partner, whether due to an accident or natural causes, inevitably leaves the surviving partner forced to make some important financial decisions, with long-term implications—decisions that would be tough enough to make even without the emotional upheaval.

The first thing you should know if you are the surviving partner is that you don't have to do everything all at once; in fact, you shouldn't make any big financial decisions for at least three months. Allow yourself time to grieve.

Financial planning has never been a slam-dunk easy job, but the *absolutely* worst time to try sorting out investments, taxes, insurance needs, a will, or even a month's stack of bills is when you are in a state of emotional shock. You'll inevitably make mistakes. You are not likely to have the presence of mind to read the fine print or shop around for the best deal, so you can end up spending more than necessary or trusting the wrong people. This is a time when financial matters hardly seem important, yet in the back of your mind you know that the roof over your head could disappear if you don't do *something*, an awareness that adds so much stress, you might find yourself just about ready to crack up.

Consider what happened on our show after September 11. For three weeks afterward none of our listeners felt like talking about money, no matter what their situations. In the face of such devastation, people put ordinary concerns on hold, *especially* money-oriented concerns. We changed the format of our show for those first three weeks—actually, our listeners changed it for us—and talked with people about more fundamental needs, such as keeping the family safe, connecting more regularly with friends, and even sparing a kind word for a stranger. These conversations seemed to help our callers heal. They certainly helped us.

The experience really drove home the point for us that when you've suffered a devastating loss, the first thing you should do, no matter what the shape of your finances may be, is **create a support network.**

You shouldn't go it alone right now, and you'll be better able to handle money decisions once you feel that your emotional needs are being met. You can turn to family and friends for love and comfort, but this is a good time to expand your social network to include more people who have been through the same experience.

We recommend contacting the AARP Widowed Persons Service; this particular AARP program is geared to widowed partners of all ages, and has many community-based chapters offering support. They're at 601 E. Street NW, Washington, DC 20049; 202-434-2260; and on the Web at www.aarp.org/griefandloss/commsupport.html.

If you're widowed with young children, you might also contact Parents Without Partners, Inc.,1650 South Dixie Highway, Suite 510, Boca Raton, FL 33432; 800-637-7974; chapter fees vary. On the Web at www.parentswithoutpartners.org, PWP is a global organization with members who are divorced, never married, and separated as well as widowed, offering discussion meetings, special programs, study groups, publications, and social activities.

Griefnet, at www.rivendell.org, operates online support groups for adults and children who have experienced loss of all kinds, including a group geared to gays who are grieving.

Do

Put any money you receive from life insurance or other benefits into a money market fund or a CD rather than trying to invest it immediately. If you need to have money coming in regularly, divide the money into four quarters and put one-fourth of the money in a 30-day CD, one-fourth in a 60-day CD, one-fourth in a 90-day CD, and one-fourth in a 180-day CD—of course, in a bank that is FDIC-insured. Conservative? Very! Safe? Very! That is what you need right now.

Watch out for scamsters who prowl the obituary or divorce notices looking for victims, then call them posing as investment advisers.

Don't

1. . . . **listen to ANYONE who tries to give you investment advice.**
    Often heard from family members after a spouse's death: "He would have wanted it that way!" Who are they to make such assumptions?

You need a support network, but not a network of financial advisers, however well-meaning people may be.

Selling assets too quickly to get cash may lead to an ill-timed sale. Make no irrevocable decisions for at least three months. Don't sell the house, change your investments, give your insurance proceeds to a financial planner to manage, or invest in a business. If you get calls from financial planners, hang up immediately!

2.   . . . **neglect your credit history.** If all your credit cards, mortgages, car loans, and other debts are held jointly by you and your spouse, your entire credit history could be erased when your spouse dies. This is especially true if you're a woman. Protect yourself by calling your credit card companies immediately and asking to have your spouse's name removed from the credit card and have a new card issued in *just* your name.

What should you do first if you find yourself widowed? To help you through this difficult time, here are steps that help you get a grip in your finances:

Financial Moves You Must Take Care Of

There are many details you will have to deal with early on. Because we know finances are the *last* thing you want to think about, we've developed a schedule for taking care of business while grieving. Take one thing at a time, one week to one month after you are widowed. Here are the items you need to address, listed in order of priority:

Get 15 certified copies of your spouse's death certificate from your State Department of Vital Records. To save time and energy, ask the funeral parlor to get these for you. Each copy will cost about $6. The funeral parlor will tack the cost onto their bill, and all expenses can then be paid by your spouse's estate. You'll need these certificates to close or rename accounts, apply for benefits, and collect insurance proceeds.

If you have dependent children, look at your own life insurance policy and see if the payout would take care of them if anything happened to you. If it's too low, increase your coverage. Make an appointment with a lawyer to update your will/trust and beneficiaries designations on retirement plans, insurance policies, and jointly held assets.

If you don't already have one, open a checking account in your name. If you and your spouse had joint checking and savings accounts, now is the time to put these accounts in your name. This is an important step to take toward establishing or building your own credit history. It wouldn't hurt to also get a credit card in your name if you don't already have one.

While you're at the bank, you should also set up a new "estate" checking account to keep your money separate from the money in your spouse's estate. You will use this account to pay for estate-related expenses and deposit estate-related income. Otherwise, you could wait up to two years to be reimbursed for expenses you pay on the estate's behalf.

Apply for your Social Security survivor benefits. Many people think of Social Security as a retirement program, but a portion of Social Security taxes go toward survivors' insurance. The Social Security Administration says the value of the survivors insurance you have under Social Security is likely to be more than the value of your individual life insurance. Have it directly deposited into your checking account.

Your dependent children can receive 50%–70% of your spouse's Social Security benefits until they reach age 19 as long as they are full-time students. You can collect 100% of your spouse's benefit once you reach age 65 (71.5% if you want to start collecting benefits at age 60; or age 50 if you're disabled). A disabled child can collect the benefits for life.

When you go to your local Social Security office, make sure you bring a certified copy of your spouse's death certificate, marriage certificate, your birth certificate, and the birth certificates of any children who are under the age of 18. You'll also need your spouse's last paycheck stub or income tax return (to verify income) and Social Security number.

Do you know where your spouse's paycheck stubs are? Do you know if he or she even saved them? September 11 taught us that a young person can die prematurely, unexpectedly, with no emergency preparations. See the section titled "Lessons from Two World Trade Center Widows" in the next section for a list of financial details you both should know about each other just in case something we all hope never happens again does happen.

To find the nearest Social Security office, click on www.ssa.gov/regions/regional.html, call 800-772-1213 or TTY number 800-325-0778, or look in the blue pages of your phone book.

Apply for life insurance and pension benefits. Your spouse may have had life insurance policies through work, professional or fraternal clubs, alumni associations, or even through a credit card's "credit life" insurance. Write each insurance company a short letter that says, "My spouse passed away on [date]. Please forward to me all life insurance proceeds, payable to the beneficiary listed, for any life insurance policies in effect as of the date listed above." The proceeds from life insurance policies are almost always exempt from income tax. Apply for pension benefits the same way, by writing to every employer for whom your spouse ever worked.

Make a thorough search for assets your partner left behind. A detailed estate inventory may uncover forgotten assets such as savings bonds, insurance policies, veteran's benefits, stocks and bonds, and so on. See your attorney and the company benefits administrator. Review past tax returns, bank/brokerage statements, and other financial statements. Check safe-deposit boxes.

Following these strategies may not ease your grief, but it will help you get through a rough time with a lot less emotional turbulence.

Lessons from Two World Trade Center Widows

We'll never forget the very special guests we had on our show on November 27, 2001. Margie lost her husband, Joel, who worked on the ninety-fourth floor of WTC Tower 1 at a meeting on the morning of September 11. He called his wife and children on his cell phone, and was last seen helping other people get out as the building collapsed. Liz's husband, Robert, was a senior vice president at Fiduciary Trust International, and was working on the ninety-sixth floor of WTC Tower 2, with no chance to get out. Neither woman was prepared for widowhood. Their ordeal of getting their financial lives back in order—not to mention the other aspects of getting on with life—can be instructional to all of us in our efforts to become more financially secure in an insecure world. Here are some lessons we learned from our guests:

Why is it so important not to make decisions in a time of stress? Margie and Liz learned about that when they were told about the federal government's Victims Compensation Fund. They could sign up to receive money from the fund, but the document also stipulated that victims had to waive the right to file lawsuits over the terrorist attack—and they didn't even know how much they would get from the fund, or what future discoveries might make a lawsuit seem a good idea. Neither widow signed, knowing this was no time to accept a half-baked promise.

What should you both know about each other's finances? Liz's husband had a will. He kept it in his desk at the World Trade Center, so the only copy in existence is gone. In her case the loss of the will was the least of her worries, because, fortunately, the assets were jointly held and she was the beneficiary of his retirement account.

If you or your spouse keep assets in your own names, however, or if you are an unmarried couple, a will or trust is crucial. So is having copies of your estate documents that each of you can easily find.

You should keep copies of all of your important papers in a safe-deposit box or a fire-safe file cabinet with a lock, available at most office-supply stores. Here are papers that you should keep in this personal vault:

Insurance policies, with a list of all beneficiaries
The most recent statements from all of your retirement accounts. Update these regularly.
Birth certificates for both of you and your children

Social Security cards

Deed to your house

Car registration papers

Up-to-date list of investments

The Most Commonly Asked Questions About Widowhood from Our Audience

Q: **Is a lump-sum insurance policy death benefit taxable?**

A: It is not subject to federal income tax. State tax laws about this vary, so consult with your accountant or state tax department. You can link to state revenue tax departments on the Web at www.taxes.about.com/blstate.htm.

Q. **How do I invest the proceeds from the death benefit so that I can support my family by myself?**

A: The biggest problem with a lump sum is that it tends to overwhelm people. Do nothing for three to six months other than putting the money into a series of bank CDs with staggering maturity dates so that you will be able to use it in small payouts if you need it. If your lump sum is more than $100,000, the maximum amount that is protected under FDIC insurance, divide it up into money market accounts or CDs in different federally insured banks.

During that time you can start looking into conservative stocks and bonds, and, if you're comfortable with the idea, start an investment portfolio (see Chapter 5). If you have young children, you may want to invest money for their education. However, if you're at all uncomfortable with risking your principal, we say keep it in safe instruments, such as Treasuries or plain vanilla money market accounts and CDs. Don't listen to people who try to offer you investment advice. You may be better off having the money in accounts that provide a low but steady interest rate than losing it.

Q: **Am I responsible for my spouse's debts?**

A: Not necessarily, but the estate is. If you are not a signatory on the credit cards or loans, you are not, but as your spouse's heir, the estate has to pay them off.

Q: **How and when should I inform creditors and the IRS that my spouse is deceased?**

A: Make at least 15 copies of the death certificate and within 30 days you should send copies to creditors, the IRS, Social Security, the insurance company, the broker, and credit card companies. To spare yourself the continuous pain of seeing the deceased one's name in print, also contact any companies that are still sending bills in his or her name.

Q: **Are there special IRS concessions to surviving spouses with children? What is the best tax-filing status for me?**

A: There is a special concession for surviving spouses with dependent children. It's known as "qualifying widower." You can file under this status for the first two years following your spouse's death, as long as you don't remarry during that time. It is the best deal for most widowed people, because it lets you retain joint filing status. After the two years, you can file as head of household if you are still supporting your children, aging parents, or other dependents.

Q: **Am I entitled to all of the benefits in the deceased spouse's retirement plan?**

A: If you are the present spouse, yes. If you are the divorced spouse, it's still possible. That's why one of the first calls you should make is to the benefits officer of your ex-spouse's company.

Q: **Is the distribution from the retirement plan taxable? Do I take a lump sum or roll it into an IRA?**

A: Our good friend Ed Slott, a CPA who is the country's leading authority on tax and estate planning for retirement savings, says it is taxable UNLESS the plan is a Roth IRA, in which case all distributions are tax-free. The fact that you will pay taxes on all distributions is as good a reason as any to NOT take a lump sum. You can roll it over into an IRA in your name or into your current plan. If you are 59½ or over, you can start taking distributions from your spouse's plan.

Your inherited IRA can last much longer, since a new set of rules governing minimum withdrawals went into effect in 2002. "Under the old rules," explains Slott, "many beneficiaries ended up using the 5-year rule, which meant that the entire inherited account had to be withdrawn by the end of fifth year following the year of death." Now you can take annual distributions based on actuarial tables that calculate your life expectancy. This way you can also take smaller distributions, which means lower taxes. Children who inherit IRAs from their parents can take the payouts over their own life expectancies; but they should keep the IRA in the deceased parent's name, as rolling it over into their own IRAs will effectively end the IRA and leave them with an income tax bill, as well as an estate tax bill if the estate is large enough.

For up-to-date information about retirement fund distributions, see Ed's Web site: www.irahelp.com.

Q: **Are Social Security benefits available to me and my children if my spouse dies?**

A: Yes. Call Social Security at 800-772-1213; TTY number: 800-325-0778. Generally, you can't collect survivors' benefits if you remarry. However, if you remarry after age 60 (50 if disabled), you will still be entitled to benefit payments on your former spouse's record. If you remarry at age 62 or older, you may get benefits on the record of your new spouse if they are higher.

Q: **How do I check if the amount of my deceased spouse's plan distribution is correct?**

A: It's a very tricky system to figure out, which is why the National Center for Retirement Benefits, a company in Northbrook, Illinois, has done a booming business in sleuthing through pension plans to discover errors that would have resulted in employees and employees' beneficiaries missing out on money that was due them. The NCRB charges you only if its investigation results in a larger sum of money for you; then they charge 20% of the amount they recover. Among the errors the company has found, according to the information on their Web site:

- The plan calls for all compensation to be used in determining your retirement benefits, but bonuses and overtime were deleted from the computer run, resulting in a portion of the contributions and benefits that should have been accumulated for you being unpaid.

- The administrators of a profit-sharing plan have valued the account on the basis of the fair market value of the assets at the beginning of the year, instead of at the end of the year, when the stock market increased substantially.

- The administrators have used the wrong years of service for your spouse in determining your benefits.

- The wrong computer disk is being used to update files. Your current benefit statement reflects the same information that was on your benefit statement four years ago!

Check out dozens of other potential errors on the company's Web site, www.ncrb.com, or contact the National Center for Retirement Benefits at 800-666-1000.

Q: **If we lived together but weren't married, can I collect the benefits from my deceased partner's plan at work?**

A: That depends on the company's policy. Most companies will allow an unmarried partner to be named as beneficiary of the retirement plan. So you can collect the benefits, but here's the problem: You can't roll it over into your own IRA. You have to take the distribution, which means you have to pay income taxes on it, although you can spread the distribution out over five years. The best thing to do is ask the employer, while your partner is still alive, if you can set up the plan as a joint annuity, so that you get the payouts in the form of an annuity. Don't sit back; discuss the options with your partner's company retirement plan administrator and your accountant *before* you become a widow(er) of a de facto relationship!

Don't Count on Job Security

Here's another kind of financial emergency that hits all too many people broadside. The once-sacred covenant between employee and employer is about as rare today as finding a live person answering a corporate switchboard. The new mantra is: Your job is temporary, your career path is uncharted, and the future of the company for which you work is unclear.

Technology is not necessarily your friend. It won't do your job in your place, but technology has caused rapid changes in the way business is done today. Indeed, the march of technology means every company has to be ready, at a moment's notice, to change product lines and corporate structures. In the blink of an eye, *you* could be expendable. We all could. We know that radio stations change formats all the time.

So be ready to open your parachute if someone kicks you out the door. Don't expect a golden parachute. It hardly ever happens anymore.

We all know people who were laid off, but, for weeks or months in advance of that layoff, denied the obvious clues of what was going to eventually happen—sort of keeping their head in the sand. Take one of our callers, from Gainesville, Florida, who never thought it would happen to him. Even though he received a series of unfavorable job reviews, which in retrospect he realized he should have challenged, he was surprised when the new human resources director at his firm laid him off. Those are two of the most blatant ploys that companies in trouble use. The senior managers pick out the sacrificial lambs (from their own ranks on down) and give them poor performance reviews. Then they bring in a new human resources person to wield the ax, basing his decisions of who goes and who stays on, you guessed it, performance reviews. When the ax falls, it's too late to challenge your job reviews.

Stick up for your rights and fight for fair reviews.

Still, let's be realistic. The odds are that just about everyone, at least once in his or her career, is going to be blindsided in the workplace with an unexpected pink slip. But *you* are not going to sulk and plot how to get even. Pull up your socks and get back to work—the work of selling yourself.

Both wage earners in your family should have a layoff strategy working before the you-know-what hits the fan. Here's how you can minimize the personal and financial trauma that comes when your job is eliminated. Follow these steps and you'll be at your professional and personal best whether your job is in jeopardy or not. Who knows, you might make a leap and land on a higher peak.

- *Revive your network.* Get a "Job Lead" file going before you actually need it. Get in touch with old colleagues, bosses, subordinates. Even doctors and lawyers, and friends. Get involved with professional associations and attend social functions for people in your field. You don't have to tell people you are job hunting—in fact, don't, if word could get back to your present employer—but let people in the know be aware that you wouldn't turn away from a lead. Start a list of people you know who might have leads. Develop your list at the *first* hint of trouble, not when you need a job. And get in touch now. It's going to be a LOT easier to ask for help from someone with whom you have stayed in contact—rather than only when you need help.

- *Dust off your résumé.* Update it and have it ready. And even if you aren't actively looking for a job, it doesn't hurt to put your résumé in the hands of headhunters and people in your field.

- *Keep your eyes peeled for warning signals.* Has anybody in your company been laid off recently? Don't stop with this piece of information. Ask around about their "deal." What important things didn't they receive? Knowing will give you insight into the kind of layoff package you might have to press for.

- *Figure out what you'll do about health insurance.* You are perfectly within your rights to have a confidential discussion with someone in your company's benefits office. Ask about the whole benefits package for employees, then ask how these benefits would be affected by a layoff. If you are covered by COBRA, as most employees of both the private and public sector are, your employer must provide anyone who is laid off the same level of coverage for 18 months, even if you go to work in another job with an inferior health insurance plan during those 18 months. The kicker, though, is that you will have to pay the premiums for coverage, and we've never been able to figure out how someone who is unemployed can be expected to pay COBRA's rates. Even at a lower, advantageous group rate, COBRA usually runs hundreds of dollars per month, and that's just for an individual. Sometimes you can negotiate to get your employer to continue paying your health insurance for at least as long as the period covered by your severance pay. But for backup, investigate less expensive plans that might be available at group rates through professional associations.

- *Work out a "lean and mean" success plan.* (Remember, we don't call it a budget!) Which expenses could you cut or scale back to survive a layoff? Some people might call this a budget for hard times, but why think so pessimistically. Your employer, if he or she has half a brain, has wielded the ax as part of a lean and mean success plan. So why shouldn't you think the same way? It's a lot easier, and a LOT less emotionally taxing, to figure out a budget when you're working rather than after you've been laid off. Maybe your first cutback will be a birthday gift you were thinking of giving your boss—sometimes revenge *is* sweet.

- *Check your state's unemployment benefits program.* Make sure you will be entitled to unemployment, and find out how long the benefits will last. In most states anyone who has been laid off after a minimum of six months with the company is entitled to collect benefits for 26 weeks. There is no shame in collecting what is due you. In many states you can file your weekly claims by telephone rather than having to stand in line at the unemployment office. And if you do have to go to the office, you will probably be amazed at the number of professional-looking people there.

Do *not*, however, let yourself be coerced into resigning if things are tough at your company. Hang in if you must, and swallow your pride. If you resign, you *will not be able* to collect unemployment benefits.

You can find news and resources for people who have lost their jobs, plus a few laughs at the company's expense, at www.laidoffcentral.com.

In most states, an entrepreneur whose business fails cannot receive unemployment insurance. However, if you lose your job or your business because of a major disaster and are not eligible for regular state unemployment insurance, you may be able to get Disaster Unemployment Assistance (DUA), which comes through the U.S. Department of Labor and is available to those whose employment or self-employment has been interrupted. More information is available at the DOL Web site, www.ows.doleta.gov.

- *Sharpen your professional skills.* Go to conferences and training programs, take courses, read professional journals, and stay on top of developments in your field. Vow to learn at least one new skill every year. This way you'll have capabilities that are in demand.
- *Rehearse your negotiation tactics while you're still employed.* Figure out what sort of severance and benefits package you might be able to ask for. You might even want to line up a lawyer. All of this will be easier when you're still getting a paycheck and

Daria Gets Dealt a Dirty Deal

I know just what kind of nasty games an employer can play to avoid paying unemployment insurance. How do I know? Because it happened to me.

When I was pregnant with Meredith, I was working for a driving school as an office manager and receptionist. My employers knew I was planning to quit before the birth. Well, one month before my due date, I gave my two weeks' notice. I was fired on the spot!

The next day I went to the unemployment office and filed my claim. But the week after Meredith was born, my ex-employer called to offer me my job back. I, of course, turned it down, and BINGO—they were off the hook for unemployment insurance and I lost my checks!

If your employer puts the screws to you by orchestrating a "resignation" instead of laying you off, you might have to sue to get the compensation to which you are rightfully entitled.

can plot a strategy without losing your cool. The best time to negotiate a separation deal is right at the time you're laid off. If you have been a valuable employee, if you've been there a long time, if you've had a cordial relationship with your boss, remind him or her of that. This might be an emotionally trying time for the person who has to lay off a large number of staffers. Concessions are in order. What is the worst the company can do if you ask for an extra month of severance and benefits? Let you go?

If the Ax Has Already Fallen

With the advent of outsourcing jobs to any number of different foreign countries, a "jobless" economic recovery and several other factors, millions of Americans find themselves without a job.

We hope that you are not a statistic or ever will be one . . . but if the ax falls . . .

First, try to *stay calm*. Sit down with your family, and tell them you'll have to do some belt-tightening. Tell them how important their emotional support is to you, and ask for their help.

In the first week, develop a success plan. You'll just have to spend less if you have less income, so think of ways to cut corners. You will, however, have to factor in some job-hunting expenses: transportation to interviews; printing and mailing your résumé; and, if you haven't been fully wired at home, getting a computer and subscribing to an Internet provider to send letters and hunt for jobs online. In some areas, the local unemployment office provides computers and Internet hookups. If you're in the lurch, consider a second-hand computer, or borrow your children's computer as part of the family effort. You will be able to take tax deductions for any expenses that involve looking for a job in the field in which you've been working, so keep the receipts in a file for that purpose.

Also in week one, start calling people on your "networking" list. Try to budget for some lunches and conferences that might net you job leads. This is money invested; put your efforts into selling yourself and making the expenditure pay off.

Helpful Web Sites and Books

Help When You're Going Through a Divorce

www.divorce-online.com

www.divorcesource.com

www.fathersdivorceline.com

http://pages.prodigy.com/divorceplus/div00.htm

www.split-up.com

Dividing Retirement Assets

Your Pension Rights at Divorce: What Women Need to Know ($24.95) explains what a wife facing divorce should know about her rights under six different retirement systems, but it's a good book for men to read, too. Order from the Pension Rights Center, 1140 19th St., NW, Suite 602, Washington, DC 20036-6608; 202-296-3776; e-mail: PnsnRights@ aol.com; www.pensionrights.org.

Pension Issues & Divorce ($29.95). Order from divorcesource.com—800-680-9052, www.divorcesource.com. The site also has a wealth of information about divorce issues and a summary of divorce laws in each state.

Hiring a Private Detective to See If Your Spouse Is Hiding Assets

www.secret-subjects.com

www.dripcentral.com

www.KnowX.com

Social Security Benefits

www.ssa.gov

800-772-1213, TTY Number: 800-325-0778

Social Security Survivors Benefits, Publication No. 05-10084; August 2000, ICN 468540. Order from the Social Security Administration Web site: http://www.ssa.gov/pubs/ 10084.html

How to Get Every Penny You're Entitled to From Social Security, by Michael Bosley and Arthur Gurwitz, Perigee Books/Putnam, $9.95.

Support for Widows

AARP Widowed Persons Service—http://www.aarp.org/griefandloss/commsupport.html

Parents Without Partners, Inc.; www.parentswithoutpartners.org

Griefnet—www.rivendell.org

Finding Out If a Pension Plan Has Errors

National Center for Retirement Benefits—www.ncrb.com, 800-666-1000

Unmarried Couples

Living Together: A Legal Guide for Unmarried Couples, from the publishing house NOLO Press. The list price is $34.99, but you can order it at a discount through NOLO: www.nolo.com/lawstore/products, or call 800-728-3555.

Tax and Estate Planning for Your Retirement Savings

Ed Slott's Web site—www.irahelp.com

Resources for Coping With a Layoff

www.laidoffcentral.com

Your Rights as a Taxpayer

Tax-litigation consultant Dan Pilla—www.taxhelponline.com, or call 800-346-6829.

Stand Up to the IRS, by Frederick W. Daily, 6th edition. $24.95. Order at 30% off from NOLO at www.nolo.com/lawstore/products.

SECTION III

Financial Protection
for the Future

CHAPTER 10

The Only Insurance You Need

WE CAN'T TELL YOU how many times a listener will call our radio or television show (CNNfn) and say, "Dolans, I know you hate insurance, but . . ."

Seems we've developed a reputation. So let's set the record straight: We don't *hate* insurance. We believe it makes perfect sense to buy insurance for the protection of your family in case something should happen to you, your family, or what you own. It also makes a lot of sense to use life insurance for certain estate planning techniques. But insurance should not be used as an investment.

But here's what makes us livid: stories from listeners like Allen in Pennsylvania, who had $400 per month to invest, and someone who stood to gain a fat commission from the recommendation suggested he "invest" in a life insurance policy. Life insurance was never meant to be an investment. It was invented to protect families in case a breadwinner dies or is unable to work. The industry began creating all of these fancy hybrid products just to sell more life insurance.

The life insurance industry is loaded with bogus sales pitches. There are insurance agents who will try to convince you to use your insurance premiums to fund your retirement on the grounds that the insurer will put your money into savvy investments and have a nest egg ready just when you'll need it. *Don't believe a word of it!* We've seen policies that give you investment or savings components so complex they do everything but dance. Most of them are not worth a bucket of warm spit as insurance coverage, and even less as an investment. They're designed strictly to make money for the insurance company.

Fact: Insurance is vital to your financial planning, and we're going to give you all the basics in this chapter. That said, it's going to be a short chapter, because it doesn't take long to run through the insurance policies you need.

Insurance is basically for protecting your most valuable asset: your family (life) and your home and possessions (homeowner's), your car (auto), and your health (health insurance, disability, long-term care). Pay for the insurance protection you need, but don't try to turn it into an asset in its own right.

Life Insurance—Most of What You *Don't* Need Is Here

The purpose of life insurance is to replace your income if you die, so you need a life insurance policy that, if you die, will pay benefits to anyone who depends on you for financial support. If you are supporting a family, you need life insurance. If you have children, you need insurance at least until they finish college. If you have special-needs children, you might need a life insurance policy that will protect them at every age. If you have a nonworking spouse, you need life insurance to protect your spouse at least until your Social Security and retirement income kick in.

If you are single with no dependents, you probably don't need life insurance at all; certainly you don't need more than what your employer might automatically provide. Don't let anyone tell you otherwise.

How Much Life Insurance Do You Really Need?

Although there is no "one size fits all" formula, we recommend as a guideline a policy that would pay your family—your beneficiaries—six to eight times your annual income if you are a family's major breadwinner. If you and your significant other are more or less equal breadwinners, you should each have a policy that provides six to eight times your annual income—that is, a policy that would replace your contribution to the total household income if you weren't around. If you don't have children, make each other the beneficiaries.

The death benefit that your family receives is not subject to federal income tax or state income tax. In many cases, this will mean that you can calculate the size of the policy you need by your after-tax income rather than your gross income. However, the death benefit is counted as part of your estate, which means that there will be tax consequences if your estate is large enough to be subject to the federal estate tax, and there might also be state inheritance taxes, depending on your state's laws (see Chapter 12 for more on federal estate taxes and state inheritance taxes).

Callers are always asking us how much life insurance a nonbreadwinning partner (for instance, a stay-at-home mom) needs. If a wife—or a husband—is at home taking care of the family, he or she needs a policy that will provide at least half the breadwinner's annual income. Why? Because who else is going to take care of the kids and the house if the homemaker partner isn't there? Those duties are worth significant bucks on the open market if you have to find a full-time housekeeper and a nanny to perform these tasks, not to mention plumbers, caterers, baby-sitters, tutors, and so on.

The needs are virtually the same for couples who aren't married. If you live together and each of you is self-supporting but you share household expenses, you might each want to take out a policy that would replace your contribution. If the policy is in your name, most insurance companies let you name anyone you wish as the beneficiary. If you are a same-sex couple and your state has laws that would make it difficult for your partner to collect, you may set up a living trust as the owner and beneficiary of the policy, while your partner is named as beneficiary of the trust. The beauty of a living trust is that it does not go through probate and its instructions are generally very detailed. It's a boon to many gay couples because the family of the deceased partner would usually have a much harder time contesting the surviving partner's rights to the assets contained in a living trust than they would contesting a will. (See Chapter 12 for more on setting up a living trust.)

If You Have a Young Family

In most cases all you need is a simple old-fashioned, inexpensive *term policy*. All this does is pay your family money to replace your earnings if you die. Period.

There are several types of term policies. Our favorite type for most people is a **guaranteed level premium policy**. Term insurance is best for people who need coverage for a certain term or time period. If your policy has a level premium, the payments will stay fixed for the entire term, which can be as long as 30 years. At the end of that period, if you still need the policy, the renewable provision will allow you to continue coverage without having to prove all over again that you are insurable. However, the rates will be much higher at that stage.

Life Insurance Through Your Company

Many employers offer a certain amount of life insurance as part of the employee benefits package. Often you get a menu that allows you to choose a policy that would pay a death benefit to your survivors equal to several times your annual salary. If the policy offers only three or four times your annual income and you have a family to support, we suggest you buy a supplemental term policy that will also provide several times your annual income.

The length of the term is something you should measure according to your family's needs. If you have a child who is two years old, you'll have 20 years until he or she is finished with college and no longer needs the protection of your life insurance. If you have a mortgage, figure how many years you have left until it's paid; your life insurance would help your family pay it off if something happened to you.

Term life has become such a competitive product, you ought to be able to get all of your protection with a term policy for as long as you need insurance. See the end of this chapter for a list of Web sites that will help you find the best policy. Our personal favorite is www.quotesmith.com.

When Does a "Convertible" Policy Make Sense?

A convertible policy starts out as a term policy but has an option to convert to a policy that has cash value (meaning that after you've had it a number of years you can redeem it for a certain amount of money—not that we recommend this). A cash-value policy is referred to in the insurance industry as a **"permanent" policy,** which means it remains in force as long as you pay your premium, rather than expiring at the end of a term. It makes sense to have a convertible policy, because it will stay in effect even if you should happen to develop health problems that would disqualify you from low-cost term insurance.

It may also make sense to buy a convertible policy if you will have dependents when you're in your fifties or sixties and beyond. That's because term premiums will be expensive if you have to buy or renew a term policy when you're past 50. For that reason, a convertible policy is a good idea if you had children in your forties or fifties and will need protection for them when you're at an age when term insurance would be expensive. A convertible policy also makes a lot of sense if you have a disabled child who will need financial support well into his or her adulthood and your senior years.

Most term policies actually have a convertible option, but not all offer it for the full term. This is something you must look for in any life insurance contract before you commit.

We're not fans of the tax-deferred **"savings"** feature of permanent insurance. As we explain on the next page, all too often life insurance policies are billed as investment and savings vehicles.

Speaking of investment, many life insurers are reeling in their (your!) investment portfolios from a shaky market. They are suffering, in many cases, because variable life insurance policies and variable annuities, insurance projects that are very stock market sensitive, have tanked in value.

Our friend Glenn Daily (a fee-only insurance adviser in New York City who has been a tireless crusader for honest industry practices; get his advice on the Web at www.glenndaily.com) recommends the 10-year term policy sold by Ameritas (800-745-

6655 or www.ameritas.com), which lets you pay low premiums yet also hedge against future uncertainties. With this policy, you can apply for a new term policy in 10 years if you are still in good health. If you are not in good health, Ameritas allows you to convert to one of its "low-load" cash-value policies, so called because there are no agent commissions built into the contract. These cash-value policies give you a decent investment along with life insurance coverage, since most of your money goes into the policy instead of into the agent's commission.

If You Are Getting Close to Retirement

Not everyone needs life insurance at this stage of life. If you are a couple of "empty nesters" with a house that's paid for and you both work or have other sources of income, it might make sense to spend your money on something else—perhaps a long-term-care insurance policy to assure that you can pay for health care in your old age. (See Chapters 8 and 12.)

However, you do need life insurance if you have any of the following:

- ✓ young children
- ✓ a disabled adult child
- ✓ an outstanding mortgage on your home or vacation property
- ✓ any large outstanding loans, such as a home equity loan
- ✓ a nonworking spouse who is much younger than you are

What Do the Dolans Have Against Some Kinds of Cash-Value Insurance Policies?

We don't like the way agents pitch it as an "investment," and what's more, we think investments within an insurance policy turn out all too often to be bad investments.

There are many variations on the permanent insurance theme, with an array of names that a customer might find confusing. That's all to the good as far as salespeople are concerned—their goal is to make the policy sound complicated so that you'll think you need to leave the details in their hands. You'll hear such names as:

Modified-premium whole life
Limited-payment whole life
Single-premium whole life
Flexible-premium adjustable life
Interest-sensitive whole life
Universal life
Variable universal life

Basically, **whole life** is a permanent policy in which the premiums are the same for the entire life of the policy. You accumulate a cash reserve within the policy, but the insurance company, not you, decides where it is invested. Typically, the company invests it in low-risk securities, such as corporate bonds and mortgage-backed securities. If you cancel your policy—which you should do cautiously if you no longer need life insurance at some point—you receive the cash value back in a lump sum. But don't expect this lump sum to buy you a dream castle! Administrative costs and agents' commissions will eat up enough that the cash-value side is more or less a joke if you're expecting—or are led by an insurance agent to expect—serious growth.

Universal life refers to policies that combine the protection of term insurance with a savings or investment component.

Whatever the kind of policy, you can be sure that the increase in value will, generally, be modest at best, if there are any profits at all.

Even among the better life insurers, a policy must be held more than 20 years to realize a decent return on premiums paid. You wouldn't believe how much of your money can disappear in sales commissions and related expenses.

Saddest of all are the industry statistics indicating that close to 20% of all cash-value policies terminate in the first year, and that 40% terminate in the first 10 years or so because the policyowners don't keep up the payments. If you surrender the policy early on, you get nothing, plus you will be required to pay surrender fees. Some agents will promise that you'll get your money back if you surrender the policy in 10 years, but what they don't tell you is that you won't get the interest. So if you already own a policy that builds cash values—that would be a whole life, universal, or variable life policy—it may be best to hang on to it. Once the huge sales commissions are paid, you will have some cash value if it's a good policy, while if you were to surrender it prematurely you'd lose the money you've put in.

This is not to say that some cash-value policies aren't better than others, or that a good cash-value policy can't be used as a sophisticated estate-planning tool—though it's appropriate only for high-net-worth individuals and couples who are not worried about liquidity. If you fit that category, life insurance can be an ideal wealth-transfer asset, because the benefits are not subject to income or capital gains taxes, so they can produce an after-tax rate of return that is stronger than that of many taxable investments.

You might also be able to maximize the benefits of a whole life policy by purchasing a hybrid policy, in which a small portion—perhaps 10%—is whole life, and the rest is term insurance. With this blend, the commissions are much lower than with a full cash-value policy, so that more of your money goes to work.

However, not just any policy will do. Here's more advice from another industry reformer, Jim Hunt, a life insurance actuary and former insurance commissioner of Vermont:

- Buy cash-value policies only from mutual insurance companies, which are owned by their policyholders, rather than companies that are owned by, and hence beholden to, stockholders. Hunt recommends the large mutual insurance companies Northwestern Mutual, Massachusetts Mutual, Guardian Life, and New York Life.
- If you do buy a cash-value policy, make sure the first year's surrender value is at least 50% of the first year's premium.

We don't like the way so many insurance agents misrepresent the earnings you are likely to get. Watch out for the "vanishing premium" trick on a whole life policy. You pay the premiums for 7 to 12 years, and the insurance company will invest the money "so smartly that in that many years the premiums will come out of their earnings." At least that's what the sales agent tells you. Why do we say it's a load of bull? Because we hear from so many listeners who are still paying premiums more than 12 years later!

Another investment policy that we hear a lot about is the "variable life" policy. The investment component goes into mutual fund–like pools called subaccounts, and in many cases the death benefit is linked to the value of the investments.

Can you think of a worse idea in a bear market?

Dolan Ah-Ha!

Yet even in this market, agents will tell you that the account will grow, or could grow, by 10% a year. . . . PLEASE!! They might even try to tell you it will beat the market. Don't believe it! If the investment value drops, you may have to pay higher premiums to keep the insurance component intact—so your investments will cost you more rather than less when the market is down.

In all of these policies, the company makes the investment decisions. Even if you buy a variable universal policy that lets you choose your investments among several mutual fund–like accounts offered by the insurance company, that's still a limited range of choices. In universal life policies you have some flexibility to decide how much goes for insurance and how much into investments, but the company determines the rate of return. Guess what: the company is in all likelihood going to pay as little as it can to *you*, so as to maximize its profits. Even if the current interest rate were to go up, the administrative charges are *typically* higher, especially in a variable policy, than the average premiums for a term policy!

Between the cash-value premium and the term premium, you would be better off if you buy a term policy, take the difference, and invest it yourself.

The bottom line with some insurance "investments" is that some companies will often deduct exorbitant fees and commissions from *your* cash value.

However, if you're thinking at all of putting money into a cash-value policy, or if you already have one, Jim Hunt runs a service that, for a nominal fee, will check the average annual rate of return for you (as opposed to the rate the sales agent promised you) and see if you'd do better by investing the money elsewhere and paying for a term policy. An explanation of how the service works is available on the Web site of the Consumer Federation of America (CFA) in Washington, D.C., www.consumerfed.org. On the home page, click on "Finance," then go to "Insurance," then click on "Life: Evaluate Your Policy." You can also contact Hunt at jameshhunt@cs.com or by phone at 603-224-2805. The cost is $50 for the first illustration of a standard policy; $75 for a "second-to-die" policy (a policy on both spouses that pays the death benefit only upon the death of the second insured); and $35 for each additional policy illustration submitted at the same time.

Peter Katt, a fee-only insurance adviser based in Michigan who is also a vocal proponent for industry reform, will give you a more detailed analysis of a policy for an hourly rate of $285. Contact him at:

Katt & Co.
890 Treasure Island Drive
Mattawan, MI 49071
Phone: 616-372-3497
E-mail: Pkatt@PeterKatt.com
For more information, see his Web site—www.peterkatt.com

When Should You Cancel Your Life Insurance?

Do you have a spouse or domestic partner who is self-supporting and would not suffer financially if you died tomorrow?

Name Your Dependents as Beneficiaries, Not Your Estate

A frequent mistake people make when they buy life insurance is to name their estate as beneficiary. This is a good way to keep your money *away* from your spouse, your partner, or your children. They'll get what's left after it goes through probate and creditors take their chunks of your estate (see Chapter 12). On the other hand, when you name specific loved ones as the beneficiaries, upon your death they get the money right away, exempt from probate and creditors.

Dolan Bottom Line

Stop paying for a term life policy when you have no more financial obligations that your family would need to pay if you weren't there to take care of them.

However, if you own a cash-value policy and no longer need the protection, be cautious about rushing to cancel it. Some policies might be worth keeping, at least for a short time, because of decent returns, a possible tax benefit, or simply because the surrender charges will cut too deeply into your cash value. The Consumer Federation of America's service can also help you recover as much of our past premiums paid as possible. Again, for information contact Jim Hunt at jameshhunt@cs.com, or by phone at 603-224-2805.

Are you single, widowed, or divorced with no dependents?

Are your children grown-up and no longer asking you for handouts and loans to get them through the rigors of adulthood?

Have you paid off all of your mortgages on your primary home and any other property you own?

Are you and your spouse retired and living off investment income, with no major financial obligations?

Are your parents either dead or self-supporting?

If you no longer rely on your earnings from work, you don't need life insurance. Call your insurance agent to cancel your existing policy, and if he tries to pitch some fancy-schmancy policy for this new stage of your life, *just say* "NO!"

How to Get a Claim Paid

The last thing you feel up to doing when a loved one has just died is filling out papers, but unfortunately, this is what you will have to do to actually collect the death benefit on a life insurance policy. Here is a checklist of the things you have to do, in order of importance:

- ✓ **Call your insurance agent or company**. He or she will be able to send you what forms you need. If the insurance came through your loved one's employer, call the human resources department to ask for the proper forms.
- ✓ **Obtain a copy of the death certificate.**
- ✓ **File your claim**. Every adult beneficiary of a life insurance policy has to fill out a "proof of death" form and submit it to the insurer, along with a copy of the death certificate. If you don't already know, find out what the payment plan will be. Some plans allow the beneficiaries to select whether they want the payment in a

lump sum or regularly scheduled payouts. Sometimes, especially if the beneficiary is a minor child, the insured person might have arranged to have a life insurance settlement, in which the insurance company invests the funds and pays the beneficiary interest.

The processing period will take no longer than a week, provided you have all of the papers necessary.

How to Find a Good Low-Cost Policy

Here are Internet sites that can help you find good term life insurance policies:

Quotesmith: www.quotesmith.com or 800-556-9393

Accuquote: www2.accuquote.com or 800-442-9899

Insweb: www.insweb.com

NetQuote: www.netquote.com

Term4sale: www.term4sale.com. This site will give you a list of "low-load" life insurers that do business directly with customers.

Here are insurers that we recommend:

Ameritas, based in Lincoln, Nebraska. 800-552-3553, www.ameritasdirect.com

Guardian Life Insurance: 866-425-4542, www.glic.com

Massachusetts Mutual: 800-272-2216, www.massmutual.com

Dolan Bottom Line

Do you know exactly how much of a life insurance payout you are due? Too many couples never discuss what life insurance protection they have. Talk about it together while you're both still alive and healthy. Do you have group policies through your employers? Do you know how much they'd pay? Keep copies of your policies in a fireproof, locked file box, along with wills and other vitally important papers. (See Chapter 12 for a list of the documents you should file in a safe place, NOT just on a computer program!)

New York Life: 800-710-7945, ext. 951, www.newyorklife.com

Northwestern Mutual, home office phone: 414-271-1444, www.northwesternmutual.com

State Farm Insurance, home office phone: 309-766-2311, www.statefarm.com

TIAA-CREF (Teachers Insurance and Annuity Association College Retirement Equities Fund): 800-223-1200, www.tiaa-cref.org Formerly restricted to employees of educational institutions, TIAA-CREF now has insurance products that are available to the general public in most states.

USAA: 800-531-8000, www.usaa.com

Northwestern Mutual and Guardian policies can be purchased only through agents. If you are interested in a cash value policy, insist on one in which the first-year surrender value is at least 50% of your first-year premium. The other insurers listed here do not pay agent commissions, so their cash-value policies provide much better value as a rule.

Insurance Information Inc., 800-472-5800, will provide you with quotes from other low-fee companies. Make sure your policy is rated either A or B by Weiss Ratings. They're the toughest insurance raters around. You can get a report on a company from Weiss by calling 800-289-9222 or by ordering through their Web site: www.weissratings.com.

Pitches You'll Hear

Forewarned is forearmed. If you are ever confronted by an insurance agent trying to sell you more than you need, remember that plain vanilla term insurance is not the best deal for the insurance agent, but it is for the customer in most cases. People who go into insurance sales are trained for weeks to win gullible customers through a strange combination of hypnotically friendly persuasion and a series of well-rehearsed pitches that sound as if they make a lot of sense and often prey on your guilt. But you don't have to be gullible! Know the realities behind these commonly used pitches.

The Pitch "Term insurance is only a temporary solution to your life insurance needs."

The Reality You don't *need* life insurance at every stage of your life. The time you're most likely to need it is precisely when it costs the least—when you are young. (If you have no dependents, you don't need it at all. If your employer offers it as a paid benefit, it's usually a small payout; perhaps equal to one year's salary. Accept it graciously; and if you're single, make your parents or a sibling the beneficiary and hope they never get the payout!) If your children are grown and self-supporting, and if your spouse has retirement funds or investments to live on, the money the agent is asking you to fork over for life insurance would be better spent going into investments that don't carry such heavy charges.

The Pitch "Cash-value policies pay dividends and provide you with a savings fund."

The Reality Cash-value polices don't function the way investment or savings accounts do, because they are illiquid. When you surrender a cash-value policy in the first 10 years, you lose most of the value. In many cases, you'll get much more bang for your buck from a dividend-paying stock, and more safety and liquidity from a money market fund or a CD.

The Pitch "Buy this policy to protect your loved ones."

The Reality Insurance is often sold by guilt association. "Don't you really love your loved ones?" the agent asks you, just as he learned in the training program. We've even heard of agents using a nasty fear ploy: "Make sure your children don't *sue* you for not looking out for their inheritance"!

To protect your loved ones, you buy term life. Insurance should not be used to leave your heirs an estate that you couldn't build up through your working years. It doesn't work, no matter what the salesperson tells you. The investment dollars will not build up enough to make much of a dent.

We heard from a couple in their sixties who had no debts and had finished putting their kids through college. An insurance agent was telling them to spend a prodigious amount of retirement dollars on an insurance policy so that when they were no longer around, they could make their children rich. We think this is a stupid way to spend your money. Consider taking a vacation instead. If you haven't accumulated an estate that will make your kids rich by the time you've retired, it ain't gonna happen. You've given them an education, a work ethic, a sensible attitude about how to handle their money—the tools to make their way in the world. The commissions from an insurance policy might enhance the estate of someone who sells such policies, but the "investments" aren't going to do a thing for yours!

The Pitch "There are no hidden fees in this policy . . . believe me!"

The Reality Check the small print for hidden fees. One notorious example is the annual premium that you're allowed to pay in monthly installments—but the installments add up to anywhere from 4% to 17% more than the annual premium that you've been quoted.

Dolan Ah-Ha!

Often the same insurance agent who sold you a lousy policy will call you again and say, "I have a much better policy, so I'm getting you out of the first one." All he's doing is churning commissions.

   You should say: "Excuse me. If the first one didn't work out so well, why would I give you money to hit me over the head a second time?" Or something to that effect.

The Pitch "We'll invest your [cash-value policy] premiums so well that after maybe five or six years' worth of premiums paid, you won't have to make any other payments for the life of the policy."

The Reality The key word is "maybe." This is known in the industry as the "vanishing premium" trick. The fact of the matter is that many insurance companies are crummy investors, so it's more likely that you'll be paying premiums for many years to come.

Another Racket: The "Specialty" Policy

The insurance industry loves to come up with new products, which is why you often find a financial institution presenting you with a dizzying array of specialty policies designed to pay off for a single event. You might have heard of mortgage life insurance policies, which pay off your mortgage if you die. There is accidental death, which pays out only in case of an accident. There are policies that cover your credit card debts or car loans, so that your loved ones can pay off these bills if you should die or become disabled and unable to work. Some waive the monthly payments for a time if you lose your job.

   The Reality: If you should die unexpectedly or become incapacitated, do you think money with these strings attached would be the best thing for your family? The payout from a term life insurance policy is meant to pay off such financial obligations, and your survivors should have the flexibility of using the money for whatever they need most at the time.

Don't Buy Insurance Through a Credit Card Company Unless It's Your Last Resort

You know how we feel about frivolous use of credit cards. The same goes for the insurance that credit card companies offer. The ratio of claims to premiums in these policies is typically low. Credit card insurance is sold without regard to the insured's age, though there

TIMPANOGOS HIGH SCHOOL

Dolan Bottom Line on Disability Insurance

According to the American Council of Life Insurers, nearly one-third of all Americans will suffer a serious disability sometime between the ages of 35 and 65. What should you do to protect your family in case you become disabled? Individual disability policies, which pay 50% to 80% of your income if you are unable to work because of a disability, are expensive. Those who need it the most are people who are self-employed or in private practice and would be unable to keep their businesses going if they became disabled. Certainly lawyers, physicians, dentists, and small- or medium-sized business owners should have disability policies. Upscale professionals may be the people most able to afford this insurance, but everyone should have some coverage if possible.

There are short-term and long-term disability policies. A savings nest egg equal to three to six months of your income can replace a short-term disability policy, and we think it's better to save your money for this purpose than to buy an expensive policy. Some people are fortunate enough to have long-term disability coverage through their employers. Most other people rely on disability benefits under Social Security. If you can afford an individual long-term disability policy, or a supplemental policy to your employer's, Jim Hunt recommends the policies sold by Northwestern Mutual and USAA Life.

may be a limit of 65 to 70 years old, and without regard to the insured's health, though a preexisting illness might disqualify you. Because these policies are open to almost anyone, however, they are the most expensive insurance policies out there.

Some Annuities: A Whole Other Category of Bad Investments

As bad as we think permanent or whole life insurance investment policies are, the insurance industry has done itself one better by coming up with annuities. The variable type of annuity is a worse "investment" than life insurance (if that's possible!).

Annuities 101: An annuity is a contract, generally with a life insurance company, in which earnings are tax-deferred and a fixed or variable payment is guaranteed for as long as you live.

Fixed annuities have yields that are guaranteed for a year or more. In an **immediate fixed annuity**, you invest a lump sum, but payments on it start right away. However, most annuities sold today are **deferred annuities**, meaning that the period payment is deferred indefinitely in exchange for either a single premium or multiple premiums. Many banks are big on fixed annuities. They love to grab senior citizens out of line and sell annuities as an alternative to CDs. Right now they're a big trap, because a first-year or one- to five-year rate on some annuities will pay more than a CD, but the problem is that it's not an alternative to a three-month to one-year CD, because a fixed annuity is a long-term investment. If you want to get your money back prematurely you're going to get hit with all kinds of penalties. Fixed annuities might make sense as a portion of your investment capital ONLY if you're looking for a safe investment that you don't have to touch for at least five years.

Variable annuities: We don't like them. They are essentially tax-deferred mutual funds. The payout varies with the value of the account. Invariably—no pun intended— these are sold to people who think they're paying too much in taxes and who are not happy with the current interest rate paid on fixed annuities. Sure, the pitch—that you are getting a mutual fund investment but your earnings are tax-deferred—sounds appealing, but the annuity salesman is leaving out the most important point: If you're paying too much in taxes, why *defer* the liability? Furthermore, when you do take distributions out, all of your earnings get taxed as ordinary income whether you've held it in the annuity for one year or 101 years. And they're expensive!

Better: Buy tax-free municipal bonds instead and *never* pay taxes on the income. The other problem with variable annuities is that they simply don't work. They're too expensive. When the market isn't doing well, variable annuities do worse than the average mutual fund because of all the expenses that come out.

Annuities for the most part are sold to too many people for all of the wrong reasons. In particular, insurance agents prey upon senior citizens, scaring them into believing annuities are the answer to every investment need. The high fees, the long-term nature of the

Dolan Ah-Ha!

While waiting for a flight at Logan Airport in Boston over the summer, we got into a discussion with an annuity salesperson from a highly rated insurance company. She was on a business trip to Tampa, selling annuities to bankers and brokers, who then sell to you. We started talking about "guranteed" annuities "guaranteeing" 7% on a 4% Treasury bond environment. By the end of the discussion we learned that the companies offering those ultra-high returns (not her company) had done so by investing huge sums of money in WORLDCOM bonds! Needless to say, those insurance companies' credit ratings have since been lowered, and the continuing payment of 7% is in jeopardy. Beware an ultra-high yield guarantee.

investment, and the high taxes when the policyholder or his heirs take payouts make annuities particularly inappropriate for senior citizens, yet many agents have attended seminars that teach them how to charm the money right out of this presumably gullible market.*

The Most Morbid Insurance Investment of All . . . Avoid Them!

We mean that literally. Some financial advisers out there are telling clients to put money into **viaticals.** These are life insurance policies on terminally ill people. Not people you know, so you have to take the financial adviser's word on "your" patient's condition, and even that he or she exists at all. There is a charitable component: Your money allows the sick person to receive a lump sum that represents part of the face value of his life insurance while he's still alive and might need it to cover medical expenses. The idea is that when the patient dies, you get part of the payout. It's developed a market among people who have AIDS and have spent all their money on medical care. But fraud runs rampant in this line of business.

Viaticals are typically sold to senior citizens, and are often touted as "low risk" or "guaranteed." Because of the abuses, they are neither! We say, stay *far away* from these . . . and don't trust anyone trying to sell you this kind of "investment." Period.

Health Insurance:
A Big Issue That Keeps Getting Bigger

Most Americans get their health insurance through their employers' health plans. But according to various government and industry estimates, anywhere from 15% to 30% of Americans are not insured at all. The reason, for many, is that they can't afford the costs of health insurance premiums. We hear from people who are self-employed, running small companies, out of work, or even working for small companies or nonprofits that require employees to pay most of the policy premiums—and their biggest expense is often health insurance. Some of these listeners are domestic partners, gay or straight, and can't get coverage through their employed partner's company. While the number of employers that offer domestic partner health insurance benefits is increasing, the costs of health insurance in the United States are a national scandal. Be outraged; be very outraged.

---

* "Annuities 101: How to Sell to Senior Citizens," by Ellen E. Schultz and Jeff D. Opdyke; *The Wall Street Journal*; Tuesday July 2, 2002, page C1.

Write to your senators and congressional representative. But what can the Dolans do about the problem?

We can't solve it, but we can tell you how to find health insurance if you're out of the employment loop.

Don't take chances with health insurance. No matter how young and healthy you may be, you never know when you might suddenly find yourself in a hospital, faced with the costs of a major medical condition. (It could be due to an accident.) In that case, you could find that you'll have to wipe out most of your savings or other assets to pay the costs.

If You're Out of Work or Self-Employed

Many professional associations offer group health insurance for members who are not presently employed or are self-employed. Another option is the National Association of the Self-Employed, which you can find online at www.nase.org. Membership is available in three different tiers that cost $96 a year for "Access" level, or $420 a year for "Premier Resource" level, but benefits for all categories include the opportunity to buy health insurance—at an additional charge. The costs vary greatly, depending on your state and how many family members you have to insure. Since the NASE only administers the policies, rules governing whether you can insure an unmarried partner will depend on your state and the policy available there.

If you're self-employed, showing a profit on your federal tax return, and paying for health insurance, you can, as of the 2003 tax year, take a deduction from your gross income of 100% of the premiums you pay on behalf of yourself and your dependents. (You can deduct 70% of the premiums for the 2002 tax year.) Anyone can deduct health care costs, including insurance, if the costs exceed 7.5% of your adjusted gross income.

www.insweb.com has information about small business insurance, including group health insurance for businesses employing two to 99 people.

Flexible Spending Accounts and Medical Savings Accounts

We're advocates of the Flexible Spending Account (FSA), which is offered to employees by many large companies. An FSA is a tax-sheltered account that you open at the start of the calendar year. A couple filing jointly may contribute up to $5,000 a year and use the money throughout the year to pay for family medical expenses that your health insurer won't reimburse. All of these expenses are in pretax dollars. The only hitch to FSAs is that if you don't spend the money by the end of the year, you don't get it back. Dentists and optometrists tend to get busy in December, with patients seeking to spend their FSA money on tooth capping, eyeglasses, and such.

But if you're self-employed or working for a small business with fewer than 50 employees, the IRS has gone one better and created a variation called the Medical Savings Account (MSA). With an MSA, you don't have to spend all the money each year. You can let it accumulate so that you'll have a tax-sheltered nest egg for medical expenses when you retire, and you pay no taxes on withdrawals as long as you use the money for medical expenses. The hitch is that until 2003, MSAs that are exempt from federal income taxes are part of a demonstration project, and limited to the first 750,000 people who sign up each year.

If you are paying for a high-deductible health insurance plan, we think MSAs are a great way to supplement your coverage and cut your costs. An individual can contribute up to $1,495 a year, a family up to $3,487.50.

If you have a child or disabled parent or spouse, you can open a **dependent care account** with pretax dollars. This account does not pay for medical care, but you may use the money you contribute (up to $5,000 a year for a married couple filing jointly or a single head of household) to pay for day care at home or in a day-care center, housekeeping expenses relating to the care of the dependent, nursery school and kindergarten expenses, and after-school care for children under 13.

Catastrophic Health Insurance

We hear from listeners who are thinking of saving money on health insurance by buying a policy that covers catastrophic care only. These policies are offered through Blue Cross, Oxford, and some other carriers, though the availability is limited in some regions. A catastrophic policy costs much less than policies that give you full medical coverage—typically around $200 to $400 every three months per individual, though rates will vary depending on your age and location. If you're in good health, a catastrophic policy is better than nothing, but not much better. It will pay for the hospital stay if you should need major medical care. Here's the catch: In most cases, the doctors who treat you will bill you separately. Your hospital room and the inedible food will be covered—and these are not insignificant costs. However, you could still wind up paying thousands of dollars for such costs as ambulance, anesthesia, the physician's fees for surgery and follow-up visits, medicine, X rays, and tests.

Health insurance scams. With policy costs constantly rising, unlicensed operators offering fraudulent policies are preying upon small-business owners, the self-employed, and other individuals. Before you buy any policy, check with your state department of insurance to be sure the plan is licensed. Watch out for premiums that seem too good to be true: lower-than-average prices and no questions about your health condition. Another sign of a scam is when an insurance agent claims the policy is exempt from state rules and falls instead under federal ERISA laws. A legitimate ERISA plan will be offered only through an employer, not through an agent.

> ## Dolan Bottom Line
>
> You can often save money on *any* insurance policy, whether it's health insurance, disability insurance, long-term-care insurance, car insurance, or homeowner's insurance, if you buy a policy with the highest deductible you can afford.

Health insurance you don't need. We're hearing from people who wonder if they should buy single-purpose health insurance policies, such as cancer insurance. In our opinion, this is a worse idea than mortgage life insurance! If you had cancer you wouldn't qualify for a cancer insurance policy, and if you are healthy, why start placing bets on a specific illness? A one-size-fits-all health policy that covers physician care, hospitalization, and major medical is what everyone needs.

Long-Term-Care Insurance

We believe in long-term-care (LTC) policies, just in case you need nursing home care in your later years (maybe sooner!?). (See Chapters 8 and 12.) This is not to be confused with acute care for specific medical episodes, which is in part covered by Medicare.

Even if your children are planning to live nearby, they may not be equipped to assume round-the-clock care for an aging parent physically or mentally unable to get around independently. But before you buy, see if there are other options. If you're a member of a church or synagogue, for instance, the congregation may have some provisions for aging members. You may also be able to find a life insurance policy—even a term policy—that has **accelerated benefits,** meaning a one-time payment on the policy available only if the insured is diagnosed as terminally ill. The payment will usually be equal to only about 50% of the death benefit, and will be deducted from the face value. Many companies allow you to add an accelerated death benefit rider at any time.

What you should know before you purchase an LTC policy is that there are rackets in this branch of the industry, too. Peter Katt reports that many companies have recruited former nurses to sell LTC insurance, many of whom approach prospective customers with the enthusiasm of zealots. Do your own research; don't let someone "sell" you on a policy.

Basically, you have three choices:

1. You can buy a low-premium policy through such online sources as www.quotesmith. com. The less expensive policies, however, may not pay the best benefits.

2. Buy a policy from a highly reputable firm, such as Northwestern Mutual, which is priced to pay benefits rather than to sell—meaning it will cost you, but you can expect good coverage.

3. Buy a lump-sum policy in which your money is "floated" until you need long-term care. You pay, say, $100,000 up front. The policy might earn interest for the insurance company, but you don't get the interest; you get $100,000 worth of long-term-care financing if and when you need it.

Be sure to see Chapter 8 for more info on LTC insurance.

Homeowner's or Rental Insurance

Insure 100% of the replacement value of your house, not the market value. Call a couple of local builders and ask how much construction costs per square foot are. Multiply the average cost by your home's total square footage and insure that amount. Don't insure the land unless it's on a fault line or shore line.

Insure 100% of the *replacement value* of your possessions, not the *current value*. We strongly recommend making a videotape of the possessions, in the places you keep them, and putting the videotape in a bank safe-deposit box. Put valuables on a separate rider and take out at least $100,000 in personal-injury liability insurance to protect yourself from being sued by someone who is injured on your property. Renters should have a tenant's policy that covers fire, burglary, and personal injury liability.

We believe in buying insurance directly from the company. This way you won't have agent commissions plowed into the premium. Get a quote from your insurance agent, then call USAA (800-531-8000), GEICO (800-841-3000), and State Farm (check your local phone book) to compare rates.

If you consolidate your homeowner's and car insurance with the same company, most companies will allow you a discount of up to 10% on both policies. Also, if you have installed storm shutters, shatter-proof windows, a security fire alarm system linked to local authorities, and outdoor motion sensors, tell your insurance company! You might save some big bucks!

Auto Insurance

Make sure your auto insurance includes a "claims cost ceiling"—the dollar amount the insurer will use to determine when to raise your premiums—of at least $2,000. Otherwise, they can jack up your premiums after even the smallest claims. Check to make sure they won't raise your premium after one speeding ticket, too. Almost all of us get a ticket at some point, and you shouldn't have to pay for one mistake.

The next time you're in the market for a new car, ask your insurance agent to quote you the difference in collision and comprehensive premiums for the different cars you're considering. It could save you another 25% in premiums! Our favorite direct writers—again, USAA, GEICO, and State Farm—are good places to start price-shopping.

Car insurance rates are higher than they were just a few years ago, thanks to more high-cost accidents with SUVs—and State Farm Mutual Automobile Insurance keeping its rates artificially low to capture more market share, forcing many competitors to do the same. Compare insurance rates online at these sites:

www.bankrate.com
www.Amica.com
www.Insweb.com
www.insurance.com
www.progressive.com
www.Geico.com

If you install a car alarm, you'll get a discount on comprehensive coverage of about 15%.

If you have teenagers driving your car and they're good students, report that to the insurer. You may be able to knock off 5% to 25% of the price you'd ordinarily pay for having a car insured for the highest-risk drivers of all. (See Chapter 6 for money-saving car insurance tips!)

Liability Insurance

How much liability insurance should a car owner have? We asked associate underwriters Linda Horvath and Bobbi Cavin at Amica, who said the industry generally recommends that you have enough liability insurance to cover $300,000 worth of personal damage, $300,000 in per-accident damage to the vehicle, and $100,000 in property damage. Unless your health policy covers all of your costs in an auto accident, you should tack on liability coverage that will take care of the damage if an uninsured motorist hits your car; this is usually a low-cost addition to the liability policy.

If you are a homeowner, you should have at least $300,000 of liability coverage on your homeowner's policy. All of these amounts may be supplemented with an umbrella policy.

Do You Need an Umbrella Policy?

An umbrella policy typically provides $1 million to $5 million in additional coverage to your auto, homeowner's, and boat liability policies. If you were to exhaust the insurance compensation you already have for these assets, the personal umbrella policy would kick in. If you frequently travel overseas and drive in foreign countries, you should also get an inexpensive umbrella policy to protect you against collisions with uninsured motorists overseas, as that is not covered in a standard auto liability policy. A commercial umbrella policy will cover liability for rental units.

How do you calculate whether you need an umbrella policy? Add up your assets—the worth of your home, money in the bank, stocks, bonds, and available funds from a 401(k) or other retirement plan. Then add up your liability coverage on your home, auto, and boat policies. If you were faced with a serious liability claim, would your insurance coverage be equal to or greater than the total value of your assets? If so, you don't need more coverage. No one can collect on a judgment against you for more than you are worth. However, if your total coverage is less than the total value of your assets, an umbrella policy will guard against the loss of your assets if you should ever be hit with a liability claim.

Helpful Web Sites and Books

General Consumer Information

www.personalinsure.about.com

www.glenndaily.com

www.peterkatt.com

Tools and Techniques of Life Insurance Planning, by Stephen Leimberg and Robert J. Doyle, Jr., National Underwriter Company; $44.95.
Order from Leimberg Associates, Bryn Mawr, Pennsylvania. Phone: 800-543-0874. www.leimberg.com

Reasonably Priced Life Insurance

www.bankrate.com

Quotesmith: www.quotesmith.com

Insweb: www.insweb.com

NetQuote: www.netquote.com

Term4sale: www.term4sale.com

Ameritas: 800-745-6655, www.ameritas.com

USAA: 800-531-8000, www.usaa.com

Insurance Information Inc.: 800-472-5800

To get the Weiss ratings on an insurer: 800-289-9222, www.weissratings.com

Evaluating a Cash-Value Policy

Consumer Federation of America: www.consumerfed.org, or 603-224-2805

Getting a Life Insurance Claim Paid

The American Council of Life Insurance: www.acli.com

Health Insurance for the Self-Employed

National Association of the Self-Employed: www.nase.com

www.insweb.com

Up-to-Date Policy and Legislative Information About Insurance Coverage for Same-Sex Domestic Partners

Human Rights Campaign: www.hrc.org/issues/family

Car Insurance

www.bankrate.com

www.Insweb.com

www.insurance.com

www.progressive.com

www.Geico.com

www.Amica.com

CHAPTER 11

Retirement

YOU HAVE WORKED HARD. You've saved some bucks along the way, and you've invested conservatively in the past two decades, which was a time of unprecedented economic prosperity. You should be in pretty good shape for your golden years—at least you thought so until the stock market took a nosedive, until one corporate scandal after another brought down even the safest stocks. Right now you're thanking your lucky stars that at least you didn't work for Enron. But you worry, as all Americans do, that more corporate skullduggery could surface—maybe even at your company!

These are trying times for people with retirement in sight—and as well for those in the early to middle stages of planning their retirement. These days we often hear from diligent savers who have seen their tax-deferred retirement accounts decimated in the bear market and are now putting off retirement. Even more often we hear from listeners whose debts match or exceed their retirement savings. We get callers who regret that they bought that third car or vacation home, and now all of a sudden they don't have enough for retirement. We hear from retirees and about-to-be-retirees who figure they'll be fine as long as they never, ever get sick, because more and more insurers are dropping coverage of unconscionably expensive prescription drugs, and employers are asking both current employees, as well as retirees, to pay a higher share of policy premiums. A caller from Wisconsin joked that he had enough for retirement as long as he didn't eat from Wednesday till Saturday each week. Funny until you realize the truth behind the joking.

By 2030 some 69.4 million people living in the United States will retire. That's more than double the number of retired Americans at the beginning of the millennium. People now in the workforce will live for 20 years or more after they retire, statistically speaking. That means you need to structure your finances so that your 401(k)s, IRAs, and other tax-deferred retirement accounts grow untouched as long as possible. You just might live to be 100. Time after time, our listeners have called us with good news and bad news. The good news is they are still kicking butt at an advanced age. The bad news is they fear they will outlive what they have managed to save and invest.

In this chapter we'll show you the ins and outs of planning in uncertain times, so that you *can* plan a long and happy life.

We don't know of many people who *aren't* looking forward to a day when they can choose what they'll do with their time. "Retire" is becoming a misnomer, because by the time the baby boomers start hitting 65 they are likely to stay active for a long time, even after they leave their jobs and draw on pensions and Social Security payouts. There are plans in New York City now for a senior living center for aging baby boomers that will have a pool and health club.

But here's a bulletin: Baby boomers are now saving about *one-third* of what they need for retirement. People nearing retirement age now are delaying retirement because the value of their retirement portfolios has declined so badly. Senior citizens represent the fastest-growing group of bankruptcy filers.

Many future retirees will have a second career. Some will continue working because they have interests they want to pursue and miss the stimulation and interaction they had in the workplace. Others, however, will work because they can't make ends meet if they don't. How do you make sure you fit into the first category? By saving NOW. Retirement may be the *last* thing on your mind if you're 20-something, but it's never too early.

Dolan Ah-Ha!

We took our first step toward building our retirement savings before we even got married, when we sat down and cut up all our credit cards. Well, okay, all 11 of Ken's credit cards, since those were the ones with balances on them. You'll never have a secure retirement if you amass debts that you can't pay off during your working years.

Talk About Active Retirement

"Active retirement" is a contradictory phrase, so all bets are on that by the time the baby boomers reach retirement age there will be a new word for this stage of life. Already, *The Journal of Financial Planning* has reported some statistics that dispute the idea of retirement as a time of rest:

1. A survey by Allstate Financial, titled *Retirement Reality Check*, found that three out of four baby boomers think they will never completely retire.
2. A January 2002 poll of 1,001 nonretired American investors conducted by the Gallup Organization for UBS, titled *Retirement Revisited—2002, a UBS Index of Investor Optimism*, found that 83% of those surveyed planned to work in retirement.*

* *The Journal of Financial Planning*, May 2002.

Are You Saving Enough for Retirement?

Consider your sources of retirement income:

- ✓ Tax-deferred retirement accounts
- ✓ Cash value on your home
- ✓ Investments
- ✓ Social Security
- ✓ Pension

How much money will you have from these sources when you retire?

Realistically, most people need about 70% to 80% of their preretirement income, plus an inflation calculation of about 3% per year. If you're anywhere close to retirement, add your annual income over the last five years and divide that by five to get your average annual income, and figure that you need 80% of that.

75% of your income   _____

How many years until you retire?   _____

Multiply the 75% figure by 3% for each year between now and your
projected retirement. This will give you a rough estimate of the
inflation rate.   _____

This is the amount you will need in your first year of retirement to
maintain your present standard of living.   _____

If you're in debt, you may come far short of reaching that goal. So . . . get out of debt!

Now subtract from that 75% figure the amount you expect to collect annually from Social Security. You'll have an idea of that from the Social Security statements you receive periodically. Call 800-772-1213 if you haven't received a statement. Interruptions of your career in which you made less or were not working will bring down the Social Security taxes you paid and hence the money in your Social Security account.

Social Security   – $_____
Subtract the income you expect to have from other sources, including:
Traditional employer pension   – $_____
Second-career income   – $_____
Other   – $_____
The total is what you need to earn from retirement accounts or
other sources each year: $_____

Retirement Account Calculator
1. The average annual interest rate of your IRAs, 401(k), and any other
    retirement accounts combined: _____
2. Multiply by the dollar amount you save annually   _____
3. Multiply by the number of years you plan to participate   _____
4. Your contributions to the plan at retirement will be $ _____
5. Your life expectancy at retirement will be (see the tables at the
    IRS site or www.irahelp.com)   _____
Divide line 4 by line 5 $ _____

You will need to withdraw approximately this much in minimum distributions each year.

How does this figure match up with the amount you need?

Note: We haven't factored in compounding here. Your investments will compound within your retirement account as long as they are appreciating. We're showing you how to make simple, conservative estimates, which, given the ups and downs of the market, will put you on safer ground than making calculations that assume your investments will do well every year.

You can find a more detailed quiz on the Web site of the American Savings Education Council at www.asec.org.

How Will You Find the Money You Need?

C'mon—get serious . . . and realistic!

Unload Your Laggard Investments

Double-check your portfolio for losing investments. Dump these investments now, before you compound your losses!

Minimize Your Debt

As we have told you many times, if someone tries to sell you an investment that promises a guaranteed return of 12%–24%, show him the door! But in a sense, you *will* realize these incredible returns on your money every month if you pay off your debts and stop paying out high credit card interest rates. Invest an extra $50 a month toward your credit card bills, starting with the debt that has the highest interest rate first so you stop incurring high finance charges. Once you've paid off all your nondeductible debt, start investing an extra $50 or more toward your mortgage principal each month. Before you know it, your debts will be a bad memory.

Better yet, once you've paid off your debts, you may find that you need a whole lot less money to live a comfortable life—which could mean that your dreams of an early retirement could become a reality.

How Much Can You Spend in Retirement?

It's only a guideline . . . but use the chart on p. 317 to get an idea of how much of your investments you can spend each year if your aim is to die broke. First, find the row that matches your stock and bond allocations. Then go across to the number of years you expect the money to last. The answer is the percentage of your investments you can spend the first year. For each following year, increase the dollar amount of your withdrawal about 3% to account for inflation.

How the IRS Will Let You Catch Up Until 2011

If you're close to retirement age and haven't saved much, the 2001 Tax Act has some provisions that enable you to catch up if you act now. This is an amazing disappearing tax act that expires on December 31, 2010, unless Congress votes before then to extend it. But until 2010 you have a guaranteed chance to increase your tax-deferred retirement savings.

Stocks/ Bonds	Average annual return	Years in retirement				
		10	15	20	25	30
70%/30%	10.0%	12.7%	9.6%	8.1%	7.3%	6.7%
60%/40%	9.5%	12.4%	9.3%	7.8%	6.9%	6.3%
50%/50%	8.8%	12.2%	9.0%	7.4%	6.5%	6.0%
40%/60%	8.2%	11.9%	8.7%	7.1%	6.2%	5.6%
30%/70%	7.6%	11.6%	8.4%	6.8%	5.8%	5.2%
20%/80%	7.0%	11.3%	8.1%	6.4%	5.5%	4.9%

For the year 2004 you can put as much as $13,000 into an employer-sponsored **401(k)** retirement plan, a nonprofit employer-sponsored **403(b)**, a government employer-sponsored **457(b)**. The maximum annual contribution increases by $1,000 each year to $15,000 in 2006, when it will be adjusted for inflation for the next four years. If you were born before 1955, you can contribute an additional $3,000 to the plan in 2004. That additional annual contribution rises by $1,000 each year until 2006, then is also subject to the inflation adjustment for four years. Then, in 2011, the limit goes back to where it was in 2001, to $10,500.

If you are a sole proprietor, a small business owner, or an employee of a business with fewer than 100 employees, your maximum allowable contributions to a **SIMPLE (Savings Incentive Match Plan for Employees) IRA or SIMPLE 401(k)** (or Savings Incentive Match Plan for Employees, available to sole proprietors or small businesses with fewer than 100 employees) go up to $9,000 in 2004 or $10,000 if born before 1955, rising by $1,000 each year until 2005, when the figure becomes indexed for inflation. If you are over 50 you can contribute an extra $1,000 in 2003. That figure goes up by $500 each year until 2006, then becomes indexed for inflation. The limit goes back to $6,500 in 2010.

If you are self-employed, you can contribute up to 25% of your annual compensation up to $40,000 to a **SEP (Simplified Employee Pension) IRA.**

If you work on your own or own a small business with fewer than 100 employees, you can receive a new tax credit of up to $500 toward the cost of setting up a retirement plan for yourself and your employees.

Employer-sponsored **qualified retirement plans**, which include **profit sharing** and **money purchase plans**, may contribute up to $40,000 a year. People 50 and over may contribute an additional $1,000 a year.

Traditional IRA and **Roth IRA** contribution limits are $3,000 in 2003, and rise to $4,000 in 2005, then up to $5,000 in 2008. If you're over 50 you can contribute an extra $500 each year from 2003 to 2005, then an extra $1,000 from 2006 to 2010.

We won't try to guess what's going to happen in Washington in 2010 and we don't recommend that you try either. Predicting both politics *and* the future is a thankless game. But right now, you can work on getting your own retirement house in order by following our steps toward a secure retirement, starting with our catch-up plan.

The Dolan "Catch-Up" Plan for a Secure Retirement

Here are some very general guidelines about how to plan. We're not going to give you portfolio allocations because, as much as we dislike giving such advice across the board for investing, we like it even less when it comes to retirement portfolios. Our generic rule of thumb is DON'T RISK YOUR RETIREMENT MONEY!

At Any Age

- Invest the maximum allowable contribution in an IRA. If your adjusted gross income is $110,000 or less ($160,000 for married couples filing jointly) and you can live without the tax deduction now, invest in a tax-free Roth IRA. Note that the amount you can contribute is phased down if your income is $150,000 to $160,000 for joint filers and $95,000 to $110,000 for single filers. These income caps are set by federal statute, so they will not rise or be subject to adjustment for inflation unless Congress passes an amendment to the present laws. You are *not eligible at all* if your income exceeds the limits. Unlike the traditional IRA, with a Roth you don't get to deduct the money you put in from taxes this year, but the earnings completely escape taxation, even when you start taking distributions. You are not required to start taking distributions from a Roth at age 70½, so the earnings may continue to grow tax-free, and you may even continue to make contributions as long as you are earning income. This is a *very* good deal for a population that is expected to live to a very ripe old age. (For more information about Roth IRAs, go to the IRS Web site: www.irs.gov.)

- *Be realistic.* Don't expect your retirement nest egg to produce the 9% to 10% average annual returns that some financial planners and pension benefits managers still claim is the norm. In these uncertain times we'd rather you err on the low end and estimate a maximum of only 5% to 6% a year, an average return that factors in the economic roller coaster we've all been riding, as well as the unimpressive track record of 401(k) plans. Assume inflation will average somewhat under 3% a year.

In Your Twenties

At this age $12,000 might as well be a billion dollars, but you may start with modest contributions. Put just 5% to 10% of your salary into a 401(k) or 403(b) (the same kind of plan, but offered by nonprofit organizations to employees) through automatic payroll deductions, so that you won't miss the money. Invest the money in dividend-paying stocks and some selected growth stocks. As a general guideline only, we'll say keep at least 50% in fixed income investments. You've heard that you can afford to take risks when you're young, but we don't believe in taking big risks with your retirement savings. Steer clear of your company's stock. (See our 401(k) warning at the end of this section.) If you're self-employed, start exercising just a little discipline and put 5% to 10% of what you earn each year into a SEP IRA or a Keogh Plan.

In Your Thirties and Forties

You are reaching your peak earning years, but if you have children, saving and investment becomes even more important now. Ideally, around 15% of your gross income should go into a retirement account. (Start with 10% if 15% is too much of a strain!) If you need some of that money to go toward your children's education, invest less in your retirement plan, but be sure to put money aside each year. Start paying off your debts *now*.

In Your Fifties

By now you should have a sense of how much money you'll need when you retire.

Invest as much money as possible in tax-deferred retirement accounts. Invest for value, in stocks that pay dividends and high-grade bonds, plus a strong component of

Dolan Ah-Ha!

As of 2006, Roth 401(k)s and Roth 403(b)s will likely enter the scene as another option in the qualified retirement plan spectrum. These plans will have an interesting twist: They will be available through employers even to people who earn too much to contribute to a Roth IRA. (As mentioned above, the limit is $110,000 for single filers and $160,000 for married couples filing jointly.) Like the Roth IRA, your contributions will not be tax deductible, but earnings will grow tax-deferred and distributions will not be subject to federal income tax if you hold the account for at least five years and take distributions only after you reach the age of $59\frac{1}{2}$, are disabled, or use the distributions for certain qualified expenses involved in first-time homebuying.

Treasuries or money market funds. If you're now 50 and you save $5,000 a year, assuming a 5% annual return, you would retire at 70 with a nest egg of about $175,000. If you know you'll need more than $175,000, you'll need to increase the amount you save each year. Can you save $7,500? $10,000? Your total retirement savings will rise accordingly. (We are estimating conservatively to factor in the beating retirement accounts have taken in recent years, but over time a good investment portfolio can earn an average of 8% a year.)

In Your Sixties

If you still need funds for your retirement (and who can't use a few more bucks?), there are several measures you can take now.

Use as many other sources as you can before you tap into retirement accounts that the bear market has beaten down. Your home may be your most useful asset if you're getting ready to retire.

If your home has appreciated since you bought it, you can sell it and pocket gains of up to $250,000 for individuals, or $500,000 for couples, without paying capital gains taxes. If you move into a less expensive home, you can put the gains into your investment portfolio.

If you find yourself house rich but cash poor, and are having trouble maintaining a reasonably comfortable standard of living, you might consider a reverse mortgage. This is a loan that allows homeowners 62 and over to draw down the equity while still living there. You have to pay back the loan, but it isn't due until you die or move out—at which point the house is sold to cover the loan. A federally insured home equity conversion mortgage can be paid in a lump sum, monthly installments, or a credit line to draw from as needs arise. AARP has information at its Web site, www.aarp.org. Also, check out www.reverse.org. For a list of reverse mortgage lenders in your area, go to www.reverse-mortgage.org. There are some good reverse mortgage plans . . . and some *really* bad ones that will rip you off. Be careful . . . your home's equity is not a "no brainer" pot of gold!

For an emergency fund, take out a home equity line of credit. It's easier to qualify while you're working. Don't use it unless you have an emergency, but have it as backup.

What's the Difference Between a 401(k) and a Defined Benefit Pension Plan?

Both are "qualified" pension plans.

A defined plan is a traditional employer pension plan. It promises to pay a specified amount to you, calculated by your salary and number of years of service, and is insured by the Pension Benefit Guaranty Corporation under Title IV of the Employee Retirement

Income Security Act of 1974 (ERISA). (This is not a guarantee that your plan is fully insured. See "Five Retirement Myths" in this chapter.) In some cases all contributions are made by the employer; in others, employees make the contributions, often with the employer matching the amount. Defined plans went out of favor when 401(k)s came in because the defined benefit plans, traditionally often funded largely by employer contributions, were more expensive to the company.

However, because employees can now make a higher level of contributions (up to $40,000 a year, as with all qualified plans), these plans are starting to become popular again, particularly among smaller employers, says Priscilla Weber, owner of Weber Financial Services in Los Angeles, a company that administers qualified pension plans for companies large and small. Benefits are usually distributed as annuities.

In a 401(k), you choose the investments. A 401(k) is not insured, but it is your investment account, managed by a private administrator. It is *not* affected by your company's fortunes unless you've put the bulk of the portfolio into company stock. The value of your 401(k) is based on the market value of the stocks, bonds, and/or money market instruments in which you've invested. You must take a minimum annual distribution by the time you are 70½. You may take a lump-sum payout, but you will pay hefty taxes on it in the year that you take the distribution unless you roll it over into another retirement account, such as an IRA.

Under Any Qualified Pension Plan

The minimum distributions for all retirement plans are based on actuarial tables calculating your life expectancy. Find these tables in Publication 590, Appendix C at www.irs.govpubirs-pdf/p590.pdf. or at Ed Slott's IRA Tax Center, run by Ed Slott, at www.irahelp.com. If there is an age difference of more than 10 years between you and your spouse, you may take distributions based on joint life expectancy tables, which means your minimum distributions can be lower than they would otherwise be for the older spouse, and therefore incurring lower taxes. If the spouse who owned the retirement plan dies, the surviving spouse uses his or her life expectancy tables.

What Happens to Your Pension Plan If Your Company Goes Out of Business?

If you have a 401(k), or any other qualified pension plan, the account belongs to you, not your employer. Assuming you've heeded our advice and haven't put the bulk of your retirement investments into company stock, you should have money due to you that you can roll over into an IRA or into your new employer's plan. The money from any kind of qualified pension plan cannot be used to pay the company's creditors. However, sometimes the firm that administers the plan refuses to release the accounts to the employees until certain administrative fees are paid by the employers. Call the Department of Labor's Pension and Welfare Benefits Administration's help line, 866-275-7922, if your funds are being held up. A benefits advisor will research your claim and follow through, and if many employees' accounts are involved, the enforcement arm might take over.

401(k) Warnings

Warning #1: Stay Away From Your Company's Stock.

We can't say this too many times. Put no more than 5% of your 401(k) money in your company's stock, even if the company matches only that contribution. Actually, we'd prefer to see *none* in there. We know that it's emotionally difficult *not* to put a big slug of your retirement bucks in a company that you know so well because you work there! But you don't *run* the company and probably aren't intimate with all the day-to-day details. Your fortunes are tied to the company for your paycheck, so at least diversify in your retirement investments. You've heard the CEO's pronouncements that it's growing by double digit percentage points every year. If you're tempted to believe this, we have one word for you:
    E-N-R-O-N.

Warning #2: Watch Out for Signs of Fraud

An antifraud campaign conducted by the U.S. Department of Labor (DOL) found a small fraction of employers that abused employee contributions by either using the money for corporate purposes or holding on to the money too long. From the DOL, here are 10 warning signs that your contributions are being misused:

1. Your 401(k) or individual account statement is consistently late or comes at irregular intervals.
2. Your account balance does not appear to be accurate in statements.
3. Your employer has not transmitted your contribution to the plan on a timely basis.
4. Your account has a significant drop in value that cannot be explained by market conditions.
5. Your statement shows your contribution from your paycheck was not made.
6. Investments listed on your statement are not what you authorized.
7. Former employees are having trouble getting their benefits paid on time or in the correct amounts.

8. You find unusual transactions, such as a loan to the employer, a corporate officer, or one of the plan trustees.

9. There are frequent and unexplained changes in investment managers or consultants.

10. Your employer has recently experienced severe financial difficulty.*

Warning #3: Watch Out for Excessive Fees

Christine Dugas, one of our favorite writers for USA Today, wrote an excellent article on 401(k)s. She said that not only did a bear market hurt most 401(k)s but fees for record-keeping, managing the investments, and optimal plan services also weigh heavily on retirement savings. Here's the box that ran with Christine's article . . . talk about a fee "wake-up" call!

Impact of 401(k) Fees

Over time, even a small increase in fees will substantially erode the retirement savings in a 401(k) plan. The chart assumes a starting balance of $50,000 and an annual return of 8%.

	Balance after			
Fees	5 years	10 years	20 years	30 years
0.5%	$71,781	$103,052	$212,393	$437,748
1.0%	$70,128	$98,358	$193,484	$380,613
1.5%	$71,781	$93,857	$176,182	$330,718

Source: Hewitt Associates

How Will You Pay for Health Care When You're Retired?

"If I'd known I was going to live so long, I'd have taken better care of myself." That quote has been attributed to a lot of famous old people. Eubie Blake, the celebrated ragtime pianist who died five days after his hundredth birthday, said it. George Burns said it. So have other nonagenarians and centenarians.

*For more information, go to www.dol.gov/pwba/pubs.

Another major concern: health care in retirement. A health care policy can cost more than $10,000 per year and that's not counting the cost of pharmaceutical benefits.

It's a fact . . . health benefits for today's retirees are shrinking, and those of us who will retire in the years ahead will have to shoulder even more of the health care burden ourselves. According to *The Wall Street Journal*, in a study of 56 retiree health plans offered by companies with at least 5,000 active employees, Watson Wyatt Worldwide, a Washington, D.C.-based consulting firm, found that 17% of the companies have "virtually eliminated" their liabilities for such benefits by reaffirming retirees to pay the FULL premiums, and 20% have already eliminated such plans altogether for new hires. So where do we start?

You must consider the efficacy of long-term-care insurance, which is best purchased while you are still working. Some employers are offering long-term-care policies for employees.

We talked about long-term-care policies for your parents in Chapter 8. Now it's time to think about getting them for yourself and your partner. See our cost table in Chapter 8. Medicaid kicks in if you spend down everything. If you are in a nursing home paid for by Medicaid, your spouse still has some protection in most states. Generally your spouse can keep at least $1,451 a month in income and half of your combined assets up to a maximum of $87,000, and the state cannot force you to sell your home while your spouse or dependent children are living, even if they don't live there. (These figures vary by state.)

It's impossible to know what prescription drugs you might need when you're a senior citizen, but suffice to say, for those who are now seniors, and those who will be, the costs are out of line. It's a problem for most seniors without substantial means. Medicare HMOs are dropping prescription drug coverage left and right. You can, however, check out **state pharmacy assistance programs**. More than 30 states have some kind of pharmacy aid program to help seniors who aren't below the poverty level. Contact your local chapter of AARP for information.

Online, the Disability Resources Web Watcher has a link to assistance programs funded by Medicare at www.disabilityresources.org/RX.html.

Alternative Lifestyles and Retirement

If you want to see a senior citizen free-for-all, just wait till widowed, divorced, single, and gay baby boomers start retiring and seeking companionship. Demographers expect the portion of senior couples who cohabit to grow dramatically in the 2010 and 2020 censuses. But even as of 2000, the U.S. Census found that almost twice as many seniors as a decade before were living as cohabiting couples. The 2000 census data showed that unmarried-partner households increased 72% over 1990. Studies have shown that between 1996 and 2000, households made up of cohabiting opposite-sex senior couples rose 46%, a bigger jump than that of their middle-aged counterparts. Other reports that included same-sex couples showed the number of senior cohabitants rising 73% between 1990 and 1999, from 127,000 to 220,000.

Though there appear to be many reasons for seniors to avoid a formal commitment, including a reluctance on the part of older women who are divorced or widowed to take on the conventional wife role again, pragmatic concerns govern the decision for many couples. For one thing, cohabitation allows couples on fixed incomes to share expenses without taking on major financial obligations, such as being responsible for each other's long-term medical care. Studies have found that cohabiting seniors often provide for their partners in their wills, but still leave the bulk of their estates to their children.

What Are Your Rights If You Aren't a Married Couple?

As we mentioned earlier in this book, the rights of same-sex couples living together are being discussed and legislated as you read this page! At the moment, you do not have rights to each other's Social Security benefits at death. Even gay couples in a marriage or civil union that has been recognized as such in their state are ineligible for Social Security spousal or survivor benefits. That means if you are living on one partner's Social Security benefits, all of the money will dry up when that person dies. A term life insurance policy with the partner as beneficiary may be a smart contingency strategy.

You may name your partner as beneficiary of your retirement plan, but there will be fairly dire tax consequences if you die first. Unlike a spouse, an unmarried beneficiary can't roll over his deceased partner's IRA or qualified retirement plan savings into his own IRA without having the money taxed as distributions. One concession is that the beneficiary can spread the distribution over a five-year period. As an alternative to direct distributions from a retirement plan, you might be able to take the payouts in the form of a joint annuity if your employer allows you to name a nonspouse as a joint annuitant. You, as the pension fund holder, might also take out an annuity for your own life with a guaranteed payout for 10 or 20 years, which will protect your surviving partner if you should die.

Misinformation Runs Rampant. Here Are Five Retirement Myths—and the Facts

Myth #1: Getting married when you're retired will cost you your Social Security or pension benefits.

Many older couples fib to their families and say they skipped off to Vegas and tied the knot—even though they're really just living together—because they're afraid of losing their retirement benefits.

Fact If you're age 60 or older and were widowed, you CAN get remarried and still collect on your deceased spouse's record. The survivor benefit is equal to your deceased spouse's full benefit, which may be more than your own benefit or the 50% you're entitled to from your new spouse's benefits. For more information, call the Social Security Administration at 800-772-1213 or visit the Web site at www.ssa.gov.

Myth #2: Thanks to the Pension Benefits Guarantee Corporation (PBGC), your pension benefits will always be safe.

Fact The PBGC doles out only a fraction of the actual benefits owed if a company's pension plan fails. You can expect to get only one-fifth of the monthly pension you would have been due, for an annual pension of $11,097 to $31,705. In addition, the PBGC doesn't cover any of the major benefits like severance, vacation, or sick pay. All those benefits will disappear if your pension collapses. Which is why we strongly urge you to check the safety of your employer's pension plan!

Myth #3: Your pension plan administrator will make sure you get all the benefits you're owed.

Fact Math or "actuarial" errors (like using an incorrect interest-rate assumption) and administrative errors are all too common when it comes to calculating your pension benefits—and we're not talking about mistakes that cost you little amounts, either! Thanks to these errors, you could be losing 20% to 50% of your lump-sum or monthly pension payment. One way to protect yourself is to have your benefits reviewed by an independent pension consultant. The best service we've found is The National Center for Retirement Benefits, Inc. (800-666-1100; 666 Dundee Road, Suite 1200, Northbrook, IL 60062; http://www.ncrb.com). They review, analyze, and—if need be—audit your pension plan participation to make sure you're getting all your benefits. Their fee is 20% of any additional money they find for you—and if they don't find any money for you, you pay nothing. See "Pension Plan Ah-Ha!" on p. 328.

Also, you can make your own calculations with the pension calculator on the Web site of the American Academy of Actuaries, at www.actuary.org.

Myth #4: In retirement, you need to avoid losses and preserve your principal at all costs.

Fact While we do think older investors should be more cautious than 30-year-old investors, we never want you to forgo growth entirely as a guideline. Keep 60%–80% of your money in fixed investments and invest the balance in conservative growth investments that pay good dividends if you can afford to lose money. Your exact investment strategy depends on

Dolan Bottom Line

The best way to protect your pension benefits if you are planning to retire in the reasonably near future is to make sure that all of your pension documents are accurate *months* before you retire.

Keep a file of start date, pay stubs, and documents outlining changes to your company's plan, plus your individual pension statements.

Get a copy of your program's summary plan description (SPD). This document outlines such important issues as calculations of pension benefits, what benefits are included in the plan, and eligibility requirements.

Every year, be sure you get a copy of your pension plan's annual report. If you don't get it in the mail or through interoffice delivery, *ask for it!* It's also available from the U.S. Department of Labor's Pension and Welfare Benefits Administration (PWBA) through its public disclosure room in Washington, D.C. Contact the PWBA by phone at 866-275-7922, or online at www.dol.gov/dol/pwba.

your particular circumstances. More discretionary assets will allow a higher percentage of stocks and mutual funds.

Myth #5: Social Security benefits are enough to make up the shortfall between your pension and your living expenses.

Fact This is one of those maybe/maybe not myths: The average annual Social Security benefit is approximately $17,000 a year for couples and just under $10,000 a year for single recipients—along with your pension benefits, which may or may not be enough to pay your living expenses. How much can you expect to get? Visit the Social Security Administration's Web site at http://www.ssa.gov/online/ssa-7004.html to download a Request for Earnings and Benefit Estimate Statement (Form SSA-7004). Or call the Social Security Administration's Information Hotline, toll-free, at 800-772-1213. Odds are you'll need to rely on your own investments to make up the shortfall between your living expenses and your pension and Social Security benefits.

Early Retirement

We'll never forget a call from a man named Roger in Oregon who was practically in tears on the phone with us. He was let go from his job *three months* before he was to become

Pension Plan Ah-Ha!

When you get change at the supermarket, do you check to make sure it's accurate? Allen C. Engerman, president of the National Center for Retirement Benefits, Inc. (800-666-1000, www.ncrb.com), sees no reason not to be just as careful about examining the sum that's in your qualified pension plan when you are getting ready to retire. This is *your* income, after all. Besides, when the NCRB investigates, they find errors around 50% of the time! Guess who profits from the errors in most cases. "Out of thousands of investigations, we've found only five or six errors that would have benefited the employee," says Engerman.

In most cases, errors found by NCRB net the client an extra $5,000 to $40,000 in the pension plan. The company has, however, found errors that, when corrected, add as much as $60,000 to $100,000 to the plan.

NCRB works mostly with defined-benefit pension plans, but the company can go after your 401(k) if you believe there might be an error in the investment value.

eligible for retirement benefits, after many years of service to his company. Can you imagine a company doing that? Believe it. Last we heard, Roger was still fighting his case in court.

Lean and mean employers like young blood, particularly because young staffers are less expensive (though not necessarily smarter) than experienced old hands—that is, if you don't factor in the cost of training and mistakes over time. Few senior managers do because they are mostly concerned about quarterly performance figures. Don't get us started. . . . Anyway, the current efforts to streamline corporate operations make older staff members particularly vulnerable. "Older" can mean as young as 40 in some companies. The sort-of-good news is that if you have a long record of service to the company, you may be offered a "golden hand-shake" in the form of an early-retirement package as an incentive to leave the company.

Should You Take an Earlier Retirement Than You'd Planned? Can You Afford to Accept the Offer?

If you haven't built up a strong retirement account, losing a job could be rough going. On the other hand, it might present a golden opportunity to take a lump sum that you can invest wisely while looking for a more rewarding second career, or another job in the same field if things aren't too tough all over.

What you *must* find out, as soon as you start to hear rumors of packages in the offing at your company, is how serious the problem is. Are there hints, or official announcements, of bonus cuts and salary freezes, too? If the company is talking cutbacks, there is a strong chance that you could be laid off in the next few years whether you accept a golden handshake or not. We think you should start scouting around for another job right away, and if you get an early retirement offer, snap it up. If you turn it down, you might not have another chance.

Many early-retirement packages compute your pension benefits by adding three years to your age and three years to how long you worked at the company. Then they offer a lump sum payout equal to half your weekly salary, multiplied by your years of service.

For example, if you worked for a company for 20 years, earning $2,000 a week before taxes, you should expect a lump-sum payment of at least $20,000. A really sweet deal would be one that adds five years to both your age and your years of service, plus two weeks' worth of pay for every year you've been there. In this case, your lump-sum payment would be $80,000 ($4,000 x 20).

To make sure you're getting the sweetest deal possible, however, be prepared to negotiate. Find out what others in your industry with your level of experience have received. In addition to money, try to get extended health insurance benefits and a longer period to exercise your stock options—until the company gets back on its feet, perhaps. The bigger the company and the more eager the company is to reduce the staff, the better position you are in to strike some bargains.

Get all figures IN WRITING!

An early-retirement offer can truly provide you with a springboard to a better retirement. You can use your lump-sum payout to finance your own business, or to give your retirement nest egg an added cushion. Unless you make a killing on the package, or on the sale of your house or another property that has greatly appreciated, you will probably have to continue seeking work, but with a decent-sized package you may be able to do something you've always wanted to do—perhaps work part-time, or for a nonprofit organization whose goals you support, or start a business, or even go back to school and master a new field.

Your Postretirement Career

Truth be told, most people who have enjoyed successful careers get bored with a retirement that's all play and no work. Sure, you probably don't want to be the oldest living burger-flipper—unless you have a plan to write a book about the experience—but there are many other options. Make a list of all the jobs you wish you'd had, then look for opportunities to do them! Here are some suggestions that come from people we've heard from on our show:

- Take a temporary or permanent part-time job in the same career field.
- Do bookkeeping or accounting work for one or two small businesses.
- Teach at a high school or community college.

- Work part-time or telecommute from home with your current employer.
- Help people with disabilities.
- Take up garden design and landscaping.
- Start writing columns for local papers.
- Become an aerobics instructor.
- Become an adventure tour leader.
- Create your own business.
- We even heard about a 90-year-old retiree who developed a new system to teach music to kids.

If you start a small business from your home, you may be able to qualify for extra tax breaks. (See Chapter 3, "Is Your Home Your Workplace? Deduct It!") You can get group savings on health insurance and other benefits, including a newsletter that publishes marketing, finance, and management advice, from the Home Office Association of America, which you can join for $49 a year, or $100 a year if you're living overseas. Contact the association at 212-588-9097 or 800-809-4622, or online at www.hoaa.com. You can also get advice online from *Home Office Magazine*—www.homeofficemag.com. To get started, we recommend reading *The Best Home Businesses for the 21st Century: The Inside Information You Need to Know to Select a Home-Based Business That's Right for You*, by home-based-biz gurus Sarah and Paul Edwards. Published by J. P. Tarcher, $17.95. Available at bookstores or online at www.amazon.com.

Your Pension Plan

The Distribution

When you retire or when you reach the age of 70½, whichever comes first, you have to start taking a distribution that is no less than a so-called "required minimum distribution" from your retirement plan, an amount based on the prior year's account balance divided by the number of years you have left to live according to the actuarial tables the IRS uses. The required minimum is recalculated each year based on this formula.

If you fail to take the minimum in any given year, you'll be subject to a 50% tax penalty on the amount you were supposed to withdraw unless the value of your plan has declined so much that it's lower than the required distribution amount. (Small comfort!)

Here is a very important question that we field all the time:

"How should I take my retirement benefit payment?" Should I:

- take 100% of my benefit and have no payment go to my spouse/partner when I die? or

- take a reduced benefit and have a payment continue to go to my spouse/partner if he or she outlives me?

Although we are simplifying this question—because specifics vary from plan to plan—we emphatically want to make a point. Let's look at the two options:

Option #1: The employee (in this case, the husband) is about to retire.

He may receive the full monthly payout (let's say $1,000) for his lifetime.

Because he chose the 100%-of-benefit option, if he predeceases his wife, his pension check stops.

The wife then will receive $0/monthly benefit.

Option 2: The husband could opt to take 85% of the monthly benefit ($850).

Should he predecease his wife, she would receive ½ of his benefit ($425) for the rest of her life.

Our Opinion

Some financial planners suggest that you take the full 100% benefit and buy life insurance so that the surviving spouse would receive a lump insurance sum to make up for the loss of monthly pension income.

This is a bad choice unless the surviving spouse is a genius money manager who could invest the insurance settlement sufficiently well to support him- or herself. But, more important, this strategy needs to be implemented many years before retirement to be effective.

Your Best Bet

Unless your spouse is a very savvy investor who could make or exceed your lost monthly benefit by investing insurance proceeds, most couples are better off selecting the "less than 100%" benefit so that the surviving spouse would have a dependable and predictable source of income for his or her entire lifetime.

However, if you are an unmarried couple, the surviving partner will not be able to get tax-deferred treatment for the balance of the pension plan. In that case your best options are either term life insurance with your partner as beneficiary, or, if your employer's plan allows it, taking the distribution in the form of an annuity that covers both of you.

Be wary of insurance salespeople who use the sales pitch that you should take the "100% option" and buy an insurance policy to care for the surviving spouse. It's a good way to sell more insurance, but not the best use of your investment dollars.

Questions to Ask Your Pension Plan Administrator
When You Join the Company

1. When do I become eligible to join the plan?
2. Is there a matching contribution—and, if so, how much?
3. What are my investment options in the plan?
4. Is an investment in company stock required?
5. Is there a hardship withdrawal provision?
6. Where will I find advice on the best investment options for my situation?
7. Does my employer or the plan administrator offer financial planning services to help me evaluate my 401(k) as part of my overall retirement savings?
8. Are annuity options available?

Social Security

When should you start drawing Social Security benefits?

The age at which you may start collecting Social Security benefits has gone up. People who turned 65 last year didn't qualify for full benefits until two months after their birthday. Those born after 1959 will not be able to collect until they are 67. The minimum age for collecting benefits is still 62, but the penalty for early collection is now steep—anywhere from 20% to 30%. The stiffest penalties apply to those who were born after 1959, meaning your benefits would be reduced by 30% if you retire at 62.

There is, conversely, a bonus in place if you wait to collect . If you wait until you're 70 to retire, you will be able to add as much as 8% for each extra year you work to the monthly benefit you'll eventually collect.

Questions Often Asked About Social Security: *

Q: **How do I apply for my benefits?**

A: Apply as soon as you are eligible. The Web site www.ssa.gov has an online benefits planner link that you can use to check out your options. You may also want to talk with a Social Security representative in the year before you plan to retire, because it may be to your advantage to start your retirement benefits before you actually stop working. You can complete the application online, by calling 800-772-1213, or by visiting or calling your local Social Security office. (Check the phone book or the Social

*Questions come from the Social Security Administration Web site—www.ssa.gov. Click on "Frequently Asked Questions" to search for answers to your questions.

Security Web site for locations.) Be sure to ask what documents you will need to sign up; for starters, you will need your Social Security card (or a record of your number) and your birth certificate.

Q: **Will my Social Security benefits be taxed?**

A. For about 20% of all recipients they are taxable. Your benefits are usually taxed if half the annual amount you receive plus your other income exceeds $25,000 for a single person and $32,000 for a couple filing jointly.

Q: **Will money withdrawn from my retirement accounts be considered earnings that reduce my benefits?**

A: No. Social Security counts only the income you earn from a job or your net profit if you're self-employed. Nonwork income such as pensions, annuities, investment income, interest, capital gains, and other government benefits will not affect your Social Security benefits.

How Much Will *You* Get from Social Security?

Most of the baby boomers we know, ourselves included, aren't 100% sure that Social Security will still be around when we hit retirement age. How big of a monthly Social Security check can you expect?

The Social Security Administration sends out to every American worker, about 60 days before your birthday, a Personal Earnings and Benefits Estimate Statement, which outlines what you can expect as a retirement benefit.

If you haven't seen yours by the time you've blown out the candles on your cake, get a copy of your earnings record and check what the Social Security Administration (SSA) has recorded as your contributions against the Social Security contributions you've made (which you'll find listed on your year-end pay stubs and W-2 forms). You'll find the SSA's

Dolan Ah-Ha!

According to the National Economic Council Interagency Working Group on Social Security, Social Security is particularly important to women. Elderly unmarried women—including widows—get 51% of their total income from Social Security. Unmarried elderly men get 39%, while elderly married couples get 36% of their income from Social Security. For 25% of unmarried women, Social Security is their only source of income, compared to 9% of married couples and 20% of unmarried men.

information on Form SSA-7004, your Personal Earnings and Benefits Statement. Go to www.ssa.gov/online/ssa-7004.html, where you can download a request form for your Form SSA-7004. Or call the SSA at 800-772-1213. While you are at it, ask for a copy of their booklet "Retirement Benefits" (Publication No. 05-10035)—a guide to Social Security retirement benefits.

Fill out this form (it takes only a minute) and mail it back to the SSA. About three weeks later, you'll get your Personal Earnings and Benefits Statement, which will tell you how much you may expect to receive from Social Security, based on their records of your lifetime contributions.

By checking your records against theirs, you'll spot mistakes quickly. It's much easier for the SSA to correct an error *before* they start paying benefits to you than after!

You may find that your spouse's benefit is more than twice yours, in which case you would be better off applying for your 50% spousal Social Security benefit instead. Do the math and see which one pays you more each month.

If you'll be getting a government pension, this money may offset your Social Security benefits, and you may wind up with a lower monthly check. Fortunately, private pension benefits don't usually affect your Social Security benefits—except in one instance, when your deferred-compensation payout could cause problems.

If you're expecting to get any deferred compensation—severance pay or sick pay, for example—make sure you mention this to the SSA, or your benefits will be reduced $1 for every $2 you're paid over $8,280, if you're under age 65. Your benefits will be reduced $1 for every $3 you're paid over $12,500, if you're age 65–70. As long as you let the SSA know in advance that the payments you're receiving were for work you did *before* you retired, your benefits will remain intact.

Where's the Best Place to Live When You Retire?

Every six months or so you'll see another magazine article about the "best places to retire." Funny how the media keeps coming up with new places. As one locale becomes overexposed and, with the overexposure, overpriced, the writers of those articles have to keep combing the warm parts of two hemispheres for something new to hype. A fun job, to be sure, but if a place sounds idyllic, by the time you read about it, it may have become so overrun with retirees that the beach feels more like the freeway at rush hour and the cafés are charging more for a glass of wine than you'd pay for a week's worth of groceries at home.

The best way to find your retirement Eden is to scout it out yourself. Take extended vacations to various places you find interesting. Once you pick a location you love and can afford, buy yourself a retirement home and either use it as a weekend getaway (if it's nearby) or consider renting it out until you're ready to make the big retirement move.

Pick a location that you can enjoy year-round and that has enough facilities and resources to meet your changing needs. Make a list of the things that are most important for you to have in your life and look for a location that matches these needs. Also, make sure the cost of living is reasonable, so you can live as well or even better in retirement than you do today!

To help you in your search for the perfect retirement location, we asked our friend Peter Dickinson (author of *Sunbelt Retirement*, *Retirement Edens Outside the Sunbelt*, and *Travel and Retirement Edens Abroad*) for some pointers on selecting good places to retire. According to Pete, the best locations have these six common traits:

1. A Bountiful Climate

Temperature extremes aren't good for you at any age, but they can be lethal as you get older. Whether you like the four seasons that come with areas in Tennessee, or whether you prefer the year-round climate of a place like San Diego, you'll enjoy your retirement more if you look for average temperatures of 66°F and humidity of 55% or less.

2. A Lower Cost of Living

By retiring to a location where living costs are below the national average, you can live better for less. For instance, if you move from New York City to San Diego, you would cut your cost of living at least 46%! Don't forget to factor in state and local taxes, which together should be less than 10% of your income. Check out www.valic.com/291e.html for a list of the top 10 low-tax retirement areas.

3. Good Available Housing at a Reasonable Cost

Ideally, when you move, you should be able to sell your current home and use the proceeds to pay off the remaining mortgage on your retirement home—and even sock a bit of it away in your retirement nest egg!

4. Adequate Medical Facilities

As we age, having quick access to quality medical care becomes much more important. Any retirement location you select should have at least one doctor for every 750 residents. Also, compare costs, to see how they stack up against what you're currently paying for medical care. A semiprivate hospital room, for example, should cost less than the national average of $375 a day.

5. Good Cultural and Recreational Facilities

Make sure that all your favorite cultural and recreational activities are available throughout the year. You shouldn't have to drive 50 miles each weekend to see a good play or to play a challenging golf course, if that's what you enjoy doing.

www.content.gay.com/channelshome/hero_seniors_991221.html has information on the myriad new retirement communities coming up for gay residents.

6. Special Services for Retirees

A good base of retirement-related services is a must. These services should range from in-home health care and senior centers to transportation programs and special community discounts.

We also believe you'll find the best deals in areas that are one to two hours from big airports. Steer clear of spots like Vail and Telluride, where the rich and famous have already staked their claim and pushed up prices. There are plenty of other wonderful areas that have yet to be overdeveloped.

To get more information about great places to retire, check out www.valic.com/251a.html.

Helpful Web Sites and Books

General Retirement Information

American Association of Retired Persons: www.aarp.org

www.benefitscheckup.org—helps eligible seniors find programs to assist with finances, housing, and other needs

www.quicken.com/retirement

www.retirement-living.com

www.retirementhavens.com

Calculating How Much Money You Will Need in Retirement

T. Rowe Price Retirement Income Calculator, at www.troweprice.com, helps retirees and soon-to-be retirees determine if their future income goals are realistic in light of their asset base.

The Retirement Savings Time Bomb . . . How to Defuse It, by Ed Slott (Penguin); $10.50 on Amazon.com

FirstGov for Seniors; benefits for federal employees: www.seniors.gov

Office of the Secretary of Defense; military retirement benefits: www.pay2000.dtic.mil

The American Savings Education Council's Ballpark Estimate: www.asec.org/ballpark—in English and Spanish

Retirement Living

www.bankrate.com—refinancing a mortgage, setting up savings, moving to a new city with a different cost of living

www.bestplaces.net—where to retire

www.retirementliving.com—excellent source of tax information in individual states

Reverse Mortgages

www.reverse.org

www.reversemortgage.org

Retirement Plans and Social Security

Social Security: www.ssa.gov

www.pensionrights.org

Up-to-date information about IRA rules and policies: www.irahelp.com, www.irs.gov

Federal Pension and Welfare Benefits Administration offers help with private-sector pension plans at 866-275-7722, or www.dol.gov/dol/pwba

The Great 401(k) Hoax: What You Need to Know to Protect Your Family and Your Future, by William Wolman and Anne Colamosca. Perseus Publishing, 2002. $26.

The Pension Book: What You Need to Know to Prepare for Retirement, by Karen Ferguson and Kate Blackwell. Arcade Publishing, New York. $12.95. Order from Pension Rights Center, PRC Publications, 1140 19th St. NW, Suite 602, Washington, DC 20036—www.pensionrights.org.

Checking to See If the Value of Your Retirement Plan Is Accurate

National Center for Retirement Benefits: www.ncrb.com, 800-666-1000

Alternative Lifestyles and Retirement

www.asaging.org/lgain—section of the American Society on Aging's Web site that hosts the Lesbian and Gay Aging Issues Network

www.gfn.com—Gay Financial Network has information about retirement issues for gay couples.

Women and Retirement

www.womensfinancialhealthnetwork.com

Health Care Policy Information

The Henry J. Kaiser Family Foundation: www.kff.org

CHAPTER 12

Protecting Your Assets
and Your Estate

THINK ESTATE PLANNING is just for fat cats? Think again. This is a chapter for everyone—unless, of course, you don't mind your loved ones getting only a fraction of your hard-earned assets after you die, while the IRS and lawyers take the rest. Nor is this a chapter just for heterosexual married couples, or just for senior citizens. Single or married; gay or heterosexual; young children, grown children, or no children—you need to have your finances in order so that if you should die or become incapacitated, the people closest to you will not have to deal, at an emotionally difficult time, with money headaches.

It makes us all shiver to realize we won't be around forever, but the fact is, there are all kinds of reasons to have a will and a plan.

Let's make one thing clear *before* we begin . . . we are *not* estate planning/trust attorneys. There is *no* substitute for sitting down with an attorney who specializes in these matters and discussing your particular situation and needs. However, what this chapter will do is alert you to the importance of "pre-planning." Every technique and strategy will not be appropriate for every reader . . . but we want you to know they exist. Keep an open mind . . . let's go. . . .

Q: **Do I really need a will? It's a pain to sit down with an attorney, with my busy schedule. Anyway, when you're dead, you're dead.**
A: We love those "information boxes" (that's what we call them) that appear regularly in *USA Today,* but a recent box really caught our eye. It was titled, "Why no will?" Listen to this: 74% of Americans with minor children don't have a will. The result:

- Letting a state court decide who will be the guardian to your underage children if you die unmarried, or if you and your spouse die at the same time.
- Taking the risk that your children from your first marriage don't receive a fair share of your estate.
- The state court will appoint an administrator for your estate, who will take a fee from your assets and decide how they will be distributed.

Still think a will is too much trouble?

Property is more than money and investments. We've often seen—maybe you have, too—adult siblings and their spouses and children squabble over furniture, pianos, silver and china, diamond rings, and items of purely sentimental value when their parents die. We knew a woman who painted. She never became famous, but she had a prolific output of canvasses that her extended family and a large circle of friends divided up, not always equitably, when she died in her seventies. A simple will would have eliminated the arguments.

Second marriages, children from previous marriages, adopted children, single-parent households, same-sex relationships, and unmarried domestic partnerships make estate planning one of the most complex games in town. If you have any next of kin, any complexities in your home life, any people or organizations you want to help, you need to plan with an estate-planning attorney. Don't ask a financial planner or an accountant to structure an estate plan for you. Don't even use "legal" recommendations from a financial planner. This is a job for a lawyer who specializes in estate planning!

In many cases, a will is not enough; you might also need a trust. (See the section on trusts in this chapter.)

People who don't have children often don't get around to estate planning. Ditto, married couples who hold all of their assets jointly. If you are single, or with a partner who is self-sufficient, you might think you have no need for a will. If you're young and not a property owner, you might think you have no assets to leave behind.

However, if you want the people you love to get *something*, you have to spell it out—especially if you don't have a spouse or children. If you die without a will, an administrator appointed by the state will look for your closest next of kin. That would be, in more or less descending order of closeness: spouse, children, grandchildren, parents, siblings, grandparents, nieces and nephews, cousins. If you have none of these relatives living, the court administrator will look for distant cousins.

You might prefer to will your possessions to a significant other, or friends or family members who need and would appreciate them. You might, on the other hand, care deeply about a cause. But if you want your money to go to that cause, you have to leave specific instructions to that effect. As we'll explain later in this chapter, a trust will make it easier for your chosen beneficiaries to get and keep your bequest.

Q: Help! I can't find my deceased spouse's will. What should I do?

A: This happens all too frequently. We mentioned in Chapter 9 the importance of keeping your wills and other important papers in a fireproof file cabinet, so that you're prepared for any emergency. If your spouse left an informal will, handwritten on notepaper, it *can* still be valid in most states if it had a notary witness signature—but only if you can FIND it! Here is what will happen if there is no will, or the original signed copy of the will is nowhere to be found.

The least dire scenario will occur if you were married—as opposed to just living together—and held your assets jointly. In that case, as the widowed spouse, you will automatically be the owner of the assets. (Joint property, however, may not be desirable if the estate is going to be larger than the amount exempt from federal estate taxes, because it will be taxed when the second spouse dies.) If your spouse's retirement accounts and brokerage account named a beneficiary, which most do, the money will go to that person.

However, in the absence of a will, other assets will be placed in the hands of a court-appointed administrator and the property distributed according to your state's laws on intestate succession. The estate will be charged for a surety bond on the appointed administrator to insure against misappropriation or finding that this stranger has run off with your family's fortune. The administrator is required to collect estate taxes and death taxes, pay off all debts and expenses of administering the estate, plus receive a commission for his or her services. After all of these items are paid off, the remaining assets are distributed to next of kin. Most often the spouse gets at least one-half of the estate and children get the remainder. If there is no living spouse, children, or grandchildren, the court will start going down that next-of-kin order we described.

The Amazing Phony Estate Tax Repeal

If your estate is under the threshold established by federal law, it will not be subject to federal estate taxes, though your heirs might get a nasty surprise in the form of a state inheritance tax bill.

If the Feds Have You by the Tail

Remember the rumors you heard back in 2001 about the end of estate tax? It is true that under the Economic Growth and Tax Relief Reconciliation Act of 2001, fewer estates will be subject to federal taxes, but only until 2011. The value of an estate that is exempt from federal taxes will keep rising until 2010, when federal estate tax disappears altogether. But that happens for only for ONE YEAR! The estate tax is *scheduled to return in full force in 2011*, with the first $1 million exempt and a tax of up to 55% on the assets above $1 million. We've heard that people have actually asked tax lawyers about the costs, and the legality, of keeping a rich relative who has been declared brain dead on life support until 2010. It's too bizarre to make up!

Here is the federal tax schedule for the decade.

Year	Estate Exemption	Top Estate Tax Rate
2004	$1.5 million	48%
2005	$1.5 million	47%
2006	$2 million	46%
2007	$2 million	45%
2008	$2 million	45%
2009	$3.5 million	45%
2010	unlimited	0%
2011	$1 million	55%

Your State Might Have You by the Unmentionables

The U.S. government has been touting the reduction and repeal of the estate tax as if it's going to preserve every hard-earned cent you've ever made.

Here is what is actually going to happen between now and 2011. As the federal tax rates go down, Congress will reduce the credit an estate can claim for state taxes paid. Modest estates will suffer more than large ones, because the credit will be a greater proportion of the total assets. Furthermore, not all state exemptions are going to rise with the federal number. Particularly in higher-tax states, total estate taxes are likely to be higher than ever! According to the Seattle law firm Perkins Coie (www.perkinscoie.com) in Washington State, state taxes on estates of residents who die in 2002 could be as high as $33,200.

Dolan Ah-Ha!

What the government has done is obscure the fact that in many states the taxes paid on estates will actually be higher. By any other name, this is smoke and mirrors.

In the past 20 years or so, many states have replaced inheritance taxes with a so-called pickup tax, which is a state estate tax calculated by the amount of credit allowed against the federal estate tax. This way the total federal and state taxes paid on an estate would be limited to the gross amount of the federal estate tax. Many states are now "decoupling" from the federal rate, however, because otherwise, with less money being paid in federal estate taxes, the states would stand to lose billions of dollars. Heirs of an estate used to receive a dollar-for-dollar credit against their federal tax liability for state estate taxes paid, but the credit is being phased out by 2005. Many states may go back to imposing inheri-

Don't Overlook the Gift-Tax Exclusion

The annual gift-tax exclusion is often overlooked as a way to give away money and reduce your estate while you're alive. This can be a useful way of reducing the taxes on your estate. The most common technique is to gift money to children and grandchildren. They can invest the money—or you can invest it for them—and the earnings will be taxed at their rates rather than yours. An individual can give away $11,000 per year per "giftee," and couples can gift $22,000 a year together to each recipient without incurring gift-tax consequences.

The lifetime exclusion—that is, the amount of money you can give away over your lifetime without anyone paying gift taxes—is $1 million as of 2003. These are a separate animal from estate taxes; if your estate is under the tax threshold, your lifetime gifts will still be taxed if they exceed $1 million. As you can see from our table of estate exemptions and tax rates, the gift tax is not going away with the federal estate tax in 2010. Gift tax could take a bite out of the tax-free portion of an estate.

You can, however, give in excess of $1 million by using the annual gift-tax exclusion. You can also bestow money to your children, grandchildren, or other "giftees" for their education or medical expenses while you are alive by giving money directly to the college, hospital, or other institution. This money will not be subject to gift tax or counted under the exclusion.

tance taxes to replace lost revenue. Minnesota, Rhode Island, and Wisconsin are among those states that have taken action to preserve their estate tax without relying upon revenue from the federal credit, and others are expected to follow.

How is the value of the estate determined? By current market rate. Your home will be assessed at today's market value, not the price you paid.

What Does the Shifting Law Mean to You Now?

Estate tax laws are moving under our feet. This means that many families have to keep revising their estate plans. Your will needs flexible language. One of the best ways to protect your heirs now is by setting up a **disclaimer trust.** Under this provision, all of your assets go to your surviving spouse, but he or she has the option to disclaim the assets and put them into a **credit shelter trust** if it turns out to be advantageous tax-wise. The

There Are No Estate Taxes on the Assets You Leave Your Spouse Unless . . .

There's one concession the IRS allows. When you die and leave everything to a surviving spouse, there is an unlimited marital deduction that exempts all assets passing to a surviving spouse from the federal estate tax. Unless . . .

Tax-free status holds no water if you aren't married. If you've been an unmarried same-sex or opposite-sex couple for 30 years it doesn't matter—the estate will be taxed. If you are a married homosexual couple, the union may be recognized in your state, but the federal law could be another matter. Inheritance laws are muddled in this area. See an estate-planning attorney familiar with the laws governing gay marriage in your state.

If you are married but your spouse is not a U.S. citizen, there will be taxes on your estate. You can't get around the tax penalty by holding property jointly. If the surviving spouse is not a U.S. citizen, the law will presume that your joint property belonged strictly to the deceased. If, however, the surviving spouse paid for an entire house or portfolio or other property and can prove it with documentation, the tax will be waived. You should, at least, consider setting up a **Qualified Domestic Trust (QDOT)** for the noncitizen spouse. Your property goes to the trust rather than directly to your spouse, but your spouse is entitled to receive the income from the trust. Any distributions of principal to the noncitizen spouse, however, are subject to estate taxes, although exceptions may be allowed for certain needs, such as medical expenses, education, and support of a child or other dependent. After the spouse's death, the assets will be subject to estate taxes.

credit shelter trust provides income for your surviving spouse, and for your children if it is set up for them, but the principal can be invaded only for health, education, support, and maintenance expenses.

An Important "Don't":

Don't write a will stipulating that your children will receive the "maximum exemption amount" allowed by law. You could accidentally disinherit your spouse this way. Suppose you leave an estate of just about $3.5 million in 2009; with this wording your children would get the entire estate and your widowed spouse could be left out in the cold. Many lawyers suggest that wills spell out the maximum sum you want to leave to your children.

Two Important "Dos":

Do make sure you know how you want your assets distributed before you set foot in your lawyer's office. Go in with a letter of instructions. If you start trying to plan while you're conferring with an estate-planning lawyer, the clock will be ticking away with billable minutes.

Do choose a primary executor and a co-executor. We recommend picking a family member as primary executor and a trusted financial adviser or estate-planning attorney as the backup. This way, your family benefits from the input of both: one executor who knows the next of kin well and one who is familiar with administering estates. Expect your estate to pay executor fees that equal 1% of the estate's value, or slightly less, for a large estate, and 3%–5% of the value of a modest estate. Family members who take commissions from the estate have to report that money as income.

Where There's a Will, There Is *Not* a Way to Bypass State Snags and Probate

While we believe in wills, we also know a will may not be enough. Wills generally have to go through probate. The probate process can be a lengthy one that includes proving

Divorced? Remarried?
Don't Forget to Rewrite Your Will

Did you know that a divorce invalidates your will? If you divorce, you will need to start your estate planning all over again, with a new will. If you remarry, you have to draw up yet another will. If you have a living trust, you will also have to change the terms.

the validity of the will in court (usually a routine procedure), identifying and inventory-ing the property, having the estate appraised, paying debts and taxes, then finally distrib-uting the property according to the directions in the will.

For years, the very word "probate" has made people shudder, because the legal process of "proving" and appraising the will has been notoriously time-consuming and expensive. It can still be—plus, it's all a matter of public record, a fact that can make families of the rich and high-profile squirm. However, in some states the probate process has become less onerous; it has been streamlined in Alaska, Arizona, Colorado, Idaho, Maine, Michi-gan, Minnesota, Montana, Nebraska, New Jersey, New Mexico, North Dakota, Oregon, Pennsylvania, South Carolina, and Utah. In California and Wisconsin, the executor can handle the probate proceedings without an attorney, which is one way to reduce the costs. In most states a certain amount of property can pass to heirs free of probate or at least with a simplified probate process.

Still, there are reasons that heirs prefer to avoid probate. It can tie up the property for months, sometimes as long as a year. The attorney and court fees may take up as much as 5% of the estate, a proportion that comes off the top *before* the estate's debts are tallied up. There may also be appraiser's fees and often other expenses.

The argument in favor of probate (you'll hear this from lawyers) is that it prevents fraud and protects heirs because creditors' claims are promptly resolved; in fact, creditors get anything that is due *before* the heirs get what's left.

It may take months, even years, to distribute the assets of the estate, but usually the estate has only nine months from the time of death to pay off debts and taxes. We've seen hundreds of cases of large estates with few liquid assets in which heirs wind up selling the home, the car, even the investments at "distressed sale" prices to pay off the IRS.

How Do You Avoid Probate?

All About Trusts

Property that passes to heirs outside of a will is not subject to probate. In our view, the best way to avoid probate is through a trust in addition to a will. A trust, to use a simple descrip-tion, is a legal document that holds assets and is run by trustees for the benefit of the par-ties named as beneficiaries. A trust can be revocable, which means the donor, the person who sets it up, has the right to terminate it, or irrevocable, which means it cannot be ter-minated. A trust, which has more detail, will be much harder to contest than a will. The balance of power is different. Although the laws can vary by state, generally the executor of a will cannot approve the distribution of assets to heirs until the entire will is approved by the family. A trust, on the other hand, passes directly to the beneficiary.

Why Unmarried Partners Should Consider Setting Up Trusts

Wills are also inadequate if you want to leave assets to a domestic partner who is not your legally wed spouse. We had a call one day from a gay man in Florida who had lived with his partner for more than 20 years. His partner had told him that he was going to leave him everything he owned—and he did, in a will.

The problem was, the deceased partner's family members, eager to split at least some of the spoils, were making our caller's life a legal hell. They were disputing the will in court. After months, he hadn't seen a penny of the estate.

This kind of scenario is the norm rather than the exception when someone leaves a large chunk of money or property to a gay partner, or even an opposite-sex partner. The parents and siblings of the deceased will come running, saying this person is not next of kin and not entitled to an inheritance.

In the case of our Florida caller, if his partner had set up a trust naming him as the beneficiary, the family would have had to sue him for the money. While there are no guarantees as to who would have won, he would be likely to have the upper hand in court as long as the trust was properly set up, and, unless some sharpshooting attorney managed to get the assets frozen, he would have had access to the income from the trust while the battle raged on.

When you move in with someone, you should each set up a living trust immediately, just in case of a tragic emergency. Lambda Legal, the gay civil rights organization, reports that at least 20 of the people killed in the terrorist attacks of September 11 were lesbians and gay men who died without a will, leaving behind partners who, in the midst of their grieving, had to battle with "in-laws" and the government. Don't let this happen to you or the person you love! Lambda has a network of cooperating attorneys who can help you set up an estate plan geared to a gay partnership. For information, check their Web site at www.lambdalegal.org.

Trusts are different from wills in a number of important ways:

- Trusts do not go through probate, and the assets go to your heirs right away.
- You can use the assets from a trust while you are alive. If you become mentally or physically unable to take care of yourself, a successor trustee can use the assets to care for you.
- You can be the trustee of your own trust. If you're married, your spouse can be the trustee with you.
- Trusts are generally written with more detail than a will and therefore are harder to dispute successfully.

Trusts will NOT, however, escape estate taxes. If you leave a large enough estate, the money held in trusts will still be taxable.

See a good estate lawyer if you want to set up a trust. Ask friends, family, and colleagues for references. If you can't find one through your own network, try the local listings on the Web site www.lawyers.com or www.martindale.com.

There have been scam artists marketing boilerplate living trusts that don't meet the legal requirements. AARP reports that, in surveys it conducted between 1991 and 2000, the number of moderate-to-high-income respondents who had living trusts rose 53%. More shocking, however, was the *125% increase* in living trust arrangements among low-income respondents—people with incomes of $25,000 or less, who probably didn't need trusts at all. How does AARP account for the rise? In a word—salespeople. Salespeople eager to line their own pockets.

The Living Trust—You MUST Know What This Is

A living trust is the only estate-planning strategy that guarantees your assets will be distributed as you wish, without going through probate. We like revocable living trusts better than irrevocable trusts, which can't be changed while you're alive, because they offer flexibility, privacy, and speedy asset distribution.

With a *revocable living trust,* even after it's established you can easily make changes during your lifetime. A trust is usually set up to pay you income while you're living, but you transfer "ownership" of the assets into the trust. You name beneficiaries, but you may change them at any time while you're alive. You can also give specific instructions as to how your assets are to be disbursed.

Set Up a Revocable Living Trust If . . .

If probate is costly in your state, if you own a business or out-of-state property, if you are concerned that someone will challenge your estate, or you are worried about who will take care of your assets and *you* if you become incapacitated, a living trust is crucial to the peace of mind of all concerned.

If you're in a gay relationship, even if your family is very accepting of your partner, funny things can happen when a loved one dies. Setting up a living trust will make it much easier for your life partner to get what you want him or her to have.

If you want to leave money to various members of your family, or even people who aren't related, you can place assets into a trust that you control for the benefit of the people you would like to name as heirs. You indicate who will receive what, but you can change the terms at any time. Another benefit: You may, if you so choose, set up the trust with some language stipulating how you want the money used—for example, a few thousand for a nephew to pay for college, a few hundred to help out a needy child you mentored in a volunteer program.

Setting Up a Living Trust

When you set up a living trust you are the trustee, or manager of the trust. You then name your children, spouse, other trusted relatives, or your significant other as "successor trustees" and "beneficiaries." The cost of setting up a living trust is about $2,500 (could be more or less depending on competition). **Don't try to do it yourself using one of the kits out there. Use an estate-planning attorney and do it right!**

A Trust for Every Need

For nearly every estate-planning problem, there is a trust designed to facilitate the distribution of your assets when you are no longer around.

Here are some of the most common types of trusts and their uses:

Special Considerations for Your Children

For a conventional nuclear family with minor children, a **revocable living trust** is a sensible way to set up an inheritance that goes to the children if both parents die while the children are still young, with an arrangement dictating that the children will get money from the trust each year. The traditional method is to have the trustee hold on to the principal and give the children income from equity dividends and bond interest. These days, however, many trusts are invested for growth or total return rather than income, so the arrangement might be to pay the children 3% to 6% of the value of the trust each year, with special provisions if they prove they need more for valid reasons. Some parents set up similar trusts even for grown-up children, rather than bestowing an inheritance in a lump sum.

You might also make provisions for your grandchildren with a **dynasty trust.** This trust makes use of the generation-skipping transfer (GST) tax exemption, which allows you to create a trust for grandchildren free of federal taxes if it's no more than the amount that is exempt from generation-skipping taxes and estate taxes in the year you die.

What if your family life is a little more complicated, however? If, to name one common example, you are in a second or third marriage and have children from a previous marriage? Sure, you assume you can trust your spouse to honor your wishes. But no one, absolutely no one, should leave such matters to chance. All too often, a husband will die and leave his estate to his second wife, who then remarries and brings his money into the new union, thus cutting off his children from his first marriage. You can protect your

TIMPANOGOS HIGH SCHOOL

children with a **qualified terminable interest property trust, known as a "Q-Tip," or "ABC" trust.** This trust is set up with your surviving spouse as beneficiary, and provides her (or him) with a lifetime income, but you leave explicit directions as to how the funds are to be distributed upon your spouse's death; in the case we've outlined, you would specify that the trust then goes to your children.

What if you have children with special needs? If you have a child who is either physically or mentally unable to be self-sufficient, and will need your support in adulthood, you should set up a **supplemental needs trust** in case you aren't there to provide for him. People with such special needs can receive government benefits through Supplemental Security Income and Medicaid, but they'll be disqualified from those benefits if they hold assets in excess of $2,000. For that reason, you should NEVER gift money to special-needs children under the **Uniform Gift to Minors Act** (known as an **UGMA or UTMA** account), because the money will become the property of the child when he or she turns 18. (We're not crazy about this kind of gifting for *any* children. See Chapter 7.) The supplemental needs trust, on the other hand, puts your money into the hands of a trustee who manages it on behalf of the person with special needs. The money can be used only for staples that the government doesn't provide, such as food, shelter, and clothing. This kind of trust has to be structured carefully to comply with the letter of the law, and it could reduce Social Security benefits, so be sure to work with a special-needs attorney.

If You Are Married With Children and Have an Estate That Will Be Above the Tax Threshold

An **A-B trust** is a living trust with two subtrusts; basically, it cuts your estate in two. Let's assume you die before your spouse. Upon your death, the trust automatically divides into

Family Limited Partnerships: Another Way to Protect Your Children

If you have children from one marriage, or two marriages, and have remarried, consider setting up a Family Limited Partnership (FLP) with yourself as general partner and your children as limited partners. The children are treated as passive investors in the family assets. The main purpose of an FLP is to give property to your children now, so that the property will not be included in your estate and subject to estate taxes. However, a secondary benefit is that since your children already own the family assets on paper, they won't be able to lose them to a stepparent or stepsiblings.

two. One is a marital trust for your spouse. The other is a family trust for your children. You make sure that the assets in the family trust fall below the estate tax liability threshold. When your spouse dies, her trust passes along to the children—but in her name, so unless it's above the threshold, it is not subject to estate taxes.

Qualified Personal Residence Trust

If you are a single parent or a widowed parent, and therefore will not be willing your property to a spouse, or you have a partner or foreign-born spouse as your heir, a **qualified personal residence trust (QPRT)** makes it possible to minimize gift and estate taxes by transferring a residence at a discount to its actual value. You transfer your primary home or your vacation home to an irrevocable trust, with yourself as the prime beneficiary and your children as remainder beneficiaries. You act as both trustee and beneficiary for a fixed term. Five to 10 years is typical. In your dual role you control the property but are also able to use it, though you also have to pay for the maintenance, the property taxes, mortgage, and any other normal property owner's expenses. At the end of the term, the property passes outright or in further trust to your heirs. The value of the gift is based not on the market value, but on the discounted present value of your beneficiaries' right to acquire the property in the future, determined by IRS tables.

If you, say, gift a house worth $1 million at the time you set up the trust, retaining the right to occupy it for 10 years, your heirs get the house with the value calculated as $1 million *minus* the so-called value interest retained during the 10 years that you remained in the house. If the value interest is 35%, they get a gift valued at $650,000, or 65% of the original value. (It is counted as a gift at the time you set up the trust, not when you die.) If you live out the term of the trust, the property is not included in your estate. However, the disadvantage to your heirs is that the original price will be used as the cost basis when they sell it, so if the home has greatly appreciated the capital gains tax might be high. See a tax adviser before you set up this trust.

Using a Life Insurance Trust to Pay Your Estate Taxes

Remember when, back in Chapter 10, we mentioned that there is an estate-planning technique that has an insurance component? This is how it works:

The beneficiary of a life insurance policy generally does not pay income taxes on the payout, but the payout is considered part of the taxable estate of the deceased if the estate is large enough. You may make your living trust the beneficiary of the insurance proceeds and thereby avoid probate, but the estate still has to pay federal estate taxes and state inheritance taxes if the estate is valued beyond the threshold.

You can, however, make things easier for your heirs by setting up an **irrevocable life insurance trust (ILIT), sometimes called a "wealth transfer trust,"** which will pay the estate taxes due on your death. Here's how it works: The ILIT is the owner and beneficiary of your life insurance policy; you are never the owner, so the policy is not part of your taxable estate. The trust doesn't die, so life insurance proceeds collected by the trust are not subject to federal estate or income taxes.

Since there's no way to know who will die first—you or your spouse—we recommend buying second-to-die insurance, so you don't have to set up two separate ILITs. Second-to-die insurance pays only after both you *and* your spouse die, which makes it less expensive because you don't have to buy two separate policies. The tax advantage is that the policy escapes estate taxes when the second spouse dies. One caution: Plan your ILIT with a competent estate-planning attorney and life insurance agent, to assure yourself that you receive the full benefits of this trust.

The trust is also immune from the claims of creditors or divorce courts in most cases. Considering the litigiousness of so many estates, this is a significant advantage. It can be an effective vehicle for someone who is divorced, or for a blended family in which exes might hover around in hopes of enlarging the settlement when the estate is being divided.

The premiums you pay in are subject to gift tax. However, you can set up the ILIT as a **Crummey trust,** in which case the premiums are defined as a "present gift"—as opposed to a "future gift." A future gift, promised for a date in the future, is subject to gift taxes, but a present gift is covered by the $11,000 (but scheduled to increase regularly with inflation) annual exclusion for gifts. That's $11,000 a year that each parent can put into the trust for each child, which buys a heck of a lot of life insurance. (The trust got its name from the Crummey family, who went to court against the IRS to set up such a trust—and won!) You are not the trustee; nor, usually, is your spouse. Most people name a trusted financial adviser, attorney, or responsible family member as trustee.

Want to transfer an existing life insurance policy into a trust? You can "gift" it to the trust, but you may encounter a gift-tax penalty if the gift is valued at more than your $11,000-per-year exclusion, which you will get if you set it up as a Crummey trust. Find out the present face value (the amount your heirs would receive if you were to die tomorrow). Don't make the transfer if you'd pay hefty taxes.

Other Ways to Avoid Probate

Payable-on-death accounts. You open an account at a bank, savings-and-loan, or credit union, naming a beneficiary who automatically gets the money when you die.

Transfer-on-death accounts. Similar to a payable-on-death account, but typically used for investment portfolios. If you were to "gift" an investment portfolio to your spouse, partner, children, or other relative, they might be stuck with hefty capital gains taxes when they sold the investments, because the original price would be used to calculate their cost basis. The gains might be particularly high if you held the portfolio for many years. However, with a transfer-on-death account, the beneficiary receives a step-up in basis on the securities, meaning that the cost basis is calculated according to the market value of the securities on the day you died. Therefore, the capital gains tax is likely to be lower.

Jointly owned property. Some people also set up joint ownership with their children, or a parent or sibling, or a domestic partner, assuming this will make easy work of willing a major asset such as a second home, a car, or an investment account. The intended person will get the assets, all right, but there may be some unintended consequences. For one thing, the assets will not be exempt from estate taxes if your estate is large enough to qualify. Then there is the method of calculating the value of an investment portfolio or property handed down this way. Although the money you put into the property will be valued at its price on the day of your death, the survivor's money will be valued at the original purchase price, leading to some hefty potential capital gains taxes. (The determinant factor here is whose money it is, so each party should keep meticulous transaction records.) If you have a very large investment portfolio, it makes more sense to keep it in your name, as a transfer-on-death account, so that the beneficiary, whoever he or she may be, gets the step-up in basis on the whole portfolio.

Messy stories abound of people setting up joint ownership in the form of *joint tenancy with rights of survivorship* with a nonspouse if they don't keep track of exactly what was contributed by whom. Here's one potential scenario you want to avoid: Say you are unmarried and set up an investment account with your brother. You are the one with the deep pockets who funded the account. But your brother dies first, leaving you the account, which by law is considered an inheritance. If the account is large enough, you could be subject to inheritance taxes on your own money, or your money could be subject to estate taxes while you are still alive! You should be able to escape such taxes, however, as long as you can produce a full set of statements for the life of the account, showing that the funds invested were yours.

One other concern about co-ownership: Do you trust your co-owner? It's easy for a co-owner to clean you out when you're alive. We've heard horror stories of generous people setting up co-owned accounts with irresponsible children or grandchildren, only to have their good deeds punished.

Retirement Accounts

An important component of many estates is the assets that sit in IRAs, 401(k)s, and other retirement plans. When you open a qualified retirement account, the sponsor will usually ask you to name a primary and secondary beneficiary. (Ask for these forms if your broker or pension administrator has forgotten to give them to you.)

Our friend and IRA guru Ed Slott advises that for estate-planning purposes you divide your IRAs into several different accounts—as many as you have heirs—and designate a different party for each account: one for your spouse or partner, one for each child, and so on. You can move money back and forth between the accounts without incurring taxes; that's a new IRS rule.

New rules also make it easier for your heirs to defer taxes on the money in your retirement accounts instead of having to claim the account in one lump sum, with all of the income tax consequences. Your spouse may elect not to claim the account within nine months after your death. Then your contingent beneficiaries—that could be your children—will get the account. At that point, the accounts will be subject to estate taxes if they are large enough. Your children will also have to take distributions, which are subject to income taxes. But here's a nifty way your children may avoid paying a whopping income tax bill: They can make withdrawals from your retirement accounts over *their* lifetimes. Your children and grandchildren, or other nonspouse heirs, can split an inherited IRA among themselves. With a conventional IRA, each pays income taxes on the money as they withdraw it; with a Roth IRA, all withdrawals are tax-free. The caveat with either is that your heirs have to break up the money into separate accounts before the end of the year after you die; otherwise they'll have to make withdrawals based on the life expectancy of the oldest heir according to the IRS mortality tables. You can create a trust for each beneficiary that dictates how much they may withdraw each year if you want to keep an eye on your children's and grandchildren's spending habits from the grave.

Charitable Estate Planning

We're in agreement with Warren Buffett, who made a good point in a now-famous quote dating back to a 1986 *Fortune* magazine interview. He said he was leaving the bulk of his fortune to charity because one should leave "enough money to your kids so they can do anything, but not enough so they can do nothing."

If you are fortunate enough to have an estate so large that you would be able to provide for your loved ones *and* leave money to a charity or a worthy nonprofit organization—congratulations!

There are a number of estate-planning strategies that will provide you with the satisfaction of knowing that you've helped someone in need *plus* received a present or future (for your estate!) tax benefit in return for your generosity.

Here are some ways that you can set up a charitable legacy with even a modest estate:

Charitable Remainder Trusts (CRTs)

This is an irrevocable trust that allows you to take an immediate income tax deduction, avoid capital gains taxes on highly appreciated assets, receive a stream of income for life, and then leave a charitable bequest when you die. CRTs provide for two sets of beneficiaries. First, you and your spouse or partner are provided for with income from the trust while you are alive. The IRS requires that you take at least 5% a year in distributions. After the two of you are dead, the charities you name receive the principal. Although the trust is irrevocable, you may change the charitable beneficiaries at any time. If the trust is structured properly, you can even serve as the trustee, so that you control the investments. Because the assets are earmarked for a charity, the trust pays no capital gains taxes.

Donor-Advised Charitable Funds

For less than $5,000, you can establish a fund that will distribute money to a charity or cause. In recent years, many financial institutions have gotten in on the philanthropic act with donor-advised charitable funds. While the managers of these funds don't claim to be experts at picking worthy recipients, they *are* in the business of building the assets you have available for giving (as much as any mutual fund manager is in the business of building your assets; see Chapter 5). In most cases you can tell the fund managers where you want the money to go and name your heirs as successor advisers. You can get an income stream from the fund if you set up a charitable remainder trust and make a donor-advised fund the beneficiary. There are many such funds sponsored by banks around the country, but here are the most established ones:

Fidelity Investments Charitable Gift Fund 800-682-4438; www.charitablegift.org; minimum contribution $10,000

National Philanthropic Trust 888-878-7900; www.nptrust.org ; minimum $25,000

Vanguard Charitable Endowment Program 888-383-4483; www.vanguardcharitable. org; minimum $25,000

Give Your Home to Charity

No heirs? Or maybe you want to shelter your home from estate taxes. You may donate your house—or any other real estate property you own—to charity. It's called a **retained life estate**. You write up a trust that decrees that you and your spouse or partner will continue living in the house, but after your deaths the house is going to _____ (pick your charity). You calculate your life expectancies according to the IRS mortality tables, and the projected value of the house at the projected time of your death becomes the amount you can declare as a charitable deduction from your income taxes for the year you set up the trust, as well as a deduction from the value of your estate. If the value of the income deduction exceeds the limit you can deduct in one year, you can spread it out over the next five years.

If you have at least $2 million to set aside from your estate or shelter from estate taxes . . .

You Might Start a Foundation

Bill and Melinda Gates have done it. So have many Americans with much smaller endowments. You should have at least $2 million to start in order to make the foundation gifts worthwhile and still cover your legal expenses and overhead. You will also need to spare some time to run the foundation while you're still alive, which is why many people wait until they're retired. You need to have a passion for a cause, but if nothing comes to mind off the top of your head, there are estate planners who, for a fee, will help you do some head-searching to identify a focus for your foundation. From there, you need to see a lawyer who specializes in nonprofit tax issues in your state who can help you file for tax-exempt status. Then you set aside an endowment that is kept invested except for the percentage that you give away each year. The law requires that you distribute only 5% a year. You can stipulate that the monies will all be paid out in a lump sum when you die, or you can set up a family foundation that your children will run after your death. It could be a way to encourage your kids to "not do nothing."

Protecting Yourself If You Become Incapacitated

According to insurance morbidity tables, most people are six times more likely to become disabled in the next year than to die. If you become incapacitated and unable to express your wishes for your estate, you go to probate court—while you're still alive, under guardianship or conservatorship.

The best way to protect yourself might be through a trust. We think a revocable living trust is a far superior strategy to setting up a durable power of attorney, which names someone to act on your behalf if you are incapacitated. A trust gives you more of a say over what is to be done when you're not there to speak for yourself. You name a successor trustee who would take over as the guardian of your estate if you were unable to look after your own affairs, and you can leave instructions that must be followed if you should become disabled or die.

The Living Will

Also called a "physician's directive," this specifies your wishes in case you become incapacitated. A living will is used most often to state a wish to refuse medical treatment that would artificially prolong life.

We believe that a living will is a gift to your family or other loved ones. It relieves them of the pressure of making a life-and-death decision, perhaps second-guessing what they think you'd want. The person who has the power to act as your representative is not supposed to be deciding on what's best for you, but on what *you would want* to have done to you. Some states also allow you to set up a "health care proxy" or "health care durable power of attorney," which gives someone else the right to make medical decisions for you if you become incapacitated. Our good friend Peter Strauss—a partner in the law firm Epstein, Becker & Green in New York City specializing in estate planning, and coauthor of the book *The Senior Survival Guide* (see more advice from him on pp. 360–61)—suggests that your documents give someone **springing power of attorney**, which guarantees that this person has permission to act on your behalf only if you should become incapacitated. "That's reassuring to many people who don't want to feel that they're giving a lot of power to their children or their friends when it isn't necessary," he told us on *The Dolans*.

Dolan Dilemma

We want to make one thing very clear before we dive into the murky and treacherous waters of qualifying for Medicaid benefits. When we discuss this subject in print, on the air, or during our public appearances, we are very much caught in the middle of a moral quandary.

Is it appropriate for us to discuss strategies that may assist you in qualifying for government benefits to pay for such important concerns as a prolonged nursing home stay, even if you have all or some of the assets needed to fund that care? On the other hand, should we advise you (or your parents or other loved ones) to go through your (or their) life savings to pay for this care—without government assistance?

We can't make that decision for you. We will, however, outline the problem and some possible solutions to this incredibly complex ethical and financial dilemma.

Now that you know how we feel, here are the main examples of what Medicaid defines as countable and noncountable assets:

Countable assets, which you must spend down before Medicaid will pay for your long-term health care:

- Cash over $2,000
- Stocks
- Bonds
- Retirement accounts
- Bank savings or CDs
- Treasury securities
- Savings bonds
- Investment property
- Vacation homes
- Second car

Noncountable assets, which you can keep while receiving Medicaid:

- Your primary residence
- Up to $2,000 in cash (in most states)
- One car
- Personal jewelry
- Prepaid funeral
- Household effects
- Term life insurance (term only, because it has no cash surrender value)

Noncountable assets vary by state. Check with your state's welfare department.

Your home is noncountable while you are alive or while a spouse or minor or disabled children are living there, but once both spouses have died, Medicaid can lay claim to it. But if you're widowed or single and in a nursing home, you are vulnerable. The government has told states they can put a lien on the house, although they can't take it away if you express an intent to return home. If you have an unmarried partner living there, he or she will probably have no rights against Medicaid, so you need to do some advance planning.

We warned against this in our last book, and we're still getting calls from older couples or widows who say that a well-meaning friend, or even a lawyer or accountant, has advised them to give their home away to their children to protect their assets against Medicaid.

Here are two things that could go wrong if you make this move, which isn't necessary anyway:

1. If you give your home to your children, or anyone else, *their* cost basis for tax purposes is *your* basis, usually what you originally paid for the house. If the capital gains are massive, they'll pay when they sell it.

2. Worst of all, the owner you've designated could conceivably steal your house and throw you out!

How to Make Countable Assets Noncountable

Before you start thinking about transferring assets to make them noncountable, you should know that the transfer creates a period of ineligibility for Medicaid. It's called the "look-back" period. The look-back period is three years for outright transfers and five years for transfers into or out of most trusts. What it means is that if you've transferred assets and then applied for Medicaid benefits within this period, the state will then calculate a certain number of months of ineligibility, beginning from the date of the transfer. The formula is this: The value of your transferred assets divided by the average monthly cost of nursing home care in the area (determined by the local Medicaid office) equals the number of months you are ineligible. A large enough transfer within the look-back period will create a period of ineligibility longer than the look-back period itself.

However, you can, during that time, spend countable assets to acquire noncountable assets. See if you can help out your spouse or children by buying some noncountable assets with countable funds. You can pay off loans, too.

You may shelter countable assets by setting up an irrevocable trust that prevents the trustee from giving you the money. (A revocable trust is worthless in protecting assets from Medicaid.) If the trustee can give you some of the assets—meaning if he's able to by the terms of the trust—those assets must be spent before Medicaid will pay. You should not be the trustee. If your aim is to shelter countable assets, set up a trust that does not allow the trustee to give assets or income to you, but does allow distributions to a third-party

Warning to Those Who Marry Late in Life

It's nice to fall in love at any age of your life, but Strauss says you have to be pragmatic about protecting your assets, especially when you marry late in life. He cautions women in particular, since women are likely to outlive their husbands, not to marry a man who doesn't have LTC insurance. If your husband is uninsured, think of the worst-case scenario:

He needs nursing home care. Because you're married you are liable for the expense until you've spent down most of your assets and can qualify for Medicaid. Then there will be little or no money left for *your* old age. Pretty frightening.

Advice from *The Dolans* with
Estate-Planning Attorney Peter Strauss

We talked about financing elder care for aging parents in Chapter 8, but it's equally important to make sure that you have a "just in case" plan in place for *yourself*. For more advice on covering yourself if you should ever become incapacitated, we turned to Peter Strauss.

"One out of two persons over the age of 85 will need significant assistance in performing the daily activities of life," he told us.

Figuring out how you are going to pay for long-term care is something you should do when you are healthy. There aren't many options. As we mentioned in Chapter 8, you can finance long-term care with:

Long-term care (LTC) insurance (see Chapter 9)

Your assets

Medicaid, the payor of last resort

If you don't know where to find the bucks to pay for long-term-care insurance, Strauss has these suggestions:

1. A reverse mortgage. As we explained in Chapter 11, if you are house-rich but cash-poor, you may convert the equity in your home into cash. The lender makes monthly payments or a lump-sum payment to you, based on a percentage of the value of your house. You continue to live in your home and hold the title, and it doesn't have to be sold until you are ready to move out or until you die. You can use the money to pay the premiums on long-term-care insurance.

   The good news is that Medicaid does NOT count a reverse mortgage when they add up your assets that affect eligibility. Our concern is that if all you have in terms of assets is your primary residence, you probably can't afford LTC insurance.

   New York City apartment owners be warned: You can't get a reverse mortgage on a cooperative residence.

2. If you're married and one of you enters a nursing home, the spouse who remains at home may try exercising "spousal refusal." You sign a legal form, called a *spousal refusal form,* stating that your assets should not be considered part of your spouse's property, and therefore you do not have to spend down before Medicaid will kick in. New York and Florida recognize this practice. Most other states don't, but they should, because it is based on a federal law. You need to structure this with an estate-planning attorney who is familiar with elder law,

however, because you run up against the risk of finding that your state has filed suit to try to get at your assets.

In spite of the complexities, Strauss says don't give up on this as a possibility. "Don't," he adds, "let an insurance company or nursing home tell you you can't get Medicaid because you're too rich." If the state does sue the spouse who signed the refusal form, you might still come out saving money. First, even if the state wins the case, it does not mean that Medicaid will collect 100% of what it has paid out. Second, if you do get a court order to reimburse Medicaid, the rate that Medicaid paid for the nursing home will be less than the rate the nursing home would have charged you.

3. As we pointed out in Chapter 10, some life insurance policies have an accelerated-benefits rider. If the policyholder is terminally ill, he or she can receive a one-time payment, usually equal to about 50% of the death benefit. This money can be used to finance long-term care.

beneficiary. Also, don't try this with your home. In nearly every state, you cannot qualify for Medicaid if you have your home in a trust.

You should make your children or your domestic partner that beneficiary, but if you're married you shouldn't make your husband or wife the beneficiary of the trust, because a spouse can keep half of your countable assets up to an amount that is indexed for inflation each year. The exact dollar amount may vary from state to state.

You could just transfer assets to your children or other family members or even friends. However, be sure you consider all of the possible consequences first. The recipients might incur large capital gains if they sell your assets. If your assets include qualified retirement plans, the recipient will face huge tax consequences. If the recipient has children in college or planning to go to college, the transfer might risk the children's eligibility for financial aid. If the recipient of your assets gets a divorce, the assets could end up in the hands of the ex-spouse. If the recipient runs a nonincorporated business and the business fails, the assets could be claimed by creditors. Besides all of these legal concerns, consider whether other family members will be resentful of your "giving" assets to one particular person—as well as whether this person will do right by you and your assets.

You May Be Able to Argue with Medicaid and Win

If you transfer assets, then due to totally unforeseen circumstances end up in a nursing home in less than three years, you might be able to get Medicaid to waive the transfer rule

IF you can show you were in good health when you made a transfer of the countable asset and therefore had no reason to expect that you'd be in this position so soon after. You should also be able to show that you had enough countable assets at that time to cover your reasonably expected health care costs, and had already established a pattern of giving away assets for estate-planning purposes or helping your kids through college. It does require a lot of foresight, no question.

This is assuming you want to receive Medicaid. Maybe you'd rather spend your own money, even if there may be little or nothing left for your heirs. It's nice to leave your children something, but the decision is up to you. If it were up to us, there would be a wider range of products and legal provisions to help people finance long-term care.

How to Find a Trustworthy Estate Attorney

As with any search for a good and trustworthy lawyer, knowledgeable colleagues, friends, and legal professionals you already know in your area are your best references. However, if you are stuck, we recommend these two excellent online services, which have state-by-state directories to lawyers with any specialty you name:

www.lawyers.com
The Martindale Hubbell directory, online at www.martindale.com

Also . . . ask your business associates and friends if they work with an estate planner with whom they are pleased.

Helpful Web Sites and Books

Basic Information About Wills and Trusts

Legal Information Network: www.itslegal.com

www.nolo.com

Save Wealth: www.savewealth.com

www.smartmoney/ac/estate

Make You Own Living Trust, by Denis Clifford, 5th edition. Nolo Press. $39.99. Phone 800-728-3555, or order online at www.nolo.com. This is a helpful reference to the subject, though we don't recommend you actually set up a trust yourself.

Asset Protection

How to Protect Your Life Savings from Catastrophic Illness, by Harley Gordon. Financial Strategies Press. $19.95. Available in most major bookstores.

Directories of Lawyers and Information About Estate Law

www.lawyers.com

www.martindale.com

Legal Information for Same-Sex Couples

Lambda Legal: www.lambdalegal.org

Elder Law

www.seniorlaw.com

The Senior Survival Guide, by Peter J. Strauss and Nancy M. Lederman. Facts on File, Inc., 2003. $35.

Long-term-Care Insurance

www.longtermcareinsurance.org

www.prepsmart.com/longtermcareinsurancetips.html

Medicare/Medicaid

www.benefitscheckup.com

www.hcfa.gov/medicaid/medicaid.htm

www.medicare.gov

INDEX

KEN AND DARIA DOLAN host a daily national television show on CNN.fn, Dolans Unscripted, which covers personal finance and airs in more than 25 million homes across America. They also host one of the nation's most popular syndicated weekend radio shows about money/business/lifestyle matters.

Special Offer

Receive Ken and Daria Dolan's New Online Newsletter <u>FREE</u>.

As a special thank you for reading
Don't Mess with My Money, you're invited to receive
Ken and Daria's brand-new online newsletter <u>FREE</u>.

Ken and Daria's "Money News You Can Use" is
a weekly online newsletter chock-full of advice,
information, and straight talk on
money matters from A to Z.

Sign up for your free membership today by visiting www.dolans.com.

WWW.DOLANS.COM